*A Mirror of Jewels which Clears Away Errors*
A Critical Guide to the Buddhist Sacred Sites
of the Nepal Valley

# *A Mirror of Jewels which Clears Away Errors*
# A Critical Guide to the Buddhist Sacred Sites of the Nepal Valley

FRANZ-KARL EHRHARD

Lumbini International Research Institute
2020

Lumbini International Research Institute
P.O. Box 39
Bhairahawa, Dist. Rupandehi
NEPAL
E-mail: lirilib@gmail.com



ISBN: 978-9937-0-7876-4

First published in 2020

Printed in Nepal by Dongol Printers, Kathmandu

# CONTENTS

*Nevertheless, the exhaustion was worth the effort, and when I saw Nepal, a country planted, [as if it were,] by the local deities, I could not get enough of looking at its outward excellence; its people, I fancied, were minor gods of the desire realm.*[*]

—Mar-pa Chos-kyi blo-gros (1000?–1081?)

# Preface

After translations of his description of the religious geography of the Mang-yul Gung-thang region of the southern part of South-western Tibet and his investigation into the history of a little-known bKa'-brgyud-pa school from the Himalayan borderlands, the translation of a third work by Brag-dkar rta-so sPrul-sku Chos-kyi dbang-phyug (1775–1837) is being offered in the following pages. Originally only available as an incomplete *dbu med* manuscript in the author's collected writings, the text exists now in a second version, in the new typeset edition published by mKhan-po bShad-sgrub bstan-'dzin, Kathmandu. The text is a pilgrimage guide to various Buddhist sites of the Nepal Valley, the two most prominent ones being the stūpas of Svayaṃbhūnāth and Bodhnāth. Similarly to what was done in the case of the guidebook to the 'Phags-pa lha-khang in sKyid-grong, early printed guidebooks are critically evaluated, while the lore surrounding other individual sites is assessed based on various literary sources. In several respects, the present work can be compared to another such pilgrimage guide composed by the Fourth Khams-sprul bsTan-'dzin Chos-kyi nyi-ma (1730–1779), who cites the epigraph quoted above in it.

A critical edition, an annotated translation and a photographic reproduction of the original *dbu med* manuscript are presented here. I gratefully acknowledge the interest in the text taken by students during reading classes at the Ludwig-Maximilians-Universität in Munich (Institute of Indology and Tibetology) and the Ruprecht-Karls-Universität in Heidelberg (Centre for Asian and Transcultural Studies) in the winter terms 2018/19 and 2019/20. Special words of thanks go to Philip Pierce, South Asia Institute, Patan, who not only checked the English but also corrected the translation with great care and patience; and Ralf Kramer, Bavarian State Library, Munich, who assisted with the final editing. The indices were prepared by Dr. Michael Pahlke, and through the kind help of Dr. Christoph Cüppers the study has been included in the publications of the Lumbini International Research Institute.

Heidelberg, in the spring of 2020

[*] gTsug-lag 'phreng-ba: *rJe btsun mar pa'i rnam par thar pa grub pa'i ngo mtshar brjod pa*, fol. 45a/6–7 (*'on kyang ngal dub bya rin chog / yul lha las btabs pa'i [= btab pa'i] bal po mthong / phyi 'dod [= don] yon tan lta bas chog mi shes / mi 'dod khams lha phran yin no snyam*).

# Part One

# Introduction

## *1. Descriptions of the World*

Of all the Tibetan works dealing with geographical knowledge, not only in the sense of the Buddhist canonical description of Jambudvīpa, but of descriptions of lands like India and Nepal, two texts come immediately to mind: the 'General Description of the World' (*'dzam gling spyi bshad*) of Sum-pa mkhan-po Ye-shes dpal-'byor (1704–1788) and the 'Extensive Description of the World' (*'dzam gling rgyas bshad*) of the Fourth bTsan-po No-min-han bsTan-'dzin 'phrin-las (1789–1839). The first work was written in the year 1777 and focuses on India and its peoples and regions, together with details of the major tantric places of pilgrimage; it then goes on to Nepal, pauses over Tibet, provides information on Manchuria, Korea and Japan, and leads finally to China and Russia. It has been observed that, while the author was by no means ready to abandon the authority of traditional book learning, he also recognized the need to supplement texts with eyewitness accounts. It is thus an important source for understanding the geographical conception of 18th-century Tibetan intellectuals.[1]

The section of the text dealing with Nepal follows the one on India and guides the reader after this passage from India to Nepal on to 'Snowland Tibet' (*bod kha ba can*) and further lands. It contains the following passage:

> Bal-yul, [or] Nepal, is a great country [consisting] of three royal domains, which are known as Yam-bu (i.e. Kathmandu), Ye-rang (i.e. Patan) and Kho-khom (i.e. Bhaktapur). Among these, in the territory of Yam-bu: [1] on the peak of a dense forest is an elevated dome called the 'Self-Arisen Caitya 'Phags-pa shing-kun'; [2] the teaching thrones of the first four Buddhas of the Fortunate Aeon (i.e. Vipaśyin, Śikhī, Viśvabhū and Krakucchanda); [3] the Bya-rung kha-shor Stūpa, close to a thousand cubits [in circumference], which is said to be one of the eight caityas known to have been erected by the Ma-mos in eight countries when once they were pacified by Heruka and his fierce entourage; [4] the Five Rocks site, where Hārītī, the *gtor-ma* mistress, was pacified together with her five hundred sons; [5] the skull of Śāriputra in the royal palace of Yam-bu. [All this] is said to exist. Many [other] unique sacred sites are located [there in Nepal], including [6] Pham-[m]thing, the site of a nine-hooded serpent, and [7] the five great towns [as well].

---

[1] Concerning the work of Ye-shes dpal-'byor, including a description of its contents and a full translation of the section on the Mongol domains, see Kapstein (2011:343–350). Consult Kim (2013:166–173) on the ethnic identity of Ye-shes dpal-'byor, a learned dGe-lugs-pa teacher of Mongolian origin from Amdo, and his works relating to history and geography.

> In this [country] there are great riches, trade is carried on in silver taṃka [coins], and bronze and copper craftsmanship is widespread.[2]

This account starts with the three cities of the Nepal Valley and closes with their economic relevance and their Buddhist art. The central part of the description concerns various religious places. First comes the Self-Arisen Caitya 'Phags-pa shing-kun (i.e. Svayaṃbhūnāth) and its teaching thrones of the first four Buddhas of the *bhadrakalpa*. The majestic stūpa of Bya-rung kha-shor (i.e. Bodhnāth) is identified next as one of a series of caityas erected at eight different sites according to Buddhist tantric literature. As the name of the residence of Hārītī suggests—located on the hill of Svayaṃbhūnāth—it was a naturally formed stone image of the deity; special mention is also made of a relic of Śāriputra, placed in front of the royal palace in the centre of Kathmandu, obviously in a caitya. Bhaktapur and Pātan are passed over, but the village of Pham[m]thing (i.e. modern-day Parphing) is highlighted among religious places outside the valley. The statement that there exist a further five settlements is puzzling, as the existence of "five great towns" (*grong khyer chen po lnga*) is generally associated with five sacred spots located around Svayaṃbhūnāth.

As already observed in the context of the description of India and its holy places, it seems that Sum-pa mkhan-po derived his information mainly from Buddhist literary sources, and this can in particular be seen in the case of Bodhnāth with its reference to the Heruka myth found in Tibetan commentarial literature of the Buddhist tantras.[3]

---

[2] Ye-shes dpal-'byor: *'Dzam gling spyi bshad ngo mtshar gtam snyan*, p. 23.5–17 (*bal yul nai pa la yam bu yu ring [= ye rang] kho khom zhes pa'i rgyal khag gsum gyi ljongs chen po yod / de las yam bu'i sa cher ni nag tshal stug po can zhig gi rtse'i rang byung mchod rten 'phags pa shing kun zhes pa'i bum pa yan thon pa dang / bskal bzang gi sangs rgyas dang po bzhi'i khri dang / sngon herukas drag po 'khor bcas btul dus yul brgyad du ma mo rnams kyis mchod rten brgyad bzhengs par grags pa'i nang gi gcig yin zer ba'i mchod rten bya rung kha shor khru stong du nye ba dang / gter [= gtor] bdag 'phrog ma bu lnga [= lnga brgya] btul ba'i gnas brag lnga dang / yam bu'i pho brang du 'phags pa sha ri'i bu'i dbu thod yod zer / klu gdengs ka dgu ldan gnas pa'i pham thing sogs gnas khyad par mang po dang grong khyer chen po lnga yod cing yul der 'byor ba rgya che la / der dngul gyi ṭaṃ kha'i tshong byed cing li dang zangs kyi bzo shin tu dar ro*).

[3] On the presentation of India in the work of Ye-shes dpal-'byor, and especially the long description of the eight "charnel grounds" (*śmaśāna*) according to the Tibetan commentarial literature—and his being at a loss when it came to identifying the geographical locations—see Huber (2008:53–56). For the pacification of the Ma-mo deities according to the dGe-lugs-pa commentarial literature, see, for example, Ngag-dbang brtson-'grus: *dPal rdo rje 'jigs byed kyi chos 'byung khams gsum las rnam par rgyal ba dngos grub kyi gter mdzod*, vol. 1, pp. 12.10–17.12.

Given that the teaching thrones of the four Buddhas of the *bhadrakalpa* might be an outgrowth of the teaching thrones of Buddha Śākyamuni and his disciples Śāriputra and Maudgalyāyana, and that these sites and the relic of Śāriputra are found in a popular pilgrimage guidebook to Nepal, such literary sources surely informed Sum-pa mkhan-po's descriptions, either directly or by hearsay. The details concerning Hārītī as a deity receiving *gtor-ma* offerings and Pham-[m]thing as the place where a nine-hooded nāgā had resided further hint at later, too, more learned treatises having reached the author in Amdo.[4]

The first version of the 'Extensive Description of the World' was completed in the year 1821 in Beijing and seems to have been in this initial stage focused mainly on India and Nepal. As a world geography—covering not only countries in South-east Asia, but also Australia and New Zealand, Africa, the Middle East and Europe—it was first printed in Beijing in the year 1830. Its author was a member of an incarnation lineage with close ties to the Manchu court, starting with the First bTsan-po No-min-han 'Phrin-las lhun-grub (1622–1699), a disciple of the Fifth Dalai Bla-ma Ngag-dbang Blo-bzang rgya-mtsho (1617–1682). The Fourth bTsan-po No-min-han had access to European visitors and other sources about the lands beyond India and China. Concerning the homeland of Śākyamuni, he relied on Buddhist literary sources, including a guidebook focusing on pilgrimage; after obtaining this book he set about composing his own guide to India's sacred sites.[5]

As the itinerary from the Tibetan plateau passed first through the Himalayas, the geographical description of the individual countries starts with Nepal. The two routes taken are those through sKyid-grong and gNya'-nang, the travel time to the Valley and its three major cities being six or seven days. It is stated that given the richness of its religious and material life, it is no mean realm. Along with Kathmandu, Patan and Bhaktapur, further villages are named, and the number of districts is given as eighty-four. In the initial passage, concerning the great number of religious objects encountered in the country, the author makes clear that he relied on a written source and on eyewitness accounts:

---

[4] A long excursus on the Yakṣinī Hārītī and her role as a protector of the Buddhist doctrine and her being worthy to receive *gtor-ma* offerings is contained in the guidebook of the Fourth Khams-sprul; see bsTan-'dzin Chos-kyi nyi-ma: *Yul chen po nye ba'i tshandhoha bal po gnas kyi dkar chag gangs can rna ba'i bdud rtsi*, pp. 219.6–222.2, and Macdonald & Dvags-po Rin-po-che (1981:266–267). For the toponym Pham-[m]thing and its etymology—deriving from Newari for a nine-hooded serpent—see the translation below, note 133.

[5] For a first assessment of the composition of the *'Dzam gling rgyas bshad* and its author, see Wylie (1962:xii–xxi); a full translation of the Nepal section is contained in Wylie (1970: 11–36). The world description and its detailed account of Magadha and neighbouring regions have been dealt with by Huber (2008:56–57). Consult Yongdan (2011:78–93) for the background of the work and its sources, including the pilgrimage guidebook to India.

In the city of Yam-bu (i.e. Kathmandu): [1] the two brothers Jo-bo Dza-ma-li and A-kaṃ Bu-kaṃ among the Four Brothers Ārya [Avalokiteśvara], called by the Newars 'Ka-ru dzu-dzu' (i.e. *karuṇarāja*), [2] the Mother [i.e. the *Śatasāhasrikaprajñāpāramitāsūtra*] brought from the realm of the nāgas by the protector Nāgārjuna, [3] the image of Tārā known to have protected the two Jayamalla brothers, the kings of Citor, from fear, and [4] the caitya which contains the skull of Ārya Śāriputra and so forth; many blessing-bestowing religious objects [exist there]. In addition, there are countless temples and statues of individual Buddhist and non-Buddhist [dieties], including Gur-mgon, Four-Armed [Mahākāla], Gaṇapati [and] Hanuman; this is explained in the register, and I have heard it directly from those who have knowledge about it.[6]

It has elsewhere been noted that the presence here of the Tārā image conflates historical events with legends, and refers obviously to the goddess Tulāja or Taleju and her introduction to Nepal by Narasiṃha Malla (d. 1326). It can be argued that this story was based on an account reported by a traveller who had visited the temple of the deity in Bhaktapur. The three other objects—the Buddhist statues, a particular manuscript and a reliquary, the last of these being also recorded in the work of Sum-pa mkhan-po—are based on the above-mentioned popular pilgrimage guidebook. Special importance is given to the Avalokiteśvara statues, although only the so-called Jo-bo Dza-ma-li is located in Kathmandu; the name A-kaṃ Bu-kaṃ actually represents a pair of such icons of Padmapāṇi Lokeśvara found in Patan. This is stated correctly in the guidebook, which also contains the narrative of Nāgārjuna's discovery of the *Śatasahasrikaprajñāparamitā* manuscript and the caitya with Śāriputra's relic.[7]

---

[6] bsTan-'dzin 'phrin-las: *'Dzam gling rgyas bshad snod bcud kun gsal me long*, pp. 43.13–44.1 (*grong khyer yam bur 'phags pa mched bzhi'i nang tshan jo bo dza ma li dang a kaṃ bu kaṃ'am bal po rnams kyis ka ru dzu dzu zer ba sku mched gnyis dang / mgon po klu sgrub kyis klu'i yul nas spyan drangs pa'i yum / yul ci to ra'i rgyal po dza ya ma lla spun gnyis kyi 'jigs pa las bskyabs par grags pa'i sgrol ma'i snang bsnyan dang / 'phags pa śā ri'i bu'i dbu thod bzhugs par grags pa'i mchod rten sogs rten byin rlabs mang po dang / gzhan yang mgon po gur dang / phyag bzhi pa dang / tshogs bdag pa dang / ha nu mantha sogs phyi nang so so'i lha sku dang lha khang shin tu mang bar dkar chag las bshad la / rgyus yod dag las kyang dngos su thos*), and Wylie (1970:14–18).

[7] Concerning the origin of the Tārā image, which is also mentioned in the Tibet section of the *'Dzam gling rgyas bshad*, see Wylie (1970:16–17, note 22); consult Bajracharya, Michaels & Gutschow (2016, vol. 1:79–83) regarding the introduction of the deity by Narasiṃha Malla according to the Wright chronicle. The fact that only the Jo-bo Dza-ma-li is located in Kathmandu while the other two statues are located in Patan is noted in Wylie (1970:14–16, note 20). The pilgrimage guidebook placed Jo-bo Dza-ma-li in Kathmandu, together with a well from which the four Avalokiteśvara Brothers are said to have arisen; see Ngag-dbang rdo-rje: *Bal yul mchod rten 'phags pa shing kun dang de'i gnas gzhan rnams kyi dkar chag*, p. 46.21–22 (*yam bu na jo bo mched bzhi'i 'khrungs pa'i tsan dan gyi khron*

If one searches the text for further references to the guidebook, it turns out that the Fourth bTsan-po No-min-han mentions it on two more occasions. The first one concerns the description of a hill about half-a-day's journey north of Kathmandu and known to Tibetans as Ri-bo 'big[s]-byed. It is said that on top of this hill can be found the actual teaching throne of Buddha Śākyamuni, and not far from it two caityas containing the relics of his parents. Although this claim is hard to believe, according to sources like the Vinaya literature such shrines could have been erected by kinsmen of Ārya Ānanda from the Śākya family after they had come to Nepal.[8] The register is finally quoted in regard to Yang-le shod and mTsho dkar-nag, two sacred sites in the south of the Nepal Valley; again, the written source is corroborated by eyewitness accounts.[9]

In both the descriptions of the world by Sum-pa mkhan-po and bTsan-po No-min-han, the popular guidebook is used to some extent for identifying Buddhist sacred sites in Nepal, while at the same time it is checked against accounts of persons who had visited the country, during which some reservations against its claims are expressed. It was obviously not the only source, as already seen above, where more learned treatises were used for the depiction of individual sites.

---

*chu dang / 'ja' [= dza] ma li dkar mo*). For the reference to the latter two statues in Patan and the literary source for these Buddhist icons, see ibid., p. 46.31–32 (*ye rang na maṇi bka' 'bum na gsal ba'i jo bo a khang dang u khang gnyis*). In addition to the caitya with Ārya Śāriputra's skull, the guidebook mentions a similar caitya with relics of Śākyamuni's disciple Ārya Kāśyapa; see ibid., p. 46.22–25 (*rgyal khang gi mdun na yam bu ya 'gal gyi che ba shā ri'i bu'i dbu thod dang / 'od srungs kyi ring bsrel bzhugs pa'i mchod rten gser zangs las grub pa yod*). Concerning the narrative of Nāgārjuna's discovery of the Buddhist manuscript, see the translation below, note 96.

8 See bsTan-'dzin 'phrin-las: *'Dzam gling rgyas bshad snod bcud kun gsal me long*, pp. 45.20–46.3 (*grong khyer yam bu'i byang phyogs nyin phyed tsam gyi sar ri bo 'bigs byed du grags pa'i ri chen po yod pa'i rtse mor rgyal ba śākya thub pa'i bzhugs khri dngos dang / de dang mi ring bar śākya thub pa'i yab dang yum gyi sku gdung mchod rten yang yod ces dkar chag na bshad 'dug par yid ches dka' mod / 'on kyang shākya rnams 'phags skyes po'i dmags gis bcom skabs su dga' bo'i nye rigs shākya 'ga' zhig bal yul du thon par 'dul ba lung sogs las gsungs pas / de rnams kyis bcom ldan 'das kyi yab yum gyi ched du bzhengs pa zhig yin nam snyam*), and Wylie (1970:22–23). The guidebook adds the teaching thrones of Śāriputra and Maudgalyāyana to Śākyamuni's; see Ngag-dbang rdo-rje: *Bal yul mchod rten 'phags pa shing kun dang de'i gnas gzhan rnams kyi dkar chag*, p. 45.29-33 (*shing kun gyi nub byang na ri bo 'bigs byed kyi rtse la ston pa'i bzhugs khri / shā ri'i bu dang mo'u 'gal gyi bu'i bzhugs khri rnams yod / ... / de'i byang 'khris na / yab sras gtsang dang yum sgyu ma lha mdzes kyi mchod rten re yod*).

9 See bsTan-'dzin 'phrin-las: *'Dzam gling rgyas bshad snod bcud kun gsal me long*, pp. 50.21–51.3 (*yang de'i slob dpon chen po padma ka ra'i sgrub phug yang le shod du grags pa dang / klu dkar nag gnas pa'i mtsho gnyis bcas rten dang gnas chen mang po yod ces dkar chag las bshad la mjal ba dag gi ngag las kyang thos so*), and Wylie (1970:31). Compare Ngag-dbang rdo-rje: *Bal yul mchod rten 'phags pa shing kun dang de'i gnas gzhan kyi dkar chag*, p. 46.34–35 (*lho nub na yang le shod kyi brag phug dang mtsho dkar nag yod*).

*2. Pilgrimage Guidebooks*

Before introducing the guidebook, I take a closer look at the popular guidebooks to Nepal and note which of them are currently available. One work which has up to now not surfaced is the 'Description of Sacred Sites' (*gnas bshad*) written by one mNga'-ris grub-chen. It is quoted twice in the world description of the Fourth No-min-han, the first reference concerning various sacred spots near the hill at the foot of the Svayaṃbhū Caitya, which is known to Tibetans as Bya-rgod phung-po ri; once again these statements are listed with some reservation:

> Also in its neighborhood is [1] a hill said to be Gṛdhrakūṭa, [2] another one said to be the place where a thousand Buddhas of the Fortunate Aeon first generated *bodhicitta*, and [3] what is said to be the site where the poultry woman who erected the Bya-rung kha-shor [Stūpa] achieved buddhahood. According to mNga'-ris grub-chen, many such astonishing sites exist [there], [and] although he has described them as such, it is hard to accept. Nevertheless, these are places that confer blessings.[10]

One finds mNga'-ris grub-chen again—this time explicitly named as the author of a guidebook—in the section dealing with Namo Buddha, the pilgrimage site to the east of Bhaktapur featuring a caitya containing relics of Śākyamuni from one of his previous existences. This time the authority of its explanation of the multiplicity of relics is accepted.[11]

Although we do not have access to this work I propose that it be seen in close context with the previously mentioned popular guidebook composed by Ngag-dbang rdo-rje, a disciple of the 'Brug-pa bKa'-brgyud-pa yogin Rang-rig ras-pa (1619–1683); the latter one circulated as a block print, whose colophon provides the following information:

---

[10] See bsTan-'dzin 'phrin-las: *'Dzam gling rgyas bshad snod bcud kun gsal me long*, p. 46.7–12 (*yang de'i phyogs dang nye sa zhig tu bya rgod phung po'i ri yin zer ba'i ri zhig dang / bskal pa bzang po'i sangs rgyas stong gis thog mar thugs bskyed pa'i gnas yin zer ba zhig dang / bya rung kha shor bzhengs mkhan ma [*add: *bya rdzi ma] de sangs rgyas pa'i gnas yin zer ba sogs ya mtshan can mang po yod ces mnga' ris grub chen gyis bshad 'dug pa ji bzhin du khas len dka' yang / gnas byin rlabs can 'dug yin tshod*), and Wylie (1970:22–23). For the place generally associated with the enlightenment of the poultry woman, see the translation below, note 87.

[11] For the reference to the work of mNga'-ris grub-chen in the context of Namo Buddha, see the translation below, note 111. See Wylie (1970:xvii, 23 & 25) for translations of these quotations and concerning the Fourth No-min-han's access to such a guidebook; indeed, according to Wylie (1970:18, note 28), the author relied chiefly on this work.

> Thus this short register was set down by Ngag-dbang rdo-rje from Nas-lung, one nourished by the instructions of the noble Rang-rig ras-pa.[12]

The wording suggests that there existed a more extensive version of the guidebook to the sacred sites of Nepal and that its author was possibly Rang-rig ras-pa himself, to whom the epithet 'Mahāsiddha of mNga'-ris' applies, inasmuch as his birthplace was located in Spi-ti in Western Tibet. This is learned from a biographical account which describes him as an influential master of the 'Brug-pa bKa'-brgyud-pa school who counted among his disciples the Sixth 'Brug-chen Mi-pham dbang-po (1642–1712). Proof that such a 'register of Nepal' (*bal po'i dkar chag*) existed can be found in the diaries of Si-tu Paṇ-chen Chos-kyi 'byung-gnas (1700–1774), who made use of it when relating details about a temple in Saṅkhu and its sacred objects. Before proceeding to the Kathmandu Valley at the beginning of the year 1724, he stayed for three days in this village, visiting also nearby Cāṅgu, making use of this particular guidebook the whole while. Taking a critical stance towards some of the legends told by Tibetan pilgrims, he noted: "I had seen them also in the way they were recorded in the 'Register of Nepal' by the 'Brug-pa Rang-rig [ras]-pa." It is quite possible that it was the same guidebook that contained the details of the sacred spots near Bya-rgod phung-po ri and the relics in Namo Buddha, as related above.[13]

I have already assessed the editorial history of Ngag-dbang rdo-rje's short, and more popular, guidebook and shown that in contrast with two later xylograph editions—one from the 18th and one from the 20th century—the original xylograph was produced together with a register of the contents of Rang-rig ras-pa's reliquary. The latter was erected near the Bodhnāth Stūpa shortly after the

---

[12] See Ngag-dbang rdo-rje: *Bal yul mchod rten 'phags pa shing kun dang de'i gnas gzhan rnams kyi dkar chag*, p. 47.23-25 (*de ltar dkar chag mdor bsdus 'di ni / rje btsun rang rig ras pa'i man ngag gyis 'tsho ba / nas lung ngag dbang rdo rjes bkod pa dza yan tu [= jayantu]*). For biographical data concerning Ngag-dbang rdo-rje, who served as Rang-rig ras-pa's 'steward' (*gnyer pa*), see Ehrhard (2013:104). Consult Dawa (2016:206–209) regarding the village of Nas-lung—or Na-zlum—which lies west of what is now called Old Dingri; it is known for being the place where the first print edition of Mi-la ras-pa's biography and songs was produced at the end of the 15th century.

[13] For the account of Rang-rig ras-pa's life in a work dealing with the 'Brug-pa bKa'-brgyud-pa school and its Mahāmudrā doctrine, see Chos-kyi dbang-phyug: *dPal ldan gzhung 'brug bka' brgyud gser 'phreng gi bla ma brygud pa'i rnam thar dang / phyag rgya chen po'i spyi don ngo mtshar snyan pa'i sgra dbyangs*, pp. 67.9–67.18. The birthplace is given as 'Śrī Mañju in the region of Spi-ti in mNga'-ris' (*mnga' ris spi ti'i phyogs shrī mañju*). The reference to the 'Register of Nepal' is contained in Chos-kyi 'byung-gnas: *Ta'i si tu 'bod pa karma bstan pa'i nyin byed kyi rang tshul drangs por brjod pa dri bral shel gyi me long*, p. 114.4 (*'brug pa rang rig pas kyang bal po'i dkar chag tu de bzhin bris pas mthong mod*). See the translation below, note 108, for the legends surrounding the temple in Saṅkhu and Si-tu Paṇ-chen's critique of them.

death of the 'Brug-pa bKa'-brgyud-pa yogin. The actual pilgrimage guidebook is followed in the original xylograph edition by a description of the circumstances in which this caitya was erected and who performed the consecration ceremonies. This text is part of a collection of several xylographed works, among which, it may be speculated, one might also find the extensive pilgrimage guidebook ascribed to Rang-rig ras-pa himself.[14]

Ngag-dbang rdo-rje's work was composed in the year 1686 upon the death of Rang-rig ras-pa and, as the title suggests, was primarily concerned with describing Svayaṃbhū and the sacred sites in its vicinity; this covers exactly half of the text. The motivation for the composition was obviously the renovation of the Mahācaitya achieved by the 'Brug-pa yogin in the year 1683, as recorded in the text. The author made use of an earlier guidebook, also produced at the time of a renovation of the stūpa in 1413. This guidebook bears the title 'A Register of Noble Shing-kun, Reliquary of All the Buddhas of the Three Times' (*dus gsum sangs rgyas thams cad kyi thugs kyi rten 'phags pa shing kun gyi dkar chag*). Although it is still not possible to identify beyond his name the individual responsible for this early register of Svayaṃbhū and other sacred sites in Nepal, he may be among persons whose identity has already been discussed in another context.[15]

Among the sacred sites in the vicinity of the Self-Arisen Mahācaitya, the above source mentions the mountain Ri-bo 'big[s]-byed, the teaching throne of Buddha Śākyamuni, and the two caityas containing relics of King Śuddhodana and Queen Māyādevī. As seen above, these have found their way into geographies of the world, and the popular guidebook was especially influential in cirulating these statements. One can also detect in the early guidebook the dominant role of Nāgārjuna said to have acted as custodian of Svayaṃbhū and to have discovered texts in the realm of the nāgās, although in this source it is a Buddhist tantra and not, as recorded in the later guidebook, a manuscript of the *Śatasahasrikāprajñāparamitā*. Things changed when new literary sources became available to Tibetans, especially the different versions of the Buddhist Purāṇa devoted to Svayaṃbhū.

---

[14] See Ehrhard (2013:104–107) concerning the xylograph of the guidebook executed after 1950 and its predecessor—produced by a native of Western Tibet—adding a section with spiritual exhortations for pilgrims. The print of the *Bal yul shing kun sogs dang rje rang rig pa'i gdung rten gyi dkar chag* has the margin *ga* and was probably accompanied by the extensive version of the guidebook.

[15] A full translation and transliteration of the register from the year 1413 can be found in Ehrhard (2013:76–87). The person who requested the text is called Mang-thos Chos-skyabs dpal-bzang, and the author's name is Punyaśrībhadra, i.e. bSod-nams dpal-bzang[-po]. The designation "dpal bzang[-po]" (*śrībhadra*) is typical of individuals who were taken up into the ordination lineage of Śakyaśrībhadra (1140–1225). For the problems of identifying one bSod-nams dpal-bzang-po from this lineage, see Jackson (1990:4–6) and van der Kuijp (1994:602–605).

The two visits of the Eighth Si-tu Chos-kyi 'byung-gnas to the Nepal Valley in 1723/24 and 1748 have already been considered on the basis of his diaries which are important sources for the intellectual history of the 18th-century Tibetan cultural world. During both stays Si-tu Paṇ-chen had meetings with numerous local dignitaries, including the Kathmandu kings Jajajjaya Malla (r. 1722–1734) and Prakāśa Malla (r. 1735–1768). Interested in Sanskrit literature, he acquired manuscripts and discussed translation problems with learned Brahmins; during his two visits he also came across manuscript versions of the *Svayaṃbhūpurāṇa* and recognized that this was the main Buddhist source for the origin of the Nepal Valley, its Self-Manifested Caitya and further sacred sites. A diary entry during his first visit states: "The reason for these sacred sites of the realm of Nepal and so forth is to be found in the extensive and condensed *Svayaṃbhūpurāṇa*; one day I want to expand on this."[16]

The rediscovery of the *Svayaṃbhūpurāṇa* and its importance as the basic reference source for later descriptions of the Nepal Valley has been described elsewhere, and Si-tu Paṇ-chen, who was intent on branding certain legends current among Tibetan pilgrims as invalid, viewed the acquisition of the condensed version as particularly important in order to establish the authenticity of a number of sacred sites.[17]

It is known that the initiative for translating the Sanskrit text into Tibetan had come from Kaḥ-thog Rig-'dzin Tshe-dbang nor-bu (1688–1755), who was engaged in a renovation of the stūpa of Bodhnāth at the time of the second visit

---

16 See Chos-kyi 'byung-gnas: *Ta'i si tu 'bod pa karma bstan pa'i nyin byed kyi rang tshul drangs por brjod pa dri bral shel gyi me long*, pp. 125.7–126.1 (*bal yul skor gyi gnas 'di rnams kyi rgyu mtshan sogs rang byung mchod rten gyi sngon rab [= rabs ] rgyas bsdus rnams su 'dug pa slad nas spro bor 'dod do*). On the diaries of Si-tu Paṇ-chen, the intellectual climate of his age and the importance of the diaries, see Smith (2001:89–95); consult Verhagen (2013:316–323) for his activities during the sojourns in Nepal, his interest in Sanskrit language and linguistics, and his intercultural contacts. A first translation of the relevant sections of the diaries was made by Lewis & Jamspal (1988:194–210).

17 For the rediscovery of the *Svayaṃbhūpurāṇa* by Si-tu Paṇ-chen, Newar and Tibetan Buddhists in early 18th-century Nepal and the text as the basic reference for the Kathmandu Valley guides, see Decleer (2000:33–59). One example is the caitya in the centre of Kathmandu said to contain the skull of Śāriputra and singled out in both world geographies as a particularly sacred site. It is identified by Si-tu Paṇ-chen as a non-Buddhist shrine of Mahādeva on the basis of both its outer shape and its content; see Chos-kyi 'byung-gnas : *Ta'i si tu 'bod pa karma bstan pa'i nyin byed kyi rang tshul drangs por brjod pa dri bral shel gyi me long*, p. 122.3–4 (*bod rnams kyis yam bu ya mgal [= 'gal] gyis [= gyi] che ba ste yam bu'i grong na 'phags pa śā ri bu'i [= śā ri bus] ya mgal [= ya 'gal] bzhugs pas 'khyad par du 'phags pa zhes zer zhing bzhugs pa'ang grong dbus su mchod rten zhig la nges 'dzin mod / de ni shin tu ma brtags pa ste mchod rten de ni phyi rol pa'i lha chen po mchod rten yin pa'i pyhir ro / mchod rten kyi dbyibs gru bzhi su la mang gi rnam par byas shing nang gi snying por mtshan ma'i dbyibs kyi dbus su linga yod pa'am gzhan yang rung ste 'di 'dra'i rigs shin tu mang ba rnams phyi rol pa'i rten du shes dgos so*).

of Si-tu Paṇ-chen to the Valley. The Eighth Si-tu-pa himself, though, did not dig deeper into the subject. His disciple, the Fourth Khams-sprul bsTan-'dzin Chos-kyi nyi-ma (1730–1779) for his part composed a guidebook which relied on the *Svayaṃbhūpurāṇa*; he took Si-tu Paṇ-chen's translation into account and mentioned, next to the extensive and condensed versions, also a medium-length one. The title of the work is 'A Register of the Sacred Sites of Nepal, the Great Upaccandoha Land, Nectar for the Ears of Those from the Glacier Country' (*yul chen po nye ba'i tshandhoha bal po'i gnas kyi dkar chag gangs can rna ba'i bdud rtsi*).[18] In going through this guidebook one finds on several occasions critical statements concerning stories made by 'foolish Tibetans' (*bod blun*), the circulation of which was due to a register that contained such narratives. This work is called by the Fourth Khams-sprul the 'Tibetan register' (*bod kyi dkar chag*), and in one case he refers to it as a text composed by Ngag-dbang rdo-rje from Nas-lung, the disciple of Rang-rig [ras]-pa; it was thus again the popular guidebook that was meant and obviously not the extensive version referred to above. The first case concerned the supposed concealment by a great number of Buddhist Arhats of the original Self-Arisen Caitya up to its dome under a heap of earth. The second case concerns the legend that Nāgārjuna had cut his hair at this spot, accompanied by the wish that a variety of trees should grow up at this site in the future: the reason for the celebrated name 'Noble All Trees' (*'phags pa shing kun*). These two claims are listed in the popular guidebook in one narrative.[19]

---

[18] Concerning the translation of the *Svayaṃbhūpurāṇa* by Si-tu Paṇ-chen, both the text and its colophon, see the translation below, note 4. An edition and transliteration of the text of the Fourth Khams-sprul was made available by Macdonald (1975:89–144); for a translation, see Macdonald & Dvags-po Rin-po-che (1981:238–273). This work, an extensive survey of the sacred sites around the Kathmandu Valley, was written by the disciple of Si-tu Paṇ-chen in 1756; see bsTan-'dzin Chos-kyi nyi-ma's autobiography: *Rang tshul lhug par smras pa ma bcos gnyug ma'i rang grol*, fol. 222b/4. For the itineraries of the Fourth Khams-sprul, both the descent from sKyid-grong to Nepal and back to Tibet according to his autobiography, see Quintman (2014:89–90).

[19] See bsTan-'dzin Chos-kyi nyi-ma: *Yul chen nye ba'i tshandoha bal po'i gnas kyi dkar chag gangs can rna ba'i bdud rtsi*, pp. 167.6–168.1 (*'di nyid sngon bang rim seng khri dang bcas pa la phyis dgra bcom pa rnams kyis bum pa man chad sa 'og tu bsnubs pa yin zer ba ni bod kyi blun po rnams kyi snyams snang*) and p. 173.2–4 (*ming gi sgra bshad kyang slob dpon klu sgrub kyis dbu skra gtor nas ri 'di la shing sna kun tshang ba skye bar gyur cig ces smon lam btab bzhin du byung bas 'phags pa shing kun tu grags zhes zer / 'on kyang de lta bu'i ming dang dang lo rgyus gnyis la mi 'thad par mngon te)*, and Macdonald & Dvags-po Rin-po-che (1981:242–243 & 245). For Ngag-dbang rdo-rje's version of this narrative, see: *Bal yul 'phags pa shing kun dang de'i gnas gzhan rnams kyi dkar chag*, p. 44.29–34 (*de nas bya rgod phung po'i ri nas dgra bcom pa nyi khri gcig stong gis sa blangs nas mchod rten gyi bum pa man chad nub nas klu sgrub kyis dbu skra bcad nas gtor te khyad par 'phags pa'i mchod rten 'di la shing sna kun skye bar shig ces smon lam btab pas shing sna kun tshang bar skyes pas phyis 'phags pa shing kun tu grags*).

Another point where the register is quoted comes at the legend involving Śāriputra and Ānanda cleaving the hill around the lake with their mendicant staff and club so that the water which had covered the land of Nepal drained away. A small lake was left behind, but it was poured out by Gaṇapati, who later dissolved into a boulder. The Fourth Khams-sprul states that this self-arisen effigy—according to the register—still exists in Bungamati near Patan. This is an interesting case of intertextuality between the two registers of 1413 and 1686: the legend of the cleft hill was taken from the former work, while the localization of the stone image of Gaṇapati in Bungamati is only found in the later work. The story of the the lake and its name is recorded in the registers according to the *Ārya-gośṛṅga-vyākaraṇa-sūtra.*[20]

The remaining three references made by the Fourth Khams-sprul to the popular guidebook relate to the story of Nāgārjuna's discovery of the *Śatasāhasrikaprajñāpāramitā* in the nāga realm; the existence of a sacred site called Chumig Byang-chub bdud-rtsi on the way to India; and finally the fact that the protective deity residing at Svayaṃbhū is Vinayaka, i.e. Ganeṣa.[21]

The Fourth Khams-sprul not only took the *Svayaṃbhūpurāṇa* translation as a basic reference source for the description of Nepal and for evaluating claims in the previous guidebook; he also investigated the local lore of specific sacred sites, and ended up producing a kind of ethnographic account of Buddhism in the Valley shortly before the Gorkha conquest of the Valley. He personally vis-

---

[20] For the legend of the cleft hill, see bsTan-'dzin Chos-kyi nyi-ma: *Yul chen nye ba'i tshandoha bal po'i gnas kyi dkar chag gangs can rna ba'i bdud rtsi*, pp. 174.6–175.2 (*bod rnams kyi ngag rgyun ltar bris pa'i dkar chag la ni mchod rten śā ri'i bu dang kun dga' bos 'khar sil dang dbyug tho thogs nas bshos pa la lhag ma cung zad cig lus pa tshogs bdag gis bshos nas tshogs bdag pha vaṃ (= bong) gcig la thim pa'i rdo glang chen 'dra ba de yi rang [= ye rang] phyogs dbu khang na da lta yang yod ces bris 'dug*), and Macdonald & Dvags-po Rin-po-che (1981:246). Compare Ngag-dbang rdo–rje: *Bal yul 'phags pa shing kun dang de'i gnas gzhan rnams kyi dkar chag*, p. 44.21–26 (*mtsho go ma de pa'i rgya gar log shig tu bcom ldan 'das kyis lung bstan pa bzhin du śā ri bu dang kun dga' bo stan las langs ste mkhar gsil dang dbyigs to thogs nas mtsho bshos / der lhag ma cung zad lus pa tshogs bdag gis bshos nas tshogs bdag pha bong zhig la thim pas rdo glang chen 'dra bar ye rang gi phyogs dbu khang na da lta yang yod*). For the quotation from the Buddhist sūtra in the earlier guidebook, see *Dus gsum sangs rgyas thams cad thugs kyi rten 'phags pa shin kun gyi dkar chag*, p. 85.2–4, and Ehrhard (2013:78–79). For the Fourth Khams-sprul's critical assessment of the name of the lake and its proper form according to the *Svayaṃbhūpurāṇa*, see the translation below, note 24.

[21] On Nāgārjuna's discovery of a manuscript in the nāga realm and on the Chu-mig Byang-chub bdud-rtsi site, see the translation below, notes 96 & 139. The last reference is found in bsTan-'dzin Chos-kyi nyi-ma: *Yul chen nye ba'i tshandoha bal po'i gnas kyi dkar chag gnags can rna ba'i bdud rtsi*, p. 215.2–3 (*vāyu pu ri ni śāntiśris rlung lha gnas par bka' bskos pa'i sa yin pas vāyu pu ri ste rlung gi grong zhes bya / bod kyi dkar chag las bi na ya ka la gnas par yang bshad*), and Macdonald and Dvags-po Rin-po-che (1981:264). Compare Ngag-dbang rdo-rje: *Bal yul 'phags pa shing kun dang de'i gnas gzhan rnams kyi dkar chag*, p. 45:28–29 (*'di'i gzhi bdag bi na ya ka yin sprul bas gar yang khyab*).

ited most of the described places and produced a learned pilgrimage guidebook for future travellers. Two generations later a similar text was written by a Tibetan visitor with the same objectives, including also details of the royal genealogies of the kings of Nepal.

### *3. A Critical Chronicle*

This work bears the title 'A Definitive Presentation of the History of the Sacred Sites and Religious Objects of Nepal: A Mirror of Jewels Which Clears Away Errors' (*bal yul gyi gnas dang rten gyi lo rgyus nges par brjod pa 'khrul spong nor bu'i me long*) and was written by Brag-dkar rta-so sPrul-sku Chos-kyi dbang-phyug (1775–1837). We are well informed about the course of his life and the important role he played on behalf of Tibetan Buddhism in the southern borderlands as throne-holder of the famous Mi-la ras-pa site in Mang-yul Gung-thang. He is known for his guidebook to the Avalokiteśvara statue called 'Lord of sKyid-grong' (*skyid grong jo bo*) in writing which he relied on, and also discussed, previous pilgrimage guides. Among his many writings one finds 'biographies' (*rnam thar*) of his teachers and 'family lineage histories' (*gdung rabs*) along with an 'abbatial history' (*gdan rabs*) and the monastic guidelines for Brag-dkar rta-so. Most of the works are dated, the guidebook to the Ārya Wa-ti bzang-po, for example, having been written between the years 1825 and 1828. Among the texts redacted in the year 1816 are the abbatial history of Brag-dkar rta-so and the monastic guidelines.[22]

It is known that Chos-kyi dbang-phyug travelled to the Nepal Valley on two occasions and that the first journey occurred in 1792 at the age of seventeen in the company of his elder brother, the artist Kun-bzang phrin-las dbang-phyug (1772–1812). Besides the stūpas of Svayaṃbhūnāth and Bodhnāth, they went to the top of the hill Ri-bo 'big[s]-byed and viewed its Buddhist caves. They also set eyes on the Ārya 'Dza-ma-li in Kathmandu and the two Avalokiteśvara statues in Patan. After paying reverence and uttering prayers at the site of Yang-le shod on the southern border of the Nepal Valley, they continued their journey to the pilgrimage site of Chu-mig Byang-chub bdud-rtsi, the autobiography mentioning that the elder brother inquired into the history of the sacred spot by interviewing a local Brahmin and putting down the information in the form of 'notes' (*zin bris*). The second visit occurred ten years later, in the year 1802,

[22] For a sketch of the life of Chos-kyi dbang-phyug, based on his autobiography, and a transliteration and translation of the guidebook to the Ārya Wa-ti bzang-po, see Ehrhard (2004:89–107 & 151–305). A transliteration and translation of the family lineage history of the Gur-rigs mdo-chen tradition is contained in Ehrhard (2008:35–95). Consult Sernesi (2019:398–412) on Chos-kyi dbang-phyug as historian and polymath, the abbatial history of Brag-dkar rta-so and his writings of local history. His medical activities and a work on the history of Tibetan medicine redacted in 1817 have been dealt with by Van Vleet (2012:37–69).

after a journey to Yol-mo, present-day Helambu, where the elder brother had been engaged previously in painting the murals of Padma chos-gling temple. Having set foot on sacred sites in Yol-mo, namely the Yang-dag mchog-gi sgrub-phug cave and the [dB]yang[s]-ri [ma] hill, Chos-kyi dbang-phyug set out once again for the stūpas of Svayaṃbhūnāth and Bodhnāth. While in Kathmandu, he stayed in the residence of a Newar Vajrācārya called Paṇḍita Śrī Harṣa.[23]

The work devoted to the sacred sites and religious objects of Nepal was originally accessible as a *dbu-med* manuscript that lacked the last folio [= A]. In the newly typeset *dbu-can* version [= B] this folio was added, but without the verso of the missing page. It is thus not possible to date this text of Chos-kyi dbang-phyug's. Nevertheless, the autobiography contains a reference that the text was given its final redaction together with the abbatial history and the monastic guidelines of Brag-dkar rta-so, so that it can be ascribed to the year 1816. The incomplete colophon lists the sources used for this chronicle; one finds again the guidebook of Nas-lung-pa Ngag-dbang rdo-rje, the disciple of Rang-rig ras-pa, as the most prominent among them, while the register of Rang-rig ras-pa's reliquary shrine, which accompanied the original version of the guidebook consulted, is also acknowledged. Although the colophon breaks of in the middle of a sentence, one can clearly see that the author makes a distinction between the guidebook—"based on mere guesses"—and the correct statements contained in the register. A second guidebook, which also circulated in the form of a xylograph, was written by Karma Blo-bzang, a former throne-holder of Brag-dkar rta-so; this work was available to Chos-kyi dbang-phyug, obviously from the monastic archive.[24]

Although we do not have access to the second guidebook it can be speculated that it was composed shortly before the ones of Ngag-dbang rdo-rje and of mNga'-ris grub-chen, mentioned above. It is known that Karma Blo-bzang made a great number of offerings to the Buddhist sacred sites of the Nepal Val-

---

[23] The two visits to Nepal are described in the autobiography, the first one occurring after the Sino-Nepalese war of 1788–1792; see Ehrhard (2004:92 & 95). For his critical assessment of a Buddhist cave located on 'Big[s]-byed hill and his look into the history of Chu-mig Byang-chub bdud-rtsi, see the translation below, notes 99 & 139. For the topography of [dB]yang[s]-ri ma hill and Yang-dag mchog-gi sgrub-phug in Yol-mo according to ritual literature and a travelogue, see Mathes (2013:38–41).

[24] For the reference in the autobiography to the fact that the chronicle was given its final shape as one of the first works of Brag-dkar rta-so sPrul-sku together with the abbatial history and the monastic guidelines of Brag-dkar rta-so, see Ehrhard (2004:100). It should be noted that at this time religious teachers from Bhutan were staying at Brag-dkar rta-so. Later they returned to their home country after having taking part in a renovation of the Svayaṃbhū Stūpa to repair damage suffered by the *yaṣṭi*; this had occurred in 1813 and is recorded in the autobiography. Concerning the incomplete colophon of the chronicle, see the translation below, note 153. Karma Blo-bzang is counted as the eleventh throne-holder of Brag-dkar rta-so; see Sernesi (2019:395).

ley in the later part of his life and that a previous journey might have resulted in this particular work. A passage in the autobiography of Karma Blo-bzang deals with this journey to the Nepal Valley and mentions which sites were visited and were regarded as Buddhist ones:

> The two stūpas of the sacred land of Nepal (i.e. Svayaṃbhūnāth and Bodhnāth), sTag-mo lus-sbyin, Yang-le shod, the Asura rock cave, the Ramadoli Charnel Ground, the Charnel Ground of [Vajra]vārāhī, [s]Tham vihāra, the Nepalese Rin-chen tshul vihāra, 'Big[s]-byed hill, the Accomplishment Cavern of Nāgārjuna, [the site of] the Eighty Siddhas, sNye-shang[s] dKur-ta (the Ka-te Cave [of Mi-la ras-pa]), the Golden Cave of Nepal, the Tārā of Bhaktapur, the Lords A-khang [and] Bu-khang [and] the Self-Arisen Cakrasaṃvara of Patan, the meditation object of Indrabhūti, the Nepalese caves of Tilopa and Nāropa and so forth: [Karma Blo-bzang and his companions] themselves went [to them] turn by turn and offered butter lamps, religious worship, *gaṇacakra*s and prayer flags at what are definitely Buddhist sacred sites.[25]

Most of these places are also treated in detail in Chos-kyi dbang-phyug's chronicle. Some of them—for example, the caves associated with the mahāsiddhas Tilopa and Nāropa—he does not accept as authentic. These various destinations of Tibetan pilgrims are described in the work's fourth chapter, a discussion of the subsidiary sacred sites in the Nepal Valley.

The most space—chapters two and three of the text—is given over to a treatment of Svayaṃbhūnāth and Bodhnāth. The former chapter is the more extensive of the two, containing long quotations from the translation of the *Svayaṃbhūpurāṇa* done by Si-tu Paṇ-chen. A particular feature of these two chapters is, besides their attention to the literary sources, the historical overview of the successive renovations of the two Buddhist monuments in Nepal. Among the literary sources used, one especially finds biographical works, including the life-stories of gTsang-smyon Heruka (1452–1507), lHa-btsun Rin-chen rnam-

---

[25] See Karma Blo-bzang: *mKhas grub chen po karma blo bzang ba rnam thar mchod sprin rgya mtsho*, p. 516.3–9 (*bal gnas mchod rten gnyis / stag mo lus sbyin / yang le shod / a su ra'i brag phug [/] dur khrod ra ma mdo [= do] li / phag mo dur khrod / thang bhī ha ra / bal yul rin chen phug [= tshul] gyi gtsug lag khang / ri bo 'bigs byed [/] klu sgrub [*add: *sgrub] khang / grub thob brgyad cu [= bcu] / snye shang dkur ta'am ka te'i phug pa / bal yul gser phug / kho khom sgrol ma / jo bo a khang bu khang / ye rang bde mchog rang byon / indra bho ti'i [= indrabuti'i] thugs dam rten / bal po tai lo na' ro'i [= nā ro'i] phug pa sogs rang res phyin zhing nang gnas yin ches [nges] rnams su dkar me dzu tsa [= pū tsa] tshogs 'khor dar cog [= lcog] phran bu re phul*). The offerings took place when Karma Blo-bzang had nearly reached the age of seventy years and before the consecration of his monastery Bragdkar bsam-gling in sNye-shang[s] in the Nepalese Himalayas in the year 1664; see Ehrhard (2013:235).

rgyal (1473–1557) and gNas Rab-'byams-pa Byams-pa phun-tshogs (1503–1581); the latter two individuals served as throne-holders of Brag-dkar rta-so and are counted as the first and second ones according to the abbatial history.[26]

The individual renovations of Svayaṃbhūnāth and Bodhnāth are not covered in detail in the Fourth Khams-sprul's guidebook; only the auspicious circumstances at the beginning of the one undertaken by Kaḥ-thog Rig-'dzin are recorded on two occasions, his authority also being acknowledged in regard to the sacred site of Yang-le shod. Chos-kyi dbang-phyug's chronicle, too, takes note of statements made by Tshe-dbang nor-bu; in particular, explicit references concerning a footprint of Padmasambhava in the vicinity of Bodhnāth and the existence of Buddhist caityas ascribed to King Aśoka in Kathmandu and Kīrtipur, a spiritual song of the master being quoted in the latter regard.[27]

The renovation of Svayaṃbhūnāth by Kaḥ-thog Rig-'dzin is recorded in the chronicle, and the existence of a register is adverted to for the relevant details. Here one has to consider the fact that Chos-kyi dbang-phyug was well acquainted with the writings of Tshe-dbang nor-bu, and indeed authored two biographies of him, in the years 1818 and 1819. Among the sources used for these works—and also for the chronicle—one must count the 'official letters' (*chab shog*). One can point this out, for example, in a missive of the master from the year 1752:

> The Indians in Nepal call it Svayaṃbhūcaitya, literally the Self-Manifested Stūpa. There are claims that it appeared from light [emitted by] the lock of hair on the forehead of Buddha Śikhī. [There are] a great number of śāstras of disciples of our teacher (i.e. Buddha Śākyamuni) that follow this [belief], and in Nepal there is also now a register [of these events] (i.e. the *Svayaṃbhū-purāṇa*). Early on Mahācārya Vasubandhu came from the land of

---

[26] lHa-btsun Rin-chen rnam-rgyal and gNas Rab-'byams-pa Byams-pa phun-tshogs were also active in renovating the so-called 'Phags-pa lha-khang, the temple of the Ārya Wa-ti bzang-po in sKyid-grong; their biographies had also been used by Chos-kyi dbang-phyug in the guidebook devoted to the temple and the statue in Mang-yul, see Ehrhard (2004:260 & 370–371, notes 96 & 97). On their position as throne-holders of Brag-dkar rta-so, see Sernesi (2019:395).

[27] For the two references in the Fourth Khams-sprul's guidebook, see bsTan-'dzin Chos-kyi nyi-ma: *Yul chen po nye ba'i tshandoha bal po'i gnas kyi dkar chag gangs can rna ba'i bdud rtsi*, p. 171.1–3 (*'gyang tsam na nas spungs kyi ri bo la mchod rten chen po zhig gsos kyi tshe rig 'dzin tshe dbang nor bur dkar phyugs kyi lha mthu bo che rnams kyis phul ba'i rdo gter 'thon pa'i shul dang chu mig gsar pa bcas yod*) and p. 208.4–5 (*da lta rang byung mchod rten gyi zhig gsos rdo gter cing chu mig gsar ba rdol ba 'dir tsho do ste nas spungs*), and Macdonald and Dvags-po Rin-po che (1981:244 & 261). For Kaḥ-thog rig-'dzin's remarks concerning Yang-le shod in the same guidebook, see the translation below, note 127; the references concerning the footprint of Padmasambhava and the caityas ascribed to King Aśoka are contained in the translation below, notes 85 & 119.

> Madhyadeśa in India to see the Svayaṃbhūcaitya; this appears in authentic histories. Among others, the noble [and] magnificent Lord Atiśa (982–1054), when on his way to Tibet, claimed to have seen the Svayaṃbhūcaitya. All this is very well known in the Holy Land (i.e. India). Tibetan learned and realized persons of the intervening period identified [the stūpa] with the Go-ma-sa-la-gan-dha told of in the *Gośṛṅga-vyākaraṇa-sūtra*, [while now] it is known as 'Phags-pa shing-kun in the whole of Tibet. As for a while now it has been greatly dilapidated, I have long entertained the wish to renovate it, now that the renovation of the Bya-ri kaṃ-sho-ma [stūpa] (i.e. Bodhnāth) has been accomplished; but at no time did my analysis [of the situation] come to fruition.[28]

These details of the Svayaṃbhū Stūpa are echoed at the beginning of the second chapter of the chronicle, with only Nāgārjuna being added to the list of Indian Buddhist masters who had venerated the stūpa. The mentioned identification of Svayaṃbhū with the Go-ma-sa-la-gan-dha stūpa received Chos-kyi dbang-phyug's particular attention, and he devoted a part of the first chapter of his work to this subject. He traces it back to the earlier guidebooks (described specifically as printed books), while among the various literary sources once again the authority of Kaḥ-thog rig-'dzin is evoked. Although in conclusion it is made clear that the two countries of Li-yul and Bal-yul are distinct, the question of the location of the former country is left open in the light of conflicting statements by previous scholars.[29]

---

[28] See Tshe-dbang nor-bu: *Chab shog khag*, p. 727.17–27 (*... bal yul du rgya gar ba rnams kyi (= kyis ) swa yam bhūcyaita [= caitya] zhes rang byung mchod rten chen po sangs rgyas rin chen gtsug tor can gyis dpral ba'i mdzod spu'i 'od zer nas grub pa'i yin tshul bdag cag gi ston pa'i gdul bya de yi rjes su 'brang ba'i bstan bcos ches mang ba dang bal yul du dkar chags da lta yang gnas zhing / sngon slob dpon chen po dbyig gnyen gyis kyang yul dbus nas bal yul du rang byung mchod rten gzigs par phebs pa lo rgyus khungs ma rnams nas 'byung zhing / jo bo dpal ldan a ti sha yang bod du phebs pa la rang byung mchod rten gzigs pa'i zol mdzad pa sogs 'phags yul nyid du shin tu grags che zhing bod yul bar skabs mkhas dang grub pas glang ru lung bstan pa'i mdor gsungs pa'i mchod rten go ma sa la gandhar ngos bzung zhing / bod yongs su 'phags pa shing kun tu grags pa de zhig [= re zhig] grum gog nyam shin tu che ba yis / de la zhig gso'i blo 'dod bya ri kam sho ma'i zhig gsos grub pa nas tsam ring mo zhig nas byung yang res rang gi brtag ma 'chub [= chub]*). There exist ten official letters addressed in the year 1752 to the Seventh Dalai Bla-ma sKal-bzang rgya-mtsho (1708–1757), touching upon the pending renovation that arose out of a diplomatic mission to Ladakh on behalf of the dGa'-ldan pho-brang government; for two further letters as sources of the chronicle, see the translation below, notes 101 & 150. These letters and further missives have also been used for investigating the attempt of Kaḥ-thog Rig-'dzin to reform Kaḥ-thog monastery and to install the Tenth Zhva-dmar-pa (1742–1792) as throne-holder; see Ronis (2009:101–132).

[29] Another missive of Tshe-dbang nor-bu, this time quoted verbatim, is turned to when tackling the localization of Li-yul. This letter was addressed to Gung mGon-po skyabs (c. 1690–

Throughout the chronicle various canonical and non-canonical Buddhist works are quoted, including the previously mentioned biographies, further historiographical writings, and particularly hagiographies and prayers devoted to Padmasambhava. In this regard, two recensions of the *Zangs gling ma* are taken note of along with the *thang yigs* that go back to O-rgyan gling-pa (b. 1323) and Sangs-rgyas gling-pa (1340–1396). In the final chapter, dealing with the dynastic genealogy of the Nepalese kings, statements and spiritual songs by Kaḥ-thog Rig-'dzin are again referenced, this time in regard to the master's acquaintance with the last Malla ruler of Kathmandu and the first member of the Shah dynasty. As with the guidebook of the Fourth Khams-sprul, the importance of the rediscovery of the *Svayaṃbhūpurāṇa* as a basic reference is testified to in the chronicle. This is true not only in the context of the narratives of the origin of the Mahācaitya and the sacred sites in its vicinity, but also in a quite unusal way in connection with the figure of Padmasambhava, whom Chos-kyi dbang-phyug identifies with none other than Zhi-ba'i dpal, the first vajrācārya according to the Buddhist Purāṇa. This seems to be a unique insertion made by him into the narratives associated with the sacred sites and religious places of the Nepal Valley.

It is not known to what extent the Fourth Khams-sprul's guidebook and Brag-dkar rta-so sPrul-sku's critical chronicle were consulted by later Tibetan pilgrims when visiting the actual sites. If one considers the distance covered on foot, the itinerary surely required some two weeks. There are two short guidebooks from the 20th century which were used during these trips, once again available as block prints and providing the Nepalese toponyms corresponding to the Tibetan names. As both these short works lead up to Chu-mig Byang-chub bdud-rtsi in the south of the Valley, we may surmise that it was again the earlier guidebook of Nas-lung-pa Ngag-dbang rdo-rje which served as the model for their itineraries.[30]

As observed in the case of the world geographies, certain details of the more learned treatises informed their description of Nepal. But it seems that even for the scholar who was depicting a country he had not seen, as well as for Tibetan

---

1750?), the author of a history of Buddhism in China known as *rGya nag chos 'byung*. On the latter work and its author, who was of Mongolian origin and had married into the lineal Manchu royal dynasty, see Mala (2006:145–147) and Zhang (2017:570–572). The text is also referred to in another statement by Kaḥ-thog rig-'dzin concerning an early renovation of the Bodhnāth Stūpa; see the translation below, note 77.

[30] The itinerary as recommended in the Fourth Khams-sprul's guidebook is contained in Dowman (2020:401–402). For the short guidebook of the Newar Bhikṣu Ngag-dbang rdo-rje, see his *Bal yul gnas yig* and the translation in Dowman (1981:205–284). The work also circulated as a xylograph, executed in 1954 in the Kimdol vihāra; see Ehrhard (2004:64, note 11). The itinerary of this work and a second short guidebook produced by a teacher from Ladakh called Padma 'gro-'dul bde-chen rdo-rje are described in Kaschewsky (1982:433–437).

travellers passing through the country on their way to India, the popular guide-book still supplied useful knowledge, whether about places imagined or visited in person.

# Part Two

## Bal yul gyi gnas dang rten gyi lo rgyus nges par brjod pa 'khrul spong nor bu'i me long zhes bya bzhugs so //

**[A: 1b] [B: 1b]** oṃ svasti / bal yul gyi gnas dang rten gyi lo rgyus nges par brjod pa 'khrul spong nor bu'i me long zhes bya ba / rgyal ba sras dang slob mar bcas pa gus pas 'phyag 'tshal lo //

dpal ldan yon tan mi zad shin tu rgya che rin chen 'byung gnas gting dpag dka' //
brtse[1] chen thugs rje'i dbugs ba[2] dkar pos legs 'khrigs gzhan phan rlabs phreng phyogs brgyar g.yo //
byang chub snying po'i rin chen rdul brtsegs rab brtan[3] ye **[B: 2a]** shes rta gdong bsreg za 'bar //
sa gsum rigs ldan skal bzang chu klung grangs med yongs 'du sangs rgyas mchog de rgyal //

sras bcas rgyal ba'i thugs rje'i tshon ris 'bum //
gsal bar shar ba'i dge **[A: 2a]** mtshan byin ldan pa //
phun tshogs ne pā la[4] yi gnas dang rten //
ngo mtshar yon tan gleng la su mi gus //

gang dag kun rmongs phyogs rer zhen pa'i gtam //
ngo sor khyer bas[5] cal sgrogs rjes 'brang ba[6] // **[B: 2b]**
mang mthong 'dir ni tshad thub sngon byung gi[7] //
lo rgyus rjes zhugs cha tsam spro bas 'god //

gang yang 'dzam bus mtshan pa'i gling gi bye brag dam pa'i chos kyi 'byung gnas 'phags pa'i yul dang / gangs can bod yul gyi mtshams sum can[8] gyi yul rgya bod kyi khyad par 'byed pa'i slad du sa la babs pa lta bu'i ljongs ne pā la[9] zhes bya ba'i yul gang na bde bar gshegs pa'i ring bsrel gyi snying po **[A: 2b]** can chos gzugs kyi rten dang / sku gzugs khyad par can dang / gtsug lag khang dang / grub brnyes dam pa mang pos zhabs kyi bcags shing byin gyis brlabs pa'i gnas khyad par 'phags pa du ma zhig yod pa las / de dag la sngon byung gi lo rgyus dkar chag zhib mor 'khod pa khungs[10] ldan zhig mig dang rna ba'i yul du

---

[1] A: rtse
[2] B: dbu ba
[3] A: brten
[4] A: nai pa la
[5] A: gyer bas
[6] A, B: 'breng ba
[7] A: gis
[8] B: rtsen
[9] A: nai pa la
[10] A: khung

spyad byar ma gyur pas ji bzhin brjod par rngo mi thogs[11] shing bal yul rang du grags pa'i lo rgyus dag kyang phal cher ngag sgros 'chol pas yid brtan du rung dka' bar snang la / bod blun rgan po dag gis byas **[B: 3a]** pa'i lo rgyus dang / zin bris / brda' chad tsam gyis bal yul du ma grags shing / gnas kyi ming tshun chad kyang sna tshogs su smra ba'i khungs[12] med rnams dang / 'ol tshod kyi[13] brdzun gtam 'ba' zhig bab col tu[14] smra bas phyogs 'dzin gyi dbang gis ngo sor brjod pa de dag ni blun pos blun po'i tshogs kyi mgo bskor ba yin pa'i phyir /

ji skad du yang[15] sa skya legs bshad las /

> blun po log pa'i lam 'gro na //
> blun pa nyid du go bas chog //
> mkhas pa log pa'i lam 'gro na //
> rgyu mtshan gang zhig dpyad dgos so //

zhes pa ltar / shes ldan rnams kyis[16] gtam du bya ba ma yin zhing nyan par rigs pa yang ma yin no //

skabs dir tshad mar gyur pa'i gtam gyi gzhi ni / 'phags **[A: 3a]** mchog klu sgrub zhabs kyis mdzad par grags pa'i dkar chag lha mdong lo tsa ba[17] bshes gnyen rnam rgyal gyis[18] bsgyur ba zhig yod par grags kyang / sngar dpe rgyun mthong byar ma gyur cing / phyi snyigs dus kyi thams cad mkhyen pa chen po si **[B: 3a]** tu dharmākara'am[19] / bstan pa'i nyin byed kyis bsgyur bar mdzad pa'i **b**al yul shing kun gyi lo rgyus dbu zhabs su paṇḍi tas byas pa'i tshigs bcad 'ga' zhig las dngos gzhi brtsams[20] kyi bka' stsal pa'i mdo nyid du bzhed pa de nyid tshad ma'i gtan tshigs gtso bor bzung nas rang blos ji ltar 'tshal ba'i lo rgyus gtam du bya ba la lnga ste / bal yul dang li yul gyi rnam par dbye ba'i rgyu mtshan bshad pa / rang byung mchod rten chen po shing kun gyi lo rgyus bshad pa / mchod rten bya rung kha shor gyi lo rgyus bshad pa / yan lag gi gnas dang rten gzhan[21] dag gi lo rgyus bshad pa / zhar byung 'phros su bya ba'i gtam gzhan yang brjod pa'o //

---

[11] A: rngo thog
[12] A: khung
[13] A: kyis
[14] A, B: 'chol du
[15] B: om. yang
[16] A: kyi
[17] B: lo tsā ba
[18] A: gyi
[19] A, B: dharma kara
[20] A, B: brtsoms
[21] A: add. gyi

[I]

dang po ni / bod snga rabs pa dag gis[22] byas pa'i lo rgyus dang ngag sgros su grags par / 'phags pa glang ru lung bstan kyi mdor bshad pa'i li yul dang / yul dge ba can sogs bal yul yin par 'dod pa dang / ri glang ru dang / mchod rten go ma sa la gandha[23] yang shing **[B: 4a]** kun nyid du ngos bzung bar byed mod / de ltar na mdo de nyid las **[A: 3b]** chu bo go ma'i 'gram zhes pa dang / sngon mtsho chen po yod pa śā ri'i bu[24] dang / rnam thos kyi bus blangs te byang phyogs gyi shod[25] gtsang por 'phos par bshad pa li yul bal yul du 'dod na / chu bo go ma dang / gyi shod[26] gtsang po sogs kyang 'di yin zhes ngos bzung bar rigs la / mchod rten go ma sā la gandha'i mtshan gyi sgra bshad kyang smra bar rigs so //

kha cig yul nyi shu rtsa bzhi'i ya gyal gau da va ri / zhes pa bal yul te / ba'i mchog sbyin zhes bya ba / ba dmar ser zhig gi 'o ma ko khoms kyi nags kyi sdong po zhig la 'thor ba'i lo rgyus can du 'dod te / gau ba lang / da na sbyin pa / va ri mchog la / 'jug tshul gsungs[27] kyang yul nyer bzhi'i gau da wa ri[28] dngos ni gau da wa ri rna ba g.yon / zhes pa la phyi[29] snyan g.yon du ngos 'dzin pas so //

bal yul gyi dkar chag dang lam yig tu btags pa par du 'khod pa 'gar / **[B: 4b]** 'jam dpal rtsa rgyud dang mdo sde glang ru dang / bka' gdams glegs bam las / bal yul dang li yul thun mong du bstan zer ba yang 'ol tshod kyi rdzun gtam kho na ste //

'jam dpal rtsa rgyud nas ni /

stobs bcu ldan pas bshad pa'i zhing //
byang phyogs yod pa'i zhing dag dang //
kha che dang ni rgya yul dang //
bal po de bzhin mang yul dang //
rgya yul che dang li yul ste //
de dag dngos grub **[A: 4a]** sgrub pa'i zhing //

zhes yul so sor dngos su bstan pa bzhin du thun mong du ga la bshad / bka' gdams glegs bam las bal yul li yul du bshad pa gtan nas med do // dper mtshon na rgya nag gi yul la che chung gi dbye ba dang / bod dang bod chen por yang

---

[22] A: gi
[23] A, B: go ma sā la gandha
[24] A: śā ri bu
[25] A: sho
[26] A: sho
[27] A: gsung
[28] B: gau dā va ri
[29] A, B: la phyis

dbye ba dngos su yod na 'dzam bu gling gi yul gru phyogs tha dad pa gcig tu sdom par 'dod pa sangs rgyas las kyang khyod cag[30] mkhas par snang ngo //

'o na li yul dngos gang zhe na / mdo glang ru lung bstan las /

> bcom ldan 'das kyis[31] bka' stsal pa / **[B: 5a]** rigs kyi bu nyon cig / nga mya ngan las 'das nas lo brgya lon pa'i tshe / rgya'i yul nas rgya yi rgyal po ca yang zhes bya ba bu stong tshang bar bdog pa zhig 'byung bar 'gyur te / bu re re yang re re gsar du[32] tshol du bcug go /

zhes pa nas /

> rgyal bu sa la nus nu ma nu des yul btab pa'i phyir rgyu des na yul 'di'i ming la nu ma nu zhes bya bar 'gyur ro //

zhes pa'i bar gyi bstan pa ltar kun mkhyen padma dkar po'i chos 'byung bstan pa rgyas par /

> sngon ston pa bzhugs pa'i dus mtshor 'khyil ba śā ri bus gseg gshang[33] gis brdol bar go ma sā la gandha zhes pa sangs rgyas bzhi'i mchod rten / zhabs rjes sangs rgyas bzhi'i skyu'i rgyur[34] byin gyis brlabs pa'i li'i ri bzhugs pa'i ston pa mya ngan las 'das nas lo brgya **[A: 4b]** phrag gnyis tsam na rgya'i rgyal po la bu dgu brgya[35] dgu bcu[36] rtsa dgu yod pa las / da dung bu dgos nas rnam thos sras la blangs pas chos rgyal mnya ngan med pa'i tsha bo skyes ma thag pa cig rnam thos sras **[B: 5b]** kyis[37] byin pa ltogs nas kha sa la gtad pas de las nu ma byung / de las 'o ma 'thung ste sa la nu zhes grags pa cher skyes pa dang / rgya rje dpung dang bcas pa chu bo shi ta[38] 'bab pa li yul du brdzangs pa[39] da lta hor sog gi yul rnams yin zhes gsungs shing /

dpal rig 'dzin chen po kaḥ thog pas kyang /

> rgyal po nus bdag byed pa'i yul drug dus sbyor skabs kyi li yul ni bod yul gyi byang phyogs su yod dgos par snang bas snga rabs kyi

---

[30] B: khyed cag
[31] A: kyi
[32] A, B: sar du
[33] A, B: shang
[34] A: sgyur
[35] A, B: om. dgu brgya
[36] A: cu
[37] B: kyi
[38] B: shi ti
[39] A: rdzangs pa

mkhas pa bcom ldan rig ral dang / phyis byung[40] gi mkhas pa kha cig gis kyang sa nu byung ba'i[41] yul zi ling gi byang gi phyogs char yod par brjod /

zhes gsungs la /

snga 'gyur gyi rgyud sku gdung 'bar ba[42] mchod rten gyi rgyud las /

byang shar mtshams na li yi[43] yul //
dur khrod 'jig rten mngon[44] rdzogs na //
dbang ldan padma chen po dang //
mi zad drag gang ba dang //
mchod rten ge'u de shan bya //
ston pas cho 'phrul bstan pa'i gnas //
chu 'byin me 'bar **[B: 6a]** 'khrul snang mang //
li rje btsan po'i rgyal khams yin //

zhes dang /

sngon he ru kas drag po btul ba'i **[A: 5a]** tshe / yul brgyad kyi dur khrod du ma mo brgyad kyi rten dngos grub 'byung ba'i mchod rten brgyad byung ba ni /

ma ga dha bde byed //
sing ga lar ri po ta la //
bal por bya tri kha shor //
sing ga gling du ge'u da na //
li yul du go ma sā la gandha //
kha cher ka ni ka //
za hor du bde spyod .... //
.... gzhon nu mchod rten no //

zhes bdud rtsi mchog gi rgyud kyi 'grel pa las kyang 'byung bas yul dang mchod rten so sor bstan pa dang /

rgyal po bka' 'bum las / li yul gyi dge tshul gnyis kyis[45] 'phags pa 'jam dpal bsgrubs[46] ste lung bstan pa bzhin bod du 'ongs pa[47] chos rgyal srong btsan sgam po dang mjal[48] nas slar yang li yul du log pa'i tshul dang / bal yul gyi lo rgyus

---

[40] A, B: 'byung
[41] A, B: 'byung ba'i
[42] A, B: add. la
[43] A: om. yi
[44] A, B: sngon
[45] A: kyi
[46] A, B: sgrub
[47] A: 'ong ba
[48] A: 'jal

so sor bshad la / gzhan yang dus kyi 'khor lo sogs du ma zhig nas bal yul dang li yul so sor bshad pas go bar nus so //

blun po 'ga' **[B: 6b]** zhig li yul zhes pa kha skad du / stod bal po li brdung sa nas smad rgya mo dar thag sa[49] yan zer ba bzhin bal po rnams li brdung ba rgyu mtshan du byas nas / li yul du 'dod pa ni shin tu 'khrul te li brdung sa thams cad li yul du ci zhig 'gyur / yang dus phyis rgya nag gi lo tsa ba[50] chen po gung mgon po skyabs kyis mdzad pa'i rgya nag chos 'byung du li yul lcang du ngos bzung ba **[A: 5b]** dang / rgya nag rang du kong wu'i zhes pa'i yul du glang ru lung bstan nas bshad pa'i gtsug lag khang dang / mchod rten go ma sā la ghan dar rgya rnams kyis ngos 'dzin pa de yod ces rgyal ba lnga pa chen pos dngos su gzigs tshul rnam thar ka pa las 'byung / de ltar yang hor sog gi yul dang ljang sogs li yul du ngos bzung nas / yul der glang ru lung bstan nas bshad pa'i mchod rten go ma sā la gan dha sogs bshad tshod dang mthun pa phal cher yod dgos par grub kyang sngar phan gang zag 'di dang 'di lta bus mthong thos kyi rgyu mtshan ma grags **[B: 7a]** shing / hor sog tu bzhed pa'ang[51] / mdo de nyid las dru gu rus sna tshogs dang / hor dang zhes dmigs su bsal bar[52] gsungs pas dpyad gzhir snang la / des na / li yul dngos 'di yin zhes mkhas grub pa mang po gung mthun pa'i ngos 'dzin thag chod pa zhig kyang ma byung ba som nyir[53] bzhag pa ltar 'dir yang tha gcig tu bzung bar ma nus so //

> dus gsum rnam 'dren kun gyis yongs bsngags shing //
> sa gsum skye dgu'i[54] tshogs kyis nyer bstan pa //
> skabs gsum mtho ris grong gis dpal 'dzin pa'i //
> rten gsum ngo mtshar gyis mdzes ne pāl ljongs //
>
> 'phags bod khyad par 'byed la gdong bzhi pas //
> ched du **[A: 6a]** byas bzhin 'dod dgu'i 'byor pa kun //
> ma tshang med rdzogs grags pa phyogs kyi mthar //
> ring ba'i phun tshogs yul der bsngags par 'os ///

bal yul gyi gnas dang rten gyi lo rgyus nges par brjod pa 'khrul spong nor bu'i me long zhes bya ba las li yul dang bal yul gcig tu **[B: 7b]** 'dod pa rnam par 'byed pa bshad pa'i skabs te dang po'o //

[II]

gnyis pa rang byung mchod rten chen po shing kun gyi lo rgyus bshad pa la / de yang / rgya gar 'phags pa'i yul du ni / sva yaṃ bhu caitya / zhes pa'i sgra las rang byung gi mchod rten grags shing / sngon sangs rgyas rin chen gtsug tor can

[49] B: thag pa
[50] B: lo tsā ba
[51] A: bzhad pa'ang
[52] B: gsal bar
[53] A: som nyer
[54] A, B: rgu'i

gyi dpral ba'i mdzod spu las 'byung bar 'dod la / 'phags mchog nā gārdzu nas[55] byon te / sri zhu rgya cher mdzad pa dang / slob dpon chen po dbyig gnyen gyi sku tshe'i smad du bal yul rang byung mchod rten nyid gzigs su byon pa'i lo rgyus 'og nas 'byung ba ltar dang / jo bo rje dpal mar me mdzad bzang po bod yul gyi mngon du byon pa'i tshe / bal yul rang byung gi mchod rten blta bar 'ong ngo //

zhes pa'i zol gyis byon pa mdzad pa sogs 'phags yul nyid du shin tu grags che zhing / bod du phal cha ba zhig gis gong du smos pa bzhin glang ru lung bstan gyi mdo bshad pa'i go ma sā la gandhar ngos 'dzin / spyir btang 'phags pa shin **[B: 8a]** kun du grags shing / zur chag gi skad dang bal skad thun mong du shin bur zhes brjod //

gang ltar rang byung gi mchod rten ni som nyi[56] med par 'di kho nar nges la / klu sgrub kyis[57] mdzad par grags pa'i **[A: 6b]** dkar chag lha mdong[58] lo tsā bas[59] 'gyur las /

bskal pa gnyis ldan dus su ni //
glang ru zhes bya'i parba ta //
bal po'i 'gro bas yongs shes 'gyur //
de ming khyad par bskal pas 'byed //

zhes[60] dang /

kun mkhyen si tu pa'i 'gyur gsar gyi mdo de nyid du rgyas par bshad pa 'dir drangs pa ni /

glang ru zhes bya'i ri bo ni //
ne pā la yi yul du yod //
de ni dus kyi khyad par gyis //
ming gi rab dbye tha dad de //
rdzogs ldan dus su padma'i ri //
gsum ldan ri bo rdo rje brtsegs //
gnyis ldan la ni glang ru'i ri //
rtsod dus ri bo glang mjug[61] go //

de nyid de'i tshe'ang padma'i ri chen po zhes pa'i ming rab tu 'jug cing 'byung bar 'gyur ro //

---

[55] A: na gardzu nas, B: nā gardzu nas
[56] A: soms nyi
[57] A: kyi
[58] A: 'dong
[59] A: lo tsa ba'i
[60] B: ces
[61] A: 'jug

de bzhin du / ’das pa dang / ma ’ongs pa dang / da lta ’byung **[B: 8b]** ba’i dus bzhi po rnams su’ang ming du ’gyur ro / da lta ni yul der gnas pa’i skyes bo rnams kyis[62] sī hang mgu[63] zhes brjod de / de yang khams sna tshogs pa du mas rnam par bkra ba nā ga ge sar[64] dang / tsampa ka dang / ba ku la ang / piṣpa la dang / ko bi dā ra[65] dang / plakṣa dang / ka pī ta na dang / tunna[66] dang / ku pa la ka dang / a sho ka[67] dang / tā la[68] dang / tā mā la[69] sogs pa’i ljon pa / khri shing sna tshogs pa bkram pa / ’dab chags sna tshogs pas sgra ’byin pa / ’bab chu sna tshogs pa ’bab pa / ri dvags mang po tshogs **[A: 7a]** pa / me tog gi rigs mang po lhag par gnas pa / ’bras bu rnam pa mang po dang ldan pa / rkang drug rnams kyis[70] glu dbyangs len pa / lha klu gnod sbyin dri za lha ma yin / nam mkha’ lding mi’am ci lto ’phye chen po grub pa’i rig ’dzin la sogs pa’i tshogs kyis[71] brten pa[72] / der sngon tshe rang byung ba’i rab mchog shel las grub pa’i mchod rten gyi rje bo dam pa khru gang pa’i tshad can yod do //

mchod rten gyi **[B: 9a]** rje bo dam pa der chos dang / don dang / ’dod pa dang / thar pa don du gnyer ba’i sems can rnams kyis[73] mchog tu dad pas mchod par bya’o //

de’ang ’di skad thos te dus gcig na / de bzhin gshegs pa dpal śākya thub pa ne pā la[74] yi yul du ri glang ru zhes bya ba’i rang byung gi mchod rten rje bo dam pa’i nub phyogs kyi logs mjug ma’i rtse mor mchod rten dang nye bar sems can thams cad rjes su ’dzin pa’i don du ’od srung chen po la sogs pa’i dge slong brgya phrag lnga’i dge ’dun chen po dang / byams pa la sogs pa’i byang chub sems dpa’i brgya phrag lnga dang / tshangs pa dang khyab ’jug dang / dbang phyug chen po la sogs pa’i lha’i tshogs rnams dang thabs gcig tu bzhugs so //

zhes dang /

---

62 A: kyi
63 B: bīhamngu
64 A, B: na ga ge sar
65 A, B: ko bi sā ra
66 A, B: runna
67 B: a svha ka
68 A, B: ta la
69 A, B: ta ma la
70 A: kyi
71 A: kyi
72 A: bstan pa; B: bsten pa
73 A: kyi
74 A: nai pā la

byang chub sems dpa' chen po byams pas zhus pa'i lan du bcom ldan 'das kyis[75] bka' stal pa / byams pa / sngon byung ba bskal pa bzang po 'dir ske rgu rnams tshe **[A: 7b]** lo stong phrag brgyad cur 'tsho ba'i tshe **[B: 9b]** 'jig rten gyi 'dren pa chos kyi rgyal po rnam par gzigs zhes bya ba de bzhin gshegs pa dgra bcom pa yang dag par rdzogs pa'i sangs rgyas gnyen ldan[76] gyi grong khyer chen por byung ngo / byams pa / de'i tshe de'i dus na byang chub sems dpa' bden pa'i chos zhes bya ba yod de / de'ang sangs rgyas rnam par gzigs de la mchod par byed do //

byams pa / bdag ni de'i tshe de'i dus na bden pa'i chos zhes bya ba'i byang chub sems dpa' de yin te gzhan du mi blta'o //

de bzhin gshegs pa rnam gzigs de mya ngan las 'das nas dus shin tu ring po zhig 'das nas bskal pa bzang po de nyid du skye rgu rnams lo stong phrag bdun cur 'tsho ba'i tshe / 'jig rten gyi 'dren pa chos kyi rgyal po gtsug tor can zhes bya ba'i de bzhin gshegs pa dgra bcom pa yang dag par rdzogs pa'i sangs rgyas a ru ṇa zhes bya ba'i grong khyer chen por byung ngo / byams pa / de'i tshe de'i dus na bzod pa'i rgyal po zhes bya ba'i byang chub sems dpa' yod de / de **[B: 10a]** yang / sangs rgyas gtsug tor can de la mchod par byed do //

byams pa / nga ni de'i tshe de'i dus na bzod pa'i rgyal po zhes bya'i byang chub sems dpar gyur te gzhan du mi blta'o //

byams pa / de'i dus su bal po yul 'di nyid kyang chur rgyang grags bdun dang ldan pa'i[77] mtsho chen por gyur te klu'i gnas zhes bya ba'i ming du grags so // **[A: 8a]**

de yang yan lag brgyad dang ldan pa'i chus yongs su gang ba / utpa la dang / padma dang / ku mud dang / padma dkar po dang / me tog rnam pa mang pos brgyan pa / ngag pa dang / bzhad dang / kā raṃḍa[78] dang / khrung khrung dang / ngur pa rnams sgra snyan par 'byin pa / chu la spyod pa'i srogs chags kyi tshogs du ma gnas par gyur pa dri bzang po'i me tog gi ljon pa dang / 'bras bu'i ljon pa sna tshogs skyes pas kun nas rnam par bkra ba / der shing rta'i 'phang lo'i tshad kyi padma chen po rin po che snga las grub pa 'dab ma stong gis sgeg cing **[B: 10b]** nor bu'i sdong bu dang / pha lam gyi ge sar dang / padma rāga 'bar ba'i ze'u 'bru dang ldan pa rab tu byung ngo / de'i ze'u 'bru la gang zhig chos kyi dbyings shel gyi rang bzhin can mtshan nyid thams cad yongs su rdzogs pa gtso

---

[75] A: kyi
[76] A: gnyer ldan
[77] A: dang zheng du
[78] A, B: kā ranta ka

> bo thu bo rnams kyis[79] 'dud par bya ba / mchod par bya ba / mos par bya ba / bsam pa las lhag pa'i 'bras bu rab tu 'byin par 'di / lha dang lha ma yin dang mi rnams kyi phan dang bde ba dang thar pa'i phyir du rang nyid rab tu skyes so //
>
> gang skyes pa tsam gyis rab tu dga' ba bzhin du sa chen po ri[80] dang bcas pa rab tu g.yo zhing me tog gi char bab pa dang / bar snang gi gnas nas lha'i rnga bo che'i sgra sgrogs pa dang / phyogs thams cad rab tu gsal bar 'gyur ro[81] / **[A: 8b]**
>
> chos kyi dbyings kyi mchod rten de da lta'i tshe yang gnas shing dus shin tu ring por yang gnas par 'gyur ro //
>
> byams pa / de ltar chos kyi dbyings kyi mchod rten 'di de bzhin gshegs pa dgra bcom pa yang dag pa rdzogs pa'i sangs **[B: 11a]** rgyas gtsug tor can gyi dus kyi tshe na rang byung du skyes pa'o //

zhes le'u dang por chos kyi dbyings kyi mchod rten gyi sngon byung gsungs shing / le'u gnyis par mchod rten chen po de la phyag dang mchod pa dang / nyams pa gso ba dang / bskor na la sogs pa'i phan yon rgyas par bstan te / le'u gsum par slar yang 'phags pa byams pas gsol ba'i lan du ston pas 'di skad ces /

> byams pa / bskal pa bzang po 'di nyid du sngon byung ba'i de bzhin gshegs pa gtsug gtor can yongs su mya ngan las 'das nas yun ring po dus'i dus na skye rgu rnams rshe lo stong phrag drug cur 'tsho ba'i tshe 'jig rten gyi 'dren pa chos kyi rgyal po thams cad skyobs cs bya ba'i de bzhin gshegs pa dgra bcom pa yangs dag par rdzogs pa'i sangs rgyas dpe med zhes bya ba'i grong khyer chen por 'byung ngo //

zhes dang /

> byams pa / dus de'i tshe byang phyogs gyi rgyud du rgya nag chen po'i yul gyi mdun na 'jam dpal gyu ri bo rtse mo[82] **[B: 11b]** lnga pa zhes bya ba'i ri yod de / ri de las 'jam dpal gyi sprul pa'i rang bzhin 'jam pa'i lha zhes bya ba'i rdo rje slob **[A: 9a]** dpon mngon shes lnga dang ldan pa / skra can ma'i sprul pa'i rang bzhin mchog sbyin ma zhes bya ba'i slob dpon ma dang / nye ba'i skra can ma'i sprul pa'i gzugs thar sbyin ma zhes bya ba'i slob dpon ma rnams lhan gcig tu chos kyi dbyings kyi mchod rten la bskur sti bya ba'i

---

[79] A: kyi
[80] A: 'di
[81] B: gyur tro
[82] B: add. 'jam dpal gtsug phud lnga pa'i ri bo

don du 'dir 'ongs nas kyang chos kyi dbyings kyi mchod rten 'di la lta bar byed do[83] //

bltas nas kyang de'i thugs rje'i blo gros 'di lta bu byung ste / gang chos kyi dbyings kyi mchod rten 'di skyes bos dben pa'i mtsho chen po 'dit padma'i ze'u 'bru la rang byung du skyes pa 'di nyid chu skem par byas nas ji ltar sa'i phyogs nyi tshe ba[84] 'dir / grong dang grong khyer dang / grong rdal dang / ljongs dang yul 'khor dang / rgyal po'i pho brang rnams rab tu 'byung bar 'gyur zhing sems can rnams kyis chos kyi dbyings kyi mchod rten **[B: 12a]** 'di la phyag 'tshal ba dang / mos pa dang / mchod pa dang / rjed pa dang / bskur sti dang / bla mar byar rung bar 'gyur ba de ltar bdag gis bgyi'o //

zhes de bzhin du yang dag par bsam nas shin tu rno ba'i ral gris ri dral te chu phyir 'gro bar byas shing / gang dang gang du yang ri bo dang ro ba gang dang gang du chu klung thams cad kyi chu bkag nas de dang der gnas pa'i ri bo dang rdo ba de dang de rnams bcad cing bcad nas chu'i rgyun **[A: 9b]** lam du byas so //

zhes gsungs pa glang ru lung bstan gyi nang nas bshad pa dang phyogs mi mtshungs shing / da lta bal po rnams kyi lo rgyus tshad mar grags pa yang / 'jam dpal gyis ral gris ri dral te chu phyir 'gro bar byas shing lhag ma cung zad lus pa yang ral gri rnam pa can du yod pas mtsho ral gri zhes grags la / 'jam dpal gyi byin brlabs pa'i mthus bal yul 'dir bzo rigs sna tshogs kyi 'byung khungs su gyur pa yin zhes zer ba **[B: 12b]** ltar bod rnams kyis kyang[85] mtsho ral grir 'bod pa dang / thang yig nas bshad pa'i bal yul nyi ma khud[86] gi mtsho zhes lo tsā ba[87] rlangs[88] dpal gyi seng ge 'das pa'i sa yang 'di nyid du grags te //

mdo de nyid las /

de nas nyin mtshan bzhis mtsho chen po'i chu thams cad legs par bskams nas / de'i tshe chu dang bas yongs su gang ba kun 'dzin[89] zhes bya ba'i mtsho 'di gcig pu nyid gnas te / gang zhig da lta skye bo rnams kyis[90] dha nā da ha zhes brjod do // 'di nyid du mtsho chen po'i bdag po karko ṭa zhes bya ba'i klu'i rgyal po gnas so // mtsho dang bar ma chad pa nyid du chos kyi dbyings kyi mchod rten gyi gzhir gyur te / rdo rje slob dpon 'jam pa'i lha'i mthu las

[83] A: blta bar byed do
[84] A: der tshe ba
[85] A: kyi'ang
[86] A, B: khung
[87] A: lo tsa ba
[88] A, B: glang
[89] A, B: add. a dha ra
[90] A: kyi

> padma chen po de yang ri 'di ltar gyur nas gnas so // rgyu mtshan de las ri bo 'di la rdo rje brtsegs pa'i ri bo zhes rab tu **[A: 10a]** grags so // gang 'dir mtshon pa'i sa gzhi'i phyogs nyi tshe ba 'di yang chu med pa nyid kyi phyir nye ba'i tstshando har gyur nas ri rnams kyis[91] kun nas yongs su **[B: 13a]** bskor te gnas so // 'di yang gangs can gyi ming can 'khor lo sdom pa'i dkyil 'khor gyi rnam pa shin tu rgyal bar dka' ba'i sa gzhi'i rang bzhin dang shes rab phun sum tshogs pa'i ye shes kyi rang bzhin can lha mo bya gdong ma 'di yang 'di nyid du gtso bor byung nas 'jig rten gsum du khyab cing skye gnas kyi rnam pas rab tu byung ngo //

zhes dang /

> byams pa / de ltar de bzhin gshegs pa dgra bcom pa yang dag par rdzogs pa thams cad skyobs kyi dus kyi tshe 'jam dpal kyi sprul pa'i gzugs rdo rje slob dpon 'jam pa'i lha zhes pas chu skem par byas nas mtsho chen po sa'i phyogs nyi tshe bar byas so //

zhes byung ngo //

de nas bal po'i yul 'dir gromg dang / grong khyer dang / grong rdal dang / ljongs dang / yul 'khor dang / rgyal po'i pho brang sogs dus nam gyi tshe byung ba ni /

mdo de nyid kyi le'u bzhi pas las /

> byams pa / sngon byung ba bskal pa bzang po 'di la de bzhin gshegs pa **[B: 13b]** thams cad skyob yongs su mya ngan las 'das nas dus shin tu ring ba zhig na / skye rgu rnams kyi[92] tshe lo stong phrag bzhi bcu tsho ba'i tshe 'jig rten **[A: 10b]** gyi 'dren pa cho kyi rgyal po 'khor ba 'jig ces bya ba'i de bzhin gshegs pa dgra bcom pa yang dag par rdzogs pa'i sangs rgyas bzod ldan zhes bya ba'i grong khyer chen por byung ngo //

zhes dang /

> byams pa / de'i tshe yang dus re zhig na / bcom ldan 'das 'khor ba 'jig de nye ba'i tstshando ha 'dir dung[93] gi ri chen po'i rtse mo gtsang zhing rgya che ba'i rtse la dge slong gi dge 'dun chen po dang thabs gcig tu byang chub sems dpa'i sems dpa'i chen po mang po dang / lha dang mi dang mi ma yin pa mang pos yongs su bskor zhing / mdun bdar te bzhugs nas 'khor thams cad kyi sdug bsngal gyi rgya mtsho yongs su skem pa zhes bya ba'i chos kyi rnam grangs ston par mdzad do //

---

[91] A: kyi

[92] A, B: kyis

[93] A: add. shā parba ta

zhes dang /

> de'i tshe yang dung gi ri'i rtse mor bcom ldan 'das dpal rdo rje sems dpa' phyag g.yas phyag sor **[B: 14a]** rnams las bsod nams kyi chu'i gnas can mchog tu zhi ba'i 'jig rten gyi mngon par 'dod pa'i 'bras bu rab tu sbyin pa bcom ldan 'das 'khor ba 'jig gi[94] chos bstan pa khyad par las chu bo gcig pu gang yang dag par phyung ngo //
>
> gtsang mar gyur pa de ni da lta yang bagma tī[95] zhes par rab tu grags pa 'di'o / de bzhin du dung gi ri bo rtse gcig la phyag sor bcu las yang dag par 'byung ba'i 'dod pa'i 'bras bu rab tu ster ba'i bsod nams kyi chu dri ma med pa'i gnas dang ldan pa'i **[A: 11a]** chu bo ste / gnyis po gang du de rnams rab tu byung nas skra dang kha spu bregs pa de dag cha gnyis su byas te cha gcig bcug pas da lta'ang de la ke śa ba tī[96] zhes rab tu grags so //

zhes gsungs pa'i chu bo bagma tī[97] ni da lta bod rnams kyis sgra zur nyams pas bag wa tir 'bod pa 'di yin la / 'di nyid kyi kyi chu 'go zur chag gi skad du / śi ti pur zhes pa'i ri ngogs su bag ces pa stag gi ming de'i gdong **[B: 14b]** brag las rang byung gi dbyibs su byas pa zhig gi kha nas 'bab pas bagma tir brjod pa yin zer / skabs 'dir ke śa ba tī zhes pa'i chu dang nor bu brtsegs pa la sogs pa'i ri bo rnams kyi ming gsungs pa ma gtogs pas slar dpyad par bya'o //

yang mdo de nyid las /

> byams pa / de ltar de bzhin gshegs pa dgra[98] bcom pa yang dag par rdzogs pa'i sangs rgyas 'khor ba 'jig gi dus kyi tshe na / thog mar 'dir grong dang / grong khyer dang / grong brdal dang / ljongs dang / yul 'khor dang / rgyal po'i pho brang rnams byung ngo //

zhes gsungs / gzhan yang le'u lnga par / chu bos phye ba'i gnas chen po bcu gnyis dang / klu'i rgyal po chen po bcu gnyis gnas pa **[A: 11b]** dang / de dag la cho ga bzhin du 'khrus bya ba dang / gso sbyong blangs nas nges par mchod pa dang / sems rtse gcig pas bsgom pa dang / bzlas pa dang / dka' thub dang / bsam gtan byed pa rnams la khyad par du 'phags pa'i dge bcu'i 'bras bu **[B: 15a]** chen po dang / zhi ba dang / rgyas pa la sogs pa'i las kyi 'bras bu ji snyed pa nas / rnam par grol ba'i grub pa'i go 'phang du 'gro ba'i bar gyi phan yon rgyas par gsungs shing / le'u drug par byams pas zhus pa'i lan du 'di skad ces /

---

94 A, B: gis
95 B: add. bsung can
96 A, B: add. skra can ma
97 A: bagma ti
98 B: gra

byams pa / sngon byung ba bskal pa bzang po 'dir / de bzhin gshegs pa 'khor ba 'jig yongs su mnya ngan las 'das nas / dus ches ring zhig nas skye rnams[99] tshe lo stong phrag gsum cur 'tsho ba'i tshe / 'jig rten 'dren pa chos kyi rgyal po gser thub zhes bya ba'i de bzhin gshegs pa dgra bcom pa yang dag par rdzogs pa'i sangs rgyas mdzes ldan zhes bya'i grong khyer chen por byung ngo //

zhes dang /

de'i tshe bi kra ma śi la'i gtsug lag **[A: 12 a]** khang chen por dge slong chos dpal bshes gnyen zhes bya ba'i mkhas pa chen pos mtshan yang dag par brjod pa rnam par bshad de / des kyang yi ge bcu gnyis kyi don bshad par ma nus so / de yang ma nus pa nyid las dus **[B: 15b]** la bab par gyur te / 'di ltar byang phyogs kyi rgyud du 'jam dpal gyi[100] ri bo rtse lnga pa zhes bya bar byang chub sems dpa' sems dpa' chen chen po 'jam dpal gnas so zhes rjes su thos na der song nas don der zhu bar bya'o / zhes nges par byas te der 'gro ba'i don la rab tu gnas so / gang zhig byang phyogs su 'ong bar byed pa de 'ongs nas kyang nyi ma 'ga' zhig la yul der phyin par gyur to / de'i dus su rdo rje slob dpon 'jam pa'i lha des chos dpal bshes gnyen 'ong bar rigs nas rdzu 'phrul chen po bstan pa'i don du / seng ge dang stag gnyis kyi gshol la zhon nas sa gzhir 'khod do / der chos dpal bshes gnyen gyis slob dpon 'jam pa'i lha rgyang ring po nas mthong ste de dang nye bar 'ongs so / 'ongs nas kyang[101] de ring bdag gi gtsug lag khang du ngal bsos[102] la gdod[103] byang phyogs kyi lam du song zhig / ces smras pas des[104] cang mi smra bar khas blangs so / rab tu zhi ba'i sngags kyi rnam pa mi shes par **[A: 12b]** mdun gyi seng ge dang stag gi rdzu **[B: 16a]** 'phrul brtul nas thong shul ni skye bos rtogs par bya ba'i slad du bzhag go / thong gshol bzhag pa'i phyogs de la da lta yang 'jam dpal gnas pa (mañjuśrībhāvanaṃ)[105] zhes bar grags so / de yang de bos pas de dang lhan cig tu 'jam dpal gyi ri bo 'di nyid du 'ongs so / gang du thong gshol la zhon pa'i gnas der da lta yang sa pā la[106] zhes 'jig rten du grags so //

zhes pa nas /

---

[99] B: dgu rnams

[100] A: gyis

[101] A, B: om. de la dri ba / bdag nyid chen po gnas 'di nas 'jam dpal gyi ri bo rtse mo lnga la thag ci tsam zhig / des smras pa / de ni thag shin tu ring ste / de bas na

[102] A: ngal so

[103] A: sdod

[104] A: de

[105] A, B: mañjuśribhabanaṃ

[106] A, B: sā pā la

'jam dpal gyis[107] gsungs pa / 'dir nor phun sum tshogs pas[108] dgos pa ci zhig yod / de'i phyir chos dpal bshes gnyen khyod la gces pas dbang bskur byin par bgyi'o / zhes zhal gyis 'ches te dbugs phyungs[109] nas chos kyi dbyings kyi mchod rten 'di na chos kyi dbyings gsung dbang gi dyil 'khor mngon sum du sprul nas / dkyil 'khor de nyid du chos kyi dbyings kyi mchod rten 'dir bkur zhing mchod par byas nas skad cig de nyid la chos dpal bshes gnyen la lha rdzas kyi tshogs mngon par dbang **[B: 16b]** bskur ro / dbang bskur ba'i rjes de ma thag nyid du yi ge bcu gnyis po de'i gdams ngag kyang bstan to[110] /

zhes dang /

byams pa / rgyu mtshan des de nas brtsams te / de bzhin gshegs pa dgra bcom pa yangs dag par rdzogs pa'i sangs rgyas gser thub kyi dus kyi tshe chos kyi dbyings kyi mchod rten **[A: 13a]** 'di nyid la chos kyi dbyings gsung gi dbang phyug ces bya ba'i mtshan byung bar gyur to /

zhes pa'i bar rgyas par bstan to / de ltar chos dbyings gsung dbang gi dkyil 'khor mngon sum du sprul te dbang bskur bzhin de'i mtshon byed du mchod rten chen po'i mdun du mchod rten chung ngu zhig gi nang du chos dbyings gsung dbang gi dkyil 'khor yin zhes pa zhig da lta yang snang la / lo rgyus dkar chag rdzun bris dag tu / dgra bcom pa nyi khri chig stong gis[111] sa blangs nas mchod rten la g.yogs pa dang / klu sgrub kyis dbu skra gtor te shing sna kun skye bar shog cig pa'i smon lam btab pas shing kun du grags zer ba ni shin tu **[B: 17a]** 'khrul pa'i rdzun ham po che che rang gar smra bar zad do //

sngar bshad ma thag nas le'u bdun par de bzhin gshegs pa 'od srung 'jig rten du byon pa'i tshe 'di skad ces /

de'i dus su byang chub sems dpa' 'jam dpal des gnas 'dir 'di ltar bya ba thams cad byas nas rdo rje slob dpon gyi cha lugs mi snang bar rang nyid lha'i lus su rang bzhin du grub pas glog bzhin song ste slar yang ri bo rtse mo lnga par bde pa chen pos gnas so / de ni 'ji ltar 'dod bzhin du 'jug pa'i phyir ro / de nas dus gzhan zhig na gau ḍa'i **[A: 13b]** yul du chos kyi bdag nyid ske dgu bde bar skyong ba rdo rje sems dpa'i sprul pa'i sku pra tsanda de ba[112] zhes bya ba'i rgyal po byung ste / des rang gi bu rgyal po grags pa mang po

---

[107] A: gyi
[108] A, B: tshogs pa
[109] A: phyung
[110] A: bstan no
[111] A: gi
[112] B: add. rab tshim lha

can śakti de ba[113] zhes bya ba rgyal srid de nyid la rgyal por dbang bskur ba byin nas / de ma thag tu 'khor bar gnas pa'i bde ba ni 'gyur ba'i sdug bsngal lo / zhes yid la byas te rgyal **[B: 17b]** srid kyi bde ba bor nas / phyogs mtshams brgyad po thams cad las yid du 'ong[114] zhing / lhag pa'i 'bras bu ster bar byed pas grub pa'i gnas su gyur pa bal po'i yul ni shin tu khyad par 'phags par shes nas de nyid du 'ongs so / 'dir 'ongs nas kyang chos dbyings gsung gi dbang phyug gi drung du rab tu byung bar byas so / śānti śrī zhes de rab tu byung ba'i ming ste de'ang rdo rje sems dpa'i brtul zhugs bzung ste skad cig de nyid la mngon par shes pa lnga dang ldan par gyur to / nam zhig na rdo rje slob dpon zhi ba dpal de nyid kyis[115] 'dir 'di bzhin du byas te / chos dbyings gsung gi dbang phyug gam rang byung bcom ldan 'das 'di'i steng nas rdul gyis g.yog par bya'o zhes yid la bzung nas de mi gsal bar bya ba dang bsrung ba'i phyir rdo bas g.yogs nas sbas par byas te / 'dod pa bzhin du mchod rten **[A: 14a]** byas so //

zhes gsungs pa 'dir legs par ltos shig / de ltar na rang byung i mchod rten dngos ni me tog padma'i **[B: 18a]** sdong po ze'u 'bru'i snying por nor bu rin po che lta bu'i shel gyi mchod rten 'od dang 'od zer phyogs bcur 'phro ba zhig tu yod par snang la / bal po rnams me tog padma'i sdong po'i rtsa ba byung ba dngos ni kho khom yin cing / de las sdong po dang yal ga rim par brgyud de[116] da lta shing kun gyi mchod rten gyi sar rang byung gi mchod rten de nyid 'khrungs pa yin zer ro / gang ltar yang rang byung gi mchod rten ngo bo ni ri'i nang du bzhugs pa la phyi rol 'gro ba'i snang ngor ri'i dbyibs dang / de'i rtse mor nang gi mchod rten gyi mtshon byed bum pa yan mngon par snang ba'i mchod rten du grub pa 'di yin no //

sngon bal po'i rgyal po 'od zer go chas lha mo 'od zer can bsgrubs[117] nas klu bi kā ra[118] sngon po bya ba'i ske ral gris bcad de klu'i gtsug gi nor bu rin po che 'o ma 'dzin zhes yod pa mchod rten gyi tog la phul / klu de nyid gnas pa'i shul la kli gtir sogs cho ga tshul bzhin byas na yo byad kyi dngos grub ster ba yin **[B: 18b]** zhes khro lo byams pa'i dpal gyi rnam thar las 'byung ba ding sang shing kun gyi byang phyogs kyi ri'i rtsa **[A: 14b]** bar yod pa'i chu mig de yin par nges so //

mchod rten chen po'i g.yas g.yon gyi mchod rten gnyis ni phyi'i dbyibs zur mang po can rtse'i gañdzi rar shang lang gi ral gris[119] brgyan pa phyi rol mu

---

[113] A, B: add. nus pa'i lha
[114] A: yid du 'ongs
[115] B: kyi
[116] A: rgyud de
[117] A: sgrubs
[118] A, B: bi ka ra
[119] A: ral gri'i

stegs byad kyi mchod rten su byas pa zhig ste / nang du ni bcom ldan 'das bde mchog lha tshogs bzhugs zhes zer ba phyi nang gi thun mong gis 'dod pas bzhengs pa zhig yin nam snyam mo //

rang byung mchod rten chen po'i phyogs bzhir grong khyer chen po lnga yod pa ni / lo rgyus kyi mdo'i bshad ma thag pa'i lung de'i rjes su /

> 'dir grong khyer chen po lnga po rnams kyang byas nas zhi ba'i dpal des lha lnga po rnams kyang bzhag ste / lnga po rnams gang zhe na / sdom pa'i lha dang / sa'i lha dang / me'i lha dang / chu'i lha dang / rlung i lha dang lnga'o // lha lnga po de rnams kyang grong khyer lnga po 'di rnams su rab tu gnas so / lha'i **[B: 19a]** dbang las grong khyer lnga po 'di rnams kyi'ang ming du 'gyur ba 'di lta ste / lha sdom pa'i gnas nyid kyi phyir śānti pu ri[120] zhes rab tu grags so // lha mo nor 'dzin ma'i gnas nyid kyi phyir nor kyi grong khyer[121] zhes bya'o // me lha'i gnas nyid kyi phyir me'i grong khyer[122] zhes bya'o // de bzhin du chu lha'i gnas nyid kyi phyir klu'i grong[123] zhes bya'o // de bzhin du rlung lha'i gnas phyir rlung gi grong[124] zhes bya'o // **[A: 16a]**
>
> byams pa / de ltar de bzhin gshegs pa dgra bcom pa yang dag par rdzogs pa'i sangs rgyas 'od srung gi dus tshe na chos dbyings gsung gi dbang phyug 'di grub pa'i slob dpon zhi ba'i dpal zhes bya bas mi gsal bar bya ba dang / bsrung ba'i don du rdul gyis g.yogs te sbas par byas so //

zhes gsungs pas / sgra zur chag pas bal po rnams kyis / saṃta pu[125] / agni pu / pāta pu / kanddhe pu zhes brjod par snang / de la grong khyer gzhan **[B: 19b]** gsum ni phyogs so sor ngos bzung byar yod pa ltar las / śānta pu ri'i gtsug lag khang gi rgyu mtshan brjod par bya ste //

sngon rgya gar du bi kra ma shī la'i[126] gtsug lag khang gi mkhas pa sgo drug gi nang tshan dpal nā ro pa dang thog mnyam du byon pa / slob dpon ngag gi dbang phyug grags pas sku tshe'i smad la bal yul du byon / gtso bor sgrub pa la gzhol zhing / sngags kyi theg pa cung zad gsungs / gzhan chos cher ma[127] ston / btshun mo mang po mnga' bas / skye bo phal cher gyis bslab pa ma thub pa yin te 'ong bsam pa las med / lan gcig rgyal pos[128] śānta pu rir 'khor lo sdom pa'i

---

[120] A: śinta pu ra; B: śānta pu ri, add. zhi ba'i grong
[121] A, B: add. bha su pu ri
[122] A, B: add. agne pu ri
[123] A, B: add. nā ga pu ri
[124] A, B: add. wa yu pu ri
[125] B: sinta pu
[126] A, B: bi krā ma shi la'i
[127] A: mi
[128] A: rgyal po

lha khang gcig bzhengs / de'i rab gnas kyi mthar tshogs **[A: 15b]** kyi 'khor lo chen po zhig bya bar 'dod nas / lha khang gi phyi rol du sngags pa mang po dag bsags / tshogs dpon du slob dpon spyan 'dren pa'i pho nya btang / slob dpon gyi spyil bu'i 'gag na bud med rgan mo zhig dang / bu mo nag mo khro gtum che ba zhig 'dug / slob dpon gang na **[B: 20a]** bzhugs byas pas nang na yod zer / des nang du phyin / rgyal po'i tshogs kyi 'khor lor slob dpon la 'byon par zhu byas pas / khyod nyid mgyogs par song / nga yang da lta 'ong gsungs / des mgyogs par phyin tsa na / śānti pu ri[129] dang nye ba'i lam gyi bzhi mdo zhig na / slob dpon btsun mo gnyis dang bcas sngar byon te khyod ma byung bas yun ring bsgugs pa[130] yin gsungs / rab gnas dngos kyi tshogs kyi 'khor lo rgyas pa bgyis pa'i rjes su / lha khang nang du slob dpon yab yum gsum bzhugs / tshogs rdzas mi drug cu lhag gcig gi skal ba blangs te song bas / rgyal po'i bsam pa / nang na mi gsum las med / tshogs rdzas 'di tsam dgos pa ci zhig yin snyam nas / sgo gseng[131] nas bltas pas / 'khor lo bde mchog lha drug bcu rtsa gnyis kyi dkyil 'khor mngon sum **[A: 16a]** du bzhugs nas tshogs rdzas la longs spyod pa mthong ste / de nyid du slob dpon 'ja'lus su bsgyur nas bzhugs pa **[B: 20b]** yin la / da lta yang de na bzhugs so / zhes jo nang rje btsun tā ra nā thas mdzad pa'i rgya gar chos 'byung las bshad / 'dir phyi rabs kyi paṇ chen nags kyi rin chen gyis[132] kyang bzhugs / dpal śa ba ri dang mjal / dkyil 'khor sprul nas bde mchog gi dbang bskur / mi 'gyur ba'i bde ba brnyes zhes pad dkar chos 'byung las so //

gtsug lag khang 'di'i sgo khang gi logs ris su rang bung mchod rtern chen po'i lo rgyus mdo 'di nyid las byung ba ltar sngon gyi bris rnying khungs dang ldan par bris pa yod do /

kun mkhyen puṇḍarikas /

> śānta pu rir gnas pa yi /
> tshogs bdag glang po'i gdong pa can /

zhes gsungs pas śānta pu ri ni gnas kyi ming kho na las gzhan du min la / spyir gnas bdag ni bi na ya ka[133]'am / ga ṇa pa ti[134] ste tshogs kyi bdag por grags mod //

bod snga rabs pa dag / dge bsnyen śānta pu ri zer ba / dge bsnyen ni / bod 'dir dge bsnyen pa cho ge[135] nyo dge sogs gnas yul **[A: 17b]** gzhi[136] **[B: 21a]** bdag spyi'i ming las dras pa[137] dang / śānta ni rgya skad sor bzhag / spu gri ni / me'i

---

[129] B: śānta pu ri
[130] A: sgugs pa
[131] A, B: seng
[132] A: gyi
[133] A, B: bi na ya ga
[134] A, B: ga na pa ti
[135] B: add. dang
[136] B: bzhi
[137] A, B: gras pa

spu gri dang / dug gi spu gri lta bur 'gres nas zer rgyur 'dug kyang / rgya 'bod 'dres ma'i skad śānta pu ri zhes brda chad med pas[138] bod rnams kyi blo bzo'i ming 'dogs kho nar zad pas gad mo'i gnas te / skabs 'dir kun rdzob kyi rdzun phugs gtibs zin to /

gnas bdag 'phrog ma ni / ha ri ti ste 'phrog ma bu lnga brgya dang bcas pa nyid las gzhan du min cing / de'i lo rgyus ni rgyas par mdo las byung ba ltar dang gzhan du gtor ma'i de nyid logs su gsal bas 'dir ma spros la / bal po rang gi lugs su 'di nyid kyi sgrub thabs las tshogs dang bcas pa yod skad la / nad rims drag po byung na 'phrog ma nyid ma mnyes pa'i cho 'phrul yin zer / sngon 'phrog ma'i sku rdo las rang byung du grub pa lha khang dang bcas pa yod kyang dus phyis[139] gor rgyal so me'i 'jus rjes med du brlags par byas pa **[B: 21b]** de'i tshab tu da lta'i sku gzugs lha khang dang bcas pa gsar du bzhengs par 'dug go //

gnas bdag gcig ni bod thang mgon por yin pa grags te / de'i tshul ni / rang byung gi rdo skur 'dod pa dang / kha cig klu sgrub kyis[140] phyag bzor[141] 'dod pa[142]gang ltar sngon ye rang dang nye ba'i ri bo phulla ḍo zhes par yod pa nam mkha' las dngos su 'phur te bod thang du bab pa bod thang mgon por grags / bal yul du du ru ṣka'i dmag byung skabs mgon po'i shangs la mtshon phul te gzhar **[A: 17a]** ba phyis rim[143] gyis gsos pa yin zer zhing / grub thob gtsang smyon pa shing kun gyi zhig gsos la byon skabs mgon po dang phyag sbrel te co pa ri'i phyi rol du bro mdzad pa bal bo'i ba ri ma mang pos mthong ba dang / gtsang smyon chen pos ras chung snyan brgyud kyi mgon por bzhed / rje rig 'dzin chen po tshe dbang nor bus kyang gtor chen mang du mdzad cing / bstod pa bzhed don lhun gyis grub pa'i[144] dbyangs zhes pa'ang mdzad do //

rang byung mchod rten chen po 'di **[B: 22a]** nyid snga phyir zhig gsos[145] kyi rim pa ji ltar byung tshul ni / gtsang smyon he ru ka pa yan / bod nas nyams gso bskur sti mdzad pa po byung ba'i lo rgyus kha gsal mi snang zhing / gtsang smyon chen por tshogs bdag gis bskul ma zhus pa ltar nyams gso mdzad / chos 'khor bcu gsum / gser gdugs mdzad / 'degs byed kyi ka ba bzhi / gañjira dang bcas pa gser zangs[146] las grub par skud la gser zho nyis stong bdun brgya lnga bcu rtsa gcig song zhes de nyid kyis[147] mdzad pa'i dkar chag las 'byung / mi ring ba na bal yul du duruṣka'i dmag chen po byung nas **[A: 17b]** shin kun gyi

---

[138] A: med pa'i
[139] B: add. rab byung bcu bzhi pa'i
[140] A: gi
[141] A: gzor
[142] B: grags pa
[143] A: rims
[144] B: 'grub pa'i
[145] A: zhig bsos
[146] A: bzang
[147] A: kyi

zangs gser thams cad bshus[148] nas khyer / mchod rten mer bsregs par byas kyang mdog mi mdzes pa tsam las skyon cher ma byung / de'i tshe[149] gtsang smyon pa'i thugs sras lha btsun rin chen rnam rgyal de nyid brag dkar rta sor sgrub pa[150] bzhugs pa'i skabs / grub thob nyid dang dag snang du mjal te lung bstan pa bzhin shing kun la **[B: 22b]** thog mar e te ka ra shing gi srog shing dang shing gdugs char khebs / de rjes rim par gser gdugs / gser tog / 'degs byed ka ba bzhi / chos 'khor bcu gsum / logs gsum gyi 'od ldan shar gyi bre logs gser zangs kyis[151] 'phur ba'i bar nyams gsos lan bzhi'i bar du mdzad / de nas lha btsun chos rje'i thugs sras skyid grong gnas rab 'byams pa byams pa phun tshogs kyis mchod rten gyi nub phyogs dang / byang ngos kyi bre'i logs rgyal mtshan dang bcas pa / chos 'khor bcu gsum gyi padma 'khor yug gser zangs kyis[152] 'phur / lha btsun rje dang / gnas rab 'byams pas[153] snga phyir gser sogs rgyu song rnams zhal gsal cher mi snang yang rags rim tsam so so'i rnam thar du gsal ba ltar ro //

de'i rjes su zhva dmar drug pa chos kyi dbang phyug nyid bal yul **[A: 18a]** gyi gnas gzigs la byon skabs mchod rten gyi nyams gso gnang bzhed kyang stabs ma 'grigs par phyogs bzhi'i sangs rgyas kyi sku bzhi'i bzhugs **[B: 23a]** khang gser zangs kyi rta bbas khang bzang bkod mdzes rnams bzhengs par mdzad / de'i rjes su grub thob chen pos bal po rgyal po pra tā pa mal la[154] gser srang sum cu so gnyis bstsal te zhig gso sgrubs[155] shig par bka' gnang ba rgyal po de kyang dang du[156] blangs te / srog shing btsugs chos 'khor tog dang phyogs bzhi'i khang bzang sku'i rgyab yol bcas gser zangs las bsgrubs[157] //

[158]rab byung bcu gsum pa lcags mo lug gi lor rig 'dzin kaḥ thog pa chen po rdo rje tshe dbang nor bus[159] nyams gso mdzad pa'i tshe lha chen po tshogs kyi bdag po dang / gzhon nu kārttikeya[160] gnyis nas rang gzugs dngos su bstan te mchod rten chen po'i nyams gso'i phrin las thams cad sgrub par khas blangs / bar skabs su mnga' ris mar[161] yul la dvags kyi rje bo 'khrugs pa'i legs 'dum[162] dang stod hor gyi dmag gi 'jigs pa skyobs phyir 'byon dgos byung ba dang /

---

148 A: shus
149 A: des tshe
150 A: bsgrub pa
151 A: bzang gis
152 A, B: kyi
153 B: ram pas
154 A, B: pra ti bhandra mal la
155 A: bsgrubs
156 A: dangs du
157 A: sgrubs
158 B: add. de nas re zhig song ba na
159 A: nor bu'i
160 A, B: gzhon nu kartika
161 A, B: mang
162 A: zlom

bod **[B: 23a]** bal mon gyi rgyal khag so so'i bar 'ching gnang dgos pa sogs kyis[163] yun ring **[A: 18b]** por 'gyang ba'i mur shing phag lor rig 'dzin rje mya ngan las 'das pas zhig gso 'phror[164] lus par slar yang rje de nyid kyi bka' chems[165] bzhin rje btsun 'brug pa rin po che thams cad mkhyen pa bka' brgyud[166] 'phrin las shing rtas rgyab gnyer dang / rig 'dzin rje nyid kyi zhabs ring gi thu bo mchod dpon rin po che bstan 'dzin rdo rje sogs kyi snying stobs chen pos zhig gsos kyi 'phro 'thud pa'i 'khur bzhes pa[167] lo ngo bdun song ba 'bru mang zhes pa sa pho stag gi lo shar ba tshun la legs par zhabs su zhugs par[168] bre yi phyogs bzhi / 'od ldan gyi ha lam pattra[169] bzhi / chos 'khor bcu gsum char khebs tog dang bcas par skud la bzhu chad bton pa'i gser btso ma stong phrag gnyis dang nyi shu rtsa gcig song bar snang zhing / de'i tshe rje 'brug pas mang yul skyid grong dngos grub phug nas dgongs pa gtad pa'i rab gnas mdzad pa'i skabs bal yul shing kun tu me **[B: 24a]** tog gi char dngos su babs pas[170]der 'dus pa bal bod rong gsum gyi skye bo kun gyi mig lam du snyon med byung bar grags la / dpa' bo rin po che gtsug lag **[A: 19a]** bas dngos kyi rab gnas mdzad cing rgyal po rje 'bangs la dngos po gnang sbyin gya nom pa dang bcas te mchod rten chen po'i gnyer dam mdzad ces thos so //

'dir snga phyi'i dngos po rgyu song gi tshul zhib pa ni rje lo ri ba kun gzigs chos kyi rgya mtshos mdzad pa'i dkar chag mdor bsdus lha'i sil snyan zhes pa zur du gsal ba las shes par bya'o //

de'i rje su zhva dmar bcu pas shar nub kyi sangs rgyas gnyis kyi bzhugs khang gser zangs kyi rta babs nyams gsos dang / dril bu chen po sogs 'bul bar mdzad 'dug / gong gi sa pho stag de nas lo lnga bcu rta lnga song bar rab byung bcu bzhi pa angi ra[171] ste chu pho spre'u lor mchod rten chen po'i srog shing yon por gyur pa phyi lo dpal gdong chu bya lo'i sa ga'i zla nang du srog shing 'gyel te **[B: 24b]** shin tu nyams chag che bar gyur pa ni skye 'gro spyi dgos kyi legs byas kyi go skabs ches cher dman cing snyigs ma lnga bod ba'i dus kyi mthar thug pa'i[172] rang rtags gsal por bstan par zad mod / de ltar[173] yang bstan dang 'gro ba'i phan bde'i lang tsho slar yang 'phel ba'i slad du lho phyogs nor 'dzin skyong ba'i dbang **[A: 19b]** phyug sgrub brgyud dpal ldan sprin gyi sgra dbyangs can kyi phrin las kyi shing rta chen po gang gi rmad du byung ba'i thugs bskyed skya rengs kyi snang ba gsar pas nye bar drangs pa'i da lta nyams

163 A: kyi
164 A: phror
165 A: bka' chem
166 B: dkar brgyud
167 A: gzhes pa
168 A, B: 'chugs par
169 A, B: parta
170 B: babs pa
171 A: angki ra re; B: anki ra
172 A: thugs pa'i
173 B: de lta na

gso rnam par dkar ba'i legs byas rgya chen por 'jug dang 'jug bzhin pa las mi ring ba lha dang bcas pa'i legs byas kyi phung po'i dpal yon las mngon par grub pa'i rgyal ba'i mchod rten nyin mor byed pa 'di nyid 'gro ba'i bsod nams kyi mkha' la 'char ba'i dge mtshan gsal bar 'gyur ba ste de dag gi tshul ni slad nas rim gyis[174] brjod par 'gyur ro //

> gdod nas rnam dag rang bzhin chos kyi dbyings //
> spros kun nyer zhi ye shes **[B: 25a]** chos sku'i khams //
>
> ma rig lkog gyur 'gro ngor thabs mkhas kyis //
> mtshon phyir chos gzugs mchod rten tshul du snang //
>
> de phyir rang byung mchod rten ngo mtshar can //
> srid gsum kun gyi mchod sdong bla na med //
> sna tshogs mtshan gyis 'gro 'dul rgyal kun gyis //
> lan brgyar sngags 'dir rnam[175] kun cis mi 'dud //

bal yul gyi gnas dang rten gyi lo rgyus nges par brjod pa 'khrul spong nor bu'i me long zhes bya las rang byung mchod rten chen po shin kun gyi **[A: 20a]** lo rgyus bshad pa'i skabs te gnyis pa'o //

[III]

gsum pa mchod rten bya tri kam sha'am / bya rung kha shor gyi lo rgyus brjod pa la / gang gi tshe bskal pa grangs med pa'i sngon rol na 'phags mchog spyan ras gzigs dbang phyug gis mgon po 'od dpag med kyi spyan sngar sems can thams cad 'khor ba'i rgya mtsho nas 'dren par smon lam btab pa bzhin mtha' yas pa'i 'gro ba dpag tu med pa'i don mdzad de slar pho brang ri bo po ta **[B: 25b]** la'i[176] rtse mor byon nas da ni sems can gcig kyang med do snyam nas gzigs pas rigs drug gi gnas na sems can chang gar ma'i sbang ma lta bu nyung du ma song bar 'dug pas da ni sems can 'khor ba'i rgya mtsho las sgrol bar mi nus so snyam nas spyan chab shor ba phyag gi srin lag gnyis kyis blangs te gtor nas ma ongs pa na spyan chab gnyis kyis kyang 'gro ba'i don byed par shog[177] cig ces pa'i smon lam btab pas sum cu rtsa gsum lha'i yul du lha'i dbang po brgya byin[178] gyi sras mo gnyis su 'khrungs te lha'i bu mo gang chen ma dang gang chung ma zhes bya ba gnyis su gyur pa gang chung mas lha'i me tog brkus pas lha'i khrims nyams nas mi'i gnas su lhungs bas[179] de bzhin gshegs **[A: 20b]** pa 'od srung[180] gi bstan pa'i dus su bal po ma gu ta'i yul grur bya rdzi ma bde

---

[174] A: rims kyis
[175] A: rnams
[176] A, B: po ṭa la'i
[177] A: shogs
[178] A, B: rgya byin
[179] A: lhung bas
[180] A: 'od srungs

mchog bya bar skyes te bya 'tsho ba'i las byed pa na / rigs ngan rta rdzi / phag rdzi / khyi rdzi / bya rdzi bzhi dang 'grogs pas bu bzhi skyes so //

'di la nyang gter thang yig[181] zangs gling mar **[B: 26a]** bu bzhi dang bu mo gcig ste ming sring lnga yod tshul kyang snang / de nas ma des bya 'tshos pa'i gla bsags pas bu bzhi khyim pa rab thang du phog slar yang gla'i lhag bsags nas nor mang po bsags te mchod rten bzhengs pa'i blo skyes nas yul gyi[182] bdag po la sa bslangs bas[183] rgyal pos kyang gnang ba sbyin pa'i tshe de ltar bya ru rung kha nas shor bas bya rung kha shor du grags zhes pa 'dug mod / de ni bod skad sgra ji bzhin pas yin pas bal po'i rgyal pos kyang bod skad du gleng ba[184] 'dra zhig tu snang la / zangs gling mar / bya 'tshos pa'i rin gyis bzhengs pas bya rin kha shor zhes dang / gzhan yang bya tri kam sho dang / bya tri kha shor dang / mon skad du / ba hu ta dang / bal po rnams kyis kha sa ti da[185] zhes pas mtshan gyi rnams grangs su mchis //

de nas bya rdzi ma bu lnga dang bran gcig / glang po che **[A: 21a]** dang bong bu gcig bcas kyis sa phag[186] bkal zhing bskyal[187] te rmangs bting nas brtsigs pas lo bzhi la bum pa man **[B: 26b]** brtsigs grub / skabs der bya rdzi ma bde mchog tshe'i dus byaspar shes nas bu bzhi dang bran dang bcas la mchod rten gyi[188] 'phro[189] bzhengs su chug la 'di'i nang du de bzhin gshegs pa'i ring bsrel bzhugs su gsol te rab gnas rgya chen po gyis shig par gdams nas tshe'i dus byas par dam tshig gi lha mo pra mo ha zhes bya bar sangs rgyas / de'i rjes su bu bzhi bran dang bcas pas mchod rten gyi[190] 'phro[191] lo gsum du brtsigs shing kun dril bas lo bdun la rdzogs par bzhengs grub / de bzhin gshegs pa 'od srung[192] gi ring bsrel ma ga dha'i[193] bre gang srog shing gi nang du bzhugs su gsol te rab tu gnas pa byas pa'i tshe bcom ldan 'das 'od srung skor dang bcas pa dang / gzhan yang phyogs bcu'i sangs rgyas dang byang chub sems dpa' dpag tu med pas byin gyis brlabs shing me tog 'thor te shis brjod rgya chen po mzad do //

de'i tshe bu bzhi bran dang bcas pas smon lam btab pa ni / rta rdzi'i bus bod kha ba can 'khyag[194] la 'khyags yul **[B: 27a]** du bde bar gshegs pa'i bstan pa rin po

---

181 A: thang yi
182 A: gyis
183 A: blang bas; B: bslang bas
184 A, B: glengs ba
185 A, B: kha pa ti da
186 B: sa bag
187 A: skyal
188 A: gyis
189 A: phro
190 A: gyis
191 A: phro
192 A: 'od srungs
193 A: ma ga ta'i
194 A, B: khyag

che 'dzugs pa'i rgyal po dang / phag rdzi'i bus[195] mkhan po / khyi rdzi'i bus[196] sngags 'chang nus pa can / bya rdzi'i bus[197] bka'i phrin blon du skye **[A: 21b]** bar smon lam btab pa na sangs rgyas dang byang chub sems dpa'i tshogs kyis[198] legs so sbyin te 'od dang 'od zer gyi gong bu gcig tu gyur pa mchod rten chen po nyid la thim pas sangs rgyas thams cad 'dus pa'i mchod rten du grags / de lta bu'i smon lam btab pa ji lta bar bod kyi yul du / chos rgyal khri srong lde'u btsan / mkhan po bo dhi sattva[199] / slob dpon padma 'byung gnas / yar lung gi chos blon sba mi khri sher / sbrang bus[200] spras ma sras su skye ba'i smon lam btab pa lha lcam padma gsal / bong bus[201] smon lam log par btab pa bdud blon ma zhang khrom par skyes / bran gyis bdud blon 'joms pa'i smon lam btab pa chos blon padma gung btsan / glang po ches smon lam log par btab pa btsad po glang dar ma / bya rog **[B: 27b]** gis bdud rgyal gsod par smon lam btab pa lha sras mu rub[202] btsan po / bram ze khye'u gnyis kyis smon lam btab pa lo tsā ba[203] ska ba dpal brtsegs / cog ro[204] klu'i rgyal mtshan / rgyal rigs kyi bu mo gnyis kyis[205] dam chos 'bri ba'i yi ge par smon lam btab pa ldan ma rtse mang dang / legs byin nyi ma ste[206] de ltar mkhan slob chos gsum 'khor bcas kyis gangs can gyi ljongs 'di'i rgud pa'i mun pa mtha' dag bsal te sangs rgyas kyi bstan pa rin po che nyi mo ltar gsal bar mdzad pa'i rten cing 'brel ba'i 'byung khungs[207] ni mchod rten chen po 'di nyid do // **[A: 22a]**

de lta bu'i mchod rten chen po 'di nyid la zhabs tog nyams gso'i rim pa ji ltar byung tshul ni / chos kyi rgyal po srong btsan sgam po'i skabs sam de'i sngon tsam du rgya nag gi rgyal po zhig gismchod rten la mchod pa dang sri zhi byas tshul gung mgon po skyabs kyis rgya nag chos 'byung bu bris zhes rig 'dzin rjes gsungs / bar skabs shig nyams gso dang zhabs tog **[B: 28a]** byed pa po ma byung bar yun ring mo zhig song ba na / dus kyi 'gyur bas mchod rten chen po ni ri dang so so mi phyed pa zhig tu gyur pas mi rnams kyi snang ngor mchod rten du btags pa tsam yang med par mngon / de'i tshe sngon gyi[208] bya rdzi ma'i bran chos kyi blon po 'gos padma gung btsan du gyur pa de nyid kyi smon lam gyi mthus skye ba'i phreng ba rim par brgyud pa las / drang so gter ston[209]

---

195 A: bu'i
196 A: bu'i
197 A: bu'i
198 A: om. kyis
199 A, B: bo dhi satwa
200 A, B: sbrang bu
201 A, B: bong bu'i
202 A: mu rug
203 A: lo tsa ba
204 A: lcog ro
205 A: kyi
206 A: te
207 A: khung
208 A: gyis
209 A: gter bton

sngags 'chang śākya bzang por 'khrungs pa des dpal bsam yas kyi gtsug lag khang chen po'i dbu rtse nas shog ril zhig rnyed par gzigs pas bya rung kha shor gyi zhig ral gso bar lung bstan te bal yul du phebs / ri dang mchod rten dbyer ma phyed pas thog mar 'di yin dgongs te ri gzhan zhig la phyag mdzad pas phye mar sang[210] / ri de yang mchod rten dang nye ba na yod skad / slar dngos rnyed de[211] sa 'og nas byung zhing kun gyi mig sngar mngon sum su snang bar mdzad de zhig gsos mthar phyin pa' tshe / chos sku'i rten **[B: 28b]** mchog mar grags pa'i bstod pa yang mdzad cing de nyid las

> lnga brgya tha ma'i dus 'dir o rgyan bkas /
> thengs gsum skul te mchod rten chen po 'di'i /
> zhig pa gso phyir sgo gsum[212] gus 'bad **[A: 22b]** pa'i /
> bdag sogs mkha' khyab 'brel tshad sems can rnams /
> kun bzang chos sku'i go 'phang myur thob shog[213] /

ces[214] gsungs / mchod rten dang nye bar sgrub chu zhig kyang yod par grags so //

de nas mi rabs kha shas song ba na / slob dpon chen po'i sprul par lung gis[215] zin pa'i grub thob chen po rje rang rig ras pas mchod rten la nyams gso dang / gañji ra bsgron[216] / brtul shugs kyi spyod pas o rgyan gyi yul sogs sku dngos kyis[217] bgrod pa'i mthar kaśmī ra'i ljongs na nā lendra'i gtsug lag khang du sku 'das pa' tshe thugs lcags spyan gsum dang sku gdung ring bsrel gyi phung por gyur pa bu slob rnams kyis[218] gdan drangs pa /

bka' chems kyi mgur las /

> nga sgom chung du va ri ka pa /
> 'gro ba o rgyan gling du bgrod /
> shi sa **[B: 29a]** rgya gar byang du byed /
> bya rung kha shor shar 'dabs su /
> mi kho bo'i gdung rten de ru bzhengs[219] /
> spyir bal po kun la bde skyid 'byung /
> sgos[220] mtha' dmag lo 'ga' zlog par 'gyur /

---

[210] A, B: song
[211] A: te
[212] A, B: sum
[213] A: shogs
[214] A: zhes
[215] A: gi
[216] A, B: sgron
[217] A: kyi
[218] A: kyi
[219] A: gzhengs
[220] A: dgos

zhes gsungs pa bzhin gdung rten bzhengs pa mchod rten chen po'i shar phyogs su bzhugs pa de yin //

de rjes bod yul mi'i rje bo pho lha ba bsod nams stobs rgyal gyi bka' bzhin skyid grong rdzong dpon lcags sprag dang / yangs grong par grags pa gnyis kyis[221] do dam gan 'khur tshul bzhin bgyis te nyams gso zhabs tog sgrub // **[A: 23a]**

de'i rjes su rje rig 'dzin chen po tshe dbang nor bus nyams gsos legs par gnang zhing rab gnas dang mar me khri tshar du mas mchod par mdzad do //

mchod rten chen po 'di ni dur khrod chen po brgyad kyi nang tshan lhun grub brtsegs pa dang / de'i mchod rten du sngar smos pa'i lung bzhin som nyi med par grub lags[222] // dur khrod kyi dbus dngos gzhi ni mchod rten nas gzhu 'dom[223] lnga brgya'i **[B: 29b]** sa na yod zhing der slob dpon chen po'i zhabs rjes kyang yod ces rig 'dzin rje gsung //

sku gdung 'bar ba mchod rten gyi rgyud las /

> shar lho mtshams na bal po'i yul //
> ta na ya ma kha bye[224] khri[225] //
> lhun grub dur khrod[226] byin za dang //
> shing bu ka ran tsit[227] 'bim pa //
> mchod rten kha shor bya tri kha //
>
> ston pa dka' thub mdzad pa de //
> bal chen rje na leb 'beb yod //
> de na zan gyi longs spyod che //
> bkra shis mchod rten hu li ka //
> 'byung po gu gu ta nag[228] gnas //

zhes dang / lha mo pra mo ha[229] gnas par bshad pa bya rdzi ma bde mchog nyid der sangs rgyas pa'i lo rgyus dang mthun zhing mchod rten la gus par mchod cing nyams pa gso ba'i phan yon rgyas pa dang / smon lam btab tshad 'grub pa'i tshul sogs zhib par[230] drang so gter ston[231] sngags 'chang śākya bzang po'i gter byon 'khrul med kha shor gyi lo rgyus chen mo las shes par bya'o //

---

[221] A: gnyis po
[222] B: la
[223] A, B: 'doms
[224] A, B: kha byed
[225] A: khrid, B: krid
[226] A: dngos grub
[227] A: tsi ta
[228] A, B: na
[229] A: phra mo ha
[230] A: zhibs par
[231] A: gter bton

phyag na padmo 'gro la rjes **[A: 23b]** brtse'i 'phrul //
cir yang ston las 'phags yul ne pāl ljongs //
khyad **[B: 30a]** par snod bcud reg bya rtsub mo'i gter //
bsil ldan yul gyi phan bde'i byung khungs[232] mchog //

sa bdag rnams kyi[233] khengs po'i ri bo kun //
rdul phran ltar byed bya rdzi ma bu yi //
'bad pas bskrun pa'i rgyal ba'i mchod sdong che //
sa la lhun po ji bzhin rnam par mdzes //

bal yul gyi gnas dang rten gyi lo rgyus nges par brjod pa 'khrul spong nor bu'i me long zhes bya ba las bya tri kha shor gyi lo rgyus brjod pa'i skabs te gsum pa'o //

[IV]

bzhi pa zhar byung yan lag gi gnas dang rten gyi lo rgyus bshad pa la / shing kun kyi nub phyogs ri bo chung ngu de ni lo rgyus kyi mdor le'u gsum pa las /

> 'jam pa'i lha de yang phyogs nyi tshe 'di nyid du yun ring por gnas te / de lhag par gnas pa nyid kyi phyir phyogs nyi tshe ba der / da lta'ang 'jam dpal gyi ri bo zhes grags pa'o //

zhes dang /

le'u bdun pa las /

> byams pa / de ma thag **[B: 30b]** der 'jam dpal gyi sprul pa'i rang bzhin slob dpon 'jam pa'i lha zhes bya ba de'i mchod rten kyang mjug ma'i rtse mo'i gnas de nyid du mthu stobs chen po rab tu gsal ba'i ched du dad pas byas so //

zhes gsungs pa de nyid yin par rtogs shing bal po rnams yang mañjuśrī zhes zer la / **[A: 24a]** bod kun 'jam dpal mchod rten zhes brjod / 'od srung mchod rten ni / kha cig glang ru lung bstan nas bshad pa'i 'od srung mchod rten yin par 'dod pa dang / yang 'phags pa 'od srung gi mchod rten yin snyam pa sogs yong srid pas de gnyis ka min pa rgyu mtshan du mas grub par nus pa la bal yul rang du'ang dmigs bsal gyi lo rgyus zhig med pas sngar ma thos so //

dbyig gnyen mchod rten ni / 'phags pa dbyig gnyen gyi sku tshe'i smad slob ma stong gis bskor nas bal yul du byon nas chos gzhis[234] mang du btsugs te dge' 'dun mang po 'phel bar mdzad / nam zhig khyim btsun gos gyon te zhing rmod pa gzigs nas ston pa'i **[B: 31a]** bstan pa nyams gso[235] zhes thugs byung nas dge

---

[232] A: khung
[233] B: kyis
[234] A, B: gzhi
[235] A: nyams so //

’dun gyi dbus su chos bstan te gtsug gtor rnam rgyal gyi[236] gzungs mgo zhabs bzlog pa lan gsum bzlos pas[237] de nyid du sku ’das / slob ma rnams kyis mchod rten yang byas pa de nyid yin par grags so //

bya rgod phung ri ’di ni / bod rnams kyis[238] btags pa’i ’dra tsam du byas pa ste / yongs du grags pa’i bya rgod phung po’i ri bo dngos ni ’phags yul kho na yod cing / gtsug lag khang ’di la bal po rnams kimṭo[239] zhes brjod do // kun mkhyen si tus ’bras spungs ri bo’i gtsug lag khang zhes gsungs /

ri bo ’bigs[240] **[A: 24b]** byed ni / ’dzam bu gling ’dir dpal gyi ri bcu gsum yod pa’i nang tshan[241] gyi ’bigs[242] byed ni ma yin te /

’bigs[243] byed dngos rgya gar ’phags yul gyi char yod la / ’di yang bod rnams kyis[244] btags ming kho nar nges bal po rnams ’dza ma[245] ’dzu zhes zer / ri’i rtse mor sangs rgyas kyi bzhugs khri yin zhes sngon rabs **[B: 31b]** su grags shing / mchod rten ni dus phyis bal po zhig gis[246] bzhengs skad /

ri de’i sked par klu sgrub kyi sgrub phug tu grags pa ni lo rgyus kyi[247] mdor bshad pa’i zhi byed lha’am / yang na klu sgrub kyi sgrub phug yin pa don la gnas te bal skad du nā ga[248] ’dzong zhes ’bod / ’phags mchog klu sgrub nyid bal yul du byon pa ni grags che la / tham wi ha ra’i[249] gtsug lag khang du bzhugs pa’i ’bum po ti rnams kyang klu sgrub kyis[250] klu yul nas spyan drangs pa de yin par ’dod pa dang / bal po rnams klu yul du byon pa yang bal yul nas mdzad pa yin zer / shing kun gyi mchod rten la sri zhu rgya cher mdzad shing / yig rnying ’ga’ zhig tu / phyag na rdo rje dbu rtsa’i[251] rgyud slob dpon ’phags pa klu sgrub kyis bal yul ’phags pa shing kun nas gter nas bton zhes kyang byung //

---

236 A: gyis
237 A, B: zlos pas
238 A: kyi
239 B: ki mo ṭa
240 A: ’big
241 A, B: nang mtshan
242 A: ’big
243 A: ’big
244 A, B: kyi
245 B: ’dzang ma
246 A: gi
246 A, B: kyis
246 B: na ga
247 A, B: kyis
248 B: na ga
249 A: thang bhi ha ri’i
250 A: kyi
251 A: u tsarya’i, B: a tsārya’i

yang ri bo 'bigs[252] byed kyi shar phyogs ri rgyud du ma he sangs rgyas pa **[A: 25a]** zer / kha cig ma he'i rdzi bo sangs rgyas klu sgrub kyi slob ma slob dpon klu'i byang chub tu 'dod pa yang lo **[B: 32a]** rgyus 'gar bris 'dug kyang ma brtag pa'i gtam kho na ste / klu byang ni / rgya gar du klu sgrub kyis ma he'i rdzi bo rgas 'khogs pa[253] zhig snod ldan du gzigs nas ma he'i sgom thabs sogs gdams pa sbyin te dus las 'das pa bram ze'i rigs su 'khrungs pa slob dpon las rab tu byung / mtshan nā ga bo dhi[254] yin zhes kun mkhyen[255] pad dkar gsungs[256] la / jo nang rje btsun dam pas de gnyis so sor gsungs pa gang ltar klu byang dngos ni / mkhas shing grub pa brnyes pa brtul zhugs kyi[257] spyod pa la zhugs pas mtshan ma taṃ gir grags te grub thob brgyad cu rtsa bzhi'i grangs su bzhugs pa de yin la / da lta yang dpal gyi ri la bzhugs par grags pas bal yul gyi lo rgyus phyogs tsam yang mi mtshungs pa'i phyir brag phug de yang gcong zhi'i[258] brag 'ba' zhig tu snang zhing zhun mar sbar te sbubs[259] shin tu dog pa ring po mthar thug par phyin pa na chu'i thigs pa[260] 'babs pa dang / tshogs bdag rang byon yin zer ba glang po'i gdong **[B: 32b]** 'dra nyams zhig las gzhan ci yang med la ma he'i rkang rjes yod zer ba sogs cal sgrogs kyi rjes su 'brang ba'i gtam kho na'o //

klu gan rkyal ni / bya rung kha shor gyi byang phyogs ri ngogs zhig tu nags tshal chu dang bcas par nī la **[A: 25b]** kanṭha te / mgrin sngon can gyi rdo sku bod rnams klu rang byon du 'bod pa de las 'dra bshus kyis[261] bzhengs pa[262] yin zer / mgrin sngon ni dbang phyug gi mtshan gyi rnams grangs te / sngon lha rnams kyis[263] rgya mtsho[264] srub pa'i tshe dug bum pa gang thon pa lha chen po'i mgrin par bzung ba[265] sngon por gyur bas mgrin sngon du grags / bod 'ga' zhig sangs rgyas klu dbang gi rgyal po'i sku yin zer ba shin tu 'khrul lo //

dzo ki a kar ni rnal 'byor nam mkha' zhes rdo rje gdan bzhi'i rgyud nas bshad pa'i gnas zhig yin par rig 'dzin rje gsungs / phal[266] skad du dzo ki a bar zhes zer //

---

[252] A: 'big
[253] A, B: khog pa
[254] A: nā ga bho dhi
[255] A: kun la mkhyen
[256] A: gsung
[257] A: kyis
[258] B: cong zhi'i
[259] A, B: sbub
[260] A: thig pa
[261] A: gyi
[262] A: gzhengs pa
[263] A, B: kyi
[264] A: rgyal mtsho
[265] A, B: gzung ba
[266] A: phral

tham wi hā ra[267] ni / sngon jo bo rje dpal mar me mdzad bzang po bod yul byon pa'i tshe bzhengs par mdzad pa de yin / wi hā ra[268] ni gtsug **[B: 33a]** lag khang ste[269] bal yul rin chen tshul [270]gyi[271] gtsug lag khang yang 'di nyid du ngos 'dzin / rgyal pos[272] bzhengs pas[273] rā dza bi hā ra[274] zhes pa zhig kyang yod tshul jo bo'i rnam thar lam yig las bshad / grub thob o rgyan pa rin chen dpal gyis bal yul gyi tham wi ha ra[275] na gsang sngags rnying ma'i rgya dpe'i ming kho na bris kyang 'bum tsam 'ong / zhes gsungs //

bal yul sang ko'i yul gyi ri ngogs su guppa ha ra zhes bod rnams kyis grub thob **[A: 26a]** brgyad cur 'bod cing / bal po rnams sa ko kha ga dzo ki ni zhes zer / de ni sngon phyogs der phyi rol mu stegs byed kyi drang srong mang du gnas shing / de dag gi mchod rten kyang mang du yod pa las sangs rgyas kyi mthus rdo'i mchod rten chen po de nyid sa las rang byung du 'phags pas[276] mu stegs byed kyi mchod rten thams cad 'jig ste mi snang bar gyur / rang byung gi rdo'i mchod rten de' 'bum pa'i srubs[277] nas chu'i rgyun snyon med du byung zhing byin brlabs[278] shin tu che bar **[B: 33b]** grags / gtsug lag khang gi nang du bzhugs pa'i rten ni badzra dzo ki nī[279] ste rdo rje rnal 'byor ma'i sku 'jim las grub pa zhig go / grub thob brgyad cu rtsa bzhis kyang byon par grags tshod du 'dug kyang lo rgyus nges pa can ma thos so / bod blun rnams grub thob rnams kyi tshogs zangs dang / sangs rgyas kyi bstan pa 'char nub kyi tshad dang / bskal pa'i me dang chu / bal mo bza'i[280] thags chas[281] yin zer ba rnams ni ma brtags pa'i[282] blun gtam kho nar zad de rgyu mtshan ci yang med do //

yang snga rabs kha cig sangs rgyas kyi 'khrungs rabs su bshad pa'i rgyal po thams cad sgrol gyi dbu sbyin par btang ba'i gnas su bzhes pa'ang mi 'thad de[283] / de ni rdo rje gdan nas dpag tshad drug cu lho nub tu phyin pa la[284] **[A:**

---

[267] A: thang bhi ha ri
[268] A: bhi ha ri
[269] A: te
[270] B: tshal
[271] A: gyis
[272] A: rgyal po'i
[273] A, B: bzhengs pa'i
[274] A, B: ra dza bi ha ra
[275] A: thang bhi ha ri
[276] A, B: 'phags pa'i
[277] A: bsrub
[278] B: rlabs
[279] A, B: badzra dzo ki ṇi
[280] A: za'i
[281] A, B: chad
[282] A: ma rtags pa'i
[283] A: te
[284] B: na

**26b]** nye ba'i tstshan do ha[285] ka ling ka zhes pa'i yul de nyid thams cad sgrol gyi 'khrungs yul yin par mkhas pa dag bzhes do //

cang khung zhes pa ni / bal po rnams ha ri 'ba' ha na lo ke śva ra zer zhing khyung gi gnas yin par **[B: 34a]** 'dod la / sngon phyag na rdo rje dngos su thim pa'i khyung rang byon zhig yod tshul dang / yang 'ga' zhig slob dpon klu sgrub kyi phyag phreng gi mdo[286] 'dzin la khyung rang byon du grub par 'dod pa dang / de nyid mjal na sa bdag gi gnod pa'i nad las grol tshul sogs grags kyang 'thad ldan gyi lo rgyus tshad mas 'dzin pa zhig mjal rgyu med nges par snang //

kurti'am[287] / mon pa rnams gu ru bad zhes zer ba bod rnams kyis[288] snyi shang kuttir 'bod pa rje btsun chen po mi las khyi ra ras pa mgon po rdo rje rjes su bzung ba'i grub gnas de ni 'khrul pa dang bral ba yin mod / 'on kyang yongs grags mgur 'bum du gsal ba'i ri brag chu sogs kyi bkod pa dang ni ches[289] mi mthun par snang la / khyi ras pa ni snyi shang pa'am ta mang par 'bod pa 'di pa'i rigs yin pas thog ma nas bod skad gyi gtam dang glu / ras gos[290] kyang med par bod kyi slog pa tim pa'i kha rgyan can / zhags pa nag po / bod kyi sha ba rwa bcu sogs 'brel **[B: 34b]** med kyi gtam mang du bris 'dug go //

stag **[A: 27a]** mo lus sbyin ni / lo rgyus rnying pa 'gar gser 'od nas bshad pa'i rgyal po snying stobs chen pos stag mor lus sbyin pa'i sku gdung mchod rten yin tshul dang / byang chub sems dpas bla gos shing gi yal gar gzer ba'i shing yang ngos 'dzin pa sogs bden bden ltar brjod zhig 'dug kyang / spyir gser 'od dam pa'i mdo sde dang mdzangs blun[291] nas stag mor lus sbyin gyi rtogs brjod gsungs pa byang chub sems dpa'am / gser 'od nas snying stobs chen po dang / mdzangs blun[292] nas sems chen chen po zhes pa'i mtshan gyi khyad par tsam las gzhan du yul dang yab yum sogs kyi lo rgyus don gcig par snang / gser 'od nas / lnga len gyi yul du de bzhin gshegs pa 'khor bcas ljongs rgyur gshegs pa na sa der sa 'og nas mchod rten byung[293] zhing byang chub sems dpa'i sku gdung bstan[294] te stag mor lus sbyin pa'i sngon byung gsungs / des na lho phyogs lnga len **[B: 35a]** gyi yul zhes rgya gar gyi lho phyogs su yod par bshad la / bal yul ni rgya gar gyi byang du ngos 'dzin pas 'gal ba'i phyir ro // bal po rnams na mo buddha ya zhes 'bod pa'ang / bod skad du sangs rgyas la phyag 'tshal gnas kyi ming du mi 'brel ba zhig 'dug pa gang ltar yang 'di **[A: 27b]** nyid kyi lo rgyus nges pa zhig ma mthong bas 'dir brjod par ma nus so //

---

285 A, B: nye ba'i mtshan dho ha
286 B: mdud
287 A, B: kunti'am
288 A, B: kyi
289 B: om. ches
290 A, B: dgos
291 A: 'dzang lhun
292 A: 'dzang lhun
293 B: phyung
294 A: stan

kho khom du sgrol ma gsung byon zhes sngon yul de'i rgyal po'i rmi lam du 'phags mas rje btsun chen po mi lar / ka shi ka'i ras dang / a ru ra rnam rgyal 'bul bar lung bstan pa'i sku byin brlabs[295] can te / bar skabs su mjal rgyu yod 'dug kyang / rjes su 'jigs pa'am phyogs gzhan du 'khyar ba'am / bod rnams kyis[296] ngos ma zin pa ji ltar yang ding sang ni mjal rgyu med skad do //

slob dpon chen pos

> bal yul gser phug na :
> e ka dza ti ral gcig ma :

zhes gsungs pa de yang kho khom dang nye bar e ka dza ti rang byung gi **[B: 35b]** rdo sku zhig mjal rgyu yod par snang //

phag mo mngal chu ni / bod rnams kyis[297] btags pa'i kha skad yin la / zur chag gi skad dang bal skad thun mong du guheshwa rī[298] zhes 'bod cing nang pa rnams śrī ma tī[299] dgyes rdor gyi yum bdag med ma'i gnas yin zer la / phyi rol pa rnams gu lang dang brel bar u ma'i gnas 'dod pa yin nam snyam //

gu lang ni / gu lang ma hā de wa[300] zhes lha chen lha chen por brjod pa dbang phug gi rten rdo las rang byung ba mi gang tsam pa sa las 'phags te thon pa phyogs bzhir **[A: 28a]** zhal bzhi phyag brgyad yod pa zhig ste[301] / de la gser gyi rgya phub dang /gser mgar[302] blugs kyi gañdzi ra / lcags kyi tri shu la tertse gsum pa yod pa de la mu stegs byed snying stobs chen 'ga' zhig sa 'og tu sgrub pa la yun ring por bsdad rjes gtsug lag khang gi rtse nas rtse gsum gyi khar lcebs te 'chi bar byed pa yin zer / sngon grub thob chen po mi tra dzo kis[303] gtsug lag khan gi gañdzi ra'i rtse mor zhag bdun du skyil krung bcas te **[B: 36a]** rdzu 'phrul gyi bkod pas mu stegs pa rnams zil gyi mnan pa'i lo rgyus khro lo'i rnam thar las byung / blun po 'ga' zhig ti lli nā ro'i sgrub phug dang / sgrub chu sogs yin zer ba rnams ni 'brel med rdzun[304] gtam kho na'o //

bal yul yam bu'i grong khyer chen po'i dbus su bzhugs pa'i 'phags pa rang byung 'jig rten dbang phyug gi snang brnyan bod rnams 'ja' ma li dkar mor grags pa'i lo rgyus zur tsam smos na / gangs can gyi ljongs su 'phags mchog 'jig rten dbang phyug rgyal po'i tshul du sku sprul pa chos rgyal srong btsan

---

[295] B: byin rlabs
[296] A: kyi
[297] A: kyi
[298] A, B: gu yi shwa ri
[299] A, B: shi rrma ti
[300] A: mahā dhe wa; B: ma hā ddhe wa
[301] A: te
[302] A, B: gar
[303] A, B: mi tra dzo ki'i
[304] A: brdzun

sgam po'i gsung rabs[305] rgyal po'i[306] mdzad pa le'u gnyer gcig pa'i brgyad pa las /

de nas yang rgyal po'i thugs dgongs la da dung lho bal gyi rgyal khams na mchod gnas ngo mtshar can 'dra e **[A: 28b]** yod na snyam nas tsan dan gyi sku rang byung mchod nas gsol ba btab pas / lha'i thugs ka nas 'od zer byung nas bal po'i yul[307] du song ngo // bal po'i yul gyi pha mtha'i lung pa cig na tsan **[B: 36b]** dan gyi nags khrod chen po gcig 'dug pa gzigs / de'i dbus na tsan dan ha ri'i sdong po la 'phags pa spyan ras gzigs gyi sku rang byung gsum 'dug pa gzigs so // de nas rgyal po'i smin mtshams kyi mdzod spu nas 'od zer gyi sna la dge slong ā ka ra śī la ma tir[308] sprul nas spyan 'dren du btang bas sprul pa'i dge slong des skyid grong du phyin pa dang / grong khyer de na lo re la grong dpon re mdze nad kyis thu lum du 'chi ba'i sdug bsngal mthong ngo // de nas bal yul du phyin pa dang / yam bu ya 'gal[309] zhes bya ba'i grong khyer na lo bskor re re la rims nad kyis 'tshol nyul[310] du 'chi ba'i sdug bsngal mthong ngo // de na bal yul gyi pha mthar phyin pa dang / rgya gar dang bal po'i so mtshams na zla ba gsum gsum na tshong dpon re gnod sbyin chen po gcig gis[311] khyer nas snga dro re re la sbos grir[312] 'chi ba'i 'jigs pa dang sdug bsngal mthong ngo //

de nas tsan da ha ri'i[313] nags gseb tu phyin pa dang tshal de'i dbus na nyin mo tsan dan gyi sdong po **[B: 37a]** la nub mo lha skur snang ngo // de nas sprul pa'i dge slong des sku gsum gyi mtshams su mtshan **[A: 29a]** ma gtod[314] nas bkas pa la de gsum gyis sgra byung ste / stod kyi de las dal gyis chod la / nga ni rgya gar dang bal po'i so mtshams su zhog[315] ces pa'i sgra byung ngo // de'i nang nas jo bo 'ja' ma li zhes bya ba tsan dan sku mdog dkar po lta bas[316] chog mi shes pa mtshan dang dpe byad[317] du ldan pa / dris dpag tshad bcu khyab pa / zhal gsum phyag drug pa / byis pa lo

---

[305] B: rab
[306] A, B: rgyal pos
[307] B: bal yul
[308] A: a kar śi la ma tir; B: a kar śī la ma tir
[309] A, B: yam 'gal
[310] A, B: chol gnyol
[311] A: gi
[312] A, B: rir
[313] A, B: tsan tra ha'i
[314] A: gtor
[315] A: bzhog
[316] A: blta bas
[317] A: dpe byed

lnga lon pa tsam zhig byung ngo // dbus kyi de las[318] dal bus chod la / nga yam bu ya 'gal[319] du zhog[320] cig bya ba'i sgra byung ngo // de kha phye ba'i[321] nang nas jo bo u khang[322] zhes bya ba sku mdog dkar po zhal gcig phyag bzhi pa / sku mtshan dang dpe byad[323] du ldan pa 'od dang 'od zer du 'phro ba gcig byung ngo // smad kyi de la dal gyis[324] chod la / nga mang yul du zhog[325] cig ces pa'i sgra byung ngo // de'i nang nas jo bo wa ti sku mdog dmar po zhal gcig phyag gnyis pa g.yas **[B: 37b]** mchog sbyin mdzad pa / g.yon padma dkar po 'dzin pa cig byung ngo //

de nas sprul pa'i dge slong des sku gsum po spyan drangs nas byon pas jo bo 'ja' ma li rgya gar dang bal po'i so mtshams su bzhugs nas gshegs su ma btub / jo bo u khang ya 'gal[326] du bzhugs nas gshegs su ma btub / jo o wa ti mang yul du bzhugs nas gshegs su ma **[A: 29b]** btub / sku rang byung gsum po de'i byin brlabs[327] kyis[328] sngar gyi 'jigs pa'i sdug bsngal gsum po de'i rgyun chad do //

zhes gsungs pa ltar jo bo rang byung mched bzhi'i nang tshan[329] 'khrul pa med pa nyid du grags shing lo rgyus cung zad rgyas pa gzhan yang yod rung 'dir yi ge'i 'jigs pas ma smos la gzhan du shes par bya'o //

'phags pa rang byung 'ja' ma li dkar mo dang nye bar / sngon chos kyi rgyal po mnya ngan med kyis[330] mnga' bangs kyi yul tha dad du skye bo rnams la yang bka' bsgos nas pho nya dang las kyi grogs thams cad gnod sbyin mthu bo che rnams kyis byas te / gnas chen **[B: 38a]** brgyad kyi mchod rten dang / rdo rje gdan gyi bar skor dang / gzhan yang byang phyogs su li yul tshun chad kyi 'dzam bu gling yul thams cad du thub pa'i ring bsrel gyi snying po can gyi mchod rten brtsigs pas nyin mtshan gcig la mchod rten brgyad khri bzhi stong grub / de'i nang tshan[331] gyi mchod rten cig da lta bal po paṇḍi ta śrī harṣa'i bsti

---

318 A, B: la
319 A, B: yam 'gal
320 A: bzhog
321 A, B: khos pa'i
322 A, B: om. u khang
323 A: dpe byed
324 A: gyi
325 A: bzhog
326 A, B: yam 'gal
327 A: byin rlabs
328 A: kyi
329 A: mtshan
330 A, B: kyi
331 A: mtshan

gnas kyi kun dga' ra ba na yod pa de yin la / kirti pur[332] du'ang mchod rten gcig yod pa'i ltas gsal por shar ces rig 'dzin rjes gsungs //

de nyid kyis /

> ring bsrel ldan pa'i mchod rten chos sku'i **[A: 30a]** brdar //
> rgyal bas gsungs bzhin 'dzam gling mdzes pa'i rgyan[333] //
> sa bdag mya ngan med pas 'bum phrag brgyad[334] //
> bzhengs las ne pāl[335] yam bu mdzes pa'i grong //
> dbus su gnas pa'i mchod rten[336] de la yang /
> bdag blo rab gus dang bas phyag 'tshal lo //

zhes bsngags par mdzad do //

de lta na mchod rten bye ba'i ya gyal[337] 'di bzhin sngar phan bod rnams kyis[338] ngo **[B: 38b]** ma shes shing yid rtog tsam yang med pas rig 'dzin rje de nyid kyis[339]ngos 'dzin par mdzad pa yin no //

bod rnams dmar ba[340] tshad pa sbyong[341] sar zer bar yod pa'i rdo sku de ni grub thob gorṣa nā tha'i sku yin te bal po rnams ma ru pa ta gorṣa nā tha zhes zer / lo rgyus rdzun[342] gtam 'gar / bcom ldan 'das kyi phyag mda' / jhai kṣim[343] las grub pa'i rgyal po sku lnga dang / pho lha tshe ring mched lnga zer ba sogs 'khrul pa'i rjes su 'brang ba'i gtam kho na ste rnam par 'khyams pa'o //

bal yul gyi bye brag pā ṭa na[344] zer ba zur chag gi skad du pā ṭan[345] du brjod pa ye rang ye rang gi grong khyer du rten bzhugs tshul ni / ston pa thub pa'i dbang po snang brnyan bal **[A: 30b]** po rnams ko ṭha bha śākya mu ni[346] zhes brjod pa de nyid bod snga rabs pa 'ga' zhig dgra bcom pa dge 'dun 'phel gyi phyag gnas ma yin zer ba dang / kha cig sngon gyi tshe bal yul e'i gtsug lag khang mes 'jig par gyur pa de'i rten gtso yin par 'dod pa dang / thub pa longs sku gsung byon ma zer ba **[B: 39a]** sogs 'dug mod / rten dngos ni sangs rgyas sprul pa'i sku'i cha

---

332 A: kyi te pur
333 A: brgyan
334 A, B: brgya
335 A: nem bal
336 A: mchod brten
337 A, B: ya rgyal
338 A, B: kyi
339 A: kyi
340 A, B: mar pa
341 A: sbyongs
342 A: brdzun
343 A: lji khyim
344 A, B: pa ṭha na
345 A, B: pa ṭhan
346 A, B: śākya mu ne

lugs can jo bo śākya mu ni[347] ji lta ba byin brlabs[348] can zhig ste[349] / sngon bal yul du du ruṣ ka'i[350] dmag byung dus / thabs gzhan gyis bzlog par ma nus pa'i tshe thub dbang gi sku brnyan de'i bzhugs khri 'og nas mon pa rdo rje ti dbyangs zhes 'bod pa'i dug sbrang chen po mthe bong tsam pa rno ba'i mchu can grangs med pa byung ste[351] dmag dpung thams cad phyir bzlog pa yin zhes bal po rang gi tshad ma'i lo rgyus las 'byung ngo //

jo bo u khang ni bal po rnams 'bung de wa zhes brjod pa / sngar smos pa bzhin rang byung 'phags mchog mched bzhi'i nang tshan[352] du gyur pa dang / yang jo bo 'bu khang[353] zhes bal po rnams tsak de war 'bod pa yang rang byung gi 'phags pa'i sku mched du **[A: 31a]** 'dod par snang / kha cig tso ba zhes pa'i yul gyi gtsug lag khang du bzhugs pa de 'phags pa u khang ngo ma yin par 'dod cing zhwa dmar drug pa'i lam yig tu yang **[B: 39b]** bshad do //

bod rnams sangs rgyas stong skur brjod cing / bal po rnams mahā buddha[354] zer ba ni / sngon bal po gur bal zhig gis rgya gar rdo rje gdan du phyin te pho brang gyi dbyibs rnams blo la nges par byas nas de'i mtshon byed 'dra mtshungs kyi mchod rten du mi gcig kho nas bzhengs pa yin zhes grags //

shing kun gyi 'dabs su 'phags mo dur khrod bal po rnams bi sa[355] zhes lun ti[356] lha khang du grags par sngon rigs ngan gdol pa mo zhig rdo rje rnal 'byor ma'i rten la thim pas phag mo'i sku byin brlabs[357] can yin par khro lo'i rnam thar las byung zhing / sku ngo bo mkha' spyod gsum las mai tri[358] mkha' spyod kyi sku yin par nges so // bod rnams mai tri mkha' spyod yin zer ba ni 'ol tshod kyi rdzun[359] gtam las gtan tshigs dang 'brel rgyu ni med do //

dur khrod ra ma dzo li ni bal yul rang du grags che ba las sngon gyi lo rgyus nges pa can ma thos so //

slob dpon sangs rgyas gnyis pa padma sam bha was byin gyis brlabs pa'i sgrub gnas yang le **[A: 31b]** shod **[B: 40a]** kyi brag phug ni / bal po rnams shi ka ṇa ran zhes brjod la / sngon slob dpon chen pos / rgya bal gyi so mtshams gnas 'dir byon / bal mo śākya de wīs[360] sgrub bde mo byas te dpal yang dag gi sgo nas

---

[347] A, B: śākya mu ne
[348] A, B: byin rlabs
[349] A: te
[350] A, B: du rukka'i
[351] A: te
[352] A: mtshan
[353] A, B: bu khang
[354] B: ma hā buddha
[355] A: bphi sa
[356] A, B: lun te
[357] A, B: byin rlabs
[358] A: mai ti
[359] A: brdzun
[360] A, B: śākya de was

mchog gi dngos grub phyag rgya chen po'i rig 'dzin grub pas / klu ging po / gnod sbyin thod ma kha / byi thur klog ma sprin gsum gyis[361] bar chad byas / lo gsum char ma babs[362] nad dang mu ge btang bas rgya gar du bla ma rnams la bar chad 'dul ba'i chos rdzang dgos gsungs pas[363] / phur pa bi to ta ma la po ti mi khur gnyis bskur bas bar chad zhi / char babs nad dang mu ge rgyun chad / mchog gi dngos grub thob / yang dag dngos grub che yang tshong pa dang 'dra bas bar chad[364] mang ba la skyel ma dang 'dra ba'i phur pa dgos par gzigs nas / yang phur sbrags ma'i sgrub skor mdzad / phur srung dang rgya bal gyi lha 'dre dregs pa can thams cad dam la btags / yang gnas der zhi ba'i **[B: 40b]** dkyil 'khor bsgrubs pas rdo rje dbyings kyi lha tshogs thams cad mngon sum du zhal gzigs te tshe'i rig 'dzin brnyes so //

kun mkhyen si tu'i 'gyur gsar gyi mdo'i le'u brgyad par ston pas bka' stsal pa /

> byams pa / 'di lta ste / bal po'i yul 'byor pa dang / rgyas pa dang / bde ba **[A: 32a]** dang / skyid pa dang / lo legs pa dang / mi'i skye bo mang pos gang bar gyur pa de nam zhig dus gzhan zhig gi tshe na bal po'i yul 'di nyid du lo bdun du char ma babs pas lo nyes par 'gyur ro //

zhes dang /

> glang ru r'i 'di la zhi ba'i grong du grub pa'i slob dpon zhi byed lha zhes bya ba yod de /

zhes pas nas /

> 'di ltar bal po'i yul 'di ni lha'i gnas grub pa'i sa gzhi[365] mthu stobs chen po'am / grub pa'i slob dpon rdzu 'phrul chen po shes rab can zhi byed lha de'ang bya ba rnams byas nas rang gi grong gyi mdun du dpag tshad kyi sa 'og tu yid bzhin nor bu dpag bsam ljon pas brgyan cing yid dga' ba'i mtho ris su shis pa'i[366] **[B: 41a]** dpal gyi bde ba'i bu gar ting 'dzin mdzad nas bzhugs so // de ting nge 'dzin de las dus shin tu ring ba zhig na ldang bar 'gyur te / langs nas kyang bal po'i yul 'dir chos ston par 'gyur ro //

---

[361] A: gyi
[362] A, B: bab
[363] A: gsung pas
[364] A, B: bar chod
[365] A, B: gzhi
[366] A, B: shes pa'i

zhes pa'i bar lung gis bstan pa bzhin zhi byed lha de ni slob dpon chen po padmā ka ra[367] nyid de /

thang yig gser phreng mar /

> de nas o rgyan gu ru padma 'byung gnas nyid bal yul du sku ngal gso zhing zla ba gsum bzhugs te: bal po'i rgyal po bha su dha ra[368] la sogs pa'i 'gro don rgya chen po mdzad: **[A: 32b]** de zhi ba'i lha zhes grags so:

zhes 'byung bas so //

'dir lo rgyus 'gyur gsar gyi mdo nyid du le'u brgyad pa'i mtha' can du gsungs pa'i bar skabs su babs pa'i lung rnams yid ches bskyed pa'i phyir yig tshogs la ma bltas par[369] dkyus su bris pa zhib tu rtogs par 'dod na rgya gzhung dngos der blta bar bya'o //

rgya gar pham mthing ni / thang yig zangs gling mar / rgya gar mtha' 'khob pham **[B: 41b]** mthing zhes bshad pa sngon rgya gar gyi sa char gyur pas rgya gar du grags par mngon pa sgra sgyur chen po mar pa lo tsā ba'i[370] bla ma pham mthing pa sku mched kyi bzhugs gnas yin par nges shing / da lta yul der phyi rol pa'i lha rten ma gtogs rten gang yang mjal rgyu med 'dra / phag mo'i sku byin brlabs[371] can de ni pham mthing pa'i thugs dam rten yin par 'dod pa dang / bal po rnams pham bi badzra dzo ki ni zhes zer //

a su ra'i brag phug ni / a su ra gu ha zhes lha ma yin gyi phug ste[372] / bal po kun da kyin ka ri zhes 'bod / thang yig tu bshad pa'i a su ra'i brag phug tu kun dga' bo bzhugs par gu ru nyid rab tu byung bar mdzad pa'i gnas de ni rgya gar du yod pa las bal yul gyi 'di min par snang zhing yang le shod dang 'brel ba **[A: 33a]** sogs rgyu mtshan mang pos mi 'thad par sems la / slob dpon chen po padma dang / rlangs[373] chen dpal gyi seng ges[374] brtan ma[375] bcu gnyis dam la btags pa'i gnas a su ra'i phrag phug **[B: 42a]** ni 'di kho na las gzhan du mi blta'o //

yang le shod nas lho nub kyi phyogs su nyin lam gcig tsam phyin pa na / rgya bal rnams ri ṣi shwa ra zhes zer / bod glen[376] rnams gu ru rin po ches gsungs pa'i[377] chu mig byang chub bdud rtsir grags pa de yin par 'dod pa'i tshul ni /

---

[367] B: padma kā ra
[368] A, B: bha su dha ri
[369] A: ma ltas par
[370] A: lo tsa ba'i
[371] A, B: byin rlabs
[372] A: te
[373] A, B: glang
[374] A: sengge'i
[375] A, B: bstan ma
[376] B: om. glen
[377] A: gsung pa'i

rgya gar mo khom pur dang bal po'i mtshams o shar gang du / pā lung / shī kha gor zhes bal po'i yul tsho gsum yod pa'i lho phyogs ri nags tshal stug por gyen chen po zhig 'dzegs pa'i phur brag skyibs chung ngu zhig gi brag ngos su mi'i gdong pa 'bur dod zhig dang / brag rtsa ru chu mig skol mo zhig ma gtogs gzhan ci yang mi snang /

lo rgyus su /

> sngon khyi ra ba zhig gis ri dwags shor bar gnas der phyin pa na drang srong ngam / dzo ki zhig mnyam par bzhag nas bsgom pa mthon ste de'i drung du song ba dang mi snang bar gyur // de'i tshe pa ṭhan zhes ye rang gi rā dza'i rmi lam **[A: 33b]** du'ang khyi ra ba mthong ba bzhin rmis te / drang srong na re / **[B: 42b]** gal te kho bo'i gnas de ngos bzung zhing mchod pa'i las byed na ci 'dod pa'i dam pa sbyin par byed do zhes zer ba'i mod la gnyid sad pas de lta bu gang na yod rtog par[378] mi nus so snyam du sems cing gnas pa na / nam zhig gi tshe khyi ra ba gleng ba'i gtam thos te rgyal po des gnas 'dir ongs pas[379] drang srong ma rnyed de brag skyibs kyi ngos su rang byung gi gdong pa yod par mthong / der dus su mchod pa'i srol btsugs te deng sang gi bar du phyogs de'i skye bo mang po dus bzang dag tu mjal mi shin tu mang ba yod zhing / phag gun[380] zhes hor zla dang po'i tshes bco lnga'i nub mo ne pāl dang / pā ṭhan sogs su dus ston la byon pa yin zer nub phyed bar ni sindhu ra'ang mi gos la byin ci yang mi byung / nub phyed nas dus ston las phyir 'khor ba yin zer zil phrom dang bcas pa'i gdong pa mngon sum du lta bu yod skad / bal po zhig gis / gnas der rdo skas dang / pā ṭhi zhes mgron khang brtsigs par brtsams pas[381] na sbas pa'i gnas **[B: 43a]** kyi[382] phyir ngoms[383] mi 'dod pa'i mtshan ma rmi lam du mthong nas gnas der shi'o //

zhes **[A: 34a]** zer ro //

tshul 'di ni phyi rol pa kho nar grags pa las nang pa'i lo rgyus shig min par rtogs kyang / 'dir the tshom bsal phyir bkod pa yin la / de ltar na /

gsol 'debs bar chad lam gsal mar /

> rgya gar bal yul so mtshams su :
> byin gyis brlabs nas byon pa'i tshe :
> dri bsung spos ngad ldan pa'i ri :

---

[378] A: rtogs par
[379] A: 'ong pas
[380] A: phag kun
[381] A, B: rtsam pas
[382] B: om. kyi
[383] A: mngoms

me tog padma dgun yang skye :
chu mig byang chub bdud rtsi'i chu /
bde ldan de yi gnas mchog tu :

zhes gsungs pa'i gnas dang / byang chub bdud rtsi chu mig ni yang le shod kyi gnas kyi[384] mtshan nyid kho nar gsungs pa[385] las / rgya gar mo khom pur[386] gyi ri rgyud kyi rtser dgun[387]kha ba bab pa'i gnas der byung ba'i chu mig lkog mo rung ba rul ba zhig la lung ston mi srid la /

o rgyan gling pa'i thang yig shel brag ma'i le'u nga bzhi par /

de nas bal yul tsha ba tsha shod byon :
chu mig byang chub ring mo zhes bya **[B: 43b]** ba :
dgun yang me tog skye der sgrub pa mdzad :
de dus sems can srog la dbang byed pa'i[388] :
sa bdag mched mo mched bzhi dam la btags :
phur pa'i[389] bka' srung bse mo mched bzhir gsol :

zhes sngar smos pa'i phur srung dam can rnams dam la **[A: 34b]** btags pa'i tshul dang mthun zhing /

myang gter thang yig zangs gling ma las /

rgya gar yul gyi tshu rol : bal po yul gyi pha rol : yang le shod kyi brag phug ces bya ba na[390] : me tog dgun yang mi skam la : bkra shis pa'i gnas der byon pa na :

zhes sogs gsungs pa[391] dang mthun pas phyin chad cal sgrog[392] ming skam gyi rjes su mi 'brangs bar / byang chub bdud rtsi ni yang le shod dang de'i mtsho dkar nag chu rgyun bzang po dang bcas pa de kho nar ngos bzung bar bya'o //

de dang rjes su 'brel bar gsol 'debs bar chad lam sel mar gsungs pa'i[393] gtsang kha la yi la thog ni ding sang bod grong lar 'bod pa 'di yin par gsungs shing / bal yul tsha ba'i tsha shod ni da lta 'dar wal **[B: 44a]** du grags pa'i ljongs dang / de'i smad mdo dman zer bar de wi gā tra[394] zhes rdo rje phur pa'i[395] srung ma ma mo bcu gnyis las bse mo bzhi'i nang tshan rdo rje ya byin gnas pa ste /

---

384 B: om gnas kyi
385 A: gsung pa
386 A: rgya mo kho pur; B: rgya mo khom pur
387 B: khun
388 B: byed ba'i
389 A, B: phur ba'i
390 A, B: om. na
391 A: gsung pa
392 A: sgrogs
393 A: gsung pa'i
394 B: de wi gā
395 A, B: phur ba'i

byang gter phur pa dang / chos dbang gi phur pa spu gri sogs gter byon phur pa'i dam can gyi bskul mang por tshig mthun par bshad la //

snga sor rig 'dzin rjer / lha chen po bi ṣṇu[396] bram ze'i gzugs kyis[397] 'ongs[398] te / lung bstan pa bzhin rang byung mchod rten chen po'i srog shing yang gnas 'di nas 'dren par mdzad pa yin no //

mtsho dkar mtsho nag tu grags pa ni / phyi rol rig byed pa rnams lha chen po dang / u ma'i gnas su 'dod **[A: 35a]** la / nang pa rnams bde mchog gi pho brang du 'dod kyang / rig 'dzin rje ni rdo rje gdan gyi byang shar lha mo re ma ti'i pho brang yin zhes gsungs so[399] //

> tshad mar gyur pa 'gro la phan bzhed mgon //
> thub dbang sras slob grub dang rig 'dzin gyis //
> byin brlabs[400] ngo mtshar gzi rgyas gnas dang rten //
> mthong **[B: 44b]** thos dran pas grol der kun dga'i dpyid //
>
> de na'ang 'khrul pa cal sgrog[401] smig rgyu yi //
> kun rmongs ri dwags mang srid rnam par khyams //
> da gdod ma nor lam zhugs[402] de dang de'i //
> yon tan rjes dran dag snang bskyed par rigs //

bal yul gyi gnas dang rten gyi lo rgyus nges par brjod pa 'khrul spong nor bu'i me long zhes bya ba las zhar byung gnas rten gzhan gyi rgyu mtshan bshad pa'i skabs te bzhi pa'o //

[V]

de na 'phros su bya ba gzhan yang brjod par bya ste / ne pā la yi yul der sangs rgyas kyi bstan pa ches dar zhing / mu stegs byed kyi grub mtha' nyung bar 'dug la / dbus 'gyur ma ga dha'i yul gyi bi ka ma la śī la'i gtsug lag **[A: 35b]** khang nub nas kyang lo brgya phrag lhag tsam gyi bar du bal po'i yul du sangs rgyas kyi bstan pa lhag par dar bar 'gyur / phyi rabs su paṇḍi ta chen po nags kyi rin chen gyi skabs dang / de'i rjes su lo mang tsam gyi bar du yang bstan pa ma nub par yod par gsungs shing / **[B: 45a]** dus kyi 'gyur bas ding sang ni sangs rgyas kyi bstan pa ming gi lhag ma tsam las thams cad phyi rol pa'i grub mtha' kho nas khyab par gyur la / nang pa cung zad yod pa rnams kyang phyi nang

[396] A, B: biṣnu
[397] A: gyi
[398] A: ong
[399] A: gsung ngo
[400] A, B: byin rlabs
[401] A: sgrogs
[402] B: bzhugs

gnyis ka'i grub mtha' 'dres mar spyod cing / nang pa sha dag gi grub mtha'i blang dor gtsang mar spyod pa ni nyin skar tsam zad do //

bal yul gyi sa yi bdag po ji ltar byung ba ni / sngon 'jam dpal gyi sprul pa rgyal po 'od zer go cha nas bzung rim par gangs can yul gyi rje bo chos kyi rgyal srong btsan sgam po'i skabs de nas kyang dus ring po'i bar sangs rgyas kyi bstan pa gus pa par mchod pa'i chos ldan gyi rgyal po mang zhig byung bar nges la / bar skabs zhig yul pa ta li pu tra[403] nas rgyal rigs mu stegs byed zhig du ruṣ ka'i[404] rgyal po **[A: 36a]** dang 'khrugs pas pham nas g.yog 'khor mang po dang bcas pa bros re kho khom du chags / rgyal po des bal po'i rgyal rigs rnying pa rnams kyang gnon par byas te mu **[B: 45b]** stegs byed kyi grub mtha' dar rgyas su btang / de rjes mi rabs kha shas nas rgyal po de'i rigs brgyud zhig yam bu'i bdag por gyur / de nas bzung rgyal po dza ya pra ka śa'i[405] bar du rgyal brgyud rim par byung ba kun sangs rgyas la ltar snang tsam las snying thag pa nas mos shing bstan pa gus pas sri zhu byed pa po cher ma byung bar mngon yang de dag gi nang nas rang rig ras pa'i skabs su gyur pa'i rgyal po pār ti wendra malla[406] zhes shing kun la nyams gso legs par sgrub tshul gong du smos zin la / rgyal rigs kyi tha ma dza ya pra ka śa[407] ste bod skad du rgyal ba rab gsal du 'bod pa de ni sangs rgyas la snying thag pa nas mos shing / bod yul gyi skyes chen dam pa bal yul du byon pa rnams la yang gus pas 'dud pa dang / khyad par rig 'dzin rje dpal dus kyi 'khor lo'i rdzogs rim sbyor drug gi man ngag legs par zhu zhing shin tu gus pa'i slob mar gyur pa zhig ste /

gsung mgur rgyal khag bcu gsum mar /

> bal yul yam bu'i **[B: 46a]** rgyal po /
> chos kyi slob mar bgyis yod /

ces gsungs /

de'i rjes su rab byung bcu gsum pa'i na tshod ldan shing phag lor gorṣa rgyal po'i dpung gis bal yul blangs so / rgyal po 'di ni / ri brag pa'i rgyal po zhig sngon grub pa'i slob dpon chen po gorṣa nā tha'i bsti gnas gorṣa gu ha zhes grub thob de'i sgrub phug yod pa'i ri'i 'dabs su slas kyi mkhar bzung bas ding sang gorṣa grags shing / kśatriya'i[408] rgyal rigs su gyur pa zhig ste / 'di pa'i rigs su gtogs pa phal cher slob dpon gorṣa nā tha la gus par byed do //

---

[403] A: pa ta li pu ṭa; B: pa tra li pu tra
[404] A, B. du ru ka'i
[405] B: dza ya pra ka sa'i
[406] B: pra ti bhantra ma
[407] B: dza ya pra ka sa
[408] B: kṣe da'i

rgyal po pṛthvī nā ra yā ṇa[409] zhes pa pha bu skabs su rig 'dzin rje la'ang gus par btud cing / rang byung mchod rten chen po'i srog shing 'dren pa'i zhabs 'gyur yang dag par zhus par snang la /

rgyal khag bcu gsum ma'i mgur las /

mon smad gorṣa rgyal po /
phyag las dge la bsgyur yod /

ces gsungs /

de nas da lta'i bar rgyal rabs bzhi tsam song bar shes so / **[B: 46b]**

gzhan yang jo nang rje btsun dam pa tā ra nā thar /

gang na sangs rgyas kyi bstan pa yod pa na / lha bzo yang mkhas par dar / gang na kla klos dbang byed pa 'dir lha bzo nub / gang du mu stegs dar sar lha bzo yang mi mkhas pa dag dar bar yod /

ces gsungs pa ltar sngon bal yul gyi ljongs su rgyal ba'i sku gzugs bris 'bur gser zangs / li sku / tsan dan la sogs pa'i shing sku dang rdo sku / lugs ma la sogs bzo khyad ches mtshar zhing legs pa dag byung zhing / bod yul du'ang ding sang gi bar kun tu khyab bzhin dang / bod snga rabs bris pa'i lha ris kyi rgyun[410] sha stag[411] byung bar mngon sum bal yul rang gi bzo rigs rnams kyi nang nas kyang ye rang gi bzo rgyun[412] zhes legs tshad du 'jog pa gsung rgyun tshad ldan las thos shing dngos su yang mthong mod / ding sang ni sku gzugs kyi bzo bkod kyang re re tsam las phal cher sgros mi gtsang ba shas che bar snang ngo //

gang sngon **[B: 47a]** rgyal ba'i thugs rje'i nyin byed kyis //
ljongs 'dir bstan pa'i pad 'tshal cher rgyas kyang //
ding dus lta ngan ring lugs ser ba yis //
phan bde'i myu gu ji snyed cig car bcom //

'on te bde gshegs gsang gsum za ma tog //
gang dag ma nyams rang rang mos dge yi //
rnam dkar sa bon bskrun la gegs med par //
rang dang bgyir rung 'di ko bskal bzang rmad //

bal yul gyi gnas dang rten gyi lo rgyus nges par brjod pa 'khrul spong nor bu'i me long las zhar byung gi 'phros don gzhan yang brjod pa'i skabs te lnga pa'o //

de ltar ne pāl yul gyi gnas dang rten //
ngo mtshar ba ku la yi 'khri shing la //
rab bsngags mdzes ma'i 'gram chang gis bran pas //

---

409 B: sri thi na ra ya na
410 B: khyun
411 B: sha dag
412 B: khyun

dpyod ldan dgyes pa'i me tog 'dzum phreng g.yo //

rdul bral thams cad gzigs pa'i spyan ldan de'i //
legs gsung dbyangs bdun rdzogs pa'i rgyud mang sgra //
sngon chad phal gyi[413] rna bar son min pa //
lhag bsam sor mos **[B: 47b]** drangs te kho bos bsgyur //

rgyal ba'i gsang gsum rten gyi ngo mtshar gtam //
gleng bas dad pa'i spu long g.yo[414] byed cing //
som nyir gyur dang khungs ldan mi ldan gyi //
dbye ba shes gyur skabs 'di'i dgos don nyid //

de phyir legs byas don gnyer blo ldan kun //
nyes bshad log pa'i g.ya' yis ma sbags par //
ngo mtshar yon tan bzhin ras gsal 'char ba //
sngon med nor bu'i me long 'dir ltos shig //

skye bar goms pa'i rnam dpyod nor dben cing //
gtsug lag gzhung brgyar sbyangs pa'i stobs bral bzhin //
ci brtol brjod pas mkhas rnams khrel gyur na //
bzod bzhes dag byed dbyangs kyis dbugs 'byin mdzod //

'dir 'bad lhag bsam 'du dge'i dngos gyur ji snyed thob pa mtha' dag ni //
ku mu da[415] ltar dri ma med cing kha ba dung dang pad rtsa ltar //
ches dkar mthu las rgyal rnams dgyes byas bstan pa rin chen mchog tu dar //
'jig rten kun tu phan bde rab rgyas phun tshogs dpal gyis 'tsho bar shog // **[B: 48a]**

'gro kun bzang po'i lam zhugs te //
chos dbyings de bzhin nyid kyi dngos //
gsung gi dbang phyug mngon gyur nas //
mkha' khyab gzhan phan 'grub gyur cig //

ces bal yul gyi gnas dang rten gyi lo rgyus nges par brjod pa 'khrul spong nor bu'i me long zhes bya 'di ni sngon chad lo rgyus phra zhib phyogs gcig tu yi ger 'khod pa med nges par snang la / rje rang rig ras pa'i slob ma nas lung pa[416] ngag dbang rdo rjes mdzad pa'i bal yul shing kun gyi dkar chag tu grags pa dang / rngog ston karma blo bzang gis mdzad pa'i bal yul gyi lam yig gnyis ka par du[417] yang 'khod pas phal cher de dag gi rjes zlos[418] byed pa mang bar

[413] B: gyi
[414] B: go
[415] B: ku mu ta
[416] B: gnas lung pa
[417] B: gsar du
[418] A: bzlos

mthong zhing / nas lung pa[419] ngag dang rdo rje[420] gyi yi ge der rje rang rig ras pa nyid kyi gdung rten gyi dkar chag de ka tsam ma gtogs gzhan mtha' dag 'ol tshod kyi rdzun gtam 'ba' zhig dang[421] [...]

[419] B: gnas lung pa

[420] B: ngag rdor

[421] B: add. 'di'i 'phro zhabs kyi shog lhe rgyab phreng kha shas ma dpe mi gsal bas bris ma nus /

# A Definitive Presentation of the History of the Sacred Sites and Religious Objects of Nepal: A Mirror of Jewels Which Clears Away Errors

May it be auspicious!

[This is] what is called 'A Definitive Presentation of the History of the Sacred Sites and Religious Objects of Nepal: A Mirror of Jewels Which Clears Away Errors'. I prostrate with reverence before the Jina and his sons and disciples!

> He whose glorious good qualities are inexhaustible and vast, an ocean, the depth of which is hard to fathom;
> whose great love is well paired with the pure breath of compassion, their rolling waves moving in a hundred directions;
> the essence of whose enlightenment is firm, [like] Mount Meru; the submarine fire of whose wisdom blazes [ever more];[1]
> who gathers completely the countless rivers of those fortunate ones of the three realms who are endowed with a spiritual lineage—may this most excellent Buddha be victorious!

> Possessing [as they do] the magnificence of [his] virtuous signs, from which arise clearly
> a hundred thousand decorative paintings of the compassion of the Jina together with his sons:
> who would not rejoice in a discourse about the wonders [and] qualities
> of the sacred sites and religious objects of marvellous Nepal?

> Those who pay heed to prattle,
> appreciating as they do talk [that shows their] craving for whatever biased stupidity there is—
> seeing many [such persons], [and] in some measure [spurred] by the enthusiasm of [my] followers,
> I here formulate a genuine history of past events.

[There is] a valley called Nepal, a region, as it were, fallen to earth [from heaven] in order to set apart India and Tibet; a land of the gods [forming] an intermediate space between the holy land—the source of the Noble Doctrine ([apart from] whatever [other] special features of the continent characterized by jambu trees [there may be])—and the glacier land of Tibet. In it there are in great numbers religious objects [serving as] visible expressions of the Buddhist doctrine that contain relics of the Sugata in their core; distinctive statues; temples; and unique sacred sites blessed [for] having been trodden by the feet of many perfected noble beings. In regard to these, no detailed authentic register of their past history has become an object for the pleasure of one's eyes and ears; there has thus been no way to communicate [that history] as it was. And also the histories known in Nepal itself, being mostly confused talk, seem hardly suitable as something to rely on. The histories composed and records [produced] by old Tibetan fools, given the simple absence of a [shared] vocabulary, are not known in Nepal. Even toponyms [are] unreliable [as] sources, being expressed in a variety of forms—expressed as unanalyzed falsities and mere frivolous anecdotes, and therefore spoken in reaction, under the sway of bias. All this is [like] a gathering of fools tricked [into gathering] by a fool.

As is said in the aphorisms of Sa-skya [Paṇḍita]:

> If a fool walks on a wrong path,
> it is enough to understand that he is a fool.
> If a learned man walks on a wrong path,
> One needs to ponder the reason.[2]

Accordingly, [these stories] are not to be repeated by knowledgeable persons, nor is it even proper to listen [to them]!

In the present context, the basis for an authoritative narrative is a translation known to exist—[done] by lHa-mdong Lo-tsā-ba bShes-gnyen rnam-rgyal (b. 1512)—of the renowned register said to have been produced by Paramārya Nāgārjuna [of events relating to the Svayaṃbhūcaitya].[3] Previously the text had not been something that one often set one's eyes on. Later, in a time of decline, the Great All-Knowing Si-tu Dharmākara bsTan-pa'i nyin-byed (1700–1774) translated the 'History of the Nepalese Shing-kun' and—except for some verses at the beginning and end composed by a paṇḍita—the main part has been accepted as a sūtra containing the words of the Buddha written out.[4] I have taken it as the main evidential basis of [my] narration, whence, in line with [what] my own mind has come up with, there are five [parts] in what is to be told of the history: [I] an explanation of why a distinction must be made between Nepal and Li-yul; [II] an exposition of the history of Shing-kun, the Self-Manifested Mahācaitya; [III] an exposition of the history of the Bya-rung kha-shor Stūpa; [IV] a discussion of subsidiary sacred sites and other religious objects; [V] further narratives told as a residual supplement.

[I]

First, in what is known of from the histories composed by early Tibetans and from how they talk, the claim is that the Li-yul (the Land of Virtuous Ones and like [epithets]) discussed in the *Ārya-Gośṛṅga-vyākaraṇa-sūtra* is [the land of] Nepal. Ox Hill and the stūpa Go-ma-sa-la-gan-dha, further, are identified with the Shing-kun [stūpa] itself.[5] But if that is so, [and] if one accepts that Nepal is Li-yul on the basis of the sūtra itself, [which] tells of what is called the 'Shore of the River Go-ma' and of the existence of a great lake in previous times which was seized by Śāriputra and Vaiśravana and changed into a stream [located in] the lower part of Gyi in the north, then it is reasonable to identify the river Go-ma, the stream in the lower part of Gyi and so forth as [part of] this [Nepal] as well. It is reasonable, too, to say [something about] the etymology of the name Go-ma-sa-la-gan dha stūpa!

Some state that what is called Godāvarī, one of the twenty-four pīṭhas, is [the land of] Nepal, known as the 'Best Gift of a Cow'—[this] in connection with the story of milk from a tawny cow being sprinkled on a tree trunk in the woods of Ko-khom (i.e. Bhaktapur). Although they say this, using *gau* in the sense of cow, *dāna* in the sense of gift, [and] *vara* in the sense of best, the real Godāvarī among the twenty-four pīṭhas is called 'Godāvarī, the Left Ear', it being identified with [the site called] sNyan-g.yon in La-phyi [Gangs-kyi ra-ba].[6]

Although some printed [works] relating to Nepal calling themselves registers or guidebooks say that the *[Ārya-]mañjuśrī-mūla-tantra*, the *[Ārya-]gośṛṅga-[vyākaraṇa-]sūtra* and the *bKa' gdams glegs bam* describe Nepal in common with Li-yul [as being one and the same], this is a mere fiction. based on [false] assumptions.[7]

In the *[Ārya-]mañjuśrī-mūla-tantra* [it is said]:

> The kṣetras described by him who possesses the ten kinds of strength
> [are] lands lying in the northern direction:
> Kaśmir, 'China' and
> Nepal; similarly, Mang-yul,
> 'Great China' and Li-yul.
> All these [are] kṣetras where siddhis are brought to perfection.[8]

As [the kṣetras] are thus actually described as individual countries, how could [one] be explained in common terms [with another]? In no way does the *bKa' gdams glegs bam* describe Nepal as being Li-yul. For example, if there actually exists a distinction between great and small in regard to China and a distinction between Tibet and Great Tibet, then to claim that different countries in Jambudvīpa are combined into one—it seems that you are more learned than the Buddha [himself].

If one asks what the real Li-yul is, then from the *Gośṛṅga-vyākaraṇa-sūtra*:

> The Bhagavan spoke: "Listen, sons of a [good] family! At the time when a hundred years have passed after my Paranirvāṇa there will appear from China a Chinese king called Ca-yang who will have fully a thousand sons; each and every son will undertake to newly seek a land of his own."

From there up to:

> Since the prince Earth-Suckled founded a land by this suckling on the breast [of the earth], the name of the place thus came to be Suckling Breast.[9]

Up to here [is] explained [more] extensively in the 'Religious History' by the All-knowing Padma dkar-po (1527–1592):

> Before, during the time when the Teacher (i.e. Śākyamuni) lived, and the round lake [of the land] had been dug away at by Śāriputra with [his] begging bowl, allowing it to drain off, the teacher dwelt on Li, a mountain [that appeared], which is blessed for having been the [material] cause of the stūpa of the four Buddhas called Go-ma-sa-la-gan-dha, [and] of footprints [and] statues of the [first] four Buddhas [of the *bhadrakalpa*]. Some two hundred years after his Parinirvāṇa there was a king of China who had nine hundred ninety-nine sons. Then, needing a further son, he besought Vaiśravana, and thus a grandson was born to the Dharmarāja Aśoka. Immediately, it being hungry for something to be bestowed, Vaiśravaṇa directed its mouth to the earth, and from there a breast arose. [The child] suckled milk from it and became [afterwards] very famous under the name Earth-Suckled. Together with the army of the king of China he was [later] dispatched to Li-yul, where the river Sītā flows—what today is called the Hor [and] Sog land.[10]

The venerable Mahāvidyādhara Kaḥ-thog-pa [Tshe-dbang nor-bu] (1698–1755)], too, said:

> Li-yul, [one of] the six countries that were taken possession of by an [earth-]suckled king at a time when his ascendant was rising, seems necessarily to lie to the north of Tibet, whence even the learned bCom-ldan rig-ral (1227–1305) in earlier times and some learned persons of later times state that the country where [the king] Earth-Suckled appeared is located in the northern part of Xining.[11]

From the *sKu gdung 'bar ba [tsha tsha] mchod rten gyi rgyud*, a tantra of the early translations:

> On the border in the north-east [lies] Li-yul;
> At the 'Jig-rten mgon-rdzogs charnel ground
> the mighty [nāgā] Mahāpadma [resides],
> and one full of ceaseless violence;
> and the stūpa called Ge'u de-shan.It is a sacred site where the Teacher (i.e. Padmasambhava) performed miracles:
> water was discharged, fire blazed up [and] many illusions [appeared].
> This is the royal domain of the ruler Li-rje![12]

Once, at a time when Heruka was vanquishing the violent one (i.e. Rudra), in the charnel grounds of eight countries there appeared eight stūpas—dwelling places of the eight Ma-mo goddesses—in which siddhis manifest.

[In] Magadha, the bDe-byed [stūpa],
in Sing-ga-la, the Ri po-ta-la [stūpa],
in Nepal, the Bya-tri kha-shor [stūpa],
in Sing-ga gling, the Ge'u da-na [stūpa],
in Li-yul, the Go-ma-sa-la-gan-dha [stūpa],
in Kaśmir, the Kanika [stūpa],
in Za-hor, the bDe-spyod [stūpa],
[in ........] the gZhon-nu stūpa.

They figure in this way, too, in the commentary on the *bDud rtsi mchog gi rgyud*: the countries and stūpas [of Nepal and Li-yul] are each presented as distinct entities.[13]

The way [it is told] in the *rGyal po bka' 'bum* is that two śrāmaṇeras from Li-yul practised the Mañjuśrī [sādhana], went according to a prophecy to Tibet, met the Dharmarāja Srong-btsan sgam-po (ca. 605–649) and returned to Li-yul;[14] and the accounts having to do with Nepal are told as if [the two countries] were distinct. Furthermore, in a manifold number [of other works]—the *Kālacakratantra* and so forth—Nepal and Li-yul are talked about as [if they were] distinct. One should be able, then, to understand [this].[15]

Some fools state that what is called Li-yul [is the land] in the saying 'from Nepal in the west, where metal [objects] are forged, over to the east, where Chinese women weave silk'; and accordingly they use [the fact] that Newars forge metal [objects] as their reason to claim that [Nepal] is Li-yul.[16] This is completely erroneous; all places where metal is forged would thus become Li-yul. Also, in the 'Religious History of China', composed by a great Chinese translator of later times, Gung mGon-po skyabs (ca. 1690–1750?), Li-yul is identified with lCang.[17] It is said as well that there are instances of Chinese identifying the temple and stūpa mentioned in the *Gośṛṅga-vyākaraṇa[-sūtra]* with Go-ma-sa-la-gan-dha in the region known as Kong-wu in China proper. How [the latter] was seen in person by the Great Fifth [Dalai Bla-ma Ngag-dbang Blo-bzang rgya-mtsho (1617–1692)] appears in the first volume of his autobiography.[18] Likewise, if the Hor [and] Sog lands, [or] lCang and so forth are accepted as Li-yul, it has also necessarily been established that in these lands a Go-ma-sa-la-gan-dha stūpa and so forth, as referenced in the *Gośṛṅga-vyākaraṇa[-sūtra]*, exist on the whole in accordance with the referenced suppositions. Nevertheless, the reason is not widely known why persons like this or that from the past until now have seen and heard [such things]. [There are those] who view [Li-yul] as the Hor [or] Sog [people], and [others who] say that the sūtra itself excludes them from being either [among] the manifold tribes of Turuṣkas or what are called the Hor [people], so that clearly things remain to be analyzed. Even though one may decide that [one region or the other] is the real Li-yul, identifying it as such in accordance with [the position of] many scholars and accomplished ones, no [firm supporting evidence] has presented itself. Leaving [the question,] as it were, as a matter of doubt, I am here again unable to take any consistent [stance].

> Universally praised by all the Guides of the three times
> and very clearly pointed out by all the throng of beings of the three realms;
> possessing splendour in virtue of its [three] cities, [which are] heavenly realms of gods,
> the valley of Nepal [is] beautiful in virtue of its three [kinds of] astonishing sacred objects.
>
> The Four-Faced One (i.e. Brahma) purposely created a unique division
> between the Holy Land [of India] [and] Tibet, and accordingly [Nepal] is famous
> for the fulfilment of all attainments one desires, nothing lacking, its marvels reaching out in all directions;
> [such] a land is worthy of praise.

The first chapter of what is called 'A Definitive Presentation of the History of the Sacred Sites and Religious Objects of Nepal: A Mirror of Jewels Which Clears Away Errors', setting forth an analysis of the claim that Li-yul and Nepal are the same [country].

[II]

Secondly, [then], an exposition of the history of the Self-Manifested Mahācaitya Shing-kun: Now, in the Holy Land of India it is called the Svayaṃbhūcaitya, literally the Self-Manifested Stūpa. It is claimed that it appeared in previous times from a lock of hair on the forehead of Buddha Śikhī. [Afterwards] Paramārya Nāgārjuna arrived, and he paid extensive homage [to it], while Mahācārya Vasubandhu came to see Nepal's Svayaṃbhūcaitya at the end of his life. [All] these stories will be told below. Likewise, the noble [and] magnificent Lord Dipaṃkarabhadra [Atiśa (982–1054)] came to Nepal to see its Svayaṃbhūcaitya when he was on his way to Tibet.[19]

These and others who, as told [here], arrived in [such] splendour are extremely well known in the Holy Land of India. As explained above, most people in Tibet identify [the stūpa] with the Go-ma-sa-la-gan-dha told of in the *Gośṛṅga-vyākaraṇa[-sūtra]*. In general, it is known as 'Phags-pa shing-kun, while in the vulgar language and the Newari vernacular it is called Shin-bur (= *seṃgu*).[20]

In any case, it alone is certainly the Self-Manifested Stūpa, without any doubt. From the familiar register composed by [Ārya] Nāgārjuna and translated by lHa-mdong Lo-tsā-ba [bShes-gnyen rnam-rgyal]:

> At the time of the Dvāparayuga
> the hill was called Gośṛṅga;

by the people of Nepal it is well known [as such].
[Each of the four] yugas has a name of its own [for it].[21]

[For comparison's sake,] the full exposition of the sūtra according to the new translation of the All-Knowing Si-tu-pa [Chos-kyi 'byung-gnas] is offered here:

The hill called Gośṛṅga
is located in the land of Nepal.
This [hill], because of the distinctions among the aeons,
is different in terms of the name [given to it in them]:
in the Kṛtayuga: Padma'i ri,
in the Tretayuga: Ri-bo rdo-rje brtsegs,
in the Dvāparayuga: Glang-ru'i ri,
in the Kāliyuga: Ri-bo glang-mjug.

[The hill] even at present [sometimes] goes by the name 'Great Lotus Mountain', and it is possible that [the name] will continue on [in the future].

Likewise, the name given [to the hill] changes as well within the four aeons of the past, future and present. The people who live in this country now call it *sī hang mgu* (= *seṃgu*). This [hill] has a wide variety of zones, whence there are trees such as blossoming nāga kesara, campaka, bakula, pippala, kovidāra, plakṣa, kapiṭṭa, tunya, kuvalaya, āśoka, tālā and tamāla; manifold tamarisks scattered about; a variety of birds emitting their calls; numerous waterfalls pouring down; numerous hosts of wild animals; many varieties of flowers growing in abundance [and] with many kinds of fruits; bees intoning their songs; [and] groups [of beings] who support it, including gods, nāgās, yakṣas, gandharvas, demi-gods, sky-soarers, mahoragas and realized siddhas.[22] There, in ancient times, existed the true sovereign of [all] stūpas, made out of most excellent self-manifested crystal and measuring one full cubit.

At this true souvereign of [all] stūpas, those sentient beings striving for the Buddhist doctrine, their [own and others'] benefit, their wishes and their liberation, may they perform [acts of] offerings with the most excellent devotion!

In this regard I once heard the [following] words: At the peak on the western rear side of this noble lord [in the form] of a self-manifested stūpa, on what is called Gośṛṅga Hill in the land of Nepal, the glorious Tathāgata Śākyamuni was staying near the stūpa in order to care for all sentient beings, together with a great saṃgha of five hundred monks, including Mahākāśyapa, five hundred Bodhisattvas—Maitreya and others—and assemblages of gods, including Brahma, Viṣṇu and Maheśvara.[23]

Answering a question from the Bodhisattva-Mahāsattva Maitreya, the Bhagavan spoke: "Maitreya! Previously, in that Fortunate Aeon when the lifespan of people was eighty thousand years, the Tathāgata, Arhat [and] completely enlightened Buddha called Vipaśyī, Guide of the World [and] Dharmarāja, was born in the great city gNyen-ldan. Maitreya! During his lifetime there was a Bodhisattva-Mahāsattva called bDen-pa'i chos; he performed offerings to the Buddha Vipaśyī.

"Maitreya! I myself was the Bodhisattva-Mahāsattva bDen-pa'i chos at that time; do not regard me as anyone else!

"After a very long time passed following the nirvāṇa of the Tathāgatha Vipaśyī, in that Fortunate Aeon when the lifespan of people was seventy thousand years, the Tathāgata, Arhat [and] completely enlightened Buddha called Śikhī, Guide of the World [and] Dharmarāja, was born in the city called Aruṇa. Maitreya! During his lifetime there was a Bodhisattva-Mahāsattva called bZod-pa'i rgyal-po; he performed offerings to the Buddha Śikhī.

"Maitreya! I myself was the Bodhisattva-Mahāsattva bZod-pa'i rgyal-po at that time; do not regard me as anyone else!

"Maitreya! At that time, too, the land of Nepal changed into a big lake measuring seven *krośa*s in length and known under the name Nāgāsthana.[24]

"Now, this [lake] was completely filled with water possessing the eight qualities [of coolness, sweetness, lightness, softness, clearness, soothingness, pleasantness and wholesomeness]; it was adorned with [such kinds of lotus as] utpala, padma, kumuda and puṇḍarīka, and many kinds of [other] flowers. Waterfowl—and [in particular] swans, ducks, cranes and geese—sounded their melodic calls. A great horde of aquatic creatures resided there, [and] as numerous trees with sweet-smelling blossoms and trees with fruit grew there, there was rich beauty everywhere. In this [lake] appeared a great lotus the size of a chariot wheel, charming in virtue of a thousand petals made of the five kinds of precious stones; it had a stem of jewels, filaments of diamonds and anthers of blazing rubies. In regard to the anthers, whichever ones were the longest and most prominent—those that were completely perfect and all of whose defining characteristics were of the nature of the crystal-like Dharmadhātu—produced fruit that surpassed ordinary thought [and] to which reverence could but be paid, offerings made and devotion shown. It was born of itself for the benefit, bliss and liberation of gods, demigods and men.

"From its merely coming into existence, the great earth and its mountains shook [with delight] as if [in] the Pramuditā [stage of a Bodhisttva], a rain of flowers descended, great divine drums sounded from the sky, and all directions cleared up.

"That Dharmadhātu-caitya [still] exists at the present time and will [continue to] exist for a long time to come.

"Maitreya! In such a way was this Dharmadhātu-caitya born of itself at the time of the Tathāgata, Arhat [and] completely enlightened Buddha Śikhī."[25]

Thus early events relating to the Dharmadhātu-caitya are told of in the first chapter. In the second chapter the benefits of prostrating to the Mahācaitya, making offerings to it, renovating it, circumambulating it and the like are extensively taught.[26] In the third chapter, the Buddha speaks once again, as follows, answering a question from Ārya Maitreya:

Maitreya! In this fortunate aeon, after a long time has passed since the parinirvāṇa of Śikhī, the Tathāgata of previous times, at the time when the life-span of the people lasted sixty-thousand years, the completely englightened Buddha, the Arhat, the Tathāgata, the Guide of the World called Viśvabhū, was born in the big city known as dPe-med.[27]

"Maitreya! At that time there was Mañjuśrī's mountain, known as 'Five Peak Mountain', at the edge of the northern region, on the threshold to the land of Great China. The vajrācārya called 'Jam-pa'i lha, in essence a manifestation of Mañjuśrī [and] possessing the five supernatural powers [of clairvoyance, clairaudience, knowledge of others' minds, miraculous abilities and knowledge of past lives], arrived from that mountain, together with the female master mChog sbyin-ma, in essence a manifestation of Keśī, and the female master gZugs-thar sbyin-ma, in essence a manifestation of Upakeśī, in order to venerate the Dharmadhātu-caitya. Even afterwards he kept directing his gaze upon this Dharmadhātu-caitya.

"After he [so] gazed upon [it], the following habitual compassion arose in him: 'In the same way as what appeared naturally [as] this Dharmadhātu-caitya on the anthers of a lotus in this big lake, which was devoid of people, [in that same way] will I make water recede from it here so that there appear, in this inhabitable region, hamlets and cities, towns and valleys, districts and royal palaces, and I will act so that sentient beings will be able to prostrate to this Dharmadhātu-caitya, be devoted [and] make offerings to it, honour it, pay service to it and take it as their teacher.

> "Having reflected thus thoroughly, he split the mountain asunder with a very sharp sword and made the water flow out. He slashed whatever [there was of] hills and rocks, no matter where, that had blocked the water of all the rivers, whichever and wherever they were—these and the hills and rocks that [still] remained there—and after slashing [them], he channelled the streams of water into [downward] courses."[28]

What is said [there] does not match up with the description in the *Gośṛṅga-vyākaraṇa[-sūtra]*. The present-day chronicles of the Newars which are acknowledged to be authoritative state that Mañjuśrī [himself] slashed the mountain with his sword and made the water flow out, while the small remainder which was left over, having the shape of a sword, came to be known as 'Sword Lake', and through Mañjuśrī's blessing it became [a place of] origin of manifold kinds of craftsmanship here in Nepal. Accordingly, even Tibetans call it 'Sword Lake'.[29] What is known as 'Lake Bal-yul nyi-ma khud', [a lake] described in the *[Padma bka'i] thang yig* [as] the place where the translator Rlangs dPal-gyi seng-ge passed away, is considered to be the very same [lake] as this.[30]

From the same sūtra:

> "Afterwards, when within four days and nights all the water from the big lake had thoroughly dried up, only the lake called Kun-'dzin, completely filled with pure water, was left over. [It is] the one people now call Dhanādaha; in it resides the lord of the great lake, the Nāgā king known as Karkoṭa. [The floor of the lake] became in perpetuity the base of a Dharmadhātu-caitya within the pure lake. By the power of the Vajrācārya 'Jam-pa'i lha, the great lotus turned into such a hill as this, and it has remained [till today]; for this reason this hill is very famous under the name rDo-rje brtsegs. Since no water remained, whatever solitary portion of land was revealed here became an *upacchandoha-[pīṭha]*. Afterwards it was completely encircled by [other] hills, and has remained [thus]. Having the shape of a Cakrasaṃvara-maṇḍala and bearing the name Himavat, it is by nature a portion of land that is very hard to conquer. And the goddess Kākāmukhī, whose essence is the wisdom of most excellent insight, appeared there personally as its principal [deity], and since then she both pervades the three worlds and appears fully in the shape of a yoni."[31]

Thus [it states], and:

> "Maitreya! Thus during the time of the Tathāgata, Arhat [and] fully enlightened Buddha Viśvabhū, the manifestation of Mañjuśrī called 'Jam-pa'i lha drained the water and turned the big lake into this solitary region."[32]

Thus it happened.

Then the time came for hamlets and cities, towns and valleys, districts and royal palaces here in Nepal.

From the fourth chapter of the same sūtra:

> "Maitreya! After a long time had passed in this previous Fortunate Aeon since the parinirvāṇa of the Tathāgata Viśvabhū, when the life-span of people was forty thousand years, the Tathāgata, Arhat [and] completely enlightened Buddha called Krakucchanda, Guide of the World, was born in the great city known as bZod-ldan."[33]

So it states, and:

> "Maitreya! Once during that time, on the pure and wide summit of the peak of the great mountain Śaṅkhaparvata here in the upachhandoha [land] of Nepal, the Bhagavan Krakucchanda together with a great saṃgha of bhikṣus was completely surrounded by many Bodhisattvas-Mahāsattvas and many gods, men and demigods, and he sat down in their presence and taught a series of teachings called 'The Complete Draining of the Ocean of Suffering of the Whole of Saṃsāra'."[34]

So it states, and:

> "At that time, further, at the top of Śaṅkhaparvata, from the fingertips of the right hand of the Bhagavan, the glorious Vajrasattva, was fully bestowed the fruit which the individuals who were present for the merit-bestowing water—[which] the world [as a whole]—obviously longed for, [namely] supreme peace; the single stream of water thoroughly overflowed with thanks to Bhagavan Krakucchanda's special teaching.
>
> "What had become pure is today very famous as [the river] Bagmatī. Similarly, once the river that is possessed of a 'tirṭha' (*gnas*) with unpolluted merit-bestowing water—[water] which completely bestows the fruit of what one longs for—had properly arisen from the [Bhagavan's] ten fingertips at the summit of Śaṅkhaparvata, then at the place of both (i.e. the river and the tirṭha) where those [among the Bhagavan's following] took monastic vows they afterwards shaved their head and beards. These they made into two [portions] and consigned one portion [to the river], whence even today [the river] is known as the Keśavati."[35]

The river Bagmati spoken of [here] is what present-day Tibetans, corrupting the pronunciation, call Bag-wa-ti. Its source is the hill called Śi-ti-pur (i.e. Śivapuri) in the vernacular. [The river] is called Bag-ma-ti because it flows out from an opening in the side of the hill as something fashioned in a self-manifesting form from a protruding rock [whose] face is called Bag, that is, ‘tiger’. Since [this name] does not appertain to the discussion in the present context of the names of the river called Keśavati or mountains such as Nor-bu brtsegs-pa, it needs to be [re]investigated later.[36]

Again, from the same sūtra:

> “Maitreya! In this way, during the time of the Tathāgata, Arhat [and] completely enlightened Buddha Krakucchanda, there appeared here for the first time hamlets and cities, towns and valleys, districts and royal palaces.”[37]

Thus it says. Further on, in the fifth chapter it talks extensively [about] the twelve mahātirṭhas separated [from one another] by the river, the sites of the twelve nāgā kings, [how] bathing at these [sites] should be done according to [customary] ritual, [how] offerings should be made without fail after performing the confessional vows and purifications, [how] one should meditate one-pointedly, recite [mantras], perform austerity rites and engage in contemplation, and what the benefits are in regard to these [acts—everything] up to reaching the full state of complete liberation [after obtaining] the great fruit of the ten exceptional virtuous acts of the Noble Ones, and whatever fruits there are of such tantric activity as pacifying [suffering], augmenting [what is good] and so forth.[38] And in the sixth chapter [the following] is spoken [by the Buddha] in answer to a question from Maitreya:

> Maitreya! In this previous fortunate aeon, after a long time had passed since the parinirvāṇa of the Tathāgata Kakutsunda, at the time when the life-span of the people lasted thirty-thousand years, the completely enlightened Buddha, the Arhat, the Guide of the World called Kanakamuni, was born in the big city known as mDzes-ldan.[39]

So [it states], and:

> “At that time the great scholar called Bhikṣu Chos-dpal bshes-gnyen was expounding the *[Mañjuśrī]nāmasaṃgīti* in the great vihāra of Vikramaśīla; he himself was not able to explain the meaning of the twelve [vocalic] letters (i.e. a, ā, i, ī, u, ū, e, ai, o, au, aṃ, aḥ). In view of this inability the time was then ripe, and so after hearing that in the northern direction, on ‘Five Peak Mountain’, was residing the Bodhisattva-Mahāsattva called Mañjuśrī, he gained certainty, [thinking]: ‘I need to go there and request the meaning [of the letters] from him’; and he held to his purpose to go there. He came in what was a northern direction, and even after arriving he went around in this region for some days. The Vajrācārya ’Jam-pa’i lha realized at that time that Chos-dpal bshes-gnyen would arrive, and with the idea of displaying a miraculous power

> he mounted a plough [drawn by] a lion [and] a tiger, [these] two, and set them to the soil. Chos-dpal bshes-gnyen then saw the vajrācārya from afar and came towards him. Upon reaching him, he asked: 'Great Being! What is the distance from this place here to Mañjuśrī's "Five Peak Mountain"?' ['Jam-pa'i lha] answered: 'It is very far, so rest today in my vihāra [and] afterwards take the route to the north.' [Chos-dpal bshes-gnyen] accepted without saying a word. Without [even] knowing the [exact] form of a completely pacifying mantra, [Chos-dpal bshes-gnyen] tamed the miraculous power of the lion [and] tiger in front of him. So that people would recognize it, he then placed the plough [on that spot]; the spot where he placed the plough is still known today as 'Mañjuśrī's Abode' (*mañjuśrī-bhavana*). Further beckoning [to 'Jam-pa'i lha], he instantaneously arrived with him on that very peak of Mañjuśrī's. The spot where ['Jam-pa'i lha] mounted the plough is known in the whole world as 'Attended by a Herdsman' (*sapāla*)."[40]

Thus it states, and then:

> "Mañjuśrī spoke: 'Here there is something which is needed more than the most excellent riches. Therefore, as you, Chos-dpal bshes-gnyen, will hold it dear, I will confer an empowerment.' Having promised this, he exhaled and directly transformed himself at this Dharmadhātu-caitya into a Dharmadhātuvāgīśvara-maṇḍala. After [Chos-dpal bshes-gnyen] had honoured and made offerings to this maṇḍala, here at this Dharmadhātu-caitya, an empowerment [featuring] quantities of divine sacred substances, was conferred upon Chos-dpal bshes-gnyen. Further, immediately after the empowerment [Mañjuśrī] transmitted the instruction [on the meaning] of the twelve vocalic letters."[41]

Thus it states, and:

> "Maitreya! It was for this reason that from then onwards, during the time of the Tathāgata, Arhat [and] completely enlightened Buddha Kanakamuni, the name Dharmadhātuvāgīśvara came into being for this Dharmadhātu-caitya."[42]

Thus the extensive presentation up to here. Further, it is said that a Dharmadhātuvāgīśvara-maṇḍala inside a small stūpa in front of the Mahācaitya is symbolic of what was actually transformed in this way into the Dharmadhātuvāgīśvara-maṇḍala, and of the empowerment; it can be seen even today. What is stated in the false histories [and] registers, [namely] that twenty thousand Arhats took up earth and covered the caitya, and because Nāgārjuna scattered his hair [over it] and uttered a prayer that all kinds of trees grow up there, that it is known as 'All Trees'—[all this] is a completely shameless, misleading lie, nothing but mere talk.[43]

In the seventh chapter [of the sūtra], immediately after what is told of above, the Tathāgata Kāśyapa comes into the world, the following being narrated in that context:

> "At that time, when the Bodhisattva Mañjuśrī had in this manner completed all his deeds at this site, he spontaneously realized his natural divine body, [his] vajrācārya's attributes disappearing, whereafter he left like lightning and resided once more with great bliss on 'Five Peak Mountain'; for he manifests according to his wishes. Afterwards, at another time, there appeared in the land of Gauḍa a king called Prachandadeva, a manifestation of Vajrasattva and a master of the Buddhist doctrine, who saw to the happiness of all beings. His own son he empowered as ruler of the kingdom—the king of great fame called Śaktideva—and immediately afterwards he became convinced of the saying 'All happiness in saṃsāra is the suffering of change.' Having rcnounced the happiness of a kingdom, he came to know that the land of Nepal was particularly noble, for it had become a place for spiritual accomplishment, more pleasing than all [others in] the eight directions, and for bestowing the supreme fruit, and [so] he went there. Once he arrived there, he was ordained in front of the Dharmadhātuvāgīśvara, received the ordination name Śantiśrī and started the Vajrasattva ascetic practice, in that same moment becoming endowed with the five kinds of supernatural knowledge. One day this Zhi-ba'i dpal, the vajrācārya, having continued to perform [his spiritual practice] there, thought: 'The Dharmadhātuvāgīśvara, the Self-Manifested Bhagavan, needs to be covered with dust from top [to bottom].' Whence, in order to make it invisible and protect it, he overlaid it with stones and concealed it, and so made the stūpa the way he wanted."[44]

Consider well what is said here! Thus the actual self-manifested caitya is seen to exist in a crystal caitya—similar to a precious jewel in the centre of anthers on the stem of a lotus flower—emitting light and rays of light in the ten directions. Newars say that the actual source—the root of the stem—of the lotus flower is Kho-khom (i.e. Bhaktapur), and that this self-manifested caitya with its gradually spreading stem and offshoots arose on the grounds of what is today the Shing-kun stūpa. However that may be, the core of the self-manifested caitya exists in the inner part of the hill; the outwardly perceived shape of the hill up to the dome on its summit, which symbolizes the caitya inside, constituted a clearly visible stūpa.[45]

Long ago the Nepalese king Aṃśuvarman performed the spiritual practice of the goddess Māricī, and then cut the throat of the nāgā Nīlavikāra with a sword and put the nāgā's head jewel, known as 'O-ma 'dzin, on top of the stūpa. If one properly performs such rituals as *gtor*[*-ma* offerings] for nāgās at the abandoned spot where that nāgā stayed, a boon of neccessities will be bestowed; this is stated in the biography of Khro[-phu] Lo[-tsā-ba] Byams-pa'i dpal (1173–1258). This [place] is without question the spring which exists [still] today at the foot of the hill north of Shing-kun.[46]

The two stūpas to the right and left of the Mahācaitya were built as stūpas having the outer form of non-Buddhist ones: many-angled and adorned on top of their *gañjira*s with sabres. It is said that in their interiors reside the assembly of Bhagavan Cakrasaṃvara's divinities; one wonders if [these two temples] were not something erected from a wish shared by Buddhists and non-Buddhists.[47]

In the four directions around the Self-manifested Mahācaitya exist five great towns. Following a prophecy [given] immediately after the [above] exposition in the chronicle–sūtra [is stated]:

> "Further, after he had created here five great towns, Zhi-ba'i dpal also installed five deities. Who were these five deities? [They were] the Commitment Deity, the Earth Deity, the Fire Deity, the Water Deity [and] the Wind Deity—[these] five. These five deities consecrated these five towns. As a result of the deities' empowerment, the names of these five towns changed, as follows: because it is the site where one commits to the deity, it is famed as Śāntipuri; because it is the site of the goddess Nor-'dzin-ma, it is called Vasupuri; because it is the site of the Fire Deity, it is called Agnipuri; similarly, because it is the site of the Water Deity, it is called Nāgāpuri; similarly, because it is the site of the Wind Deity, it is called Vāyupuri.
>
> "Maitreya! Thus, during the lifetime of the Tathāgatha, Arhat [and] completely enlightened Buddha Kāśyapa, the siddhācārya Zhi-ba'i dpal, in order to make it undetectable and protect it, covered the Dharmadhātuvāgīśvara with dust, hiding it [from view]."[48]

So it is taught, and thus Newars call [these towns], due to a corruption in pronunciation, Santapu (i.e. Śāntipur), Agnipu (i.e. Agnipur), Pātapu (i.e. Pratappur) [and] Kanddhepu (i.e. Anantapur). The last three towns exist as entities which can be identified in their individual locations; whence it remains to explain the reason for [the existence of] the vihāra of Śāntapuri.

In former times, Ācārya Vāgīśvarakīrti (10th/11th cent.), one of the six Gatekeeper Scholars of the vihāra of Vikramaśīla in India, and at first the equal of the revered Nāropa, came in the later part of his life to Nepal. He applied himself mainly to spiritual practice but expounded the Mantrayāna to some extent, without much explaining any other doctrine. He held sway over many consorts, and therefore most people were unable to train [under him], and had nothing other than the thought that they might. The king once erected at Śāntapuri a Cakrasaṃvara temple. He had in mind to perform at the end of its consecration a great gaṇacakra, and so a large number of tantric teachers came together outside the temple. A messenger was sent to invite the ācārya (i.e. Vāgīśvarakīrti) to preside over the assembly. At the barrier [in front] of the ācārya's hut were one old woman and one very fierce-looking black woman. When [the messenger] asked where the ācārya was, they replied that he was inside [the hut]. He went inside and requested the ācārya to come to the king's gaṇacakra. [The latter] replied: "You go quickly; I too will be coming presently." By the time [the messenger] was quickly setting off, the ācārya, in the company of his two consorts, had [already] arrived at a crossroads near Śāntapuri before him. He said: "You didn't show up, so we've been waiting a long time." After the extensive gaṇacakra, the central part of the consecration, had been performed, the ācārya (the father) [and] the [two] mothers—[these] three—stayed on inside the temple: they took shares of the offered substances for more than sixty persons and went inside [the temple]. Thus the king wondered: "Inside there are not more than three people; what's the need for such an amount of offered substances?" When he looked through a crack in the door, he saw the circle of the sixty-two deities of Cakrasaṃvara actually present [in the temple] and enjoying the offered substances. In that very moment the ācārya transformed himself into a rainbow and remained [in that state]; even today he remains [as such]. Thus it is described in the 'Religious History of India', written by Jo-nang rje-btsun Tāranātha [Kun-dga' snying-po] (1575–1634).[49] In the 'Religious History' of Pad[ma] dkar[-po] it is stated that Vanaratna (1384–1469), the Mahāpaṇḍita of later times, also stayed in this [temple]. There he encountered the glorious Śavaripa, [who] conferred the Cakrasaṃvara empowerment after manifesting the [corresponding] maṇḍala, [and Vanaratna] obtained unalterable bliss.[50]

On the murals on the walls of this vihāra (i.e. Śāntapuri) there are old [captions] from former times, written authentically according to the sūtra itself (i.e the *Svayambhūpurāṇa*), the source of the history of the Self-Manifested Mahācaitya.[51]

The All-Knowing Puṇḍarika (i.e. Padma dkar-po) states:

> Gaṇapati, the Elephant-faced One
> who resides in Śāntipuri ...[52]

So it is stated, and thus Śāntapuri is only a toponym and nothing else. The lord of the sacred site is generally [considered to be] Vinayaka or Gaṇapati, known as Tshogs-kyi bdag-po [in Tibetan].

Former Tibetans spoke of Upāsaka Śāntapuri. As to "Upāsaka," here in Tibet it is a corruption [arising from] the general term for a lord of a locality—Upāsaka Cho-ge, Nyo-ge and so forth. The Sanskrit "Śānta" is left unchanged, [and] as to "sPu-gri" (i.e. razor), it is said that it was mixed up with such [notions] as *fire razor* or *poison razor*, and even though there are grounds for saying so, what is called "Śāntapuri", a mixture of Sanskrit [and] Tibetan, there is no [rock-solid] evidence, whence it ends up being a mere nickname fabricated in the minds of Tibetans, a [mere] object of laughter. In this case, the fiction of what was a [mere] convention was carried to extremes.[53]

As for the local deity, [whom Tibetans call] 'Phrog-ma ('Abducting [Enchantress]'), she is none other than [the one Newars call] Hārītī—'Phrog-ma together with her five hundred sons. As her story is clarified in the extensive form in which it appears in Buddhist sūtras, and elsewhere in a separate [treatise of mine] on the essential nature of *gtor-ma* [offerings], I do not expand on it here. It is said that in the tradition of the Newars themselves there exists a sādhana together with a series of ritual acts, and that when a fierce epidemic erupts it is a magical display for not having pleased 'Phrog-ma. Previously there existed a statue of Hārītī, which came about as a self-manifestation from stone, in association with a temple. In later times the king of Gorkha, clutching [sword] blades [and] fire[brands], destroyed it without leaving any trace. It seems that the present statue together with the temple was newly erected as a replacement.[54]

One [other] local deity is known as the Bod-thang mgon-po. His mode [of appearance] is held to be as a self-manifested stone statue, while some [other] people regard it as something crafted by Nāgārjuna. Whatever the case, it was earlier located on Phulla-ḍo (i.e. Phulcokī) Hill near Patan, but [later,] flying in bodily form in the sky, it descended at [the site called] Bod-thang, [whence it is] known as the 'Protector of the Tibetan Grounds'. When an army of the Duruṣkas showed up once in Nepal, it is said that weapons were offered to the nostrils of the protector, and that what had been "shaved" [from the statue's face] was later gradually repaired.[55] When gTsang-smyon Heruka [Sangs-rgyas rgyal-mtshan] (1452–1507) arrived in order to renovate the Shing-kun [stūpa], he joined hands with the protector, and many female devotees saw him perform a dance [with the statue] outside the straw hut on wooden pillars.[56] The great gTsang-smyon [Heruka] regarded him as the protector of the Aural Transmission of Ras-chung[-pa]. Further, Mahāvidyādhara Tshe-dbang nor-bu made many offerings of large *gtor-ma*s [before the statue] and composed the [song of] praise called 'The Melody Which Fulfils Wishes Spontaneously'.[57]

As for how the sequence of earlier and later renovations of the Self-Manifested Mahācaitya came about: Up to gTsang-smyon Heruka there seems to be no distinct account of how individuals from Tibet showed up to perform the service of restoring it.[58] It was in accordance with an exhortation by Gaṇapati to the great gTsang-smyon that [the latter] undertook [such] a renovation. For the overlay made from gold and copper applied to the thirteen rings, the golden parasol [and] the four supporting pillars together with the pinnacle, 2,751 *zho*s of gold were used, as stated in a register kept by [gTsang-smyon] himself.[59] Not long afterwards a great army of Duruṣkas arrived in Nepal, stripped off all the copper and gold from Shing-kun and carried it away. Although they set the stūpa on fire, no great damage occurred except for the colouration having been spoiled. At that time, when lHa-btsun Rin-chen rnam-rgyal (1473–1557), the heart-son of gTsang-smyon, was residing for his spiritual practice at Brag-dkar rta-so, he encountered the siddha himself in a vision. According to a prophecy [made in it by the latter, he would restore], first, the *yaṣṭi*, made of etakara wood, and its cover; afterwards successively the golden parasol, the golden top, the four supporting pillars, the thirteen rings and the shield in the east, up to the point of overlaying the latter with gilded copper, [so that it was] luminous in the three directions. He performed renovation work up to four times.[60] Afterwards the heart-son of Dharma Lord sKyid-grong gNas Rab-'byams-pa Byams-pa phun-tshogs (1503–1581) overlaid with gilded copper the square shields in the western and northern directions of the stūpa, together with [their] victory banners, [and] the lotus enclosure of the thirteen rings. Although what expenditures for gold and the like [were made] by the noble lHa-btsun [Rin-chen rnam-rgyal] and [sKyid-grong] gNas Rab-'byams-pa [Byams-pa phun-tshogs]—[the one] earlier and [the other] later—are not entirely evident, they [will have been] roughly along the lines of what is elucidated in their individual biographies.[61]

Later, when the Sixth Zhva-dmar-pa Chos-kyi dbang-phyug (1584–1630) went on a pilgrimage to Nepal, he had wished to perform a renovation of the [Svayaṃbhūnāth] Stūpa, but the situation was not favourable, so [instead] he had well-designed arched shrines overlaid with gilded copper [as] residences for the four Buddha statues in the four directions [around the Mahācaitya].[62] Later the Mahāsiddha [Rang-rig ras-pa (1619-1683)] offered to the Newar king Pārthivendra Malla (r. 1680–1687) 32 ounces of gold and exhorted him to do a renovation. The king readily accepted, erected a [new] *yaṣṭi* and completed, with [overlays of] gilded copper, the rings, the top and the shrines in the four directions, adding [to the latter] curtains behind the statues.[63]

In the iron female sheep year of the thirteenth sixty-year cycle [=1751], at the time the vidyādhara from Kaḥ-thog, rDo-rje Tshe-dbang nor-bu (1698–1755), was undertaking a renovation [of Svayaṃbhūnāth], Mahādeva Gaṇapati and Kumara Kārttikeya, [these] two, manifested themselves in their own forms and promised to accomplish all works for the renovation of the Mahācaitya.[64] In the meantime, in order to mediate a long-running disagreement between the rulers of mNga'-ris Mar-yul, [that is,] Ladakh, and to ward off fear of the Western Hor army, it became necessary [for him] to proceed [to Western Tibet]. Due to his having to contain disputes among individual royal domains of Tibet, Nepal [and] Mon, [work] was postponed for an extremely long time, [until finally] in the fire pig year [= 1755] the noble vidyādhara [rDo-rje Tshe-dbang nor-bu] passed away with renovation work still left to do.[65] Once again, in accordance with the last testament of the Noble One [and] with the support of the lord, the precious all-knowing [Seventh] 'Brug-pa bKa'-brgyud 'phrin-las shing-rta (1718–1766), and thanks to the great enthusiasm of such individuals as the precious ceremony master bsTan-'dzin rdo-rje (18th cent.), the main one among the personal disciples of the noble vidyādhara, the reponsibilty for continuing the renovation was taken over, and after seven years had passed, from the beginning of the earth male tiger year (called *bahu dhānya*) [= 1758] 2,021 *zhos* of refined gold were used, having been drawn forth, after the smelting process was terminated, for proper application to the shields in the four directions [around the *harmika*], the four nearly luminous plates, the thirteen rings and the parasol, together with the top, [as these now] appear. At that time, when the noble [Seventh] 'Brug-pa [bKa'-brgyud 'phrin-las shing-rta] was performing an establishing consecration from [the practice cave called] dNgos-grub phug in Mang-yul sKyid-grong, it is known that in Shing-kun in Nepal [itself] a shower of flowers actually fell and that it flawlessly manifested before the eyes of all the people from Nepal, Tibet and the gorges—[these] three—who had assembled there. The precious [Seventh] dPa'-bo gTsug-lag [dga'-ba] (d. 1781) performed the actual consecration, and I have heard it said that besides [giving] excellent material things [as] gifts to the king [of Gorkha]—the lord and his subjects—he entrusted oversight of the great [Svayaṃbhūnāth] stūpa [to the king].[66]

Details of how expenditures [were made for] materials [used] here both earlier [and] later can be ascertained separately from a clear, short register called 'Divine Cymbals', which was composed by the noble Lo-ri-pa Kun-gzigs Chos-kyi rgya-mtsho (18th cent.).[67]

Afterwards the Tenth Zhva-dmar-pa [Chos-grub rgya-mtsho (1742–1792)] made an offering [in the form of] a renovation of the gilded-copper entrance arches of the two Buddha shrines in the east [and] west, the large bell and so forth.[68] In the water male monkey year (called *aṅgira*) of the fourteenth sixty-year cycle [= 1812]—after a period of fifty-five years from the above-mentioned earth male tiger [year] [= 1758]—the *yaṣṭi* became bent, and during the month of Sa-ga (i.e. the fourth Tibetan month) of the following year, the water [female] bird year (called *śrīmukha*) [= 1813], the *yaṣṭi* collapsed, resulting in great damage. This was the final clear demonstration that the opportunity for good deeds—the general aim of beings—had been ever more deteriorating, signalling that the end of time, when the five kinds of degeneration are rampant, was being reached. Thus, in order to increase once again the youthful age of benefit for the doctrine and the beings it was rendered forward by the new light of dawn (i.e.) the marvelous concern of the 'Mighty Protector Seizing the Riches' of the South', [who is] such a great chariot of enlightened activities of melodious glorious deeds of the practice lineage [of the 'Brug-pa bKa' brgyud-pa]; engaging in such an extensive completely virtous deed of the present renovation [of Svayaṃbhūnāth] and not long after, while having fully completed the majestic action of such a mass of good deeds, accompanied by gods: [this act of] making the victorious stūpa shine again, it brings forth auspicious omens which rise high in the sky [of the field] of good merit of beings and its ways are something to be told successively in the future.[69]

The Dharmadhātu, whose essence is completely pure from the very beginning—
the sphere of of the Dharmakāya [and] wisdom, where all elaborations have ceased—
for beings it is hidden [and] unknown; through skill in means
[and] in order to symbolize [itself, it] manifests as the stūpa, the visible Dharma.

Thus the astonishing Self-Manifested Stūpa—
an offering pole unsurpassed in all the three worlds—
with manifold names is praised by all Jinas, [those] who tame beings,
hundreds of times; how could I not bow down [before it] continually?

The second chapter of what is called 'A Definitive Presentation of the History of the Sacred Sites and Religious Objects of Nepal: A Mirror of Jewels Which Clears Away Errors', setting forth the history of Shing-kun, the Self-Manifested Mahācaitya.

[III]

Thirdly, an exposition of the history of the Bya-tri kam-sha or Bya-rung khashor Stūpa.[70] There was a time countless ages ago when Paramārya Avalokiteśvara uttered a prayer in the presence of the protector Amitābha to draw forth all living beings from the ocean of saṃsāra. Accordingly, he acted for the immeasurable benefit of the countless beings and returned afterwards to his palace on the peak of Mount Potala. Thinking that now not even a single sentient being existed anymore, he looked around and, inasmuch as in the realms of the six classes [of rebirth] sentient beings had not diminished—[they were still] like the dregs of strong beer—he thought himself now unable to liberate sentient beings from the ocean of saṃsāra. When as a result two tears dropped down [from his eyes], he took them up with the two ring fingers of his hands and flicked them away; he then uttered a prayer that in the future these two tears might act for the benefit of beings. Therefore they were born in the heaven of the thirty-three gods as two daughters of the mighty god Śatakratu (i.e. Indra), known as the divine maidens Gang chen-ma and Gang chung-ma. Gang chung-ma stole divine flowers, and so, having breached the divine law, she fell into the human realm. There, at the time of the doctrine of the Tathāgata Kāśyapa, she was born in the Maguta area of Nepal as a poultry woman called bDe-mchog. When she was raising chickens, she took up with four persons of lower caste—a horse breeder, a swineherd, a dog-keeper and a poultry man—and four sons were born.[71]

In this regard, in the *Thang yig zangs gling ma*, a treasure [discovery] of Nyang[-ral] Nyi-ma'i 'od-zer (1124–1194), it is shown, too, that there were four sons and one daughter, five siblings [in all].[72] Then this mother amassed great earnings from raising chickens, her four sons became veritable householders, and in the course of amassing more earnings they accumulated much wealth. The idea arose [in her] to erect a stūpa, and she begged the lord of the country for land, whence the king granted his consent, at which time [the words] slipped from his mouth that it would be proper to do so. It seems that accordingly [the stūpa] is known as Bya-rung kha-shor ('Authorized through a Slip of the Tongue'). As this is plainly Tibetan, one obviously has the feeling that the Nepalese king was speaking Tibetan.[73] In the *Zangs gling ma* it is called Bya-rin kha-shor ('Chicken Earnings Slip of the Tongue'), given that [the stūpa] was erected from what was earned by raising chickens. It is furthermore called Bya-tri kam-sho and Bya-tri kha-shor, and in the Mon dialect Ba-hu-ta, and by the Newars Kha-sa ti-da (i.e. Khāsā caitya), so there exist [a number of] variants of this name.[74]

Then the poultry woman, mother and sons, [these] five, and one servant, together with an elephant and an ass, loaded bricks and carried them off. After laying a foundation, they [began] erecting [the stūpa], and within four years had completed construction up to [just below] the round dome. At that time the poultry woman bDe-mchog, having realized that she would die, instructed her four sons along with the servant, [saying]: "Have the remaining parts of the stūpa erected, and then insert the relics of the Tathāgata in the interior and celebrate a great consecration ritual!" After that she passed away and attained Buddhahood as the Commitment [Deity's] goddess called Pramohā. Then the four sons, together with the servant, erected the remaining parts of the stūpa within three years; and if everything is taken into account, the complete erection was accomplished in seven years. A full Magadha *bre* measure of relics of the Tathāgata Kāśyapa was inserted into the *yaṣṭi*, and during the time when the consecration ritual was being performed the Bhagavan Kāśyapa together with his entourage and, further, the Buddhas of the ten directions and countless Bodhisattvas blessed [the stūpa]; and auspicious words were uttered extensively amidst a burst of flowers.[75]

At that time the four sons, together with the servant, uttered the following aspirational prayers: The son of the horse breeder prayed to be born as the king who would establish the Tathāgata's precious doctrine in the snowland of Tibet, a region where coldness prevails; the son of the swineherd, as an upādhyāya; the son of the dog-keeper, as a powerful mantra-holder; [and] the poultry man, as an influential minister. Whereupon the assembly of Buddhas and Bodhisattvas proclaimed: "Well done!" And transforming themselves into a ball of light and light rays, they melted into the Mahācaitya; therefore it is known as the 'Stūpa where all the Buddhas are united'. In accordance with the prayers uttered, [the four sons were born as] Dharmarāja Khri Srong lde'u-btsan, Upādhyāya Bodhisattva (i.e. Śāntarakṣita), Ācārya Padmasambhava [and] sBa-mi Khri-sher, the Dharma minister of Yar-lung. A bee uttered the prayer to be born as a well-adorned child [and became] the princess Padma-gsal; the ass uttered an improper prayer and was born as the demon-minister Zhang-khrom. The servant uttered the prayer to be born as the one who would vanquish the demon-minister [and became] Padma Gung-btsan. The elephant uttered an improper prayer [and became] the ruler Glang dar-ma; a raven uttered the prayer [to be the one] to kill the demon-king [and became] Prince Mu-rub btsan-po. Two young Brahmins uttered a prayer [and were born as] sKa-ba dPal-brtsegs [and] Cog-ro klu'i rgyal-mtshan. Two girls of royal descent uttered a prayer to become scribes who would write down the Noble Doctrine, [and they were born as] lDan-ma rtse-mang and Legs-byin nyi-ma. Thus the Upādhyāya, Ācārya [and] Dharma [king], [these] three, together with their entourage, cleared up all the deep darkness of this glacier land, [Tibet]; and the source of these positive circumstances that made the Buddhist doctrine shine like the sun is precisely this Mahācaitya![76]

As for how the succession of acts of service to and renovations of such a Mahācaitya came about: At the time of the Dharmarāja Srong-btsan sgam-po, or just prior to him, a Chinese king had made offerings to this stūpa and paid respect to it; this, as stated by the venerable [Kaḥ-thog] Rig-'dzin [Tshe-dbang nor-bu], is written in the 'Religious History of China' by Gung mGon-po skyabs.[77] A long time passed with no one coming forth in the interval to undertake a renovation [of the stūpa] or do service [to it], and the Mahācaitya, due to the changes wrought by time, became something indistinguishable from the hills [around it], so that in the eyes of the people it was obviously not something to be called a stūpa. At that time, owing to the power of his aspirational prayer, the one who had become the Dharma minister 'Gos Padma Gung-btsan, [the reincarnation of] the earlier poultry woman's servant, was born as sNgags-'chang Śākya bzang-po, the treasure discoverer from Drang-so, into a lineage within a succession—a chain—of incarnations. He discovered on the top floor of the mahāvihāra of glorious bSam-yas a written scroll, and upon investigating it [found] a prophecy relating to repairing damage done to Bya-rung kha-shor, and [so] he went to Nepal. As the stūpa could not be distinguished from the hills [around it], at first he thought: "This is the one," but after prostrating before another hill and cleaning away [his offering of] butter-flour, that hill thereupon said, "[You] are near the stūpa." Thereafter he discovered the real [hill], and [the stūpa] emerged from below the earth.[78] He made it directly visible to everyone's eyes, and once the renovation had come to an end he also composed a laudation, known as 'Most Excellent Support of the Dharmakāya'. [To quote] from it:

> Here in the final five hundred years [of the Degenerate Age], having been aroused three times
> by words of the One from Oḍḍiyāna to renovate this Mahācaitya,
> I applied myself with the devotion of my three doors (i.e. body, speech and mind) [to doing so]:

may all beings who encounter [here] the Lord and others [under him] who fill the expanse of space quickly reach the state of the wholly good Dharmakāya![79]

Thus it reads. It is known that a spring of sacred water existed in the vicinity of the stūpa.[80]

Then, when some generations had passed, Mahāsiddha Rang-rig ras-pa (1619–1683), who had been prophesied as an incarnation of Mahācārya [Padmasambhava], [performed] a renovation of the stūpa and adorned it with a [new] *gañjira*. At the end of his personal travels, [pursued] with 'disciplined conduct' (*vratācārya*), to the land of Oḍḍiyāna and other [places], he passed away at Nalendra vihāra in the Kashmir Valley; at that time his heart, tongue and eyes, [these] three, along with his bones turned into a heap of relics, and these were brought by his disciples [to the Mahācaitya].

From his parting song:

I myself, a minor meditator, will proceed to O-rgyan gling,
[the land of] beings from Du-va-ri-ka!
I will make the north of India the place of my death.
Erect a reliquary shrine at the eastern side of Bya-rung kha-shor!
Joy will [thereby] arise in general in all of Nepal;
In particular, foreign armies will be kept back for some years!

In accordance with what he said, a reliquary shrine was erected—the one located on the eastern side of the Mahācaitya [Bya-rung kha-shor].[81]

Afterwards, pursuant to an order of Tibet's ruler, Pho-lha-ba bSod-nams stobs-rgyas (1689–1747), two government officials of sKyid-grong, lCags-sprag and Yangs-grong-pa, accordingly took responsibility for managing [the undertaking], and completed the service of renovating the stūpa.[82]

Following this, Mahāvidyādhara Tshe-dbang nor-bu [himself] performed a proper renovation and a consecration ritual; and he offered ten thousand butter lamps many times over [during the consecration to the Bodhnāth Stūpa].[83]

Among the eight charnel grounds, [one is called] lHun-grub brtsegs-pa, and this Mahācaitya [is] without a doubt, according to a previously mentioned scriptural authority, the stūpa associated with it.[84] The noble Vidyādhara (i.e. Kaḥ-thog Rig-'dzin Tshe-dbang nor-bu) said that the original centre of the charnel ground is located at a place about 3,000 feet away from the stūpa, and that there also exists a footprint of Mahācārya [Padmasambhava] [at it].[85]

From the *sKu gdung 'bar ba [tsha tsha dang] mchod rten gyi rgyud*:

At the south-eastern border, [in] the land of Nepal,
[where] ten thousand *ta-na-ya-ma* [flowers exist] in full blossom,

one obtains the blessings of the lHun-grub [brtsegs-pa] charnel ground
and [finds] offering sticks [made of] *karacchada* [and] *bimba* [wood]:
[there is located] the Kha-shor Bya-tri-kha stūpa.

Where the Teacher (i.e. Padmsambhava) performed penance,
and where the ruler of this great Nepal lay down flat [before it];
[there] the pleasure [taken in eating] food is great,
[and there one finds] Hu-li-ka, the stūpa of prosperity,
[and] the site of the demon Gu-gu-ta-nag.[86]

Thus it is said, and the statement that the goddess Pramohā resides [there] is in agreement with the account of the poultry woman bDe-mchog's having attained Buddhahood at this place.[87] And the extensive benefits of making respectful offerings to the stūpa and renovating it, and the way to achieve the full measure of one's aspirational prayers and so forth is to be learned in detail from the 'Great History of [Bya-rung] kha-shor', a genuine treasure find of sNgags-'chang Śākya bzang-po, the treasure discoverer from Drang-so.

Of all the places the magic of [his] love for [all] beings
has been shown by Padmapāṇi, the holy land of Nepal,
a treasure [which, though] rough to the touch for the world and its sentient beings,
is a particularly excellent source of the benefits of a cool region.

All the proud mountains of the local deities
are reduced, as it were, to dust by what was erected through the efforts
of the poultry woman and her sons: a great victorious offering pole—
it shines forth like Mount Sumeru over the earth!

The third chapter of what is called 'A Definitive Presentation of the History of the Sacred Sites and Religious Objects of Nepal: A Mirror of Jewels Which Clears Away Errors', setting forth the history of Bya-tri kha-shor.

## [IV]

Fourthly, from the third chapter of the sūtra, the chronicle [of Svayaṃbhūnāth], an additional account of subsidiary sacred sites and religious objects. The small hill to the west of Shing-kun:

> 'Jam-pa'i lha, moreover, stayed in this confined area for a long time, and the confined area behind where he stayed is even now called Mañjuśrī hill.[88]

Thus it states.

And from the seventh chapter:

> "Maitreya! Furthermore, [there was] faith that the great power of the stūpa of the one called [Vajr]ācārya 'Jam-pa'i lha, [who is] in essence a manifestation of Mañjuśrī, would become clear at its site on the peak behind [the hill of Svayaṃbhūnāth], [and this faith] at once made this [happen]."[89]

Thus it is stated. It is in recognition of this that Nepalese call it Mañjuśrī and all Tibetans refer to it as the stūpa of 'Jam-dpal.[90] The Kāśyapa stūpa is regarded by some as being the Kāśyapa stūpa as described in the *Gośṛṅga-vyākaraṇa*; and further, although the thought might arise, for instance, that it is the stūpa of Ārya Kāśyapa, for many reasons one is able to establish that [it] is neither of these two. In Nepal itself there are no such specific accounts. This is why [its people] had not heard them before.[91]

The Vasubandhu stūpa: Ārya Vasubandhu came in the later part of his life, surrounded by a thousand disciples, to Nepal. He established many monastic estates and expanded [them into] a great monastic community. At one time he saw that a householder had put on monastic robes and was ploughing [his field]. Afterwards, it having occurred to him that the doctrine of the Teacher (i.e Śākyamuni) needed to be restored, he expounded the Buddhist doctrine in the midst of the monastic community, recited three times the dhāraṇī of Uṣṇiśa-vijayā in reverse order, and then passed away right then and there. The disciples then erected a stūpa, famed to be this very one.[92]

Bya-rgod phung[-po] Hill: Tibetans probably simply made up the name. The real Gṛdhra-kūṭa-parvata, which is very well known, exists only in India, while the vihāra [located] here is called Kimṭo[l] (i.e. Kiṃḍola) by the Newars; the All-Knowing Si-tu [Paṇ-chen] calls it 'Rice Heap Hill vihāra'.[93]

'Big[s]-byed hill: It is not Vindhya, one of the thirteen glorious mountains here in Jambudvīpa; the real Vindhya is part of the holy land of India. This again is certainly just a name given by Tibetans; the Newars call it 'Dza-ma 'dzu (i.e. Jāma-cva). On the peak of this mountain is said to be a throne of Buddha [Śākyamuni] familiar from the stories of his previous lives; the stūpa [located there] was, it is said, erected in later times by a Newar.[94]

As for what is known as Nāgārjuna's meditation cave in the middle of this hill, [regardless of whether] it was the meditation cave of Zhi-byed lha—as explained in the sūtra, the chronicle [of Svayaṃbhūnāth]—or of Nāgārjuna, it does actually exist; in Newari it is called Nāgā-'dzong (i.e. Nāgārjun[a]).[95] It is very well known that Paramārya Nāgārjuna had come to Nepal; it is also claimed that the volumes of the *Śatasāhasrikā[prajñāparamitā]* located in the [s]Tham vihāra are those brought forth from the realm of the nāgās by Nāgārjuna; and it is said that the Newars had executed them after Nāgārjuna had returned from the realm of the nāgās. He had performed extensive service for Shing-kun and in some old scriptures it is also stated that Ācārya Nāgārjuna had raised [there] the main tantra of Vajrapāṇi as a treasure.[96]

Also on the row of hills to the east of 'Big[s]-byed hill [is a site] called the 'Buffalo Buddha'. Although written in some histories, the claim of some people that the buffalo herder [known as] the Buffalo Buddha is Ācārya Nāgabodhi, a disciple of Nāgārjuna, is only empty talk. Concerning Nāgabodhi, All-Knowing Pad[ma] dkar[-po] said that Nāgārjuna had recognized that an old decrepit buffalo herder in India was a proper vessel and gave him instructions including the means of contemplating [himself as] a buffalo; and after the latter passed away he was [re]born into the Brahmin caste, ordained by Ācārya Nāgārjuna [and given] the name Nāgabodhi.[97] The noble Venerable One from Jo-nang (i.e. Tārānātha) said that these two persons are different.[98] Whatever the case, as concerns the real Nāgabodhi, he obtained knowledge and realization and remained in [a state of] disciplined conduct, wherefore he is known by the epithet Ma-ṭam-gi and is counted among the eighty-four Mahāsiddhas. As he is known to be still living today on Śrī Parvata, [this account] is not even partially similar to [that of] the Nepalese chronicles. Therefore, [it is no surprise that] this cave [of the 'Buffalo Buddha'] also appears to consist of mere limestone, and if one illuminates it with the help of a butter [lamp] and arrives at the very end of its extremely narrow interior space, there is nothing other than falling waterdrops and the sight of something like an elephant face, said to be a self-arisen Gaṇapati. The rumour that there exists a buffalo hoofprint or the like is mere talk in pursuit of nonsense.[99]

The Nāga [and] Supine One: On the side of a hill to the north of Bya-rung khashor, in a wooded grove fed by water, [one finds] a Nīlakaṇṭha. The stone effigy, featuring a blue neck, is called by Tibetans the Self-arisen Nāga and is said to have been made as a simulacrum of him. The Blue-necked One is one of the names of Śiva. Long ago, when the gods were churning the ocean, there arose a vessel of poison. It was taken into his throat by Mahādeva, and [his neck] turned blue, and thus [Śiva] is known as the Blue-necked One. The words of some Tibetans that it is an effigy of Buddha Nāgeśvararāja is completely misleading.[100]

Dzoki a-k[h]ar: [This name] means Yogāmbhara, and [the site] is a pīṭha described in the *Catuḥpīṭha-[mahāyoginī-]tantra[-rāja]*, as stated by the Vidyādhara (i.e. Kaḥ-thog Rig-'dzin Tshe-dbang nor-bu). In the vernacular language it is called Dzo-ki a-[']bar.[101]

[s]Tham vihāra: It was erected long ago when the venerable lord Śrī Dīpaṃkarabhadra (i.e Atiśa) was travelling to Tibet. Vihāra means *gtsug-lag khang* in Tibetan,[102] and [s]Tham vihāra] has been identified as the Nepalese vihāra [Tibetans call] Rin-chen tshul.[103] There is also one that was established by a king; it is thus called Rāja vihāra, as explained in the *Jo bo [rje]'i rnam thar lam yig [chos kyi 'byung gnas]*.[104] [There] it is stated that even though the

siddha O-rgyan-pa Rin-chen dpal (1230–1309) reported only the titles of Sanskrit manuscripts relating to the old secret mantras in Nepal's [s]Tham vihāra, some hundred thousand [manuscripts] have come [down to us there].[105]

On a hillslope in the Saṅkhu area in Nepal [is] Guppahara, which Tibetans call the Eighty Siddhas and Newars call Saṅko Khaga Dzoki ('Eighty Yogins of Saṅko'). This [means] that many non-Buddhist ṛṣis resided in this region in early times. There also existed many of their stūpas, but since this stone Mahācaitya was superior, in that it had manifested itself from the ground by the power of the Buddha, all the stūpas of the tīrthikas were destroyed and vanished. After the dome of this self-arisen stone stūpa [developed] a crack, a previously nonexistent stream of water emerged and is [now] famed for conferring great blessing. The religious object inside the vihāra is a statue of Vajrayoginī, or rDo-rje rnal-'byor-ma, made of clay. Although it is commonly supposed that the Eighty-four [Mahā]siddhas went [there], I have not heard any reliable account [of this].[106] Also, the rumours of foolish Tibetans regarding a large cauldron associated with the siddhas, the culmination of the rise and fall of the Buddhist doctrine, the fire and water at the end of an aeon, and the weaving implements of the Nepalese queen (i.e Bhṛkuṭī)—[these all] amount to mere foolish, unreliable talk, with no truth to them.[107]

Again, some persons from earlier times regard [this site] as the place where Prince Viśvaṃtara gave away his head, as described in the stories of Buddha [Śākyamuni]'s previous lives; this is not correct either. The [original site] is the region called Upacchandoha Kaliṅga, located 360 *dpag-tshad*s south-west of Vajrāsana and accepted by learned persons as the birthplace of Viśvaṃtara.[108]

What is called Cang-khung (i.e. Cāṅgu), the Newars call Hari[harihari]vāhanalokeśvara, and they regard it as a site sacred to Garuḍa. In early times there seems to have existed a self-arisen Garuḍa into which Vajrapāṇi had openly melded. Some people also claim that Ācārya Nāgārjuna grasped the knot in his rosary and it formed into the self-arisen Garuḍa. It is also reported, for instance, that if one looks upon this [effigy] one is cured of harmful diseases [caused by] territorial spirits. It appears certain, though, that one will not come across any authoritative historical account that accepts [such claims].[109]

What is called Kurti or Guru Bad (i.e. Guru Badzra) by the Mon-pas, Tibetans call sNyi-shang Kutti. This site of spiritual practice, where the great [and] venerable Mi-la [ras-pa] (1028–1111) took care of Khyi-ra ras-pa mGon-po rdo-rje, is not a fantasy; nevertheless, the setting of hill, cliffs, river and so forth as visualized in [Mi-la ras-pa's] very well-known 'Collected Spiritual Songs' seems for the greater part not to correspond [with this site]. As to Khyi-ra ras-pa, who is called a sNyi-shang-pa or [r]Ta-mang[s], he was [indeed] a member of this ethnic group; from the very beginning of the tradition surrounding Mi-la ras-pa many irrelevant things have been written, such as the words and songs [of Khyi-ra ras-pa] in the Tibetan language, [his wearing of] a dappled antilope skin without even any cotton clothing, [his use of a] a black noose [for hunting], [his hunting of] a ten-pronged Tibetan deer and so forth.[110]

sTag-mo lus-sbyin: There seems to be some real truth to [the statements in] a number of old histories that [at this site] is the stūpa containing the remains of the body given to a female tiger by Prince sNying-stobs chen-po, as described in the *Suvarṇaprabhāsottama[-sūtra]*, and that the Bodhisattva, with his comprehension of the life-force, identified the branch of a [nearby] tree as the [best] wood for the spike [to pierce his flesh with] and so forth, but [in any case] what in general is related in the *Suvarṇaprabhāsottama[-sūtra]* and the *'Dzangs-blun* [about the prince] in the narrative of his giving his body to the female tiger (apart from differences only in [his own] name, being called the Bodhisattva; or, in the *Suvarṇaprabhāsottama[-sūtra]*, sNying-stobs chen-po; or, in the *'Dzangs-blun*, Sems-chen chen po, is seen to be identical, [including] the country [of his birth] and the [names of] his father and mother. The *Suvarṇaprabhāsottama[-sūtra]* presents an early account of the Tathāgata travelling with his entourage to lNga-len following the summer retreat, of a stūpa appearing from below the ground in that realm, of the remains of the Bodhisattva being put on display and of his body having been given to the female tiger. Therefore, since it explains that what is called the 'land of lNga-len in the south' lies in the south of India, and as Nepal is identified [as lying] in the north of India, there is a contradiction. The Newars call [the site] Namo Buddhaya, [which means] in the Tibetan language 'I prostrate before the Buddha'; the two toponyms are thus not related [to each other]. In any case, as I have not seen an authentic history of this [sacred spot], I am not able to speak [further about it] here.[111]

In Bhaktapur, the so-called Speaking Tārā: In a previous time Ārya [Tārā] prophesied in a dream to the local king that [he] would offer cotton cloth from Varanasi and an *arura vijaya* [fruit] to the great and venerable Mi-la [ras-pa]; [this] statue [of her doing so] confers blessings.[112] Although in the interval one could go see it, later it was destroyed, went missing or was no longer recognized [as such] by Tibetans. Whatever the case, I have heard that one is no longer able to go see it nowadays.

The Mahācārya [Padmasambhava] prophesied:

> In the Golden Cave of Nepal [resides]
> Ekajaṭī, 'She of One Plait of Hair'.

This [quotation] obviously contains a reason to visit the one self-arisen stone effigy of Ekajaṭī [at a site] close to Bhaktapur.[113]

Phag-mo mngal-chu: This is the name given by Tibetans. In vernacular speech and in the common Newarī language it is called Guhyeśvari. Buddhists say that it is a sacred site of the glorious consort Nairātmyā. One may wonder whether, as claimed by non-Buddhists, it is the sacred site of Uma's union with Śiva.[114]

Gu-lang: What is called Gu-lang Mahādeva, [which can be] explained as [meaning] the 'Great God, Great God', [is] a self-arisen stone effigy of Īśvara—about the size of an average man—rising up out of the ground and possessing four faces in the cardinal directions and eight arms. [Housing] it is [a temple with] a golden roof, a *gañjira* cast [by] goldsmiths, and an iron *trīśula* with three seals [on its three prongs]. It is said that at this [place] some brave-hearted tīrthikas who have remained buried for a long time underground for their spiritual practice afterwards seek their death by [throwing themselves] from the top of the temple onto the three prongs [of the *trīśula*,] thereby committing suicide. Previously the mahāsiddha Mitrayogin (12th/13th cent.) remained for seven days cross-legged on top of the temple's *gañjira*, and by displaying this miracle intimidated the tīrthikas, an account [of which] can be found in the biography of Khro[-phu] Lo[-tsā-ba].[115] The words of some fools that this is [the site,] too, [of] the meditation caves and sacred springs used by Tilo[pa] [and] Nāro[pa]—it is mere disjointed talk.[116]

The image of the self-arisen Ārya Avalokiteśvara located in the centre of the great city of Yam-bu (i.e. Kathmandu) is known to Tibetans as the White 'Ja'-ma-li. To elaborate briefly its history, [as recounted] in the eighth chapter of the 'Twenty-One Chapters on the Deeds of the King', a pronouncement of the Dharmarāja Srong-btsan sgam-po, a physical manifestation of Paramārya Lokeśvara in the Glacier Land (i.e. Tibet):

> Then the king thought: "Now, I wonder whether there are such astonishing objects of worship in the southern kingdom of Nepal. And afterwards he made offerings to the self-arisen sandalwood statue (i.e. Ekādaśamukha Avalokiteśvara) and uttered prayers, whence a light appeared from the heart of the sandalwood [statue] and went to the land of Nepal. [Following it with his eyes,] he saw in a valley on the further side of Nepal a great forest of sandalwood [trees], and in the middle of it he saw that there were three self-arisen statues of Ārya Avalokiteśvara in the trunk of a *haricandana* [tree]. Then the bhikṣu Ākaramatiśīla appeared out of the tip of a beam of light [emitted] from the circlet of hair between the king's eyebrows. Dispatched to invite back [these statues], this emanated bhikṣu went to sKyid-grong. In this town he witnessed the calamity of each year a [new] town headman dying as a lump [of flesh] from leprosy. Then he went to Nepal, and in the city called Yam-bu Ya-'gal he witnessed the calamity of [inhabitants] each year dying as epidemics went in search [of them]. Then he went to the further side of Nepal, and on the border between Nepal and India witnessed the calamity and fear resulting from a great evil spirit kidnapping leading merchants every three months and of their dying the morning after with a knife in their stomach.

Then he went to the dense forest of *haricandana* [trees,] and in the middle of a grove [he saw what was] in the daytime a sandalwood trunk and [what] at night appeared to be a divine effigy. When afterwards this emanated bhikṣu made marks between the three statues and started to split [the wood], the three spoke with [individual] voices. From the upper one came the words: "Split slowly! And [then] place me on the border between India and Nepal!" From the interior [of the trunk] appeared the one called Jo-bo 'Ja'-ma-li, a white sandalwood statue one cannot glance at enough; it possesses the major and minor marks [of a Buddha], its fragrance pervades ten *dpag tshad*s, and it has three faces and six arms and [the appearance of] a child of just five years. From the middle one came the words: "Split slowly! And [then] place me in Yam-bu Ya-'gal!" From the exposed interior [of the trunk] appeared the one called Jo-bo U-khang, of white complexion, having one face and four arms [and possessing] the major and minor marks [of a Buddha], its light and rays of light radiating [in all directions]. From the nether one came the words: "Split slowly! And [then] place me in Mang-yul!" From inside [the tree] appeared Jo-bo Wa-ti bzang-po, of red complexion, having one face and two arms, the right one in *varada-mūdra* and the left one holding a lotus.

Afterwards, after the emanated bhikṣu had made the invitation to the three statues, he set off [with them]. Once Jo-bo 'Ja'-ma-li was on the border between India and Nepal, he could not proceed further. Once Jo-bo U-khang was in Ya-'gal, he could not proceed further. Once Jo-bo Wa-ti [bzang-po] was in Mang-yul, he could not proceed further. By the blessing of the three self-arisen statues an end was put to the three earlier much feared calamities.[117]

[These three,] as thus told, are known as the true ones among the four self-arisen [statues which are] brothers. And although a slightly more extensive account exists elsewhere, I shall not say more [by citing it,] out of fear of [uttering too many] words here; one may learn [more] elsewhere![118]

In the vicinity of the self-manifested noble White 'Ja'-ma-li: In previous times the Dharmarāja Aśoka issued an order to the people in the different countries under his rule, all the work of messengers and helpers being performed by powerful yakṣas. Stūpas at the eight sacred sites, a circumambulatory path in Vajrāsana (i.e. Bodhgaya), and in addition—in the whole of Jambudvīpa up to Li-yul in the north—stūpas containing quintessential relics of [Śākya]muni were erected, so that 84,000 caityas were completed in a single day and night. One caitya among these is the one which stands in the garden of the residence of the Newar paṇḍita Śrī Harṣa. The noble Vidyādhara (i.e. Kaḥ-thog Rig-'dzin Tshe-dbang nor-bu) said that miraculous signs of the existence of another caitya manifested clearly in Kīrtipur, too.

From [Kaḥ-thog Rig-'dzin] himself:

> Caityas together with their relics as symbols of the Dharmakāya—
> so stated the Jina—are beautiful ornaments of Jambudvīpa.
> Eight hundred thousand [of them] were erected by the ruler Aśoka.
> Among them, in the middle of Kathmandu in Nepal—the beautiful city—
> exists [one such] offering pole; before it, too,
> I prostrate with a mind full of sincere devotion!

With such words he made praise.

Thus this particular one among the ten million caityas was not recognized by Tibetans up until recent times; there was not the least inkling of it, whence it was the noble Vidyādhara himself who identified it.[119]

The stone effigy located at what is called by Tibetans a place where the 'red fever' is cured is a statue of the siddha Gorakṣanātha; Newars call it Ma-ru-ta-pa (i.e. [Kāṣṭha]maṇḍapa) Gorakṣanātha. In some untruthful accounts it is claimed [that there exist, further,] an arrow [shot by] the Bhagavan, the five *rgyal po* [spirits] made out of *jhai kṣim*, and the Five Sisters of Long Life, [who are] protective deities for male persons. These are all [just] rumours that follow upon groundless statements and linger on and on.[120]

One part of Nepal is Ye-rang, [there] called Pāṭana, [pronounced] Pāṭan in vernacular speech. There is, in the way of a sacred object in the city of Ye-rang, an image of the Teacher, the mighty [Śākya]muni, called by Newars the Śākyamuni of Kva Bahal. A number of Tibetans from previous times state that it is not an object the arhat Saṃghavardhana [produced by] hand; while some claim that it was previously the main sacred object of E vihāra in Nepal before [the latter] was destroyed by fire. It is [also] said that it is a speaking Saṃbhogakāya [Śākya]muni [image] or the like.[121] [But] the actual sacred object is an authentic blessing-bestowing Jo-bo Śākyamuni with the attributes of a Nirmāṇakāya Buddha. In previous times, when an army of Turuṣkas appeared in Nepal and could not be expelled by any other means, from underneath the throne of this image of the mighty [Śākya]muni emerged countless large mosquitoes about the size of a thumb and with sharp proboscises, which are called 'Ti-Sounding Vajras from Mon', and all the troops were [thus] driven back. This account can be found in the reliable chronicles of the Newars themselves.

Jo-bo U-khang: The Nepalese call him Bung[a] de-wa (i.e. Būga-dyaḥ). As mentioned above, [the statue] is one of the self-arisen Four Brothers Paramārya [Avalokiteśvara]. Also, the one whose name is Jo-bo 'Bu-khang, called Tsak de-wa (i.e. Cāk[-uvā]-dyaḥ) by the Newars, is obviously regarded as a self-arisen Brother Ārya [Avalokiteśvara].[122] Some people say that [the statue] which resides in the vihāra of the place known as Tso-ba (i.e. Chobāra) is the original Ārya U-khang, and it is also described [as such] in the *lam yig* of the Sixth Zhva-dmar-pa [Chos-kyi dbang-phyug] (1584–1630).[123]

What Tibetans call the 'Effigies of a Thousand Buddhas', and Newars refer to as Mahābuddha: It is known that in early times a Newar tent [and] wool trader travelled to Vajrāsana (i.e. Bodhgaya), and after he had firmly fixed in his mind the forms on the palace [temple at this site], a similar stūpa true to this model was erected [in Pāṭan] by only a single man.[124]

Adjacent to Shing-kun, on the charnel grounds of the Noble One who is called Bisa (i.e. Vidyeśvarī, here an epithet of Vajravārāhī) by the Newars—in what is known as the Lun-ti temple [there]—a low-caste butcher woman in former times melded into a statue of Vajravārāhī, whence it is a blessing-bestowing image of [Vajra]vārāhī—[an account] that derives from the biography of Khro[-phu] Lo[-tsā-ba]. It is certain that the actual effigy is a statue of the Maitrī[pāda] Khecarī from among the Three Khecarīs. Assertions by Tibetans that it is the Maitrī[pāda] Khecarī, besides being fabricated assumptions, are [just] irrelevant talk without any reason [to them].[125]

The Ramadoli charnel grounds: I have not heard any reliable past accounts [of them] other than their being very famous in Nepal itself.[126]

The Yang-le shod rock cave, a site of spiritual practice blessed by [the presence of] the ācārya [and] second Buddha Padmasambhava: The Newars call it Shi-ka ṇa-ran (i.e. Śikhanārāyaṇa). The Mahācārya had previously come to the sacred site, at the border between India and Nepal, and the Newar lady Śākyadevī made his practice blissful; by means of the dPal Yang-dag [sādhana] he reached [the stage of] a vidyādhara of Mahāmudrā, the highest [such] siddhi. As a result the nāga Ging-po, the yakṣa Thod-ma-kha and the hedgehog Klog-ma sprin created obstacles, and for three years there was no rainfall, and disease and famine were sent down. [Padmasambhava's] teachers in India therefore said that a teaching had to be dispatched in order to overcome the obstacles. A two-man load containing the volumes of the *Phur ba vidyottama[-tantra]* were dispatched, so that [all] the obstacles were cleared away: rain fell, disease and famine ended, and [Padmasambhava] attained the highest siddhi. Although the siddhi of [dPal] Yang-dag is great, it is like a merchant and therefore many obstacles [come along with it]. Whence he saw that the Phur-ba [practice], which is like an escort ]to the merchant], was necessary he performed the [dPal] Yang[-dag] and Phur[-pa] practices in a combined form, [and afterwards] bound the protectors of the Phur-pa [cycle] and all the gods, demons and arrogant spirits of India and Nepal to an oath. Further, when he performed a pacifying maṇḍala practice at this sacred site, he saw the faces of all the deities of the Vajradhātu [maṇḍala] and obtained the siddhi of Long Life.[127]

In the eighth chapter of the sūtra, in the new translation by the All-Knowing Situ [Paṇ-chen], the Teacher (i.e. Buddha Śākyamuni) spoke:

> "Maitreya! In this way, the land of Nepal prospered, developed, happiness and good fortune [prevailed], [there were] good harvests and it was filled with many people. [But then] during one period, at another time, no rain fell for seven years in this land of Nepal, so that bad harvests occurred."[128]

[Thus he] said, [and]

> "At Śāntipur on this Gośṛṅga Hill lived the siddhācārya Zhi-byed lha."[129]

[Thus he] said, [and]

> "In this land of Nepal [is] a sacred site of the gods, a powerful ground for realization. After this Zhi-byed lha—the siddhācārya, the great magician endowed with insight—had performed his deeds, he cultivated samādhi a *dpag tshad* underneath the ground in front of his own town, in a cavity adorned with wish-fulfilling jewels and paradise trees—a blissful [site] of blessed glory in a joyful heavenly abode, and remained [there]; after a long time he will emerge from this samādhi and, having emerged, will expound the doctrine in this land of Nepal."[130]

As pointed out in intervening prophecies [since the one just] stated, this Zhi-byed lha is none other than Mahācārya Padmākara.

From the *[Padma bka'i] thang yig gser phreng*:

> Then Padmasambhava, the teacher from Oḍḍiyāna, took rest in the land of Nepal, and he stayed [there] for three months. He performed great benefit for the people, among them the Nepalese king Vasudhara. He is known as Zhi-ba'i lha.[131]

For so it is stated.

Here, in order to generate faith, pronouncements that have come down in the meantime as to what is said at the end of the eighth chapter of the recently translated sūtra (the chronicle), rather than paying attention to its full wording, are written in generalities. If one wishes to understand in detail the extensive account, one should consult the actual Sanskrit source.

Indian Pham-mthing: In the *[Padma bka'i] thang yig zangs gling ma* it is described as 'Pham-mthing [at] the Indian border', it being called Indian because in previous times it was in the territory of India.[132] Obviously, this was the residence of the Pham-mthing-pa brothers, the teachers of the great translator Marpa Lo-tsā-ba. Nowadays one is unlikely to encounter anything except non-Buddhists statues in that place.[133] The blessing-bestowing image of Vārāhī, it is claimed, was the tutelary object of Pham-mthing-pa (i.e.Vagīśvara); Newars call it Pham-bi Vajrayoginī.[134]

The Asura cave: This is what is called the Asura Guhā, a cave of the demigods; the Newars call it Kun-da kyin-ka ri. The Asura cave as described in the *[Padma bka'i] thang yig* is the site where Ānanda resided and ordained Guru [Padmasambhava]. It is located in India, so that it is obviously not the one in Nepal.[135] [The notion,] too, that it is connected with Yang-le shod and so forth, should be considered inadmissible for many reasons.[136] This Asura cave is, [however,] to be regarded as none other than the sacred site where Mahācārya Padma[sambhava] and Rlang[-chen] dPal-gyi seng-ge bound the brTan-ma bcu-gnyis [goddesses] to an oath.[137]

If one proceeds about a day's journey from Yang-le shod in the south-western direction, [there is a place] called Ṛṣeśvara by Indians and Newars. [Now,] as for the claim by foolish Tibetans that it is [the site] known as Chu-mig Byang-chub bdud-rtsi, discussed by the Precious Guru (i.e. Padmasambhava).[138] [On] the border between Nepal and Indian Mo-khom-pur (i.e Makwanpur), in the southern direction, where there are three Nepalese rural villages called O-shar gang-du, Pā-lung (i.e Palung) [and] Shi-kha-gor (i.e. Shikapur), [there is] a great elevation in a dense mountain forest. Ascending to the top of it, [one finds] a bas relief human face on the rock surface of a small grotto, and at the base of the rock a spring [and] boiling water, besides which there seems to be nothing else.

In a historical account:

> Once a hunter, having lost track of a deer, came to this place and saw a ṛṣi or a yogi absorbed in meditation. He approached him, [but the latter] disappeared. At the same time the king of Pāṭan ([which is] called Ye-rang) dreamt of what the hunter had seen. The ṛṣi spoke: "If you grant recognition to my place and perform offerings [there,] I will provide you with any excellent thing you wish." And immediatelly [the king] awoke. He was unable to conceive where something like this could have happened, but he kept pondering [the incident]. One day he heard the hunter [himself] tell the story. [Afterwards] when the king arrived at this place, he could not find the ṛṣi, but he saw the surface of a grotto that had a self-arisen face [on it]. He established there the custom of making regular offerings, and up to the present many inhabitants of that region assemble [there] on auspicious days; a big crowd comes together. It is said that in the night of the fifteenth day (i.e. the full moon) of the first Mongol month, called Phālguna, people come together from Nepal, Pāṭan and so forth to celebrate a festival. In the first half of the night not even *sindhura* is put [on the rock surface] and there is no pomp; [but] from the second half of the night onwards, it is said, people [start] returning from the celebrations and the face can be seen directly in its glittering glory—thus it is reported. When a Newar started to construct stone steps and a rest-

house, called a *pāṭi*, he saw in a dream an undesirable sign on display, inasmuch as [this place] is a hidden sacred site. Afterwards he passed away at that spot.

Thus it states.

Concerning this matter, one needs to realize that, let alone from [the fact that] it is only known to non-Buddhists, the story is not a Buddhist one.[139] Here, [then], in order to clarify doubts [some] records, as [for example]:

In the *gSol 'debs bar chad lam gsal ma*:

> At the border between India and Nepal
> [he] arrived, having blessed [the surroundings,]
> a mountain with sweet and fragrant scents,
> where lotus flowers grow even in winter,
> its waters a spring of enlightenment nectar.
> At this excellent site, an abode of gods....[140]

The place referred to by these words and the spring of enlightenment nectar is said [here] to be similar in character to the sacred site of Yang-le shod. By contrast, there is snowfall on the peak of the chain of hills in the Indian [district of] Mo-khom-pur (i.e. Makwanpur). It is not possible that a piece of scripture is being quoted [here] in regard to the putrid hidden spring issuing forth at that place.

In the 54th chapter of the *[Padma bka'i] thang yig shel brag ma* of O-rgyan gling-pa:

> Then he arrived at Tsha-ba tsha-shod in Nepal,
> [the site of ] what is called a spring of enduring enlightenment,
> where flowers grow even in winter: there he performed his spiritual practice.
> At that time he overpowered the life-force of beings,
> bound to an oath the Earth mistresses, the four sisters,
> and asked them to be the Four bSe-mo [Sisters], the protectors of the Phur-pa [cycle].[141]

This accords with how the oath-bound protectors of the Phur[-pa cycle] mentioned above were bound to an oath.

In the *[Padma bka'i] thang yig zangs gling ma*, a treasure of Nyang[-ral Nyima'i 'od-zer]:

> On this side of [the border is] India; on the other side of [it is] Nepal. At what is called the cave of Yang-le shod, even in winter the flowers do not dry up. When he arrived at this auspicious site....[142]

As this corresponds [with the quotations above]—rather than giving birth to nonsense and mere names—[this site] alone should henceforth be identified as the spring of enlightenment, [that is,] Yang-le shod together with the good stream mTsho dkar-nag.

In connection with this: The mountain summit of gTsang-kha pass, as described in the *gSol 'debs bar chad lam gsal ma*, today is said to be called 'Tibetan Village Pass'; and Tsha-ba tsha-shod in Nepal is a valley nowadays called 'Darwal (i.e. Darwal).[143] In its lower part [lies] Devīghāṭ, known as mDo-dman, the seat of rDo-rje Ya-byin[-ma], one of the Four bSe-mo [Sisters] among the twelve Ma-mo [goddesses], the protectors of the Phur-pa [cycle].[144] The words in the many admonitions for the oath-bound deities of revealed Phur-pa treasure works, such as those of the Phur-pa of the Northern Treasures or the Phur-pa Razor of [Guru] Chos[-kyi] dbang[-phyug] (1212-1270), describe this similarly.

Earlier, the great god Viṣṇu came as a Brahmin to the noble vidyādhara [Kaḥ-thog Rig-'dzin Tshe-dbang nor-bu], and in accordance with a prophecy had the latter bring a *yaṣṭi* for the Self-Manifested Mahācaitya [of Svayaṃbhū] from this sacred site (i.e. Tsha-ba tsha-shod).[145]

What is known as mTsho dkar-nag: non-Buddhists who follow the Veda regard it as a seat of Mahādeva (i.e. Śiva) and U-ma. And although Buddhists regard it as a palace of Cakrasaṃvara, the noble vidyādhara [Kaḥ-thog Rig-'dzin Tshe-dbang nor-bu] stated that it is a palace of Remati, the goddess to the north-east of Vajrāsana (i.e. Bodhgaya).[146]

> The protectors, they who have become authorities in their desire to benefit beings,
> [namely] the sons and disciples of the mighty Muni; the siddhas and vidyādharas:
> seeing, hearing [and] remembering the astonishing sites and sacred objects of growing splendour blessed by them—
> in [such] liberation—[brings on] a spring season rejoiced in by all!
>
> Although this is the case, wild animals, in complete bewilderment at illusionary trees splashing into water and traps [set for them],
> wander around within many worlds (i.e. the six realms);
> now, from the very beginning, they should enter the right path,
> and should generate memories [and] pure visions of the good qualities of each and every [sacred site]!

The fourth chapter of what is called 'A Definitive Presentation of the History of the Sacred Sites and Religious Objects of Nepal', setting forth the causes behind the additional subsidiary sacred sites and religious objects.

## [V]

Now, furthermore, what else needs to be explained as a supplement: In this land of Nepal the Buddhist doctrine spread very widely, and the doctrines of non-Buddhists grew less. In particular, the Buddhist doctrine spread to the land of

Nepal for a period of about a hundred years from the west, [from] the vihāra of Vikramaśīla in the central land of Magadha; [and] it is said that in later generations, at the time of Paṇḍita Vanaratna and afterwards, for a period of many years, the doctrine did not decline. [But] nowadays, with the changing times, other than Buddhism as a mere leftover name, all people have embraced the doctrines of those outside [the Dharma]; and even if there are a small number of persons inside [it], they practise in a way that mixes the doctrines of persons both inside and outside. Behaviour according to the pure tenet of acceptance and rejection—[propounded by] Buddhists alone—is [as rare as] stars in the daytime.[147]

How the rulers of Nepal arose [in this country]: It is certain that for a long time in the past, from the time of King Aṃśuvarman (a manifestation of Mañjuśrī) onwards, and also from the time of Srong-btsan sgam-po, the Glacier Land dharmarāja, onwards, a number of religious kings emerged who devoutly revered the Buddhist doctrine. On one occasion, a non-Buddhist of royal descent from Pāṭaliputra fought against a Turuṣka king, and when he was defeated he fled with a great retinue of attendants to Kho-khom (i.e. Bhaktapur) and settled [there]. This king conquered the old royal families in Nepal and initiated the diffusion of non-Buddhist tenets. Some generations following that a descendant of this royal family became the ruler of Yam-bu (i.e. Kathmandu). From then onwards, down to Jayaprakāśa Malla, it is clear that no one among this royal lineage appeared who believed in the Buddha from the bottom of his heart and offered reverent service to the Buddhist doctrine—only mere outward show. Nevertheless, among them, the king called Pārthivendra Malla (r. 1680–1687), who lived at the time of Rang-rig ras-pa, did properly accomplish a renovation of Shing-kun, as described above.[148] The last member of this royal family, Jayaprakāśa, called in Tibetan rGyal-ba rab-gsal, believed in the Buddha from the bottom of his heart. Even in front of the revered great beings of Tibet who came [to Nepal] he bowed down with respect; in particular, he properly requested from the noble [Kaḥ-thog] Rig-'dzin instructions for the Ṣaḍaṅga-[yoga], the perfection stage of the Kālacakratantra, and was one of the latter's devoted disciples.[149]

In the spiritual song [called] 'The Thirteen Kingdoms':

> The king of Kathmandu in Nepal
> Acted like a disciple of the Dharma.

Thus it is said.

Afterwards, in the wood [female] pig year called *yuvan* of the thirteenth sixty-year cycle [= 1755], the army of the king of Gorkha seized Nepal. In regard to this king: a mountain king had once seized a retainer fortress on the side of a hill where a former resting place of the great siddhācārya Gorakṣanātha is located—the meditation cave of this siddha (called Gorkha Cave); today [the locality] is known as Gorkha. [This king] was of Kṣatriya warrior descent, [and] the majority of those belonging to this family revered Acārya Gorakṣanātha.[150]

During the time of King Pṛthvīnārāyaṇa Śāha [and his] sons, respect was also paid to the noble [Kaḥ-thog] Rig-'dzin, and [the king] is seen to have properly assisted [him] in procuring a *yaṣṭi* for the Mahācaitya [of Svayaṃbhū].

From the spiritual song "The Thirteen Kingdoms":

> The king of Gorkha in Lower Mon—
> he turned his deeds into [acts of] virtue.

Thus it is said.

It is known that some four generations have passed since then.

Further, from the venerable [and] noble Jo-nang Tārānātha:

> Wherever the doctrine of the Buddha exists, the skill of making statues has spread; wherever barbarians dominate, the making of statues degenerates; wherever non-Buddhists spread, persons without any skill in making statues also spread.[151]

As thus stated, in the past there appeared in the valley of Nepal artifacts of an astonishingly excellent and graceful quality, including painted and sculptured statues of the Jina, images in copper and bronze, wooden sculptures made of sandalwood, stone statues and cast images. Even in Tibet they have been popular everywhere up to the present. All that appeared in the way of a tradition of painting deities among the early Tibetan artists in reality was established as a proper standard known as the painting tradition of Ye-rang (i.e. Pātan), one of the artistic lineages of Nepal. This I have heard from a reliable oral source, and I have seen it with my own eyes. Nowadays it appears that even if the art of making statues exists, the style of most of them—apart from some individual [exceptions]—is greatly corrupted.[152]

> Whereas in the past, by the enlightened compassion of the Jina,
> the lotus grove of his doctrine blossomed greatly,
> nowadays, due to the hail from the enduring casting of wrong views,
> whatever sprouts of common good exist are destroyed in one stroke.
>
> Still, wherever the basket containing the three secrets of the Sugata
> has not been damaged, it has produced perfectly white seeds
> of individual respect and virtue without obstacle;
> it is fit that deeds are perfomed individually: this is a good—a very good—aeon!

The fifth chapter of what is called 'A Definitive Presentation of the History of the Sacred Sites and Religious Objects of Nepal: A Mirror of Jewels Which

Clears Away Errors', setting forth additional points remaining to be explained as a supplement.

[Colophon]

Thus [are] the sacred sites and religious objects of the land of Nepal:
on a wondrous *bakula* tree,
sprinkled with liquor from lauded lovely ladies' [mouths],
a fluttering of flowers—a garland of smiles—pleasing to the wise.

One free from dust, whose eyes see all—
his well-pronounced sayings (the sound of a *vina* perfect in its seven tones)
in the past were not planted in the ears of common folk;
having plucked them forth with fingers sincere in intent, I have [now] translated them.

The astonishing words—the three secrets of the Jina—
being spoken makes one's hair quiver.
To differentiate between what is trustworthy and what not—a matter of doubt—
is the pith of this [treatise].

Therefore, all the wise, [they] who strive towards virtuous deeds,
unstained by the rust of wrong, misguided talk—
may their face lighten up from the astonishing qualities [of this country];
may they look into this mirror of jewels, which did not exist in the past!

Devoid of the wealth of judgement one customarily generates,
and lacking power to be trained in the hundred scriptures of science,
the learned shame themselves with what they unabashedly expound;
forbear, [and] comfort [them] with purifying song.

Everything here—whatever [could be] obtained as positive facts [through] the union of effort and sincerity—
[is] as unblemished as a *kumuda* [flower] and, by virtue of its dazzlingness, similar to a conch and the root of a lotus.
May the precious doctrine which delights the Jinas spread immeasurably,
and may its benefits expand to all worlds and nourish them with the glory of its excellence!

It permeates the path that is good for all beings,

And, [as] the essence of the suchness [that is] the dharmadhātu,
may it, having manifested as the Lord of Speech,
Pervade all space and accomplish benefit for others!

It seems certain that there has not existed in the past a detailed history [written] in simple language [like] what is called 'A Definitive Presentation of the History of the Sacred Sites and Religious Objects of Nepal: A Mirror of Jewels Which Clears Away Errors'. As the well-known 'Register of Nepal's Shing-kun', composed by Nas-lung-pa Ngag-dbang rdo-rje, a disciple of the noble Rang-rig ras-pa, and the guidebook to Nepal composed by rNgog-ston Karma Blo-bzang, [these] two, were executed as xylographs, they [are the ones] generally echoed, having been consulted on numerous occasions. In this book of Nas-lung-pa Ngag-dbang rdo-rje, except for merely the register of the reliquary of the noble Rang-rig ras-pa himself, all the rest is mere fiction, based on [false] assumptions and....[153]

## Notes

1 'Mare's mouth fire' (*rta gdong bsreg za / rta gdong me*) is an allusion to the legend featuring a fire created by the wrathful sage Aurva, which would have consumed the earth had it not been cast into the ocean; a whirlpool constantly bathes it and the water smothers the flames. For the proverbial use made of this legend, see the references in Silk (2008:167, note 120).

2 This verse is contained in the eighth chapter of the *Legs par bshad pa'i rin po che'i gter* of Sa-skya Paṇḍita Kun-dga' rgyal-mtshan (1182–1251). For this work, composed between the years 1244 and 1251, and information on the various manuscripts and block prints of it, see Eimer (2014:6–25). The mentioned verse is there no. 370; id. (2014:155).

3 For a quotation from the introduction of the translation made by lHa-mdong Lo-tsā-ba bShes-gnyen rnam-rgyal, see note 21. The notion that the *Svayaṃbhūpurāṇa* was composed by Ārya Nāgārjuna may stem from the translation. bShes-gnyen rnam-rgyal is also known for having authored the second part of the biography of dBus-smyon Kun-dga' bzang-po (1458–1532), a text written down at an early age in the year 1537. An incomplete manuscript of a journey to Nepal has also survived, but it covers only the initial stages of the journey in Central Tibet; for more details, see Ehrhard (2010:236–237, note 20).

4 On Si-tu Paṇ-chen's translation of the *Svayaṃbhūpurāṇa*, see Decleer (2000:33–37), Verhagen (2008:527–536) and Verhagen (2013:320). The obtaining of a first Sanskrit manuscript occurred during the initial visit to Nepal in the year 1723, the final translation, based on a second manuscript, being completed during a further stay in the valley in the year 1748. Having received the first, quite corrupt text, Si-tu Paṇ-chen, too, mentions the "various stories by foolish Tibetans" and the previous translation of lHa-mdong Lo-tsā-ba bShes-gnyen rnam-rgyal; see Chos-kyi 'byung-gnas: *Dri bral shel gyi me long*, pp. 117.6–7 (*spyir 'phags pa shing kun gyi mchod rten chen po 'di ni bod blun rnams kyi ngag sgros sna tshogs la brten nas 'dod tshul mang zhig 'dug kyang / 'di nyid kyi dkar chag sangs rgyas kyi gsungs*

*pa'i bkar gtogs pa zhig sngar lo tsā ba bshes gnyen rnam rgyal gyis bsgyur yod 'dug kyang da lta dpe dkon par snang zhing*). The translation was made upon the request of Kaḥ-thog Rig-'dzin Tshe-dbang nor-bu, who was engaged in a renovation of the Bodhnāth Stūpa at the time; see note 83. The colopon contains his words of admonition for Si-tu Paṇ-chen, while declaring the sūtra, except for some verses, as a pronouncement of the Buddha; see *Bal yul rang byung mchod rten chen po'i lo rgyus*, p. 257.3–4 (*zhes bal yul rang byung mchod rten gyi lo rgyus 'di ni dbu dang gsham du paṇḍitas mdzad pa'i tshigs bcad 'ga' zhig las dngos gzhi bcom ldan 'das kyi bka' stsal ba'i mdo nyid du 'dug pas gnas 'dir cis kyang legs sbyar gyi skad las bod skad du sgyur cig ces*).

[5] In the early pilgrimage guidebooks, the identification of Bal-yul with Li-yul and the Go-ma-sa-la-gan-dha with the Shing-kun stūpa are to be found at the very beginning of the texts. See bSod-nams dpal bzang-po: *'Phags pa shing kun gyi dkar chag*, pp. 82.3–83.2, and the translation in Ehrhard (2013:76); compare Ngag-dbang rdo-rje: *Bal yul 'phags pa shing kun dang de'i gnas gzhan rnams kyi dkar chag*, p. 43.7–18. A direct quotation from the sūtra is marked as such in the former text; see bSod-nams dpal bzang-po: *'Phags pa shing kun gyi dkar chag*, pp. 84.3–85.4, and the translation in Ehrhard (2013:78). The relevant section describes Li-yul, Goma Lake and the mountain called 'Prophesied Ox-horn' (*glang ru lung bstan*) on top of which the Go-ma-sa-la-gan-dha stūpa was to appear in fulfilment of a prophecy by Buddha Śākyamuni; for the original, see *Ārya-gośṛṅga-vyākaraṇa-sūtra* [= *'Phags pa glang ru lung bstan zhes bya theg pa chen po'i mdo*], p. 348.1.5–5.8. The second pilgrimage guidebook includes the same details but without referring to the sūtra; see Ngag-dbang rdo-rje: *Bal yul 'phags pa shing kun dang de'i gnas gzhan rnams kyi dkar chag*, p. 44.10–24.

[6] This pseudo-etymology of the toponym Godāvarī can be regarded as a ploy to claim for Nepal one of the *upapīṭhas* that figure in the tradition of the *Saṃvarodayatantra*; for the legends identifying a site in the southern part of the Kathmandu Valley with the *upapīṭha* of the same name located in South India see, for example, Slusser (1982, vol., 1:352). The literary sources consulted by Brag-dkar rta-so sPrul-sku are in this case the early pilgrimage guidebooks to the Ārya Wa-ti bzang-po, where the legend of the cow serves to identify the tree from which the 'Brothers Ārya [Avalokiteśvara]' (*'phags pa sku mched*) arose. In his own guidebook to the statue, written between the years 1825 and 1828, he quotes the same claim in full, while also pointing out the Tibetan tradition of identifying sNyan-g.yon with a well-known meditation cave in the south of La-phyi; see Ehrhard (2004:279–280 & 396–397, notes 149–150). For a list of these twenty-four pilgrimage sites in India according to the *Cakrasaṃvaratantra*, see Davidson (2005:40–41); consult Pahlke (2012:44, note 217) concerning the actual site in La-phyi, especially the cave associated with the great yogin Mi-la ras-pa and how to locate it when approaching La-phyi from the south.

[7] In the early pilgrimage guidebook, the titles of the *Ārya-gośṛṅga-vyākaraṇa-sūtra* and the *Ārya-mañjuśrī-mūla-tantra* are referred to in both the introductory and concluding verses—elliptically as, respectively, the sūtra and tantra—and there treated as the authoritative sources concerning Nepal and the Svayaṃbhūnāth Stūpa; see bSod-nams dpal bzang-po: *'Phags pa shing kun gyi dkar chag*, pp. 82.2 & 89.6, and the translation in Ehrhard (2013:76 & 83). The later guidebook kept only the reference to the two works in the introductory verses; see Ngag-dbang rdo-rje: *Bal yul 'phags pa shing kun dang de'i gnas gzhan rnams kyi dkar chag*, p. 43.5–6. The *Bal po gnas gyi lam yig* of rNgog-ston Karma Blo-bzang is not available; see the Introduction, note 24. This printed guidebook might contain the reference to the *bKa' gdams glegs bam*.

[8] For this quotation, see *Ārya-mañjuśrī-mūla-tantra* [= *'Phags pa 'jam dpal rtsa ba'i rgyud*], chapter 10, p. 194.2.7–8. It is also cited by Brag-dkar rta-so sPrul-sku in his guidebook to the Ārya Wa-ti bzang-po as a Buddhist literary source for the toponym Mang-yul. The original Sanskrit version lists five countries, i.e. *kaśmira*, *cīna*, *nepāla*, *kāviśa* and *mahācīna*. *Kāviśa*, corresponding to present-day Afghanistan, was rendered as Mang-yul, but there is no reference to Li-yul (or Khotan) in the Sanskrit text; for this quotation and the translations of the *Ārya-mañjuśrī-mūla-tantra*, see Ehrhard (2004:279 & 393–394, note 144).

[9] The prophecy of the foundation of the land of Li-yul by a grandson of the Indian emperor Aśoka is contained in the *Ārya-gośṛṅga-vyākaraṇa-sūtra* [= *'Phags pa glang ru lung bstan zhes bya ba theg pa chen po'i mdo*], pp. 349.1.7–8 & 349.2.5. On the legend of the son who was abandoned by his father and suckled by the earth goddess, and so received the name 'Earth-Suckled' (*go-stana*)—i.e. he whose [suckling] breast is the earth—which was later transferred to the city he founded, see Brough (1947:334). It has been noted that this legend is prototypically associated with Khotan, but it can, for instance, also be found in the Buddhist *vaṃśāvalīs* of Nepal.

[10] See Padma dkar-po: *Chos 'byung bstan pa'i padma rgyas pa'i nyin byed*, p. 91.7–17. The literary source for this presentation of the legend of the grandson of Aśoka who was discarded by his father, raised by Vaiśravaṇa to the rank of a Chinese prince, and who later looked for the place of his birth with an army of ten thousand men, could be another work relating to the Buddhist country of Khotan; see *Li yul lung bstan pa*, pp. 302.5.4–303.5.1 and the translation in Emmerick (1967:15–23). Both at the beginning and end of this version, the reckoning of the period when Sa-la-nu became king of the Li country is given as two hundred thirty-four years after the Parinirvāna of the Buddha. See Nattier (1991:188–204) concerning texts like the *Glang ru lung bstan* and *Li yul lung bstan*, which are styled Buddhist prophecies, and are translations from the Khotanese preserved only in Tibetan.

[11] The term *dus sbyor* (Skt. *laghna*), referring here to the time when Li-yul was conquered by a king, describes the period a zodiac sign is in ascension at a certain place. It is one of the determinants of the *Svarodaya* (or *dByangs-'char*) astrology, which was quite widespread in Tibet; see Schuh (2012:1413 & 1505). This quotation is from a letter written by Kaḥ-thog Rig-'dzin in the year 1747 and sent from Lhasa to Gung mGon-po skyabs in Beijing. The latter is the author of the *rGya nag chos 'byung*; for this work, see note 17. For the full quotation, see Tshe-dbang nor-bu: *rGya nag tu gung mgon po skyabs la dri ba mdzad pa*, p. 725.2–5 (*li yul 'di yang ngos 'dzin tshul mi gcig pa mang ba ding seng nas mdzad pa'i chos 'byung du li yul lcang du ngos bzung ba ni bod sngags rnying pa'i gzhung lo rgyus rnam dag rnams su li yul lcang ra smug po sogs kyi khung (= khungs) dang 'brel zhing thad par snang yang rgyal po sā (= sa) nu'i bdag byed pa'i yul drug dus sbyor skabs gi (= kyi) li yul ni bod yul gyi byang phyogs su yod dgos par snang bas mkhas pa rig ral sogs snga rabs dang / phyis byung kha cig gis kyang sā (= sa) nus byung ba'i yul zi ling gi byang phyogs char yod pa brjod na de yang bden min dang / yul drug li yul gyi ngos 'dzin rgya nag su ji ltar bzhed phebs gsal dang*). The name 'Shady Willow Grove of Khotan' (*li yul lcang ra smug po*) was used by rNying-ma-pa authors such as gNubs-chen Sangs-rgyas ye-shes (9th/10th cent.) in the context of the legend according to which Buddha Śākyamuni visited the kingdom on the Southern Silk Route; see his *sGom gyi gnad gsal bar phye ba bsam gtan mig sgron*, pp. 5.6–6.2 (*rgyu'i theg pa chen po'i lugs kyis kyang sngon ston pas zhabs kyi bcags pa'i rdo rje'i gdan / bya rgon phung po'i ri dang / li yul lcang ra smug po la stsogs pa bkra shis pa'i gnas dag bya ba grub par byed pas btsal lo*). Consult van Schaik (2016:45–61) concerning this passage and the cultural relations between Khotanese and Tibetan Buddhists.

[12] See *sKu gdung 'bar ba dang tsha tsha mchod rten gyi rgyud*, chapter 6, p. 408.2–3 (*byang shar mtshams na li'i yul / dur khrod 'jig rten mngon rdzogs na / dpal ldan padma chen po dang / mi zad drag po gang ba dang / mchod rten 'ge'u te shan zhes bya / ston pas cho 'phrul bstan pa'i gnas / chu 'byin me 'bar 'khrul snang mang / li rje btsan pa'i (= btsan po'i) rgyal khams yin*). This chapter contains a description of the 'Eight Charnel Grounds' (*dur khrod chen po brgyad*) and their eight self-manifested stūpas according to the tradition of the early translations. A description of the eight sites and the names of the eight stūpas can also be found in the biographical tradition of Padmasambhava; on the country of Li-yul, see O-rgyan gling-pa: *U rgyan gu ru padma 'byung gnas kyi skye rabs rnam par thar pa rgyas par bkod pa padma bka'i thang yig*, p. 87.19–21 (*yul gyi ming ni li yul du phyin: dur khrod chen po lo ka brtsegs zhes pa: mtha' skor dpag tshad phyed dang bzhi yod pa'i: dbus na rang byung mchod rten ke'u sha: ma mo chen mo shma sha nī gnas pa:*). The same chapter of the tantra is quoted below in the context of the Bya-rung kha-shor stūpa; see note 86.

[13] The commentary on the *bDud rtsi mchog gi rgyud* has not been identified up to now. The two final lines of the quotation are incomplete. Concerning Bya-tri kha-shor in Nepal and the etymology of its name, see note 74. The 'Eight Mother-Goddesses' (*ma mo brgyad*) are a group of female territorial deities who served, after being tamed, as 'protectors of the [Buddha's] pronouncements' (*bka'i srung ma*). On these pre-Buddhist mother goddesses and the cult of a group of seven deities which was prevalent in the region of Mang-yul, see Ehrhard (2008:15–24). For the problem of the classification of the group of seven or eight Ma-mo deities according to the tantras of the early translation period, see Blondeau (2002:293–294).

[14] The legend of the two Buddhist monks from Li-yul visiting King Srong-btsan sgam-po in Tibet can be found in chapter sixteen of the work *rGyal po'i mdzad pa nyi shu rta gcig pa*; see different authors: *Maṇi bka' 'bum*, vol. 1, pp. 408.10–410.6. This popular narrative was transmitted in the Tibetan historiographical literature, including the *rGyal rabs gsal me long* of Bla-ma dam-pa bSod-nams rgyal-mtshan (1312–1375); for a translation of its version, see Sørensen (1994:303–306 & 584, note 920). In the *Maṇi bka' 'bum*'s version of the story—which, being the earliest testimony, was obviously seen as the most authoritative in this regard—Srong-btsan sgam-po features as an emanation of the Bodhisattva Avalokiteśvara. According to the version in the *Maṇi ka' 'bum*, the two monk-novices propitiated Avalokiteśvara, who then revealed that he had manifested as a king in Tibet and they should visit him. The historiographical work states that the revelation was made after the two śramaṇeras from Li-yul had practised the Mañjuśrī sādhana in vain for eight years.

[15] For the geography of the world as described in the *Kālacakratantra* and the cosmological tradition underlying it, see Schuh (2012:cvi–cvii). Jambudvīpa is pictured as shaped in the form of an inverted triangle, known as the 'Small Rose Apple Continent' (*'dzam bu gling chung ba*), and as consisting of six countries; these are called, proceeding from north to south, Glacier Land (*gangs ldan*), Śambhala, China (*rgya nag*), Khotan (*li yul*), Tibet (*bod*) and Ārya-deśa (i.e. India) (*'phags yul*).

[16] This stock phrase for the geographical extension of Tibet was transmitted in different versions. In the same saying contained in the preamble to a Tibetan law code from the 17th century, the western region is characterized in a different way: "... in short, [the whole of Tibet] from the west, where cardamon is crushed with sticks, over to the east, where silk is woven by Chinese women" (*mdor na stod dzā ti dbyug pas brdungs sa nas / smad rgya mo dar 'thag sa yan....*); see Ehrhard (2015:109 & 120).

[17] The work of mGon-po skyabs bears the title *rGya nag gi yul du dam pa'i chos dar tshul gtso bor bshad pa blo gsal kun tu dga' ba'i rna rgyan*. This history of China and Chinese Buddhism was written in the year 1736, and its author, forwarded a manuscript copy to Si-tu Paṇ-chen Chos-kyi 'byung-gnas. The work was later executed as a xylograph in the lHun-grub steng printery in sDe-dge; see ibid. pp. 265.17–266.13. The identification of Li-yul with the region of lCang was assessed by Kaḥ-thog Rig-'dzin in a letter to mGon-po skyabs; see note 11. According to him the identification is found in 'present-day religious histories' (*ding sang nas byas pa'i chos 'byung*); these seem not to include the *rGya nag chos 'byung*, as such a statement cannot be found in the work of mGon-po skyabs.

[18] See Ngag-dbang Blo-bzang rgya-mtsho: *Za hor gyi ban de ngag dbang blo bzang rgya mtsho'i 'di snang 'khrul pa'i rol rtsed rtogs brjod kyi tshul du bkod pa du kū la'i gos bzang*, vol. 1, p. 380.7–11 (*tshe bco brgyad la sngon sangs rgyas kyis lung bstan pa'i glang ru gyi gtsug lag khang mchod rten gom (= go ma) sa la gandhar rgya rnams kyis ngos 'dzin pa de chu pha ri'i sar mig rkyang gang gi tshod na yod pa kong wu'u zhes pa'i mkhar dang mi ring bar bsdad*). For a translation of this passage, see Karmay (2014:285): "On the 18th we halted at a place near the fortified town called Kong-wu. On the other side of the river, within eyesight, there was a *stupa* that the Chinese identified as Gomasala Gandha *stupa*, prophesied by the Buddha in the *Glang ru lung bstan*." This took place during the journey of the Fifth Dalai Bla-ma to Beijing in the year 1652.

[19] For accounts of Nāgārjuna acting as custodian of the Mahācaitya and Vasubandhu's stay, see notes 43 & 92. On the arrival of Atiśa at the Svayaṃbhūcaitya according to the *Jo bo rje'i rnam thar lam yig*, an apocryphal text considered to be a composition of 'Brom-ston rGyal-ba'i 'byung-gnas (1005–1064), see rGyal ba'i 'byung-gnas: *Jo bo rje'i rnam thar lam yig chos kyi 'byung gnas*, p. 257.1–9, and Decleer (1996:40). The stūpa is also mentioned at the end of the biography of Atiśa known as the *rNam thar rgyas pa yongs grags*. According to it, it was at this sacred site in Nepal that the spiritual identities of Po-to-ba (1027/31–1106), Phu-chung-ba (1031–1109) and sPyan-snga-pa (1038–1103), the three well-known disciples of 'Brom-ston rGyal-ba'i 'byung-gnas, were revealed to a yogin who had joined their company in circumambulating the Svayaṃbhūcaitya; see Ehrhard (2013:427–428).

[20] The Fourth Khams-sprul provides in his pilgrimage guide the change of the local name name Svayaṃbhūcaitya from *sīhmangu ma* (New. *seṃgumā*), i.e. the 'Mother of Seṃgu', to *singu de vo* (New. *seṃgudhyaḥ*), i.e. the 'Deity of Seṃgu'; this name was rendered by Tibetans as *shing kun*; see bsTan-'dzin chos-kyi nyi-ma: *Yul chen nye ba'i tshandhoha bal po'i gnas kyi dkar chag*, p. 174.1–2 (*de'i phyir na mtshan yang swa yaṃbhu te rang byung mchod rten du grags / de nyid sngon gyi bal skad du sīhmangu ma zhes zer ba de nyid rim pas zur chag tu da lta'i bal po tshos singu de vo zer / bod rnams kyis ni de yang zur chag ste shing kun tu 'bod par 'dug*) and Macdonald & Dvags-po Rin-po-che (1981:246). On the Newari names of the Svayaṃbhūcaitya, see von Rospatt (1999:142 ff.); consult also von Rospatt (2009:36–37) concerning the Svayaṃbhū hillock as originally the seat of an autochthonous goddess—identified simply as 'Mother' (New. *mā*)—and the building of the stūpa over the rock to serve as her residence.

[21] The quotation of the introductory verses of the *Svayaṃbhūpurāṇa* translation by Lha-mdong Lo-tsā-ba suggests that a copy of the work was still available to Brag-dkar rta-so sPrul-sku when he composed his own guidebook. In the autobiography of Si-tu Paṇ-chen, the four names of the hill which forms the base of Svayaṃbhū are given according to the corrupt manuscript of the text which he obtained in the year 1723; see Chos-kyi 'byung-

gnas: *Dri bral shel gyi me long*, pp. 117.6–118.1 (*shing kun gyi ri 'dir dus bzhi'i rim pas ming 'gyur ste rdzogs ldan gyi su go shringga parba te ste ri glang ru / gsum ldan gyi dus su padma gi ri ste rdo rje padma'i ri / gnyis ldan gyi dus su badzra ka ṭa kardo rje'i zom / rtsod dus su go putstsha par ba ta ste ri glang mjug tu grags shing*). This differs from the version which he translated in 1748; concerning these matters including the Sanskrit equivalents of the four names, see Verhagen (2008:536–537). It should be noted that in the corrupt version the name Gośṛṅga is given to the hill in the Kṛtayuga rather than, as in the translations of Lha-mdong Lo-tsā-ba and Si-tu Paṇ-chen, in the Dvāparayuga. Consult Decleer (2000:42–43) for the full context of this passage and the statement of Si-tu Paṇ-chen's that the error in regarding the Gośṛṅga hill of the Kṛtayuga as the Svayaṃbhū hillock led to the mistaken identification of Go-ma-sa-la-gan-dha with the stūpa in Nepal.

22 The description of the Gośṛṅga hillock and its flora and fauna was included by the Fourth Khams-sprul in his pilgrimage guide, where he adds two species of monkeys; see bsTan-'dzin chos-kyi nyi-ma: *Yul chen nye ba'i tshandhoha bal po'i gnas kyi dkar chag*, pp. 164.6–165.3 (*khams sna tshogs pa du mas rnam par bkra ba / nā ga ge sar dang / tsam pa ka dang / ba ku la dang / piṣpa la dang / ko bi dā ra dang / plakṣa dang / ka pī ta na dang / tu nna dang / ku ba la ka dang / a shwa ka dang / tā lā dang / ta mā la sogs pa'i ljon shing dang 'khri shing sna tshogs pa bkram pa nyin mtshan kun tu 'dab chags sna tshogs pas skad snyan 'byin cing spra dang spre'u ri dvags rnams kyis gang ba zhig yod do*) and Macdonald & Dvags-po Rin-po-che (1981:241). He further adds some observations on the special quality of the blossoms of campaka trees, which, he says, should not be confused with the ones growing in Tibet. In this regard, literary sources like the *Kāvyādarśa* and the *Bodhisattvāvadanakalpalatā* are quoted; see *Yul chen nye ba'i tshandhoha bal po'i gnas kyi dkar chag*, pp. 165.3–166.3, and Macdonald & Dvags-po Rin-po-che (1981:241–242).

23 See *Bal yul rang byung mchod rten chen po'i lo rgyus*, chapter 1, pp. 230.4–231.5.

24 The emergence of the crystal-like Dharmadhātu from the multi-petalled lotos in the lake Nāgāsthana is recounted by the Fourth Khams-sprul in a paraphrase of the *Svayaṃbhūpurāṇa*, which he refers to as the authoritative narrative among those found in either the 'Indian and Newari treatises' (*rgya bal gyi bstan bcos*); the 'Tibetan histories' (*bod kyi lo rgyus*) call the lake instead *mTsho go ma [de vi / de ba]*. His purpose was to give the correct name of the lake in contrast to the one known from the older pilgrimage guidebooks; see bsTan-'dzin chos-kyi nyi-ma: *Yul chen po nye ba'i tshandhoha bal po'i gnas kyi dkar chag*, pp. 175.2–5 (*mtsho de nyid las shing rta'i 'phang lo'i tshad kyi rin chen sna lnga las grub pa'i padma'i 'dab ma stong dang ldan pa'i ze'u 'bru la de bzhin gshegs pa rnams kyi thugs chos kyi dbyings kyi rang bzhin gyi rten rnam pa shel gyi mchod rten khru gang ba zhig sangs rgyas gtsug tor can gyi dus na rang byung du skyes pa yin par bshad / mtsho de yi ming yang bod kyi lo rgyus la ni mtsho go ma de vi zer / rgya bal gyi bstan bcos la ni klu'i gnas zhes bya bar grags so*), and Macdonald & Dvags-po Rin-po-che (1981:246). Concerning the name *mTsho go ma [de ba]* for the lake, see Ngag-dbang rdo-rje: *Bal yul 'Phags pa shing dang de'i gnas rnams kyi dkar chag*, pp. 44.13–14 & 21; compare bSod-nams dpal bzang-po: *Dus gsum sangs rgyas thams cad thugs kyi rten 'phags pa shing kun gyi dkar chag*, p. 84.2, and Ehrhard (2013:78).

25 See *Bal yul rang byung mchod rten chen po'i lo rgyus*, chapter 1, pp. 232.3–233.6.

26 The second chapter of the *Svyaṃbhūpurāṇa* has the title 'An Exposition of the Fruits of Making Offerings [to the Svayaṃbhūcaitya]' (*mchod pa'i 'bras bu nges par bstan pa*); see *Bal yul rang byung mchod rten chen po'i lo rgyus*, pp. 234.1–236.4.

[27] *See Bal yul rang byung mchod rten chen po'i lo rgyus, chapter 3, pp. 236.6-237.2.*

[28] See *Bal yul rang byung mchod rten chen po'i lo rgyus*, chapter 3, pp. 237.3–238.1.

[29] The Fourth Khams-sprul provides the Sanskrit *mādhāra* for the original name of 'Sword Lake' and *dha nā da ha* as the Newari; see bsTan-'dzin chos-kyi nyi-ma: *Yul chen po nye ba'i tshandhoha bal po gnas kyi dkar chag*, pp. 176.5–177.1 (*'on kyang de yi lhag ma mtsho chung ngu zhig lus pa ni mā dhā ra ste kun 'dzin zhes bya ba'i mtsho 'di gcig pu gnas so / zhes grags / mtsho de yi ming la da lta bod rnams kyis ni mtsho ral gri zer / bal po rnams dha nā da ha zhes brjod kyin 'dug*), and Macdonald & Dvags-po Rin-po-che (1981:247). The latter local name is also found in the next passage of the *Svayaṃbhūpurāṇa*; in a gloss on Si-tu Paṇ-chen's translation, the Sanskrit is given as *ādhara*. The lake is located one mile north of the Chobāra gorge and known today as Taudā (Great Lake); for the mention of it in the so-called Wright Chronicle, see Bajracharya, Michaels & Gutschow (2016, vol. 1:1–2, note 16).

[30] In the biographical tradition of Padmasambhava as transmitted in the extensive versions of the *Padma bka'i thang yig*, Lake Bal-yul nyi-ma khud is mentioned on two occasions: first when the master is invited to Tibet by royal messengers, and second, on the occasion when his disciple Rlangs dPal-gyi seng-ge is killed by a huge nāgā in its waters; see O-rgyan gling-pa: *U rgyan gu ru padma 'byung gnas kyi skyes rabs rnam par thar pa rgyas par bkod pa*, chapter 59, p. 147.11–17 & chapter 79, pp. 186.1–197.2. For a different account of the two episodes, see Sangs-rgyas gling-pa: *O rgyan gu ru padma 'byung gnas kyi rnam thar rgyas pa gser gyi phreng ba*, chapter 55, pp. 231.17–232.6 & chapter 69, pp. 274.7–275.8.

[31] See *Bal yul rang byung mchod rten chen po'i lo rgyus*, chapter 3, p. 238.1–4. This identification of Nepal as an *upapīṭha* can be regarded as the second tradition mentioned in the text linked to the *Saṃvarodayatantra*; for Godāvarī, see note 6. The third chapter of the *Svayaṃbhūpurāṇa* has the title 'An Elucidation of the *Upacchandoha*' (*nye pa tshandoha rab tu gsal ba*), while the passage concerning this identification and the goddess Kākāmukhī is also referred to in a long passage in the Fourth Khams-sprul's guidebook; see bsTan-'dzin Chos-kyi nyi-ma: *Yul chen po nye ba'i tshandhoha bal po gnas kyi dkar chag*, p. 187.1–3 (*des na de lta bu'i rten rang byung da lta rang cag bod yul gyi gnas chen gangs ti se dang pre ta pu ri tsā ri tra la sogs pa rnams su'ang 'byung ba bzhin du bal po'i yul 'di nyid kyang yul chen po nye ba'i tshandhohar grags pa'i snying po'i rten rang byung ni pāśu pa ti dang gu hya shwa rī zhes pa'i rten 'di gnyis yin*) & pp. 187.6–188.2 (*rgyu mtshan de phyir gu ti shwa ri (= gu hya shwa rī) grags pa'i gnas 'di yang yin lugs don dam pa'i dbang du byas na sngar yang bshad pa ltar yum rdo rje phag mo'i bhaga'am yang na sa la spyod pa'i dpa' mo'i dbang phyug bya gdong ma 'khor grangs med pa dang bcas te dgyes par rol pa'i gnas su rang byung mchod rten gyi dkar chag las bshad*), and Macdonald & Dvags-po Rin-poche (1981:251). The first section addresses the notion that a pīṭha is always characterized by one or more 'self-manifested sacred objects' (*rten rang byung*); in the case of the *upapīṭha* known as Himavat, these are the lingam and yoni of Paśupatinātha and Guhyeśvari. The identity of the female goddess is taken up in the second section, which refers to her, as does the *Svayaṃbhūpurāṇa*, as either Vajravārāhī or Kākāmukhī; consult Decleer (2000:50–51) for the identity of the latter goddess, known from the Vajrayoginī cycle.

[32] See *Bal yul rang byung mchod rten chen po'i lo rgyus*, chapter 3, p. 239.1–2.

[33] See *Bal yul rang byung mchod rten chen po'i lo rgyus*, chapter 4, p. 239.3–4.

[34] See *Bal yul rang byung mchod rten chen po'i lo rgyus*, chapter 4, p. 239.5–6.

[35] See *Bal yul rang byung mchod rten chen po'i lo rgyus*, chapter 4, p. 241.2–4.

[36] The fourth chapter of the *Svayaṃbhūpurāṇa* gives, after Śaṅkhaparvata, the names of further mountains, beginning with the one called Nor-bu brtsegs-pa. This latter is associated with the Bodhisattva Nor-bu'i gtsug and the origin of a further river known as Maṇilohinī: see *Bal yul rang byung mchod rten chen po'i lo rgyus*, pp. 241.6–242.2 (*'dod chags dang bral ba gcig ni dung gi ri 'di ni dang nye bar nor bu brtsegs pa'i ri zhes bya ba / sngon byang chub sems dpa' nor bu'i gtsug ting nge 'dzin la bzhugs nas nam zhig na rang gis gtsug gi nor bu phral te gang du sbyin pa byin pas / maṇi kū ṭa zhes grags pa'i ri bo phang ba 'dir rab tu byung ngo / der da lta'i tshe yang 'dod chags dang bral ba'i gnas der maṇi linga zhes grags so / de bzhin du dung gi ri bo'i nor bu brtsegs pa'i rtse nas 'bab pa'i chu bo 'di yang nor bu'i gtsug gi khrag lhung pa chu dang 'dres pa'i phyir da lta yang ma ṇi lo hi nī zhes grags so*). Except for the names of these mountains, other information relating to them—their exact locations and further legends—were obviously not known to such Tibetan travellers to the Kathmandu Valley as Brag-dkar rta-so sPrul-sku. For the source of the river Bagmati and its origin on Śivapuri according to the Wright Chronicle, see Bajracharya, Michaels & Gutschow (2016, vol. 1:2).

[37] See *Bal yul rang byung mchod rten chen po'i lo rgyus,* chapter 4, pp. 242.6–243.1.

[38] The fifth chapter of the *Svayaṃbhūpurāṇa* has the title 'Thorough Praise of the Tīrthas [associated with the Svayaṃbhūcaitya]' (*gnas kyi bsngags pa rnam par nges pa*); see *Bal yul rang byung mchod rten chen po'i lo rgyus*, pp. 243.1–246.6.

[39] See *Bal yul rang byung mchod rten chen po'i lo rgyus*, chapter 6, pp. 247.1-3.

[40] See *Bal yul rang byung mchod rten chen po'i lo rgyus*, chapter 6, pp. 247.4–248.3. A similar legend featuring the bhikṣu Dharmaśrīmitra and Mañjuśrī is contained in the Wright Chronicle. There the field ploughed by Mañjuśrī, located in an area lying north of the Thamel quarter of Kathmandu, is called Sāvābhūmi; see Bajracharya, Michaels & Gutschow (2016, vol. 1:5).

[41] See *Bal yul rang byung mchod rten chen po'i lo rgyus*, chapter 6, pp. 249.5–250.1.

[42] See *Bal yul rang byung mchod rten chen po'i lo rgyus*, chapter 6, p. 251.2–3.

[43] A similar critique of the popular designation 'Noble All Trees' (*'phags pa shing kun*) for the Svayaṃbhūcaitya had also been delivered by the Fourth Khams-sprul in his guidebook, wherein he points out that such a story was not known to contemporary Newar Buddhists; see bsTan-'dzin chos-kyi nyi-ma: *Yul chen po nye ba'i tsandho ha bal po'i gnas kyi dkar chag*, p.173.1–5 (*mchod rten chen po 'phags pa shing kun 'di / bod rnams la grags pa'i ngag rgyun gyi dbang du byas na bal po'i yul du 'dod cing mchod rten go ma sa la gandha yang 'di yin pa dang / de yang rgyal po bi pa de was bzhengs pa'i mchod rten du byed / ming gi sgra bshad kyang slob dpon klu sgrub kyis dbu skra gtor nas ri 'di la shing sna kun tshang ba skye bar gyur cig zhes smon lam btab bzhin du byung bas 'phags pa shin kun du grags zhes zer / 'on kyang de lta bu'i ming dang lo rgyus gnyis la mi 'thad par mngon te / ci'i phyir zhe na rgya bal gyi skad la shing kun zer ba'i skad dod lo rgyus de dang bstun na 'byung dgos pa la de mi snang zhing / da lta bal yul du yod pa'i nang pa rnams la'ang lo rgyus de yi cha tsam yang mi 'dug pa'i phyir na mi 'thad do*), and Macdonald & Dvags-po Rin-po-che (1981:245–246). For the story of the twenty thousand Arhats and Ārya Nāgārjuna in the older guidebook, see Ngag-dbang rdo-rje: *Bal yul mchod rten 'phags pa shing kun dang de'i gnas gzhan rnams kyi dkar chag*, p. 44.29–34. The story is not recorded in bSod-

nams dpal-bzang-po's guidebook, where Ārya Nāgārjuna is described as a custodian of the Svayaṃbhūcaitya.

[44] See *Bal yul rang byung mchod rten chen po'i lo rgyus*, chapter 7, p. 252.1–5.

[45] The narrative of Śantiśrī, who was responsible for covering the crystal-like Dharmadhātu-caitya and thus creating the actual stūpa of Svayaṃbhūnāth, is included in the Fourth Khams-sprul's guidebook. The detail is added that Śantiśrī put his mark on the former residence of the Vajrācārya 'Jam-pa'i lha by erecting a stūpa known as the 'Mañjuśrī Caitya' (*'jam dpal mchod rten*); see bsTan-'dzin chos-kyi nyi-ma: *Yul chen po nye ba'i tshandho ha bal po gnas kyi dkar chag*, pp. 179.1–180.1 (*de nas dus gzhan zhig na rgya gar gau ḍi'i yul du rdo rje sems dpa'i sprul pa'i sku rgyal po pra tsanda de wa ste rab tshim lha zhes bya ba byung ste de 'khor ba'i bde ba 'gyur ba'i rang bzhin can la yid 'byung nas rang gi bu shakti de wa ste nus pa'i lha zhes bya rgyal srid la bzhag nas 'ongs ste / mchod rten 'di'i drung du rab tu byung nas rdo rje sems dpa'i brtul zhugs gzung ste mtshan yang rdo rje slob dpon shanti śrī ste zhi ba'i dpal zhes bya des chos dbyings gsung gi dbang phyug rang byung mchod rten de nyid rab tu bsrung ba'i phyir steng nas rdul gyis g.yogs shing phyi rol du mchod rten kyi gzugs su byas te / rang byung gi rten de yi snying por bzhugs su gsol / de yi tshe na shanti śrī de nyid kyis rdo rje slob dpon 'jam pa'i lha gang du yun ring po bzhugs pa'i gnas dang de yi mthu stobs gsal bar bya ba'i ched du mchod rten brtsigs pa ni da lta 'jam dpal mchod rten du grags pa 'di nyid do*), and Macdonald & Dvags-po Rin-po-che (1981:248). According to the Wright chronicle, the root of the lotus flower which supports the Dharmadhātu-caitya starts at Guhyeśvari; see Bajracharya, Michaels & Gutschow (2016, vol. 1:2).

[46] For this episode in the biography of the translator, who stayed in Mang-yul Gung-thang and the Nepal Valley between the years 1196 and 1198, see Byams-pa'i dpal: *Paṇ grub gsum gyi rnam thari dpag bsam 'khri shing*, fol. 18a/2–4 (*bal yul gyi 'phags pa shing kun gyi byang nub na / sngon bal yul gyi rgyal po 'od zer go cha bya bas lha mo 'od zer can bsgrubs) nas klu'i rgyal po bi ka ra (= bi kā ra) sngon po bya ba'i ska (= ske) ral gris bcad te / de yi spyi bo na rin po che 'o ma 'dzin bya ba yod pa de 'phags pa'i mchod rten gyi tog la phul yod skad / klu de'i shul na klu gtor dang klu mchod shes pas mchod na de'i rgyud la lhag mtsho la yo byad kyi phan 'dogs byed pa gcig yod par gda' bas de la bag re mchod pa gyis dang / lo tstsha ba bya cha rkyen kyi 'phongs pa cig 'ong pa'i nyen che ba yin gsung / de mchod pa'i cho ga 'dra mnga'am zhus pas / 'phags pa shing kun gyi lho shar gyi phyogs ri'i steng gi lha khang gi sgo la 'brug ris bris pa'i gcig na / hi tu drug gul gcig yod pas de la zhus cig gsung / phyis de la zhus pas yon se ka (= gser kha) 'dra (= phra) men mang po dbul dgos par byung ste phan yon che bar byung ngo*). These details of different sites in the vicinity of Svayaṃbhū where offerings should be performed are told prior to the arrival of Khro-phu Lo-tsā-ba in sKyid-grong and his departure thence to the Nepal Valley. Byams-pa'i dpal was staying at the time at the monastery of the siddha Klong-rtse-pa (12$^{th}$/13$^{th}$ cent.) in Mang-yul, and it was the latter who related the story of the nāgā-king and the place north-west of Svayaṃbhūnāth to the departing traveller. Concerning Klong-rtse-pa and his monastery Klong-rtse dpal-gyi yang-dgon, see Ehrhard (2004:287 & 427, note 205).

[47] The question of the religious identity of the two *śikhara* temples located in front of the Mahācaitya is also raised in the Fourth Khams-sprul's guidebook; see bsTan-'dzin chos-kyi nyi-ma: *Yul chen po nye ba'i tsandho ha bal po gnas kyi dkar chag*, pp. 182.1–5 (*shar phyogs nye ba'i cha na yod pa'i mchod rten gnyis ni / kha cig gis phyi rol pa'i mchod rten yin cing gter lung 'ga' las kyang bal yul rang byung mchod rten gyi mdun du rten mche ba lta*

*bu gnyis byung ba'i dus zhes byung bas 'di lta bu shin tu mi shis pa yin zer / la la ni mchod rten de yi sgo khang sogs dngos su mthong ba'i gnas na'ang nang pa'i lha sku yang yod cing dbyibs phyi pa'i mchod rten lta bur yod kyang rdor rje gdan gyi ganddho la'i bkod pa rnams la'ang phyi nas bltas na 'di dang 'dra ba rung du yod pas nang pa'i mchod rten yin zer ba sogs bshad sgros mi 'dra ba mang du 'dug pas re zhig brtag par bya'o*), and Macdonald & Dvags-po Rin-po-che (1981:249). The prophecy from a treasure text about the time when Svayaṃbhūnāth appeared to display two fangs has still to be identified.

48 See *Bal yul rang byung mchod rten chen po'i lo rgyus*, chapter 7, pp. 252.6–253.3. The Fourth Khams-sprul's guidebook lists the five towns according to the *Svayaṃbhūpurāṇa*. In the case of Śāntipuri, the story of King Guṇakāmadeva saving the land of Nepal from a seven-year-long period without rainfall—from the eighth chapter of the *Svayaṃbhūpurāṇa*—is added; see bsTan-'dzin chos-kyi nyi-ma: *Yul chen po nye ba'i tshandho ha bal po'i gnas gyi dkar chags*, p. 180.1–6 (*de nas kyang zhi ba'i dpal gyis grong khyer lnga po rnams kyang byas te shanta pu ri zhi ba'i grong / ba su pu ri nor gyi grong / agni pu ri me yi grong / nāga pu ri klu yi grong / vāyu pu ri rlung gi grong rnams te / de rnams so sor sa yi lha dang chu yi lha me yi lha rlung gi lha ste lha lnga yang gnas bar byas pas dus ring po'i bar du yang bal po'i yul du lo legs 'bru 'phel ba sogs bkra shis pa'i dge mtshan du ma dang ldan pa la / lan gcig lo bdun gyi bar du yang char ma babs pas lo nyes chen po byung ba la bal po'i rgyal po gu ṇa kā ma de wa ste yon tan 'dod pa'i lha zhes bya bas śānta pu rir grub pa'i slob dpon zhi ba'i dpal gyis spyan sngar 'ongs nas char 'bebs par gsol ba btab des kyang der klu bsgrubs nas grub pa'i mthar klu yi rgyal po rnams sngags kyis bkug nas char 'bebs par byas so*), and Macdonald & Dvags-po Rin-po-che (1981:248–249). On the ensuing critique of misconceptions arising from this account in regard to where the nāgas had originally been propitiated by Ārya Nāgārjuna, and to the source of the central part of his rosary, see note 109.

49 See Kun-dga' snying-po: *Dam pa'i chos rin po che 'phags pa'i yul du ji ltar dar ba'i tshul gsal bar ston pa dgos 'dod kun byung*, pp. 286.3–287.6. The quite extensive description of the life of Vāgīśvarakīrti can be found in the 33rd chapter of Tāranātha's history, which deals with the reign of the Pala king Canaka and the lives of the 'Six Gatekeeper Scholars' (*mkhas pa sgo drug*) in Vikramaśīla; for an evaluation of this hagiographic account of Vāgīśvarakīrti and his role as an early recipient of the *Kālacakratantra* teachings and as a teacher within the Tārā cult, see Schneider (2010:32–34). Vāgīśvarakīrti is especially known as the author of the *Mṛtyuvañcanopadeśa ('Chi ba slu ba'i man ngag)*, 'Instruction on Cheating Death', translated by Atiśa and Rin-chen bzang-po (958–1055); on this work and further tantric writings of Vāgīśvarakīrti, see Schneider (2010:17–23 & 31–32). Concerning the association of the Śāntapuri temple and the sixty-two-deity Cakrasaṃvara maṇḍala with the Nepalese king Aṃśuvarman, see note 53.

50 For the sketch of the life of Mahāpaṇḍita Vanaratna in the work of the Fourth 'Brug-chen, see Padma dkar-po: *Chos 'byung bstan pa'i padma rgyas pa'i nyin byed*, pp. 230.19–233.19. The various spiritual encounters of Vanaratna with Mahāsiddha Śavaripa can be reconstructed with the help of the biography of the former written by 'Gos Lo-tsā-ba (1392–1481). The first face-to-face meeting is said to have occurred in Śrī Parvata in India, followed by a second—visionary—meeting in Magadha; see gZhon-nu dpal: *mKhas pa chen po dpal nags kyi rin chen gyi rnam par thar pa*, pp. 24.4–25.2 & 31.2–3. The next two meetings took place in the temple of Śāntapuri in Svayaṃbhūnāth, where Śavaripa manifested the thirteen-deity maṇḍala of Cakrasaṃvara for Vanaratna during the final vision; see ibid., pp. 36.6–7 & 68.7–72.7. Khrims-khang Lo-tsā-ba bSod-nams rgya-mtsho (1424–1482) visited the temple

of Śāntapuri in the company of Vanaratna in the year 1466; see Ehrhard (2002:68–69). At that time legends about the presence of Vāgīśvarakīrti in Śāntapuri were still alive. It is also reported that a stone image of Śavaripa was erected by the Mahāpaṇḍita on the hill to the west of Kathmandu. The Fourth Khams-sprul had access to the biography of Vanaratna, and in his guidebook provides details of the latter's sojourns in Nepal; the final section points out the initial stay at Śāntapuri, various visions he had of Vāgīśvarakīrti and Śavaripa, and the site of the relic shrine. See bsTan-'dzin Chos-kyi nyi-ma: *Yul chen po nye ba'i tshandho ha bal po gnas kyi dkar chag gangs can rna ba'i bdud rtsi*, pp. 205.6–206.4 (*spyir paṇ chen nags kyi rin chen 'di bal por rgyun ring bzhugs pa las thog mar shanta pu ri na bzhugs pa'i tshe lhan cig skye pa'i ye shes ji bzhin pa mngon du mdzad / slob dpon ngag dbang grags pa dang 'jam dpal sha wa ri dbang phyug kyang shanta pu ri dang go bi tsandra'i gtsug lag khang la sogs pa bal po'i yul 'di kun na bzhugs pa'i tshe yang yang zhal gzigs shing sbyor drug nye brgyud kyang gsungs / gnas bdag ha ri siddhi yang bran du bkol / phyis mya ngan las 'das nas sku gdung yam bu ye rang gnyis kyi bar dur khrod ra ma do li zhes bya ba na bzhugs la gzhan par bshad pa de ni da lta'ang bal po'i dur khrod du byed cing ming yang ra ma do li rang zer*), and Macdonald & Dvags-po Rin-po-che (1981:260).

[51] On the murals based on the *Svayaṃbhūpurāṇa* in the vestibule of Śāntipuri, which is open to the public, see von Rospatt (2014:45–54). Reference is made there to Brag-dkar rta-so sPrul-sku's description during his visit to the temple at the end of the 18th century, which attests that the murals were already regarded as old during that time. Consult von Rospatt (2014:54–65) for the origin of the paintings in an initiative undertaken by Pratāpa Malla (r. 1641–1674), whose various forms of engagement with Svayaṃbhūnāth also included the project of redesigning the temple's vestibule.

[52] This quotation is from a work devoted to fumigation rituals for different protective deities at various religious sites; see Padma dkar-po: *bSangs dpe bkra shis re skong*, pp. 273.4–5 *(bsre mkhar gnas pa'i ma ru rtse / beg rtse ming sring gsham pas bskor / śānta pu rir gnas pa yi / tshogs bdag glang po'i gdong pa can / skye bu chen po rdo rje legs / mched 'khor sum brgya drug cu'i gtso / de vi ko ṭi la dga' ba'i / snyon kha'i rje btsan brtsan rgod de).*

[53] On this passage and Brag-dkar rta-so sPrul-sku's critique of the pseudo-etymology of a local protector of Śāntipuri called Upāsaka Śāntaputri, see Decleer (2000:45). During gTsang-smyon Heruka's time the Śāntapuri temple was known as the 'shrine of dGe-bsnyen Śān-ta spu-gri' (*dge bsnyen śānta spu gri'i lha khang*), and a biography of the former describes a vision he had of the protective deity revealing himself to be Vinayaka, or Gaṇapati; see sNa-tshogs rang-grol: *gTsang smyon he ru ka phyogs thams las rnam par rgyal ba'i rnam thar rdo rje theg pa'i gsal byed nyi ma'i snying po*, pp. 174.4–175.5. This occurred when the Holy Madman of gTsang had returned to Nepal for his second visit around the year 1496. During the vision he was requested by Gaṇapati to undertake a restoration of Svayaṃbhūnāth, which resulted in his first whitewashing of the Mahācaitya in the spring of the following year; see Larsson (2011:215–216). In the old pilrimage guidebook, it is stated that during the Newar king Aṃśuvarman's time Ārya Nāgārjuna acted as custodian of Svayaṃbhūnāth, and that the site of the local protector, known as Śāntaputri, was his 'chamber for spiritual practice' (*sgrub khang*); see bSod-nams dpal bzang-po, *Dus gsum sangs rgyas thams cad kyi thugs kyi rten 'phags pa shing kun gyi dkar chag* pp. 85.6–87.2, and Ehrhard (2013:79, note 12). The source of the protector's name seems to be one found in the narrative of a Newar king who joined a gaṇacakra in the inner cavern of the temple and prayed to be allowed into the sacred realm again in the future; he was then transformed into an ox, and the king's bones into the sixty-two-deity Cakrasaṃvara maṇḍala. The gate to this cavern,

known as Śāntapuri, is impassable owing to a circle of swords (*gri'i 'khor lo*). The latter feature is related to prophecies about King Aṃśuvarman in the *Mañjuśrīmūlatantra*; see the historiographical work of gTsug-lag phreng-ba: *Dam pa'i chos kyi 'khor lo bsgyur ba rnams kyi byung bar gsal bar byed pa mkhas pa'i dga' ston*, pp. 173.11–174.3, and Ehrhard (2013: 77–78, note 9).

[54] Brag-dkar rta-so sPrul-sku wrote a work dedicated specifically to *gtor-ma*s and the local deities (including 'Phrog-ma and her five hundred sons to whom these kind of offerings are made); see Chos-kyi dbang-phyug: *Chu sbying gtor ma brgya rtsa phan bde'i gru rdzings kyi dmigs khrid rnam bshad*, pp. 109.4–110.2 (*rtsa bar / bdun pa 'brog gnas mched lnga dang : 'phrog ma'i bu lnga brgya dang : 'dzam bu gling gi klu gnyan sa bdag thams cad dang : 'byung ba chen po bzhi'i lha dang : lha srin sde brgyad pa 'khor dang bcad pa thams cad la ster ro sbyin no : zhes pa / 'brog gnas te gnod sbyin mched lnga dang / ha ri ti ste 'phrog ma ma bu lnga brgya dang bcas pa la bsngo zhing / klu gnyan sa bdag sogs ni sngar gong du song ba ltar ro*). Sitalā or Hārītī (the Buddhist equivalent of the Brahmanical name) is considered as the goddess of smallpox, and is ardently worshipped in the Kathmandu Valley; see Slusser (1982:328–329) concerning this mother goddess and the devastating epidemic at the end of the 18th century in which the favourite queen of King Rana Bahadur Shah (r. 1777–1799) died. The destruction of her shrine by a "king of Gorkha" can be attributed to this ruler, who was maddened with grief by this loss and had the heartless Svayaṃbhū Hārītī dragged from her sanctuary.

[55] The Fourth Khams-sprul offers a detailed account in his guidebook of the perfectly crafted Mahākāla statue, and highlights its role as a protector of the Svayaṃbhūnāth Stūpa. He refers as well to the damage caused by the Moslem army, adding a further detail on the results of the fierceful look of the statue in the direction of the Mahācaitya. The toponym 'Tibetan Grounds' (*bod thang*) is explained in the narrative: during Srong-btsan sgam-po's rule a Tibetan delegation under the minister mGar used the site for camping purposes when they came to invite the Nepalese princess Khri-btsun, daughter of King Aṃśuvarman, to Tibet; see bsTan-'dzin Chos-kyi nyi-ma: *Yul chen po nye ba'i tshandho ha bal po'i gnas kyi dkar chag gangs can rna ba'i bdud rtsi*, pp. 197.5–199.3 (*bod thang mngon po ni la las rang byung du byung ba yin par byed / kha cig gis slob dpon klu sgrub kyis nag po chen po'i sku brgya rtsa brgyad bzhengs nas bstan pa spyi dang khyad par rdo rje gdan la sogs pa gnas chen rnams kyi srung mar bskos pa'i nang tshan rang byung mchod rten chen po'i srung mar bskos pa'i sku yin cing klu sgrub rang gi phyag bzos yin yang zer / gang ltar byin rlabs kyi tshan kha mchog dang ldan cing bzo khyad kyang phul du phyin pa / lhan cig skyes pa'am rtsa ba'i mgon po sku rgyu rdo nag las grub pa zhal gcig phyag gnyis gri gug dang thod khrag thugs kar 'dzin cing kha ṭvaṃ ga (= khaṭvāṅga) phrag pa la bkal ba zhabs mnyam pa'i stabs su bam ro'i steng na bzhengs pa zhig yod / sngon dus bar skabs shig yul 'dir kla klo'i dmag byung ste sku 'di bshig par brtsams pas bshig ma nus pa ma zad bal bo'i yul kun na kla klo'i bstan pa da dung yang ma byung ba 'di yin / 'on kyang de skabs ro gdan gyi cha shas 'ga' dang sku dngos rang gi'ang shangs kyi rtse mo sogs la nyams chag phran bu byung ba 'dug / sku gzugs 'di'ang rang byung mchod rten chen por zhal bstan nas yod / shin tu gnyan pas zhal bstan phyogs kyi gdong der khrong khyer sngar chags pa rnams la'ang mi shis pa sna tshogs byung nas yul stongs pa yin zer da lta grong med / sku 'di sngon ye rang dang nye ba'i ri bo phu lla ḍo zhes pa'i rtse mor bzhugs pa nam mkha'i lam nas 'phur shing gshegs nas bod thang du phebs par grags / de la bod thang zer ba ni sngon chos rgyal srong btsan sgam po'i skabs blon po mgar sogs bod kyi gnye'o (= gnye bo) rnams der bsdad cing bal mo bza' khri btsun la rgyal po 'od zer go chas rdzongs btab pa'i*

*gnas yin pas bod thang du grags so*), and Macdonald & Dags-po Rin-po-che (1981:256–257).

56 The spectacle of gTsang-smyon joining hands with the Mahākāla statue and dancing with him is based on the biography written by lHa-btsun. There it is stated that news of this vision, which occurred specifically among Newar lay devotees called *bha-ri-mas*, was spread by them far and wide; see Rin-chen rnam-rgyal: *Grub thob gtsang smyon pa'i rnam thar dad pa'i spu long g.yo' ba (= g.yo ba)*, p. 43.5–6 (*ba ri ma rnams kyi mthong snang la mgon po dang rje nyid phyag sbrel te / tso ba ri'i phyir byon nas bro brdung mdzad pa mthong bas / ba ri ma rnams ya mtshan zhing 'jigs nas re rang gi gnas su bros / mi kun la de ltar zlo bar gyur to*). The term *co pa ri* or *tso ba ri* describes a simple shrine which housed the Mahākāla statue before the pagoda temple was built; this reference I owe to Hubert Decleer.

57 The description of the Protector of the Tibetan Grounds is taken from the colophon of the work of Kaḥ-thog Rig-'dzin, which was completed in 1754; see Tshe-dbang nor-bu: *dPal nag po chen po phyag gnyis pa'i sku brnyan rang byung bod thang mgon por bstod cing 'phrin las gsol ba'i tshig phreng bzhes don lhun gyis grub pa'i dbyangs*, p. 327.1–4 (*bal yul du bod thang mgon po zhes rdo las rang byung du grub par yang bzhes cing / kha cig gi (= gis) mgon po klu sgrub kyi phyag gis bskrun par yang 'dod la / gang ltar sngon ye rang dang nye ba'i ri bor phul la ḍo zhes pa'i rtse mor yod pa nam mkha' 'phur ste bod thang du bab par bal yul kun tu grags gyur ....*). For the description of the statue according to this text, see Kaschewsky (1982:430). gTsang-smyon Heruka's encounter with the magnificent Mahākāla statue took place during his first visit to the Kathmandu Valley around the year 1477; see sNa-tshogs rang-grol: *gTsang smyon he ru ka phyogs thams las rnam par rgyal ba'i rnam thar rdo rje theg pa'i gsal byed nyi ma'i snying po*, p. 49.2–4, and Larsson (2011:212). The statue's association with the Aural Transmission of Ras-chung-pa can be dated to the second visit and the successful whitewashing of Svayaṃbhūnāth. At that time the statue of the Bod-thang mgon-po is called a 'master of the teaching' (*chos bdag*) of the transmission, which was then being disseminated to a wide group of disciples; see ibid., p. 175.5–6 (*de nas sku dkar gyi mdzad pa rnams legs par grub pa / 'di'i res la gtso bor bod thang mgon po snyan rgyud yid bzhin nor bu'i chos bdag yin phyir / gcig rgyud bka' rgya las grol nas yi ger bkod pa la bar chad med pa'i btang rag / slar yang bsrung mar mnga' gsol ba bu slob rnams la ye shes mgon po'i dbang rjes su gnang ba rnams mdzad*).

58 On two prior renovations of the Svayaṃbhūnāth stūpa in the 13th and 15th centuries according to Tibetan sources, see Ehrhard (2013:67–70). The earlier of the two—presumably in the first half of the 13th century—was undertaken by a member of the Tshal-pa bKa'-brgyud-pa school, concerning which it has been argued that this event involved the replacement of the 'central mast' (*yaṣṭi*) under the first chief administrator of Sa-skya rule, nominated by 'Phags-pa Blo-gros rgyal-mtshan (1235–1280); see von Rospatt (2001:200–201) and von Rospatt (2011:163–168). The historiographical source for the renovation is Kun-dga' rdo-rje: *Deb ther dmar pa*, pp. 146.19–147.9. It should be noted that according to this description the new *yaṣṭi* replaced an old one said to have been erected by Ārya Nāgārjuna himself.

59 One narrative of the renovation undertaken by gTsang-smyon Heruka and his disciples in the year 1504 is that in sNa-tshogs rang-grol: *gTsang smyon he ru ka phyogs thams cad las rnam par rgyal ba'i rnam thar rdo rje theg pa'i gsal byed nyi ma'i snying po*, pp. 208.4–235.3. The register of the renovation, which contains a carefully recorded list of all the donors and their donations can be found ibid., pp. 220.6–226.2.; the full amount of gold needed for this undertaking is mentioned in ibid., pp. 224.7–225.1 (*phyed rin tsam song rtsis pa'i*

*gser zho ni / nyis stong bdun rgya [=brgya] lnga bcu rtsa gcig song / song be de dag byung du'ang shes par bya / de ltar byung shing song bar gyur pa ni / kho bos bgyis pa'i zhig bsos 'di gong gi / sbyin bdag bal bod 'dres pa'i 'khor bcas mang*). Concerning the fact that only the upper part of the Mahācaitya was renovated at that time, see von Rospatt (2001:206). Consult Larsson (2011:217–225) for the individual stages of the renovation, and in particular the four pillars that supported the regal parasol covered with an alloy of copper and gold.

60 The renovations of lHa-btsun Rin-chen rnam-rgyal occurred about twenty-five years after the one by gTsang-smyon Heruka, and after the stūpa was demolished by the Magar troops of the king of Palpa; see von Rospatt (2001:207–208). On the vision of gTsang-smyon in the year 1529 and the following events leading to the various efforts to restore Svayaṃbhūnāth, see Rin-chen rnam-rgyal: *dPal ldan bla ma dam pa mkhas grub lha btsun chos kyi rgyal po'i rnam mgur blo 'das chos sku'i rang gdangs*, fols. 32b/1–38b/1. According to this source, gTsang-smyon's disciple went back and forth between Brag-dkar rta-so and Nepal, the first journey taking place in 1530; the renovation went on for a period of almost ten years, during which time he was only able to do part of the work of adorning the *harmikā* with gilded copper shields. See Clemente (2016:105–106) for the pertinent details according to the autobiography, including the donors involved in the renovation work and other activities of lHa-btsun Rin-chen rnam-rgyal during this period.

61 For the continuation of the earlier renovation of lHa-btsun Rin-chen rnam-rgyal by his disciple from the village of gNas in sKyid-grong, see von Rospatt (2001:200–209). The details of the restoration of the remaining parts of the *harmikā* with gilded copper shields and the embellishment of the rings can be found in the latter's autobiography; see Byams-pa phun-tshogs: *mKhas grub chen po byams pa phun tshogs kyi rnam thar ngo mtshar snang ba'i nyin byed yid bzhin nor bu dgos 'dod kun 'byung dad pa'i 'debs*, fols. 90a/2–91a/3; this section contains details of the amounts of materials used for the renovation and the consecutive consecration ceremonies that took place. Consult Ehrhard (2012:165–166) for this period in the life of Byams-pa phun-tshogs and the dating of the renovation of Svayaṃbhūnāth to the years 1566 to 1572.

62 On this partial renovation of the Mahācaitya undertaken by the Karma bKa'-brgyud-pa hierarch, see von Rospatt (2001:218–219). The pilgrimage of the Sixth Zhva-dmar-pa Chos-kyi dbang-phyug to Nepal in the years 1629/30 is described by him in a separate work bearing the title *Bal yul du bgrod pa'i lam yig nor bu spel ma'i phreng ba*; concerning this text and the individual stages of the journey, see Ehrhard (2013:283–289) and Lamminger (2013: 137–160 & 223–263). During his stay he had contacts with the Newar kings of Kathmandu, Patan and Bhaktapur, and afterwards was escorted by King Lakṣminarasiṃha Malla (r. 1619–1641), Prince Pratāpa Malla and a large retinue back to Tibet. The activities at Svayaṃbhūnāth are also described in historiographical works of the Karma bKa'-brgyud-pa school, wherein it is mentioned that the original plan was to install a golden parasol, but a strong wind kept it from staying in place; see Chos-kyi 'byung-gnas & Tshe-dbang kun-khyab: *sGrub brgyud karma kaṃ tshang brgyud pa rin po che'i rnam par thar pa rab 'byams nor bu zla ba chu shel gyi 'phreng ba*, vol. 2, p. 295.5 (*shing kun la gser gdugs phul na'ang rlung chen pos mi brtan zer bas phyogs bzhir rgyal ba'i rigs bzhi bzhugs pa'i bum pa nor bu rta babs byed pa'i bkod pa mdzes*).

63 According to the Newar sources, the renovation of the Mahācaitya by Rang-rig ras-pa lasted from 1681 to 1683; see von Rospatt (2001:219–222). See note 81 for a renovation of

the Bodhnāth Stūpa by the 'Brug-pa bKa'-brgyud-pa yogin, and note 148 on the gold left over from it.

64 For the renovation of Svayaṃbhūnāth achieved by Kaḥ-thog Rig-'dzin Tshe-dbang nor-bu and his disciples in the years 1751 to 1758, see Ehrhard (2013:55–62). The biography of the master completed by Brag-dkar rta-so sPrul-sku in the year 1819 contains further details of this project, starting with the vision of Mahādeva Gaṇapati and Kumara Kārttikeya in the year 1751 at rGyal gyi śrī-ri in Tshib-ri. The master had stayed before in the monastery of Jo-nang in gTsang, where letters from both Jayaprakāśa Malla, the king of Kathmandu (r. 1735–1768), and Pṛthvīnārāyaṇa Śāha, the ruler of Gorkha (r. 1743–1775), were received, each promising to create no obstacles and to support such an enterprise; see Chos-kyi dbang-phyug: *dPal rig 'dzin chen po rdo rje tshe dbang nor bu'i zhabs kyi rnam par thar pa'i cha shas brjod pa ngo mtshar dad pa'i rol mtsho*, p. 104.21–27. Consult von Rospatt (2001:225–233) for the Newar sources of this extended renovation.

65 The diplomatic mission of Kaḥ-thog Rig-'dzin to Western Tibet in order to settle a conflict between the kingdom of Ladakh and the kingdom of Purig is described in Schwieger (1997:220–228) and Schwieger (1999:33–87). A period of 17 months was spent in Ladakh, lasting from September 1752 to February 1754. The master's final visit to the Kathmandu Valley and his reflections on the pending restoration of Svayaṃbhūnāth occurred in the autumn of 1754. Regarding this occasion, the previous efforts and individual contributions by gTsang-smyon Heruka, lHa-btsun Rin-chen rnam-rgyal and gNas Rab-'byams-pa Byams-pa phun-tshogs are mentioned as well by Chos-kyi dbang-phyug: *dPal rig 'dzin chen po rdo rje tshe dbang nor bu'i rnam par thar pa'i cha shas brjod pa ngo mtshar dad pa'i rol mtsho*, pp. 132.9–133.19. It was at that time that Kaḥ-thog rig-'dzin made extended offerings to the Bod-thang mgon-po, the 'protector of the Mahācaitya' (*mchod rten chen po'i srung ma*) and composed a laudation for the Mahākāla statue; see note 57.

66 Concerning the final stage of the renovation and the contributions by the Seventh 'Brug-chen bKa'-brgyud 'phrin-las shing-rta, the ceremony master bsTan-'dzin rdo-rje and the Seventh dPa'-bo gTsug-lag dga'-ba, see Chos-kyi dbang-phyug: *dPal rig 'dzin chen po rdo rje tshe dbang nor bu'i zhabs kyis (= kyi) rnam par thar pa'i cha shas brjod pa ngo mtshar dad pa'i rol mtsho*, pp. 138.23–140.6. The Seventh 'Brug-chen had arrived in Kathmandu in the autumn of 1754 in order to meet Kaḥ-thog Rig-'dzin, and later received from him the request to finalize the renovation, while the Seventh dPa'-bo arrived at the end of 1757, performed the consecration and afterwards entrusted (*gnyer gtad*) the king with taking care of the stūpa. The presence of the ruler of Gorkha is highlighted in this source, too; see ibid.: pp. 139.26–140.1 (*rab gnas nyin gsum ma sbyor dngos rjes gtsang du grub rjes gorṣa rgyal po mahā rā dza la dngos po'i gnang sbyin gya nom pa rtsal ba [=bstsal ba] dang lhan cig mchod rten chen po'i gnyer gtad mdzad pa rgyal po nas kyang dangs shing gus pa'i blos khas blangs dam bca' phul*).

67 The register written by Lo-ri-pa Kun-gzigs Chos-kyi rgya-mtsho is not extant. Brag-dkar rta-so sPrul-sku had access to the text and quotes individual items from it that added up to a total of 2,021 *zho*s of refined gold; see Chos-kyi dbang-phyug: *dPal rig 'dzin chen po rdo rje tshe dbang nor bu'i rnam par thar pa'i cha shas brjod pa ngo mtshar dad pa'i rol mtsho*, pp. 140.6–141.23. This section closes with further details of the material costs and wages for the full time span of the extended renovation. One of the biggest stone inscriptions at Svayaṃbhūnāth, in both Newari and Tibetan, describes the individual steps of this renovation of the Mahācaitya, again with a final tally of costs and wages; for this inscription as

contained in whole in the Wright Chronicle, see Bajracharya, Michaels & Gutschow (2016, vol. 1:115–118).

68 The stay of the Tenth Zhva-dmar-pa in the Kathmandu Valley can be dated to from the year 1784 onwards, during a pilgrimage together with a teacher from the 'Brug-pa bKa'-brgyud pa school. He became involved in a dispute about debased Malla coins between the Gorkha ruler Rana Bahadur Shah (r. 1777–1797) and a mission consisting of two Tibetan government officials, and so had to remain in Nepal until after a proper resolution could be reached; for details according to a modern historiographical source, see Ehrhard (2007:119–120). These kind of official delegations from Tibet sent in order to whitewash the stūpas of Svayaṃbhūnāth and Bodhnāth go as far back as the Tibetan ruler Pho-lha-ba bSod-nams stobs-rgyas (1698–1747) and the Seventh Dalai Bla-ma sKal-bzang rgya-mtsho (1698–1755). The renovations of the Bodhnāth stūpa by Kaḥ-thog Rig-'dzin Tshe-dbang nor-bu have also to be seen in this context; see notes 82 and 83. For accounts of the Tenth Zhva-dmar-pa's time as a hostage of the Gorkhas and his death in Nepal according to the testimony of the physician sMan-bsgom Chos-rje Kun-dga' dpal-ldan (1735–1804), see Ehrhard (2007:124–128).

69 See von Rospatt (2001:233–237) concerning this comprehensive renovation of the Mahā-caitya during the period 1814–1817, during which the replacement of the *yaṣṭi* was carried out with Bhutanese help. The group of religious teachers from Bhutan and their journey back from Kathmandu via sKyid-grong and Brag-dkar rta-so in the year 1814 is mentioned in the autobiography of Brag-dkar rta-so sPrul-sku. At that time one of these teachers, a certain mKhan-chen Don-yod rdo-rje, paid a visit to Chos-kyi dbang-phyug, who later in the year put his text on the sacred sites of Nepal into adequate shape; see Ehrhard (2004:100). A register of this renovation has not yet surfaced. In the years 1818 and 1819 another religious teacher from the above group, one mTshams-pa Rin-po-che Sangs-rgyas rdo-rje, who was responsible for the erection of a small temple to the east of the stūpa, paid visits to Brag-dkar rta-so; see Ehrhard (2004:100–101). For the official rights which Bhutan had been exercising over Svayaṃbhūnāth and Bodhnāth since the time of the regent Mi-'gyur brtan-pa (1667–1680), see Aris (1994:42).

70 In the Fourth Khams-sprul's pilgrimage guidebook, the local spelling of the name for the stūpa (Khāsā caitya) is given as Kha-shwa caitya, which is described as an (orthographical) mixture of Tibetan and Newari. It further states that the name Bya-ri kaṃ-shwa-macan be found in several writings of the Great Vajracārya Mahāvidyādhara. See bsTan-'dzin Chos-kyi nyi-ma: *Yul chen po nye ba'i tshandhoha bal po gnas kyi dkar chag*, pp. 182.5–183.1 (*mchod rten bya rung kha shor la ni / rgya bal gyi phyogs su pod la gang grags de tsam las lo rgyus gyi gtam gsar pa mi snang zhing mtshan yang kha shwa cai tya zhes bal bod kyi skad 'dra 'dres su lan kyin 'dug / rdo rje slob dpon chen po ma hā bi dya dhā ra'i [= ma hā bi dyā dha ra'i] gsung 'ga' las bya ri kaṃ shwa ma zhes bris pa mthong*), and Macdonald & Dvags-po Rin-po-che (1981:249–250). The latter individual is none other than Kaḥ-thog Rig-'dzin Tshe-dbang nor-bu, and one finds in his biography the additional alternative forms Bya-tri kha-sho and Bya-tri kam-sho; see Ehrhard (2013:100, note 8). Consult Blondeau (1994:33) for these same alternative Tibetan designations in various rNying-ma and Bon sources; there the observation is made that, far from being a mere deformation of the generally known Bya-rung kha-shor, the forms Bya-ri kha-shwa[-ka] and Bya-ri kaṃ-shwa[-ma] may reflect an older name of the stūpa. See also in this regard note 74.

71 This is a partly verbatim reproduction of the initial part of the first chapter of the history of the Bodhnāth Stūpa, a treasure text of the First Yol-mo-ba sPrul-sku (15th/16th cent.); see

Śākya bzang-po: *mChod rten chen po bya rung kha shor gyi lo rgyus*, fols. 2b/2–3a/2, and Dowman (1973:23–24). The narrative of the theft of the divine flowers by Gang chung-ma and her disregard of the divine law raised polemical objections in regard to the nature of these rules; see sNa-tshogs rang-grol: *Slob dpon rin po che padma'i rnam thar chen mo las brtsam te dri ba'i lan nges don gsal byed*, pp. 450.1–451.6, and Blondeau (1987:145). Consult Ehrhard (2018:76–88) concerning the first print edition of this treasure text, dating to the year 1556.

72 Among the various versions of the construction of the Bodhnāth Stūpa contained in rNying-ma and Bon sources, Nyang-ral's alternative account has been noted elsewhere; see the table in Blondeau (1994:43–45). It derives from the introductory chapter of a version of the treasure text known as the 'Middle[-length] Biography' (*rnam thar 'bring po*); for the relevant section, see Nyi-ma'i 'od-zer: *U rgyan gu ru padma 'byung gnas kyi rnam thar 'bring po zangs gling mar grags pa*, fols.1b/2–7a/2. Consult Lewis (2014:43, n. 2) concerning this extra chapter, and Doney (2014:67–70) on two exemplars of this recension of the first Padmasambhava biography; compare also Doney (2017:317–318) on the 17th chapter of the *Zangs gling ma* and the triad—Padmasambhava, Śāntarakṣita and Khri Srong lde'u-btsan—who spent a previous life together in Maguta as three brothers building a stūpa and uttering aspirational prayers for the spread of the Dharma in Tibet.

73 For the full account of the encounter of the poultry woman with the ruler and his granting of her wish to erect the stūpa, see Śākya bzang-po: *mChod rten chen po bya rung kha shor gyi lo rgyus*, fol. 3a/2–b/3, and Dowman (1973:24–25).

74 The alternative name Bya-rin kha-shorcan be found in the middle-length version of the Padmasambhava biography by Nyang-ral; see Nyi-ma'i 'od-zer: *U rgyan gu ru padma 'byung gnas kyi rnam thar 'bring po zangs gling mar grags pa*, fol. 4b/2–3 (*de ru kha shor te bya btsod pa'i (='tshos pa'i) bla (= gla) dang rin gyi (= gyis) brtsigs pas / der mchod brtan (= mchod rten) bya rin kha shor ba'i ming chags so*). Both Bya-tri kam-sho and Bya-tri kha-shor, listed separately by Brag-dkar rta-so sPrul-sku, seem to be cognate forms respectively of the already mentioned names Bya-ri kaṃ-shwa-ma and Bya-ri kha-shwa-ka. A variation of the latter form is also attested in Bon sources; for the narrative of the erection of the stūpa Bya-ri kha-sho[r] as related in the *Grags pa gling grags*, supposedly a work of the 12th century, see Kvaerne (2017:401–402). According to Newar sources, the Bodhnāth Stūpa was built by King Mānadeva in the 6th century in expiation of parricide. The legend goes that a bird was sent off and a large Buddhist shrine was to be erected wherever it landed; see Bajracharya, Michaels & Gutschow (2016, vol. 1:21 & 42). It could be argued that the designation 'Bird Mountain' (*bya ri*) is the related toponym. The term *kha-sa* in the local name Khāsā caitya was interpreted by the Eighth Si-tu as a corrupt form of Sanskrit *kha-ta* 'excavated'; see Chos-kyi 'byung-gnas: *Ta'i si tu 'bod pa karma bstan pa'i nyin byed kyi rang tshul drangs por brjod pa*, p. 267.5–6 (*nges rang tshos bya rung kha shor zer ba 'di la / bal po rnams kyis kha sa caitya zer / kha sa zhes kha ta zur chag pa yin pa 'dra bas / brkos pa'i mchod rten zer rgyu yin 'dra ste*), and Ehrhard (2013:98, note 6). A possible translation of the old name Bya-ri kaṃ-shwa[-ma/ka] would thus be 'Excavated Bird Mountain'. The name in the Mon dialect has not yet been found elsewhere.

75 This is a résumé of the final part of the first chapter of the history of the Bodhnāth Stūpa; see Śākya bzang-po: *mChod rten chen po bya rung kha shor gyi lo rgyus*, fols. 3b/3–4b/7, and Dowman (1973:25–29).

[76] The second chapter of the history of the Bodhnāth Stūpa deals with the prayers uttered by various persons and animals present at the time of construction, and is, like the first chapter, couched within a dialogue between Padmasambhava and King Khri Srong lde'u-btsan, with the addition of related prophecies; see Śākya bzang-po: *mChod rten chen po bya rung kha shor gyi lo rgyus*, fols. 5a/1–8a/2, and Dowman (1973:31–38). The individual who would kill Glang dar-ma is lHa-lung dPal-gyi rdo-rje, regarded as a rebirth of Prince Mu-rub btsan-po. See ibid., fol. 7b/5–6 (*da lta'i lha sras mu rub btsan po 'di yin no : ma 'ongs pa'i dus su bdud rgyal glang gi ming can byung nas : sangs rgyas kyi bstan pa bsnub pa'i tshe : byang chub sems dpa' lha lung dpal gyi rdo rje zhes bya bar skyes nas : bdud kyi rgyal po de nyid gsod par 'gyur ro*).

[77] See note 17 for the *rGya nag chos 'byung* of Gung mGon-po skyabs. No mention of a renovation of the Bodhnāth Stūpa has been identified in this work or in the writings of Kaḥ-thog Rig-'dzin.

[78] For the incarnanation lineage of the Yol-mo-ba sPrul-skus and a biographical sketch of sNgags-'chang Śākya bzang-po, see Ehrhard (2013:121–127). The narrative of the discovery of the written scrolls at bSam-yas monastery and the excavation of the Mahācaitya in Nepal by the treasure discoverer is taken from a work by the Third Yol-mo-ba sPrul-sku; it describes in its first part the lives of the individual members of his incarnation lineage. Besides the search for the real hill hiding the original stūpa, special mention is made of the emergence of a spring of sacred water at that time; see bsTan-'dzin nor-bu: *rTogs brjod mkhas pa'i rna rgyan*, pp. 30.2–31.2 (*re zhig nas dpal bsam yas su pheb [= phebs] / chos rgyal gyis [= gyi] dus su skor lam yong pa [= yongs pa] la da lta bkag pa zhig la / 'di na skor lam yod pa yin gsung [= gsungs] te / phyag 'dzub gtad pas slar brtsigs pa de 'gyel lo / de nas dbu rtser zhabs skor mdzad pas thog las shog ril zhig babs pa gzigs pas / bya rung kha shor gyi zhig ral gso bar lung gi bstan te / tsham tshob med par bal yul la 'phebs [= phebs] / de'i tshe bya rung kha shor kyang ri dang so sor mi phyed pa zhig yod de / thog mar 'di yin dgos te / ri gzhan zhig la phyag mdzad pas / phyed mar [= phye mar] sang ba yin no / zer ba'i ri de da lta yang mchod rten dang nye ba na yod do / slar dngos rnyed de zhig gsos rgyas par mdzad tshe / nye sar chu med pa las / 'di na yod tshod yin gsungs nas / der bsan pas [= gsan pas] khrol khrol zer ba'i shul 'drus pas [= brus pas] / chu thon pa yang da lta yod do / 'di lta bu ni ches ngo mtshar te / sngon rgyal 'od srung gyi bsten pa [= bstan pa] la bran du 'khrungs pa de thugs la shar 'dug go*), and Ehrhard (2013:101, note 9).

[79] According to the Third Yol-mo-ba sPrul-sku's narrative, the prayer known as "Chos sku'i rten mchog ma" was composed after the renovation of the Bodhnāth Stūpa and a magical contest between sNgags-'chang Śākya bzang-po and gTsang-pa, i.e. gTsang-smyon Heruka; see bsTan-'dzin nor-bu: *rTogs brjod pa'i rna rgyan*, p. 31.2–4 (*de'i tshe gtsang pa yang shing kun gyi zhabs tog la byon pa dang rdzu 'phrul 'gran pas / kong gi [= gis] nam mkha' sprin med pa la phaṭ ces brjod pas / sprin 'dus / phaṭ gnyis pa la 'brug sgra grag [= grags] / gsum pa ser ba phabs so / rigs sngags 'chang ba chen po 'di ni / hūṃ gsum brjod cing phyag 'dzub gug pa gsum mdzad pas / bal yul gyi nags tshal ri bo dang bcas pa thams cad mgo gug gug byed pa byung / de'i tshe chos sku'i rten ma mchog ma 'di mdzad*), and Ehrhard (2013:67, note 7). For the first encounter between the First Yol-mo-ba sPrul-sku and gTsang-pa smyon-pa according to the same source, see ibid., pp. 29.6–30.2; it is stated there that prior to his visit to bSam-yas monastery sNgags-'chang Śākya bzang-po had studied magic under the Holy Madman of gTsang.

[80] For the emergence of a spring of sacred water at the time of the excavation of the stūpa, see note 78. As recorded in his autobiography, the Third Yol-mo-ba sPrul-sku reenacted the emergence of the spring during his reconsecration of the Self-Manifested Mahācaitya at the time of the Newar king Śivasiṃha (r.1578–1619); see bsTan-'dzin nor-bu: *Rang gi rtogs pa brjod pa rdo rje sgra ma'i brgyud (= rgyud) mangs*, p. 120.2–6 (*de nas yul de'i si'u sing ma hā ra dzas [=śiva siṃha ma hā rā dzas] sbyin bdag mdzad de / kha shor zhabs drung gi dgon pa 'di thebs pa yin no / de'i sa phyogs la phyin / gad pa gcig yod pa la mdzub mo btsugs nas 'di nas chu zhig byung na byas pas / slar de'i thad nas chu dkar po che rab cig byung bar gdan sa'i drung de nyid nga la thugs zhen che bas / mi mang gi nang na sprul sku zer na 'di 'dra cig yong ba yin a / zhes yang yang gsung ba byung / rang byung gi mchod rten chen po 'di la rab gnas gsos pa'i nyin kyang me tog gi char chen po byung / smon lam 'dra btab pa thams cad kyang thebs byung ngo*), and Bogin (2013:191).

[81] This section on the renovation of the Bodhnāth Stūpa by the 'Brug-pa bKa'-brgyud-pa yogin Rang-rig ras-pa is based on a text dealing with the history of the reliquary shrine by him that contains the mentioned biographical details and the parting song. See Ngag-dbang rdo-rje: *Bal yul shing kun sogs dang rje rang rig gdung rten gyi dkar chag*, fols. 4a/3–6a/4; for a full translation, consult Ehrhard (2013:107–114). Especially noted is the installation of a *gañjira* finial together with the supporting pillar and ancillary pillars. The reliquary shrine of the master was consecrated by his disciples in the year 1686, followed years later by an additional consecration ceremony conducted by the Fourth Yol-mo-ba sPrul-sku Zil-gnon dbang-rgyal rdo-rje (1674–1716).

[82] The renovation of the Bodhnāth Stūpa under Pho-lha-ba bSod-nams stobs-rgyas lasted from 1727 to 1728. The initial order and the role of the two government officials from sKyid-grong is described in the ruler's biography; see Tshe-ring dbang-rgyal: *dPal mi'i dbang po'i rtogs par brjod pa 'jig rten kun tu dga' ba'i gtam*, p. 562.2–18, and Ehrhard (2004:381–382, note 121). Pho-lha-ba bSod-nams stobs-rgyas's motive for this renovation may have lain in his wish to successfully end a battle campaign in Central Tibet and the broader civil war of 1727–1728, and thus to establish himself as the ruler of Tibet; see Ehrhard (2013:57). The consecration ceremony was performed by Kaḥ-thog Rig-'dzin at his behest; see Chos-kyi dbang-phyug: *dPal rig 'dzin chen po rdo rje tshe dbang nor bu'i zhabs kyis rnam par thar pa'i cha shas brjod pa ngo mtshar dad pa'i rol mtsho*, p. 53.7–14 (*dgung lo so gcig pa phur bu ste sa spre lo gsar mtshams gtsang nas mi'i dbang po bsod nams stobs rgyas kyi [=rgyal gyi] bka' lung ltar skyid grong rdzong sdod lcags sprag pa dang yang grong nas gnyis kyi (= kyis) do khur bgyis te bal yul mchod rten bya rung kha shor la nyams gso gnang ba skabs 'dir mi'i dbang po'i lung gis rje 'di ni la rab gnas gnang dgos tshul phebs pa bzhin bal yul du byon.... / de nas bal yul du phebs mchod rten chen por rab tu gnas pa'i me tog 'thor bar mdzad*).

[83] According to the testimony of Kaḥ-thog Rig-'dzin Tshe-dbang nor-bu, this renovation lasted up to the fifth Tibetan month of the year 1748; see *dPal rig 'dzin chen po rdo rje tshe dbang nor bu'i zhabs kyi rnam par thar pa'i cha shas brjod pa ngo mtshar dad pa'i rol mtsho*, p. 87.20–23 (*me yos rab byung gsum pa'i lo de'i mthar mchod rten bya tri kam sho'am bya rung kha shor du grags pa'i zhig gso tshugs nas sa 'brug snron zla'i tshes bco lngar rab tu gnas pa'i cho ga bsgrub (= bsgrubs) / chu stod zla ba'i tshes lnga la kha shor nas bod du yong ba'i lam du zhugs*). This is the initial part of a letter addressed to Si-tu Paṇ-chen Chos-kyi 'byung-gnas, who was also in the Kathmandu Valley in 1748; see note 4. In 1747 Kaḥ-thog Rig-'dzin together with Si-tu Paṇ-chen and other dignitaries of the bKa'-brgyud-pa school had been in the presence of Pho-lha-ba bSod-nams stobs-rgyas in Lhasa in

order to perform rituals shortly before the latter's death. It cannot be ruled out that this particular renovation of the Bodhnāth Stūpa was again set in motion by Pho-lha-ba bSod-nams stobs-rgyas, this time to ensure the joint rule of his son 'Gyur-med rnam-rgyal and the Seventh Dalai Bla-ma sKal-bzang rgya-mtsho (1708–1757); see Ehrhard (2013:58). This is suggested by one of the songs intoned by Kaḥ-thog Rig-'dzin after the successful completion of the renovation; see Chos-kyi dbang-phyug: *dPal rig 'dzin chen po rdo rje tshe dbang nor bu'i zhabs kyi rnam par thar pa'i cha shas brjod pa ngo mtshar dad pa'i rol mtsho*, p. 87.6–11 (*sa dbang chos kyi rgyal po / 'gyur med phyogs las rnam rgyal / gangs can yong [= yongs] gi bdag po / rdo rje'i khri la bzhugs yod / gangs can yongs kyi mgon po / rgyal ba skal bzang rgya mtsho / mi rje chos kyi rgyal po / thugs yid gcig tu 'dres yod / rgyal dbang padma'i rgyal sras / rig 'dzin tshe dbang nor bu / phyogs med 'gro don skyong ba / 'brel tshad smin grol bkod yod / mthong thos dran reg grol ba'i / mchod rten bya rung kha shor / bod bal yongs kyi bde thabs / zhig gso phun tshogs byas yod / dza ya dza ya su dza ya*).

84 For the eight charnel grounds together with eight corresponding stūpas including Bya-tri kha-shor in the land of Nepal according to the unidentified commentary of the *bDud rtsi mchog gi rgyud*, see note 13. The Fourth Khams-sprul's pilgrimage guidebook contains an account of the excavation of the Bodhnāth Stūpa, which it also associates with the lHun-grub brtsegs-pa charnel ground, while terming it, too, a sacred object under the protection of one of the eight Ma-mos; all this is ascribed to the tradition of the First and the Third Yol-mo-ba sPrul-skus. The identity of Puṣkā dmar-ser (the goddess venerated in front of the small temple on the northern side of the stūpa) as one of the eight Ma-mos was nevertheless not generally accepted; reference is made in this regard to a printed register from a treasure text which supports this claim. See bsTan-'dzin Chos-kyi nyi-ma: *Yul chen po nye ba'i tshandhoha bal po'i gnas kyi dkar chag gangs can rna ba'i bdud rtsi*, 183.1–184.2 (*spyir mchod rten 'di nyid sngon gyi bar skabs su zhig ral nyams chag gi rnam pas bye ma la sogs pa'i sa rdul gyis g.yogs shing nub nas mi mngon par yod pa la gu ru rin po che'i lung bstan dus la babs pas sprul pa'i skyes mchog rig 'dzin yol ma ba śākya bzang pos bton te zhig gsos mthun rkyen tshul bzhin du bsgrubs shing rgya cher sngags pas / slar yang mchod rten chen po'i mtshan nyid zla ltar grags pa yin / des na yol mo śākya bzang po nyid dang de'i sku phreng gsum pa yol mo pa bstan 'dzin nor bu bcas kyi bzhed pa la ni mchod rten brgyad / shing brgyad / dur khrod brgyad kyi ya g.yal gcig 'di yi mchod rten dang / lhun grub brtsegs pa'i dur khrod shing sogs yin / mdun du yod pa'i srung ma 'di'ang gnas kyi ma mo brgyad kyi nang tshan puṣ ka (= puṣ kā) dmar ser rgyu ma 'dren zhing za ba bzhes pa de yin par 'dod mod / de yang khungs mchod pa'i gtam rang yin paṛ bla ma rnams mi bzhed / gzhan slob dpon chen po'i zhal gsung mar byed pa'i dkar chag gter ma spar la 'khod bzhin pa ni yod ltar la / 'dir dpyod kyi yul du ma byas*), and Macdonald & Dvags-po Rin-po-che (1981:249–250).

85 When paying his first visit to the Bodhnāth Stūpa in the year 1728, Kaḥ-thog Rig-'dzin Tshe-dbang nor-bu is said to have located the original lHun-grub brtsegs-pa charnel ground and the centre of it containing the mentioned footprint; see Chos-kyi dbang-phyug: *dPal rig 'dzin chen po rdo rje tshe dbang nor bu'i zhabs kyi rnam par thar pa'i cha shas brjod pa ngo mtshar dad pa'i rol mtsho*, p. 53.16–18 (*bya rung kha shor du bzhugs skabs lung bstan las dur khrod chen po lhun grub brtsegs pa'i dngos gzhi kha shor nas gzhu mdom (= 'dom) lnga brgya'i sar yod cing der gu ru rin po che'i zhabs rjes kyang yod tshul byung ba mngon du gyur*).

86 See *sKu gdung 'bar ba tsha tsha dang mchod rten gyi rgyud*, pp. 406.6–407.1 (*shar lho mtshams na bal po'i yul / ta na ya ma kha byed kri / lhun grub dur khrod byin za dang /*

*shing bu ka ra na cita 'bims pa dang / mchod rten kha sho bya khri kha / ston pa dka' thub mdzad pa de / bal che rje na leb 'beb yod / de na zan gyi longs spyod che / bkra shis mchod rten hu lu ka / 'byung po gu gu ta nag gnas*). Concerning the great charnel ground in Nepal, the associated stūpa and Ma-mo according to the biographical tradition of Padmasambhava, see O-rgyan gling-pa: *U rgyan gu ru padma 'byung gnas kyi skyes rabs rnam par thar pa rgyas par bkod pa padma bka'i thang yig*, p. 82.13–15 (*de nas yul gyi ming ni bal po'i yul: dur khrod ming ni lhun grub brtsegs pa zhes : dbus na mchod rten bya ri kha shor ni : ma mo chen mo kasmā rī gnas pa:*).

[87] According to the work of the Fourth No-min-han, there was a tradition which claimed that the place where the poultry woman attained Buddhahood was one of the sacred sites in the vicinity of Svayaṃbhūnāth. This claim, there said to be hard to accept, is contained in a no longer extant guidebook written by mNga'-ris grub-chen; see the Introduction above, note 10.

[88] See *Bal yul rang byung mchod rten chen po'i lo rgyus*, chapter 3, pp. 238.6–239.1.

[89] See *Bal yul rang byung mchod rten chen po'i lo rgyus*, chapter 7, p. 252.5–6.

[90] The Fourth Khams-sprul had described the Mañjuśrī stūpa in his guidebook as a relic shrine of Vajrācārya 'Jam-pa'i lha; see note 45. In a later section he noted the existence of a nearby stūpa referred to by Tibetan pilgrims as 'the Second Svayaṃbhūnāth'; see bsTan-'dzin Chos-kyi nyi-ma, *Yul chen po nye ba'i tshandhoha bal po gnas kyi dkar chag rna ba'i bdud rtsi*, pp. 215.5–216.1 (*'jam dpal kyi mchod rten ni sngar bshad zin pa ltar dang / de'i 'khris su bod rnams shing kun gnyis pa zhes 'bod pa'i rdo yi mchod rten chung ngu zhig 'dug pa ji ltar yin ma shes*), and Macdonald & Dvags-po Rin-po-che (1981:264).

[91] For the references to the Kāśyapa stūpa in Li-yul, see *Ārya-gośṛṅga-vyākaraṇa-sūtra* [= *'Phags pa glang ru lung bstan zhes bya ba theg pa chen po'i mdo*] , p. 349.3.5–6 (*'di ltar ji srid du mchod rten chu bo go ma'i 'gram zhes bya dang / 'od srungs (= 'od srung) gi mchod rten 'di gnyis rgyas zhing mtsho'i gnas su byas pa de srid du yul dge ba yang rgyas shing bzang po 'gyur ro*). Compare also *Li yul lung bstan pa*, p. 304.3.7–4.6, and Emmerick (1967:31) regarding the stūpa which contained the relics of the Kāśyapa Buddha and is to become visible again at the time of the Maitreya Buddha. The reference that the Kāśyapa stūpa contains the relics of Ārya Kāśyapa, the disciple of Buddha Śākyamuni, can be found in the old pilgrimage guidebook; see bSod-nams dpal bzang-po; *Dus gsum sangs rgyas thams cad kyi thugs kyi rten 'phags pa shing kun dkar chag*, p. 85.5–6, and Ehrhard (2013: 79). During his first visit to Svayaṃbhūnāth in the year 1723 Si-tu Paṇ-chen, too, described the minor relic shrines on the hill. According to his diary entry, the Newars regarded the Kāśyapa stūpa as a sacred site where the Bodhisattva Mañjuśrī had preached the Buddhist doctrine; see Chos-kyi 'byung-gnas: *Dri bral shel gyi me long*, p. 118.3 (*de bzhin du 'od srung gi mchod rten du grags pa 'di'ang bal po rnams ni 'jam dpal dbyangs kyis chos bstan pa'i gnas yin zhes zer*). It seems that the Kāśyapa stūpa was conflated by him with the Mañjuśrī stūpa—not mentioned in his account—during this initial tour in the surroundings of Svayaṃbhūnāth.

[92] The narrative of the origin of the Vasubandhu stūpa is also recorded in the diaries of Si-tu Paṇ-chen, which thus serves as a source for its authencity; see Chos-kyi 'byung-gnas: *Dri bral shel gyi me long*, p. 118.4–5 (*slob dpon dbyig gnyen kyi mchod rten ni 'khrul med rang du nges te / slob dpon de yul 'dir phebs na khyim btsun chos gos gyon zhing rmo ba gzigs pas thugs byung bas gtsug gtor rnam rgyal ma'i sngags bzlog nas bzlas te gshegs pa'i lo*

*rgyus kyis mtshon par nus so*). It is also mentioned in the guidebook of the Fourth Khams-sprul, who raises the point that the stūpa must have been renovated quite a number of times in view of Vasubandhu's dates; see bsTan-'dzin Chos-kyi nyi-ma: *Yul chen po nye ba'i tshandhoha bal po gnas kyi dkar chag gangs can rna ba'i bdud rtsi*, p. 216.1–6 (*'dzam gling rgyan drug du grags pa'i nang tshan 'phags pa thogs med kyi gcung slob dpon chen po dbyig gnyen de nyid kyis 'phags pa'i yul du sangs rgyas kyi bstan pa gsal bar mdzad pa'i phrin las mthar phyin nas slob ma stong gis bskor te bal yul du byon chos gzhi (= gzhis) mang po btsugs dge 'dun thug med du 'phebs pa mdzad / dus lan gcig khyim btsun chos gos skur gyon te zhing rmod pa gzigs pa'i rkyen gyis thugs skyo nas rigs sngags sku tshe la dbang thob pa yin pa'i phyir gtsug tor rnam rgyal gyi gzungs mgo zhabs bzlog pa lan gsum bzlos pas de nyid du sku 'das pa'i shul na slob ma rnams kyis mchod rten byas pa ni 'di yin / 'on kyang slob dpon 'di ni bod yul du chos kyi dbu brnyes pa'i rgyal po lha tho tho ri gnyan btsan dang thog mnyam pa'i phyir dus kyi bskal pas rjes su zhig gsos sogs yang yang byas pa ni yin nam snyam mo*), and Macdonald & Dvags-po Rin-po-che (1981:254–265).

93 The old pilgrimage guidebook states that Bya-rgod phung-po Hill was scooped out of the original Gṛdhra-kūṭa-parvata in India and brought to Nepal by the monkey god Hanuman; see bSod-nams dpal bzang-po: *Dus gsum sangs rgyas thams cad kyi thugs kyi rten 'phags pa shing kun dkar chag*, p. 88.1, and Ehrhard (2013:81). This was taken up into the later guidebook, which added a description of five stūpas and a charnel ground at this site; see Ngag-dbang rdo-rje: *Bal yul 'phags pa shing kun dang de'i gnas gzhan rnams kyi dkar chag*, pp. 45.34–46.1 The name 'Rice Heap Hill vihāra' can be found in the second part of Si-tu Paṇ-chen's translation of the *Svayaṃbhūpurāṇa*; see *Bal yul rang byung mchod rten chen po'i lo rgyus*, p. 257.5 (*chos smra ba bstan pa'i nyin byed kyis bal yul rang byung mchod rten chen po'i nye 'dabs 'bras spungs ri bo'i gtsug lag khang du legs par bsgyur ba'i dge bas skye dgu thams cad gzhom du med pa'i gnas chen po mngon du byed par gyur cig*). The Fourth Khams-sprul described the vihāra at Kiṃḍola as the residence of Tibetan religious dignitaries, including Si-tu Paṇ-chen and Kaḥ-thog Rig-'dzin; the Newari toponym Rice Heap is identified as one of three such elevations bearing the name of a cereal grain. See bsTan-'dzin Chos-kyi nyi-ma: *Yul chen po nye ba'i tshandhoha bal po gnas kyi dkar chag gangs can rna ba'i bdud rtsi*, fol. 208.2–5 (*gtsug lag khang 'dir rje karma pa zhva dmar nag / 'brug pa rin po che / kun mkhyen si tu / rig 'dzin chen po sogs dus phyis bod yul kyi bla ma rim byon rnams kyang bsti gnas su mdzad cing / bal por ji tsam bzhugs ring 'dir bzhugs par 'dug / des na de yi ming la'ang bal po'i skad du kim ḍol ste 'bras spungs dang da lta rang byung mchod rten gyi zhig gsos rdo gter thon cing chu mig gsar pa rdo ba 'dir tsho ḍo ste nas spungs / da dung phyogs gzhan zhig na o ḍi ste so ba spungs pa zhes gsum 'dug pa'i nang tshan 'dir 'bras spungs yin*), and Macdonald & Dvags-po Rin-po-che (1981:261). According to the Wright Chronicle, King Bhāskara Malla (r. 1700–1722) had a beautiful *dharmaśālā* built at Kiṃḍola during his reign; see Bajracharya, Michaels & Gutschow (2015, vol. 1:110–111).

94 Both the name Vindhya for the hill to the west of Svayaṃbhūnāth and the teaching throne of Buddha Śākyamuni on top of it are mentioned in the old pilgrimage guidebook; see bSod-nams dpal bzang-po: *Dus gsum sangs rgyas thams cad thugs kyi rten 'phags pa shing kun dkar chag*, p. 87.6–7, and Ehrhard (2013:81). The later guidebook lists additional teaching thrones of Śāriputra and Maudgalyāyana; see Ngag-dbang rdo-rje: *Bal yul 'phags pa shing kun dang de'i gnas gzhan dkar chag*, p. 45.29–30. For the localization of Ri-bo 'big[s]-byed along Nepal's border according to the origin myth of the 'Ārya [Avalokiteśvara] brothers' (*'phags pa sku mched*) contained in the relevant pilgrimage guidebooks, see Ehrhard (2004:

235 & 329, note 25). The Fourth Khams-sprul points out the fact in his guidebook that the original Vindhya is located in South India and adds that the Newari name of the hill to the west of Svayaṃbhūnāth had no Tibetan equivalent; he also refers to the teaching throne of Buddha Śākyamuni, which he, convinced of its authenticity, paid a visit to. He goes on to detail Newar funerary practices and divinations performed in front of the teaching throne; see bsTan-'dzin Chos-kyi nyi-ma: *Yul chen po nye ba'i tshandhoha bal po'i gnas kyi dkar chag gangs can rna ba'i bdud rtsi*, pp.216.6.–218.1 (*ri bo 'bigs byed du grags pa 'di yang bod rnams kyis btags pa yin mod / de yang ming tsam ni rnam rtog gi rjes 'gro yin pas ji ltar btags kyang rung ste 'gal ba med / ri bo 'bigs byed dngos ni lho phyogs na yod phyir 'di yin par bsam na mi rung / bal skad du dzā ma tsho zer gyin gda' / de nyid bod skad du gang yin ni cha ma 'tshal / ri bo 'di yi rtse na rdo brtsegs pa'i khri sangs rgyas bzhugs khri yin par grags pa de yod / spyir de yang yin pa dang min pa'i mtha' gnyis kar kha tshon gcod mi nus mod / 'on kyang yul 'dir sangs rgyas kyi zhabs kyis bcags pa ni nges pa nyid kyi phyir yin yong snyam bdag gis kyang mjal bas bzhugs khri'i mdun du rdo stengs (= stegs) shig 'dug pa la bal po'i mi shi ba phal cher gyi phung po dur khrod du bsregs zin pa'i rjes su mi thod kyi rus pa 'dir rdo stegs de'i khar brdungs pa'i thal ba rlung la 'phyur nas de gyen la song na shin po de yang mtho ris dang 'og tu song na ngan song du 'gro ba'i ltas yin zer nas brtags pa'i srol kyang yod par snang*), and Macdonald & Dvags-po Rin-po-che (1981:265).

[95] Nāgārjuna's grotto of spiritual practice is mentioned in the old pilgrimage guidebook, together with associated religious objects; see bSod-nams dpal bzang-po: *Dus gsum sangs rgyas thams cad kyi thugs kyi rten 'phags pa shing kun gyi dkar chag*, p. 87.6, and Ehrhard (2013:81). The site is said to be on the 'side' (*'dabs*) of the hill. The grotto and a spring of sacred water are referred to in the later guidebook; see Ngag-dbang rdo-rje: *Bal yul 'phags pa shing kun dang de'i gnas gzhan dkar chag*, p. 45.31–32. The Fourth Khams-sprul reports that Ācārya Nāgārjuna's pleasant private grotto was in the middle of a thick forest; inside it were stone statues of Buddha Śākyamuni and Nāgārjuna. See bsTan-'dzin Chos-kyi nyi-ma: *Yul chen po nye ba'i tshandhoha bal po gnas kyi dkar chag rna ba'i bdud rtsi*, p. 218.1–2 (*ri bo de yi mdun gyi phyogs gcig na nags tshal stugs po'i dbus su / slob dpon klu sgrub kyi gzims phug shin tu legs shing spro ba 'phel ba'i gnas nang na thub pa'i dbang po dang klu sgrub kyi rdo sku yod pa zhig 'dug*). In the Wright Chronicle, a detailed section describes Nāgārjunapāda's stay at the hill to the west of Svayaṃbhūnāth and his setting up a meditation cave in the middle of its slope; there he attained nirvāṇa, and the prominence would later become known as Nāgārjuna [Hill]. The funerary practices related by the Fourth Khams-sprul are also recorded in the chronicle; see Bajracharya, Michaels & Gutschow (2016, vol. 1:16–17). For the quotation from the eighth chapter of the *Svayaṃbhūpurāna* and more on Zhi-byed lha, including the account of his long samādhi in a 'cavity' (*bu ga*) at the end of his life, see notes 130 & 131.

[96] Among the old scriptures mentioned by Brag-dkar rta-so sPrul-sku one can refer to the old pilgrimage guidebook to Svayaṃbhūnāth concerning the raising of a treasure by Nāgārjuna. A section of the text describes his stay at Svayaṃbhūnāth, where he acted as custodian of the Stūpa, had his chamber for spiritual practice at the site of the local protector Śāntaputri and brought forth a tantra with the title *Phyag na rdo rje [db]u rtsa'i rgyud* from the realm of the nāgas. When expounding the latter work Nāgārjuna addressed the local protector to take some delight in this act; see bSod-nams dpal bzang-po: *Dus gsum sangs rgyas thams cad thugs kyi rten 'phags pa shing kun dkar chag*, pp. 85.6-86.2, and Ehrhard (2013:79). This work might refer to the *Ārya-vajra-pātāla-nāma-tantra-rāja* [='*Phags pa rdo rje sa 'og gi rgyud kyi rgyal po*], the main Kriyātantra associated with Vajrapāṇi; see Lessing & Wayman (1968:128-129). The later guidebook adds the details that there existed three different ways

from Śāntapuri, leading to the ground of Shing-kun, to the realm of the nāgas, and to the realm of the *bgegs* demons respectively. Afterward the discovery of the *Śatasāhasrikaprajñāparamitā* manuscript by Nāgārjuna is added, cosnsisting of sixteen volumes in gold script and later stored in the [s]Tham vihāra; see Ngag-dbang rdo-rje: *Bal yul mchod rten dang de'i gnas gzhan dkar chag*, p. 45.1-9. Si-tu Paṇ-chen noted in his diaries the public display of the statues and the volumes of the monastery during his visit in the year 1724; see Chos-kyi 'byung-gnas: *Dri bral shel gyi me long*, p. 126.3 (*thang bi ha ra gyi sku dang 'bum sogs spyan drangs nas khrong khyer bskor ba dang / phal gu ne'i zlos gar ltad mo gzigs*). The Fourth Khams-sprul had inspected the deluxe edition stored in the upper floor of the temple, refering to its provenance according to the pilgrimage guide book and not accepting it. He dated the *Śatasāhasrika-prajñāparamitā* volume instead to the period of Vibhūticandra (12th/13th cent.); for the [s]Tham vihāra see note 102.

97 See Padma dkar-po *Chos 'byung bstan pa'i padma rgyas pa'i nyin byed*, p. 112.3–12 (*klu'i byang chub ni slob dpon klu sgrub kyis ma he'i rdzi bo rgas 'khogs pa zhig snod ldan du gzigs nas / gang gsal dri bas ma he'o / der ma he sgom du bcug pas ma he'i rva phug la zug pa dang / bcad pas med par song ba byung nas gdams ngag sbyin te dus las 'das pa bram ze'i rigs su 'khrungs pa slob dpon las rab tu byung ste / mtshan nāga bodhi klu'i byang chub tu grags / phyi nang gi grub mtha' thams cad mkhyen pa yi dam lha'i zhal gzigs nas dkyil 'khor gyi cho ga nyi shu pa la sogs pa mdzad / brtul zhugs kyi spyod pa la bzhugs pas mtshan ma ti ma kir (= ma tam gi) grags te da lta yang dpal gyi ri la bzhugs so zhes grags so* ).

98 See Kun-dga' snying-po: *Dam pa'i chos rin po che 'phags pa'i yul du ji ltar dar ba'i tshul gsal bar ston pa dgos 'dod kun byung*, pp. 112.18–113.11 (*yang shar phyogs bhan ga la'i yul kyi bram ze rgan rgod gnyis la bu zhig kyang yod cing / longs spyod kyis dbul ba la slob dpon klu sgrub kyis gser mang po gnang bas / lhag par dad de / de gsum char gyis slob ma byas / bu des slob dpon gyi nye gnas byas shing bcud len gyi dngos grub kyang thob pa na / rab tu byung ste sde snod gsum la mkhas pa byas pa ni slob dpon klu'i byang chub pa / des kyang slob dpon klu sgrub bzhugs kyi bar du slob dpon gyi g.yog byed cing / sku 'das pa na dpal gyi ri'i phyogs cig phug zab mo zhig tu 'dug nas rtse gcig tu bsgoms pas lo bcu gnyis na phyag rgya chen po mchog gi dngos grub thob / sku tshe nyi zla dang mnyam pas gnas de nyid du bzhugs so / mtshan gyis rnam grangs nyid yod de / nāga bo dhi klu'i byang chub dang / nā ga budddhi klu'i blo'o*). For the Nāgārjuna–Nāgabodhi/Nāgabuddhi connection with Guhyasamāja literature and the awareness of such a linkage in Tibetan intellectual circles, see van der Kuijp (2007:1009–1014). Compare id. (2007:1015–1017) concerning the *dKyil 'khor nyi shu pa* as mentioned by Tāranātha and the fact that for Tibetan authors the 12th-century work of Abhayakāradatta on the spiritual careers of the eighty-four Mahāsiddhas obviously served as the literary source when it came to retelling Nāgabodhi's life.

99 The Fourth Khams-sprul had also visited the site, known to Tibetans as 'The Place Left Behind by the Buffalo Buddha' (*ma he sangs rgyas shul*). It is described by him as an important pilgrimage spot in the vicinity of the above-mentioned site of Nāgārjuna's spiritual practice, with reference being made to the legend of the latter's disciple according to the Newar tradition; the narrative reflects the Mahāsiddha's life as found in the literary sources and adapts it to the local context. The traces left behind by the 'Buffalo Buddha' were accepted as authentic by this visitor, while he associated another nearby cave with Mahācārya Vasubandhu; see bsTan-'dzin Chos-kyi nyi-ma: *Yul chen po nye ba'i tshandoha bal po'i gnas kyi dkar chag gangs can rna ba'i bdud rtsi*, pp. 218.2–219.6 (*de dang nye bar bod rnams kyis ma he sangs rgyas shul yin zer gnas skor ba kun mjal bar 'dug / bal po rnams la*

*de'i lo rgyus dri bas / sngon slob dpon klu sgrub brag phug der bzhugs pa'i tshe / yam bu grong khyer nas ma he'i rdzi bo blun po zhig gis slob dpon la shin tu dad nas yang yang mjal zhing zho dang 'o ma la sogs pas kyang mchod par byed la / dus lan gcig slob dpon grong khyer du 'byon par zhu ba la zhal gyis ma bzhes nas khyod rang yang dag pa'i don la mnyam par 'jog nus na 'dir sdod gsungs pas / des kyang de bzhin du byed pa la ma he skyong ba'i las la shin tu goms pa'i bag chags kyi (= kyis) me he rang dran zhing 'dug pa la / slob dpon gyis khyod rang nyid ma he yin par sgoms shig gsungs nas / des kyang ma he sangs rgyas shul yin zer ba'i brag phug der bsgoms pas je zhig na ma he dngos su song ste / phug pa la rva thogs da lta'i zhabs rjes 'di yang byung / yang slob dpon gyis khyod rang gi lus rnal mar bsgoms gsungs / de bzhin du bsgoms pas lus snga ma ltar song bas dbang rnon du mkhyen nas dbang bskur gdams pa byin te bsgrubs pas / lus de nyid kyis brag phug brtol nas mkha' spyod du byon pa yin zer / gnas de na zhabs rjes dang brag phug brtol ba'i shul ni da lta'ang gsal bar 'dug go / yang de dang nye bar slob dpon chen po dbyig gnyen gyi bzhugs gnas su grags pa'i brag phug shin tu nyams dga' ba nang na gtso bor ston pa sangs rgyas kyi sku rdo las grub pa'i mi tshad gnyis 'gyur tsam dang gzhan phyi pa'i lha sku 'dra thor tsam yod pa zhig 'dug*), and Macdonald & Dvags-po Rin-po-che (1981:265–266).

100 For the legend of the churning of the ocean and the name Blue-necked One for Śiva according to the Wright Chronicle, see Bajracarya, Michaels & Gutschow (2016, vol. 1:65–66). The same source mentions that there existed a primordial form of Nīlakaṇṭhanārāyaṇa and that the statue of Jalaśayananārāyaṇa was later placed in the middle of the pond by Pratāpa Malla; see id. (2016, vol. 1:106–107). The Fourth Khams-sprul identifies the effigy correctly as a statue of Viṣṇu, and adds that it displays the god lying in the pond of the nāga king Śeṣa. In addition, he mentions two Buddhist stūpas in front of the same hill. These were known to Tibetan pilgrims as reliquary shrines of Śuddhodana and Māyādevī, an identification the Fourth Khams-sprul found difficult to accept; see bsTan-'dzin Chos-kyi nyi-ma: *Yul chen po nye ba'i tshandoha bal po'i gnas kyi dkar chag rna ba'i bdud rtsi*, pp. 225.4–226.2 (*klu gan rkyal du grags pa yang bod rnams kyis btags par 'dug yin lugs lo rgyus dbang du byas na 'di yang klu she ṣa'i khrus kyi rdzing bu yin par grags pa la lha khyab 'jug gis khrus byed pa'i tshul du rdo sku gan rkyal du nyal ba 'di bzhengs pa yin 'dug / de yi ri gdong na yod pa'i mchod rten gnyis ni yab zas gtsang dang yum sgyu ma lha mdzes gnyis kyi mchod rten yin par bod rnams la grags kyang ji bzhin yin pa dka' / 'on kyang nang pa'i mchod rten sngon bstan bstan pa dar ba'i tshe bzhengs pa zhig ni yin 'dug go*), and Macdonald & Dvags-po Rin-po-che (1981:268). According to the old pilgrimage guidebooks, the stūpas with the relics of the parents of Buddha Śākyamuni were located on the peak of 'Big[s]-byed hill; see bSod-bams dpal-bzang-po: *Dus gsum sangs rgyas thams cad kyi thugs kyi rten 'phags pa shing kun gyi dkar chag*, pp. 87.7–88.1, and Ehrhard (2013:81); compare Ngag-dbang rdo-rje: *Bal yul mchod rten 'phags pa shing kun dang de'i gnas gzhan rnams kyi dkar chag*, p. 45.32–33.

101 The small hillock, whose name is also spelled Dzo-ki a-[']bar, and the corruption—during the pronunciation of mantras—of the Sanskrit name Yogāmbhara, is also mentioned by the Fourth Khams-sprul. He personally visited the site, enquired about its status as a tīrtha according to the *Catuḥpīṭha-mahayoginī-tantra-rāja*, and received the information that it was the place of Jñāneśvarī, the consort of Catuḥpīṭha. This led to a general reflection on the presence of local human ḍākinīs in Nepal and the means whereby their existence was kept secret. He also noted that at this site blood offerings were performed by non-Buddhists; see bsTan-'dzin Chos-kyi nyi-ma: *Yul chen po nye ba'i tshandoha bal po gnas kyi dkar chag rna ba'i bdud rtsi*, pp. 226.2–227.3 (*yang bod rnams kyis dzo ki a 'bar du 'bod pa'i ri de'u 'di*

*na legs sbyar gyi skad du yo gambha ra ste rnal 'byor nam mkha' zhes grags pa la rgya bal gyi sngags bklags tshul dang bod kyi go phyogs tha dad du gyur cing sgra zur chag pas dzo ki a 'bar du song ba yin / gnas 'di ni dpal rdo rje gdan bzhi'i gnas su yang grags kho bos kyang gnas 'di phyin pa'i tshe rgya gar gyi mi shig la / i hrā tirṭhi kung de ba ta kau na he zhes dris par / dzñāneśwarī he zer ba'ang grags tshod kyi gtam de dang mthun te rdo rje gdan bzhi'i yum ye shes dbang phyug ma yin pas so / spyir gnas 'di dpa' bo dang rnal 'byor ma mang po ngang gi 'du ba zhig yin 'dug cing / nai pā la'i ljongs 'di kun na zhing skyes kyi mkha' 'gro ma mi mo'i rnam pa snang ba yang ji snyed pa yod 'dug / de rnams kyang mi mngon pa'i tshul du gnas 'dir dpa' bo dpa' mo'i gral du tshogs kyi 'khor lo la 'gro ba nang mi phal gyis mthong zhing nyams 'og tu chud kyang gzhan la gsang zhing smra mi nus pa'i rigs can de 'dra mang du yod par go / phyi rol pa rnams ni gnas 'di la'ang dmar gyi a rghaṃ gyus mchod par byed do*), and Macdonald & Dvags-po Rin-po-che (1981:268–269). In this case, too, the authority of Kaḥ-thog Rig-'dzin Tshe-dbang nor-bu seems to have prompted the association of the site with the mentioned tantra. In three of his letters addressed to the Seventh Dalai Bla-ma sKal-bzang rgya-mtsho from Nepal in the year 1752, Dzo-ki a-khar is mentioned as the first stopover after leaving Svayaṃbhū; see Tshe-dbang nor-bu: *Chab shog khag*, p. 739.25–27 (*da lta rang byung mchod rten chen po'i ngogs nas thon ste bal yul gyi gnas chen dzo ki a khar zhes rdo rje gdan bzhi'i gnas su 'dod pa der 'byor ba'i skabs su ...*), p. 743.2–3 (*grub pa'i bsti gnas rdzo khi a khar ...*), and p. 743.24–26 (*da lta rang byung mchod rten chen po'i ngogs nas thon ste bal yul gyi gnas chen dzo ki a khar zhes rdo rje gdan bzhi'i gnas su 'dod pa der slebs pa'i skabs su lam yig dgos mkho sogs kyang yong tshul phebs pa thugs la btags*). There exists a commentary on the extended deity maṇḍala of the *Catuḥpīṭha-mahāyoginī-tantra-rāja*; see Tshe-dbang nor-bu: *rGyud kyi rgyal po gdan bzhi dkyil 'khor rgyas pa yi lha'i mtshan grangs gsal ba'i me long.*

102 The [s]Tham vihāra in Kathmandu and its original establishment by Atiśa are also recorded in the guidebook of the Fourth Khams-sprul, who further points out that Mahāpaṇḍita Vibhūthicandra for a long time served as abbot of the monastery, where he received the direct transmission of the Ṣaḍaṅgayoga of the Kālacakratantra from Śavaripa; also, that in later times Mahāpaṇḍita Vanaratna stayed for some time in this vihāra. As already mentioned, the manuscript of the *Śata-sāhasrika-prajñāpāramitā* said to have been recovered by Nāgārjuna at Svayaṃbhūnāth was among the valuable religious objects in the monastery; see bsTan-'dzin Chos-kyi nyi-ma: *Yul chen nye ba'i tshandoha bal po'i gnas kyi dkar chag rna ba'i bdud rtsi*, pp. 199.3–200.2 (*sthaṃ bi ha ra'i gtsug lag khang ni sngon jo bo rje dpal ldan a ti shas thog mar btab / de nas paṇḍita bi bhu ti tsandra mkhan por yun ring du bzhugs shing 'chad nyan rgya chen po mdzad dge 'dun de yang thug med du 'phel / dpal sha wa ri dbang phyug las sbyor drug nye brgyud kyang gnas 'dir gsan / de rjes paṇ chen nags rin yang cung zad bzhugs da lta de yi gtsang khang na sangs rgyas pa'i lha sku mang po mchod pa dang bcas te yod / steng khang na shes rab kyi pha rol tu phyin pa stong phrag brgya pa'i glegs bam lantsa'i yi ger byas te gser gyi bris pa'i rgya dpe yod / de yang bod kyis byas pa'i dkar chag na / slob dpon klu sgrub kyis klu yul nas spyan drangs pa'i dpe ngo ma rang yin zer ba ni mi 'thad kyang / bi bhu ti'i (= vi bhū ti'i) skabs tsam la byung ba yin par mngon no*), and Macdonald & Dvags-po Rin-po-che (1981:257). For more on the studies of Vibhūticandra in the Kathmandu Valley under Newar Buddhist masters, his travels to Tibet and his residence in [s]Tham vihāra, where the vision of Śavaripa occurred, see Stearns (1996:136–141); consult id. (1996:160) for a list of texts composed or translated there. An early Tibetan description of the vihāra is contained in the travelogue of Chag Lo-tsā-ba Chos-rje dpal (1197–1264), who also translated at least two texts in collaboration with Vibhūticandra and studied under some of the same Newar Buddhist masters; for this description, see Roerich

(1959:6.29–71.13 & 55–56). The account mentions in particular the presence of a stūpa of Buddha Kāśyapa at the site and the efforts of Atiśa to erect a temple to worship it.

[103] In the diaries of Si-tu Paṇ-chen, [s]Tham vihāra and the monastery known as Rin-chen tshul-gyi gtsug-lag khang are clearly differentiated from one another: the former being located on the north-eastern border of Kathmandu, and the latter on its outskirts in the north-western direction; see Chos-kyi 'byung-gnas: *Ta'i si tu 'bod pa karma bstan pa'i nyin byed kyi rang tshul drangs par brjod pa dri bral shel gyi me long*, pp. 122.1–3 (*skabs 'dir thang bi ha ra zhes pa yam bu'i grong gi byang shar mtshams su grong mthar yod pa de dang /.... / grong khyer gyi phyi rol nub byang mtshams su rin chen tshul gyi gtsug lag khang yin yang zer ba....*). Brag-dkar rta-so sPrul-sku's acceptance that the two names refer to one and the same place is based on the biography of gTsang-smyon Heruka written by lHa-btsun. At the time of the renovation of Svayaṃbhūnāth a gaṇacakra was performed at the monastery, during which many officials, religious persons and laypeople were present; see Rin-chen rnam-rgyal: *Grub thob gtsang smyon pa'i rnam thar dad pa'i spu slong g.yo' ba (= g.yo ba)*, pp. 114.1–2 (*gzhan yang blon po dang khra kur (= thā khur) dang bā ro dang dmangs phal ba sogs grangs las 'das pas bsu nas ba yul (= bal yul) rin chen tshul gyis (= gyi) gtsug lag khang thang bhi ha rir (= bhi hā rir) grags pa der phyag phebs / tshogs kyi 'khor lo bzang po phul ba rnams bzhes so*).

[104] The *Jo bo rje'i rnam thar lam yig* is a work ascribed to 'Brom-ston rGyal-ba'i 'byung-gnas; see note 19. For the narrative of Atiśa's sojourn in the Kathmandu Valley and the establishment of a monastic complex consisting of [s]Tham vihāra and Rāja vihāra, see rGyal-ba'i byung-gnas: *'Brom ston pa rgyal ba'i byung gnas kyis mdzad pa'i jo bo rje'i rnam thar lam yig chos kyi 'byung gnas*, pp. 264.17–292.16, and Decleer (1996:40–45). According to this Tibetan source, the original monastery was completed during Atiśa's journey to the court of the rulers of Western Tibet; further, that Rāja vihāra was erected afterwards by a Newar king whose son had served as abbot of [s]Tham vihāra.

[105] This citation of O-rgyan Rin-chen dpal concerning the library holdings of [s]Tham vihāra has not yet been identified. It is known that this master of the 'Brug-pa bKa'-brgyud-pa school stayed in Kathmandu on several occasions during his travels to India. One memorable event during his second visit has to do with the release of a large number of Tibetans from the local authorities in the Valley. According to his biography, they had left their homeland owing to a drought, and O-rgyan-pa set off from the Tibetan Plateau to lead them back; see bSod-nams 'od-zer: *dPal ldan bla ma dam pa grub chen o rgyan pa'i rnam par thar pa byin rlabs kyi chu rgyun*, pp. 176.14–178.3, and the translation and comments in Vitali (2009/10: 191–193, note 69).

[106] The question of the presence of the Eighty-four Mahāsiddhas at Saṅkhu is also raised by the Fourth Khams-sprul in his guidebook. He argues for the possibility that eighty of these great ascetics may have arrived at different times at this site, and refers in this regard to an oral account going back to Mahāpaṇḍita Abhayākaragupta ($11^{th}/12^{th}$ cent.) and Tsa-mi Lo-tsā-ba Sangs-rgyas grags-pa ($12^{th}$ cent.) concerning such a gathering that occurred at the court of an Indian king. In regard to the individual meditation caves, he also supported the view of some local informants that Śaṅkarācarya—according to him the opponent of the Buddhist logician Dharmakīrti ($7^{th}$ cent.)—had stayed at Saṅkhu. The main deity of the sacred site is identified in his guidebook as Ugratārā alias Ekajaṭī, while reference is also made to the sculpted head of a king called Bintirāja, which is accompanied by a copper cauldron, both located on the upper floor of the main temple. Left unmentioned are all the various un-

certain accounts of Newars and Tibetans concerning the latter religious objects; see bsTan-'dzin Chos-kyi ma: *Yul chen nye ba'i tshandoha bal po'i gnas kyi dkar chag rna ba'i bdud rtsi*, pp. 190.5–192.4 (*grub thob brgyad cur grags pa'i gnas na brag phug yid du 'ong ba bzhi lnga tsam 'dug / de ni bod rnams kyis grub thob brgyad cu thams cad bzhugs pa'i gnas yin zer kyang / grub chen de rnams mkhas shing grub pa'i bdag nyid rtsod med du gyur pas mtshan nyi zla ltar grags shing sangs rgyas kyi bstan pa la bya ba rlabs po che byas pa'i mdzad pa mnyam pa tsam la brten nas dus snga phyir byon kyang grang (= grangs) brgyad cur 'dren pa'i srol ni byung mod / thog mnyam zhing dus mtshungs pa dang / ye yang lhan cig tu rgyu zhing gnas pa'i tshogs lta bu ga la yin pas de ltar mi 'thad / 'on kyang paṇḍita 'jigs med dpal dang mi nyag lo tsā ba gnyis las brgyud pa'i gtam nub phyogs kanta ma ra'i rgyal po kunyja'i lo rgyus ltar / yin na mtha' man bkag rung / gnas 'dir de ltar byung ba'i lo rgyus sngar ma thos / klu sgrub kyi sgrub khang yin zer ba zhig ni yod / der slob dpon rang gi rdo sku yod 'dug pa da lta brag phug gi phyi rol 'gyang tsam na bton 'dug / gzhan brag phug phal che ba ni dpal chos kyi grags pa'i rtsod zla saṃ ga rātsryya'i gnas yin par 'dug / de nyid gnas 'dir rgyun ring po bsdad pa'i skabs kyi rnam thar dang lo rgyus thor bu ji snyed pa rgya gar ba rnams kyi ngag las 'byung ba thos / gnas 'di'i rten gyi gtso bo ni khang bzang gser gyi rgya phubs can gyi nang du lha mi u gra tā ra ste e ka dzā ṭi sku mdog dmar mo zhal gcig phyag bzhi dang po gnyis thugs khar gri thod / lhag ma gnyis ral gri dang utpala 'dzin pa dang steng khang la'ang u gra tā ra'i li sku zhal phyag phyag mtshan dang bcas gong dang 'dra ba la g.yon brkyang gis bzhengs pa dang / de yi g.yas g.yon du rgyal po binta rā dza'i dbu yin zer ba dang zangs kha sbubs bcas yod / 'di yi lo rgyus ltar snang ba mang po bal bod kyi mi mang po'i ngag las thos mos kyis de kun ma dag par 'dug pas 'dir ma bris*) and Macdonald & Dvags-po Rin-po-che (1981:253–254). For the legend of Śaṅkarācarya's stay in Nepal, his wish to debate with Buddhist masters and his encounter with the Maṇiyoginī Ugratārā on Maṇicūḍa hill behind Saṅkhu according to the Wright chronicle, see Bajracharya, Michaels & Gutschow (2016, vol. 1:38–39).

[107] The various religious objects which Tibetan pilgrims saw at Saṅkhu are also described by the Fourth Khams-sprul. He recorded the weaving implements of Bhṛkuṭī, the Nepalese wife of Srong-btsan sgam-po—located again on the upper floor of the the main temple—and the stone caitya in a separate shrine; along with the two statues of Ugratārā, venerated by both Buddhists and Hindus, he also mentions the fire and water, which he says are known as 'Fire at the End of an Aeon' and 'Water at the End of an Aeon'. To the end of this section is added the story of the Bodhisattva Prince Maṇicūḍa, who gave away the jewel of his *uṣṇīṣa*, known as Maṇiliṅga, still supposedly to be seen on Maṇicūḍa hill. The source of the Maṇirohiṇī river, also associated with the former presence of Maṇicūḍa, was nearby, as was a miraculous rock cave, whose significance is recorded as well; see bsTan-'dzin Chos-Kyi nyima: *Yul chen nye ba'i tshandoha bal po'i gnas kyi dkar chag rna ba'i bdud rtsi*, pp. 192.4–193.6 (*steng khang der bal bza' khri btsun gyi thags khri yang thog la bkal 'dug / yang khang pa gcig na rdo yi mchod rten rang byung yang yod do / de rnams bzhengs pa po dang dus snga phyis sogs ji bzhin ma shes / lha mo ugra tā ra ni phyi nang gnyi ka la so so'i lugs kyi rgyud sgrub thabs dang bcas pa yod / shes rab kyi lha khyad par can du brtsi / phyi rol pa tshos ni dmar gyi arghaṃ kyang mchod par byed / de na bskal pa'i me dang bskal pa'i chur grags pa yang yod / de yi rgyab ri'i rtse mor mani (= maṇi) liṅga zhes bya ba yod de / ri de'i ming ni nor bu brtsegs pa'i ri zhes bya / de'i rtse mor sngon byang chub sems dpa' nor bu'i gtsug ting nge 'dzin la yun ring por bzhugs nas nam zhig na rang gi gtsug gi nor bu phral te sbyin pa byin pa nyid rdo yi rang bzhin du gnas gyur pa ni da lta ma ni (= ma ṇi) liṅga ste nor bu'i mtshan pa zhes bya ba 'di yin / des na de dang mi ring ba'i cha nas 'babs pa'i chu bo 'di byang chub sems pa nor'i gtsug sbyin pa bzhugs pa'i skabs kyi khrag dang*

*'dres pas ma ni lo hi ni (= ma ṇi ro hi ṇī) ste nor bu dmar ldan zhes grags so / de dang nye ba'i zhig na brag phug gcig yod pa'i ngos la sātstsha bstan na rdo khab len gyis lcags len pa bzhin brag ngos su 'byar 'gro ba zhig kyang yod par thos so*), and Macdonald & Dvags-po Rin-po-che (1981:253–254). On Prince Maṇicūḍa, his practice of austerities in the mountain forests, where he gave away the jewel of his *uṣṇiśa,* and the creation of ten things beginning with the letter *ma*—including Maṇicūḍa hill, Maṇiliṅga, Maṇirohiṇī river and Maṇiyoginī—according to the Wright Chronicle, see Bajaracharya, Michaels & Gutschow (2016, vol. 1:24).

[108] Reference is being made here to the tale of Viśvaṃtara in the work of Āryaśūra (3rd/4th cent.); see *Jātaka-māla* [= *sKyes pa'i rabs kyi rgyud*], pp. 15.3.6–19.3.4. Various accounts concerning the chained head of a king stored on the upper floor of the main temple at Saṅkhu are mentioned by the Fourth Khams-sprul in his guidebook; see note 106. This same religious object is also referred to by Brag-dkar rta-so sPrul-sku, who rejects the origin of it as being according to the tale of the previous life of Buddha Śākyamuni. This is verified by the account of Si-tu Paṇ-chen, who stayed in Saṅkhu for three days when he was first entering the Kathmandu Valley at the beginning of 1724. There he inspected the site of the 'Cave of the Eighty Siddhas' (*grub thob brgyad cu'i phug pa*) and paid particular attention to the head of Śākyamuni Buddha attached with an iron chain to a big copper cauldron turned upside down in front of it. The belief of Tibetan visitors is reported as being that at the time of the degeneration of Śākyamuni's doctrine the head would sink deeper and deeper into the ground and that, as a sign that the time was ripe for the doctrine of the future Buddha Maitreya, an effigy of the latter would arise from below; to prevent this the head had been strapped to an iron chain and the already partly visible head of the statue of Buddha Maitreya covered with the copper cauldron. It is stated that such foolish talk can be found in the guidebook written by 'Rang-rig [ras-pa of the] 'Brug-pa [school]' (*'brug pa rang rig pa*). This may refer to the previously mentioned extended guidebook composed by mNga'-ris grub-chen; see the Introduction, note 13, and Chos-kyi 'byung-gnas: *Ta'i si tu 'bod pa karma bstan pa'i nyin byed kyi rang tshul drangs par brjod pa dri bral shel gyi me long*, pp. 114.1–4 (*'dir zhag gsum bzhugs ring sa mgo'i nye phyogs su bod pa rnams grub thob brgyad cu'i phug pa yin zer yang / gang ltar sngar grub chen mang po bzhugs pa'i gnas yin nges bcos ma'i sa 'og phug chung mang po yod pa dang / rdo rje rnal 'byor ma'i sku rang byon sogs mjal / yang lha khang zhig tu gser zangs las grub pa'i sangs rgyas kyi dbu lcags thag gis btags pa zhig dang de'i mdun du zangs shin tu che ba zhig sbub (= sbubs) nas bzhag 'dug par / bod pa rnams kyi kha ngag tu thub pa'i dbu de shā ka (= shākya) thub pa'i bstan pa nub pa'i tshes 'og tu 'bying bar 'gyur la / de nas byams mgon gyi bstan pa 'byung ba'i ltas su byams pa'i sku sa nas brdol rgyu la de dag mi 'byung ba'i phyir dbu gcig shos lcags thag gis (= gis) btags shing / byams pa'i sku'i dbu cung zad thon pa zangs kyi (= kyis) bkab pa yin no zer zhing 'brug pa rang rig pas kyang bal po'i dkar chag tu de bzhin bris pa mthong mod / de ni blun po rnams kyi kha ngag kho nar thad na ci yang ma brtags pa nyid do*). This is followed by what he takes to be authentic accounts of Śākyamuni Buddha's head and the copper cauldron as told by reliable Newar informants; see ibid., pp. 114.4–115.1, and Lewis & Jamspal (1988:195–196).

[109] The Fourth Khams-sprul also criticized as a misconception claims by Tibetan pilgrims that the self-arisen Garuḍa statue at Cāṅgu had originally formed the central part of Ārya Nāgārjuna's rosary. It was believed that the teaching throne of the master still existed at Śāntipur at Svayaṃbhūnāth and that the self-arisen effigy had manifested when he propitiated the nāgas; see bsTan-'dzin Chos-kyi nyi-ma: *Yul chen nye ba'i tshandhoha bal po'i gnas kyi dkar chag gangs can rna ba'i bdud rtsi*, pp. 180.6–181.3 (*des na lo rgyus de las 'khrul*

*nas da lta bod rnams kyis shanta pu rir klu bsgrubs pa'i bzhugs khri yod zer ba dang / de yi skabs kyi phyag phreng gi mdo 'dzin la khyung rang byon byung ba da lta cang khung 'di yin zer ba sogs ngag sgros 'phyugs mang po 'dug na'ang lo rgyus 'di bzhin go na de thams cad bye ma'i changs bu bzhin du hrul gyis 'jig par 'gyur ro*), and Macdonald & Dvags-po Rin-po-che (1981:249). This criticism of 'old talk' (*gtam rnying pa*) is taken up again at the beginning of the description of Cāṅgu; see ibid., pp. 188.6–187.2 (*de nas bal skad du tsang khung dang bod rnams kyis zur chags pas sa 'go zhes 'bod pa'i grong khyer chen po'i dbus su khyung rang byung yod / de ni klu sgrub kyi mdo 'dzin las byung ba sogs bod la grags pa'i gtam rnying pa nyid mi 'thad pa'i rgyu mtshan gong du bshad zin*), and Macdonald & Dvags-po Rin-po-che (1981:252). Si-tu Paṇ-chen had earlier during his own visit objected to this statue being recognized by Tibetans as a Garuḍa bird rather than as a statue of Viṣṇu; see Chos-kyi 'byung-gnas: *Ta'i si tu 'bod pa karma bstan pa'i nyin byed kyi rang tshul drangs par brjod pa dri bral shel gyi me long*, p. 115.3–4 (*'di la yang bod pa rnams klu sgrub kyis klu dam la brtag pa'i (= btags pa'i) phyag phreng na ga (= nāga ) pa ṇi yin zhing de la khyung rang byung yod ces dang / sku de'ang bya khyung tsam las khyab 'jug yin pa ma shes pa sogs ni der zad do*). For the arrival of Viṣṇu on Garuḍa at the Cāṅgu hill according to the Wright Chronicle, and his making himself known as Harihariharivāhanalokeśvara (one of the 108 Lokeśvaras), see Bajracharya, Michaels & Gutschow (2016, vol. 1:16).

[110] In the pilgrimage guidebook of Rang-rig ras-pa's disciple, the Mi-la ras-pa cave gNyi-shang kur-ti is placed south-east of Bhaktapur and is said to be described in the Great Yogin's 'biography' (*rnam thar*); see Ngag-dbang rdo-rje: *Bal yul mchod rten 'phags pa shing kun dang de'i gnas gzhan rnams kyi dkar chag*, p. 46.30–31. The episode of Mi-la ras-pa and his disciple Khyi-ra ras-pa can be found in the 'Collected Spiritual Songs' recorded by gTsang-smyon Heruka; see Sangs-rgyas rgyal-mtshan: *rJe btsun mi la ras pa'i rnam thar rgyas par phye ba mgur 'bum*, pp. 430.2–442.16 (*khyi ra ras pa dang mjal ba'i skor*). The secluded site, whose location is specified at the beginning of this chapter, is called gNyi-shang 'gur-rta; for the song intoned by Khyi-ra ras-pa, see ibid., pp. 438.1–439.9. The local designation Guru Bad[zra] seems to refer to Hasabadzra or Hasavajra, i.e. Laughing Vajra, the epithet by which Mi-la ras-pa was known to Newars. This is reported by the Fourth Khams-sprul, who also provided the Newar name Vagīśvarī for the site; see bsTan-'dzin Chos-kyi nyi-ma: *Yul chen nye ba'i tshandhoha bal po'i gnas kyi dkar chag gangs can rna ba'i bdud rtsi*, pp. 193.6–194.3 (*gnyi shang kur ti ni rje btsun bzhad pa rdo rje'i bsti gnas khyi ra ba mgon po rdo rje yang 'dir rjes su bzung / shva ba'i zhabs rjes kyang brag la gsal bar yod / rje btsun chen po 'di'i mtshan gyi grags pa ni bal po'i phyogs su yang che bar yod mtshan yang ha sa badzra du 'bod rnam thar zhib pa ni mi shes gsung mgur grags che ba kha shas saṃ skri ta'i (= saṃ skri ṭa'i) skad du bsgyur te don gyin yod 'dug / gnas di yi ming bal po rnams kyis vā gi shwa ri zer*), and Macdonald & Dvags-po Rin-po-che (1981:254–255). Concerning the Nye-shang-pa ethnic group, which according to the Sixth Zhva-dmar-pa Chos-kyi dbang-phyug's travelogue inhabited the regions below Helambu, see Ehrhard (2013:291); also id. (2013:290) on the ethnonym rTa-mang[s] as explained in the biography of the Third Yol-mo-ba sPrul-sku bsTan-'dzin nor-bu, who places their settlements on the northern route from Kathmandu to sKyid-grong. See Quintman (2008:373–374) for the Mi-la ras-pa sites located on or near the trade and pilgrimage routes between Tibet and Nepal that are most clearly described in gTsang-smyon Heruka's texts.

[111] The narrative of the previous life of Buddha Śākyamuni's giving his body to a female tiger so that she could feed her cubs is contained in the *Ārya-suvarṇaprabhāsottama-sūtrendrarāja-nāma-mahāyāna-sūtra* [= *'Phags pa gser 'od dam pa mdo sde'i dbang po'i rgyal po zhes bya ba theg pa chen po'i mdo*], chapter 18, pp. 98.1.2–100.5.2 (*stag mo la lus*

*yongs su btang ba*) and in the *Dāma-mūko-nāma-sūtra* [= *'Dzang blun zhes bya ba'i mdo*], chapter 2, pp. 58.2.1–59.2.7 (*sems can chen pos stag mo la lus byin pa'i le'u*). This famous story is also recounted in the guidebook of the Fourth Khams-sprul, who points out that the original *jātaka* sources should be consulted and explains that the name of the Buddha was evoked by both Buddhists and Hindus out of fear of tigers when travelling to this site; see bsTan-'dzin Chos-kyi nyi-ma: *Yul chen po nye ba'i tshandhoha bal po gnas kyi dkar chag gangs can rna ba'i bdud rtsi*, pp.194.3–195.2 (*stag mo lus sbyin du grags pa ni skyes rabs sogs las 'byung ba'i dngos gnas ran yin yin min slar brtag dgos shing / skye bo spyi la grags tshod kyi dbang di byas na bcom ldan 'das sngon byang chub sems dpa' spyad pa spyod pa'i tshe na stag mo bkres pas nyen te rjes su 'brangs pa'i phru gu za bar brtsams pa la snying rjes kun nas bslangs te lus sbyin par btang ba'i dbu skra dang rus pa sogs la mchod rten du byas pa nyid yin / gnas 'dir stag gi 'jigs pa che bas dngos ming nas ma smos par sangs rgyas kyi mtshan brjod na 'jigs pa las skyob pa'i dgos pa yod pa'i phyir da lta yang grub mtha' phyi nang gang yin kyang 'dra ste bal po thams cad kyis 'di yi ming la ni na mo budha ya zer / 'der 'gro ba'i lam dri na yang stag mo lus sbyin gang na yod ces dris na mi go na na mo buddha ya gang na yod ces dris na go ba zhig 'dug go*), and Macdonald & Dvags-po Rin-po-che (1981:255). The Fourth No-min-han, too, refers to the narrative in the *Suvarṇa-prabhāsottama-sūtra*, but he did not believe that the stūpa is the one containing the remains of the Bodhisattva; see bsTan-'dzin phrin-las: *'Dzam gling rgyas bshad*, pp. 46.19–47.10, and Wylie (1970:24–25). On that point, he quotes a second time from mNga'-ris grub-chen's guidebook, namely a statement about the multiplicity of relics of Bodhisattvas who have reached the stage called *slob pa'i lam* (*śaikṣamarga*); see the Introduction, note 11.

[112] The Speaking Tārā is mentioned already in the pilgrimage guidebook of Rang-rig ras-pa's disciple; see Ngag-dbang rdo-rje: *Bal yul mchod rten 'phags pa shing kun dang de'i gnas gzhan rnams kyi dkar chag*, p. 46.30–31 (*kho khom na sgrol ma gsung byon ma yod*). As the main religious object for Tibetan pilgrims in Bhaktapur, possessing as it does great power to bless, it is also recorded in the work of the Fourth No-min-han; see bsTan-'dzin phrin-las: *'Dzam gling rgyas bshad*, p. 44.5, and Wylie (1970:18). In the 'Collected Spiritual Songs' of Mi-la ras-pa compiled by gTsang-smyon Heruka, the chapter on Ārya Tārā appearing to the king in a dream and the latter's offerings to the great yogin follows the episode involving Khyi-ra ras-pa; see Sangs-rgyas rgyal-mtshan: *rJe btsun mi la ras pa rnam thar rgyas par phye ba mgur 'bum*, pp. 442.17–451.3 (*kho khom rgyal pos mchod cing tshe ring mas glags blta phyir myul ba'i skor*).

[113] Neither the quotation from a treasure work mentioning Ekajaṭī, the female protector of the Great Perfection doctrine, nor a cave with her effigy in the vicinity of Bhaktapur has yet been identified. According to the modern pilgrimage guide, the shrine of Caṇḍeśvarī within eyesight of Banepa is what is meant; see Ngag-dbang rdo-rje: *Bal yul gnas yig*, p. 40.33–34 (*e ka dza ti [= eka dza tī] tsan ti shwa ri [= tsaṇ ḍi shwa rī] ba ne pāl [= ba ne pa] sa mig mthong sar yod / e ka dza ti [= eka dza tī] rang ngo po [= ngo bo] gcig pa lha mo tsan ṭi ka [= tsaṇ ḍi ka] 'dra*), and Dowman (1981:282). The literary source for the Golden Cave may have been the guidebook of Karma Blo-bzang that has yet to surface; see Introduction, note 25.

[114] The Fourth Khams-sprul in his guidebook puts the location of the sacred site at the bank of the river Bāgmati and provides the names Guhyeśvari (pronounced Gutishwari by the Indians and Nepalese), the Tibetan translation of this as 'Lady of the Secret' (*gsang ba'i dbang phyug ma*), and the name '[Vajra]vārāhī's Amniotic Fluid' given by the Tibetans. This quite extensive section contains the reference to Nepal as an *upacchandoha-pīṭha* and

cites the *Svayaṃbhūpurāṇa* as the literary source for Guhyeśvari being the location of the womb of the goddess Vajravārāhī (or Kākāmukhī); see note 31. For the full passage, see bsTan-'dzin Chos-kyi nyi-ma: *Yul chen po nye ba'i tshandhoha bal po'i gnas kyi dkar chag gangs can rna ba'i bdud rtsi*, pp. 185.3–188.5, and Macdonald & Dvags-po Rin-po-che (1981:251–252). The lingam and yoni of Paśupatināth and Guhyeśvari are described as sacred objects, regarded by Buddhists as those of Heruka and Vajrayoginī, and by Hindus as those of Śiva and Śaktī. For the different ways Buddhists worship Guhyeśvari, including as Nairātmyā, see Slusser (1982:215–216 & 327). In the old pilgrimage guide, only Guhyeśvari is singled out among the many astonishing sacred sites to the south of the Bodhnāth Stūpa; see bSod-nams dpal bzang-po: *Dus gsum sangs rgyas thams cad kyi thugs kyi rten 'phags pa shing kun gyi dkar chag*, p. 88.5, and Ehrhard (2013:82).

115 In the Fourth Khams-sprul's guidebook, Paśupati (there translated into Tibetan as 'Lord of Cattle' (*phyugs bdag*)) is given as the name of the sacred image in the main temple in Gulang village. It is said to be this same lingam of Maheśvara that was shattered into pieces by the Buddhist mahāsiddha Jalandharipa. As it was not possible to investigate conditions at the time, the author relates oral accounts describing the fear of being cursed by the mahāsiddha and the erection of a wooden Buddhist caitya on this spot; see bsTan-'dzin Chos-kyi nyi-ma: *Yul chen po nye ba'i tshandoha bal po'i gnas kyi dkar chag*, pp. 184.2–185.3 (*gu lang gyi grong khyer dbus na pā shu pa ti (= pa shu pa ti) ste phyugs bdag ces dbang phyug chen po'i linga rang byung gdong bzhis mtshan pa'i lha khang shin tu mthong che ba rgya phubs can mchod rdzas sna tshogs kyi gang ba dang / de yi bgos gcig na lcags kyi tri shul la thog so do lhag tsam pa yod / gu ti shwa ri dang 'di gnyis kar dmar gyi argham gyis mchod cing shin tu gnyan par grags / linga 'di ni sngon grub thob dza landha ri pas nus pa bstan pa'i cho 'phrul gyis tshal bar gas yod ces bshad pa de gnas 'dir yin pa ni rtsod pa med la 'on kyang da lta rgyan mang pos g.yogs shing bsgribs pa dang 'khris su 'gror mi bcud bsags yod min ji bzhin mi shes pa 'dug / des na dus de skabs kyi rang byung gi rten de ngo ma'am de yi shul du byung ba gang rigs shig yin par byed dgos shing / la la dag gi zer sgros la dus deng sang yang sngon grub thob kyi dmod pas 'jigs te / dus nges can zhig la nang pa'i mchod rten shing la byas bsgribs pas 'jog pa yin kyang zer / gang ltar shin tu grags che ba'i gnas rten yin pas lo re bzhin zla dus nges pa can zhig la rgya gar pa shin tu mang pa 'dzoms nas mchod pa byed pa'i srol da lta yang yod 'dug*), and Macdonald & Dvags-po Rin-po-che (1981:250–251). For the description of the main temple of Paśupati and the magical contest performed by Mitrayogin with the non-Buddhists according to the biography of Khro-phu Lo-tsā-ba, see Byams-pa'i dpal: *Paṇ grub gsum gyi rnam thar dpag bsam khri shing*, fol. 23a/7–b/5 (*de'i og tu gu lang gser khang bya ba mu stegs kyi rten sgra can gcig yod de / mu stegs kyi lha rten rdo la rang byung ba mi gang tsam sa la 'phags te thon pa / phyogs bzhir zhal bzhi phyag brgyad yod cing drung du phyin na 'jigs kyang phro ba yang skye ba gcig yod / de la gser gyi rgya phubs nyis [= gnyis] rim brtsegs pa'i steng na gser gar bu'i 'ga' dzi ra [= gañjira] btsugs / byang gi ngos na sdong po la rtse gsum pa'i gzugs chen po gcig yod pa / phyogs kyi sgo bzhi na khro chu'i seng ge chen po gnyis gnyis sgo srung gi tshul du yod do / re zhig na gā dzi ra'i [= gañjira] rtse mor rjes mitras dkyil khrung mdzad de / mu tegs kyi rnal 'byor pa nga rgyal can yod pa lta stangs kyis bkug nas rtsod pa byas pas pham par byas / slar yang sa la babs nas brtul zhugs sna tshogs mdzad pas / mu stegs kyi nus mthu thob par grags pa'i cakra bar ti [= cakravarti] che chung bya ba ta pa ri ral pa'i cod paṇ chen bcings pas smyo bar byas te lha la phyag 'tshal bar bgro ba dang / phyag thal mo brdabs pas / sgo phyed ste 'dud pa brtsams pas / lha rten 'dar bar gyur / glo bur sa g.yo ba yang byung / me tog dmar po'i cher chen po yang babs skad* ).

[116] In the pilgrimage guidebook of Rang-rig ras-pa's disciple, the meditation caves and sacred springs associated with Tilopa and Nāropa (and a sacred spring and throne of Padmasambhava) are located to the south of Bodhnāth in the Paśupati and Guhyeśvari area; see Ngag-dbang rdo-rje, *Bal yul mchod rten 'phags pa shing kun dang de'i gnas gzhan rnams kyi dkar chag*, p. 46.15–19 (*de'i lho na tai lo ba'i sgrub khang sgrub chu yod / lhun grub brtsegs pa'i dur khrod / phag mo mngal chu yod / nā ro pa'i sgrub chu sgrub khang yod / o rgyan gyi sgrub chu dang bzhugs khri yod / gu lang ni dbang phyug chen po pho brang yin*). Si-tu Paṇ-chen visited the meditation caves said to be those of Tilopa and Nāropa during his visit to the area of Paśupati and Guhyeśvari in the spring of the year 1724; see Chos-kyi 'byung-gnas: *Dri bral shel gyi me long*, p. 126.5 (*phyi nyin gu lang du pā shu pa tir (= pa shu pa tir) te lo nā ro sgrub phug zer ba / phag mo gsang chu sogs mjal*).

[117] See *rGyal po'i mdzad pa nyi shu rtsa gcig pa*, chapter eight, in Different authors: *Maṇi bka' 'bum*, vol. 1, pp. 393.4–394.9. The same passage of the origin myth of the three self-arisen statues is also quoted by Brag-dkar rta-so sPrul-sku in the pilgrimage guide to the Ārya Wa-ti bzang-po; see Ehrhard (2004:162–163 & 235–236). It should be noted that the names of the individual statues are left out in this source, and the Vindhya mountains—there located at the border of the Nepal Valley—are referred to in order to identify the statues' place of origin; concerning this mountain range, see note 94.

[118] A more extensive version of the origin myth of the 'Four Brothers Ārya [Avalokiteśvara]' (*'phags pa sku mched bzhi*) is contained in the old pilgrimage guidebooks to the statue of Ārya Wa-ti bzang-po; for the relevant sections, see Ehrhard (2004:163–165 & 236–239). In these works, Jo-bo U-khang is localized to Ye-rang (i.e. Patan), and Jo-bo 'Ja'-ma-li to Yam-bu (i.e. Kathmandu). To Jo-bo Wa-ti bzang-po in sKyid-grong is added the Ārya Lokeśvara as a fourth statue, said also to have been brought to Tibet, where it afterwards came to reside in the Potala Palace; for Brag-dkar rta-so sPrul-sku's assessment of these various accounts, see Ehrhard (2004:170–172 & 246–249). The Fourth Khams-sprul reported 'Five Brothers Ārya [Avalokiteśvara]' (*'phags pa mched lnga*) and criticized the view that the White 'Ja'-ma-li was Mañjughoṣa. He added that it was difficult for Tibetans to enter the shrines of the three Jo-bos located in the Valley—one in Kathmandu and two in Patan—and that the faces of all the statues were masked; see bsTan-'dzin Chos-kyi nyi-ma, *Yul chen po nye ba'i tshandoha bal po'i gnas kyi dkar chag*, p. 197.1–4 (*jo bo 'ja' ma li dkar po ni 'phags pa mched lnga'i ya gyal yin cing mched lnga ga lha yi ngo ni spyan ras gzigs yin par 'dug kyang ye rang na bzhugs pa'i jo bo gnyis ka sku mdog dmar po dang 'di dkar po yin pas / kha cig 'ja' ma li 'jam dbyangs yin nam snyam pa ni nor ba'o / spyir jo bo gsum ka'i lha khang gi nang du bod kyi mi mi thar bas zhal phyag sogs ji bzhin pa rtsad ma chod / zhal ras kyang dngos su ma mthong ba de ni phyi nas mthong ba de ni phyi nas sku 'bags g.yogs pa yin 'dug*), and Macdonald & Dvags-po Rin-po-che (1981:256). On the second statue in Patan, see note 124.

[119] For the legendary account of the establishment of various caityas in Kathmandu by the Mauryan king Aśoka (and in particular the four great stūpas of Pāṭan) according to the Wright chronicle, see Bajracharya, Michaels & Gutschow (2016, vol. 1:30 & 36). The quotation by Kaḥ-thog Rig-'dzin is contained in a prayer composed in the fourth Tibetan month of the year 1754; see Tshe-dbang nor-bu: *sMon tshig sna tshogs phyogs bsdus*, p. 436.11–13. The Fourth Khams-sprul mentioned a number of these caityas here and there in the Valley; see bsTan-'dzin Chos-kyi nyi-ma: *Yul chen po nye ba'i tshandoha bal po'i gnas kyi dkar chag*, p. 170.1 (*rgyal po mya ngan med kyis bzhengs pa'i mchod rten rnams phan tshun du yod*), and Macdonald & Dvags-po Rin-po-che (1981:244). He also specifically pointed out

the one alluded to by Kaḥ-thog Rig-'dzin and identified the acting priest of the monastic complex, Samantabhadra, as the head of the Gubhāju Vajrācāryas; see bsTan-'dzin Chos-kyi nyi-ma: *Yul chen nye ba'i tshandoha bal po'i gnas kyi dkar chag*, p. 200.2–4 (*chos rgyal mya ngan med kyis de bzhin gshegs pa'i ring bsrel gyi snying po can gyi mchod rten bye ba phar gcig bzhengs pa'i ya gyal rtsod med du gyur pa zhig yam bu grong khyer du da lta nang pa gurba rnams kyis slob dpon du byed samantabhadra zhes bya ba'i bsti gnas khang pa'i dkyil du yod*). The Newar priests of this monastic compound must have hosted visiting Tibetan teachers. It is known that Brag-dkar rta-so sPrul-sku stayed in the residence of Paṇḍita Śrī Harṣa during his second trip to the Valley in the year 1802; see the Introduction, note 23. According to the pilgrimage guidebooks to the region of Mang-yul Gung-thang, further caityas associated with King Aśoka were located in this region, among other places in the temple of the Ārya Wa-ti bzang-po and in the lower part of La-ldebs; see Ehrhard (2004:262 & 374, and 289 & 442).

120 The pilgrimage guidebook of Rang-rig ras-pa's disciple contains the story of an arrow shot by Śākyamuni and his two main disciples from the peak of Ri-bo 'big[s]-byed; it is said to have landed at a site in the centre of Kathmandu. The five statues of the king-like spirit Pehar and his attendants known as 'Dispelling All Hindrances' (*bar chad kun sel*) are said to be located west of the city near the Ram-do-li charnel grounds; see Ngag-dbang rdo-rje: *Bal yul mchod rten 'phags pa shing kun dang de'i gnas gzhan rnams kyi dkar chag*, p. 46.25–29 (*bcom ldan 'das dang shā ri'i bu mo'u 'gal gyi bu rnams kyis ri 'bigs byed kyi rtse nas rdo mda' rgyab pa yam bu'i grong khyer gyi dbus na da lta yang ye re yod / grong khyer gyi nub smad na rgyal po sku lnga dzhe kṣi las grub pa bar chad kun sel bya ba yod / de'i logs na dur khrod ram do li bya yod*). According to the same guidebook, the stone arrow was located at Makhan-tol; see Ngag-dbang rdo-rje: *Bal yul mchod rten 'phags pa shing kun dang de'i gnas gzhan rnams kyi dkar chag*, pp. 38.35–39.1, and Dowman (1981:235–236). The mentioned statues represent Pehar as the leader of a band of five spirits known as *Pe har rgyal po*; see Wylie (1970:29–30, note 79). Images of Gorakṣanātha are extremely rare, but I suppose that Brag-dkar rta-so sPrul-sku is referring to the Kāṣṭhamaṇḍapa, one of his chief shrines in the Kathmandu Valley; see Slusser (1982:367).

121 The Fourth Khams-sprul included a reference to E vihāra in his guidebook and mentioned rediscovered *thang-yig* literature as the source for the narrative that Padmasambhava had shown the various hells to his female disciple Kusalī at this site; see bsTan-'dzin Chos-kyi nyi-ma: *Yul chen po nye ba'i tshandhoha bal po'i dkar chag*, p. 206.4–6 (*e bi ha ra'i [= bi hāra'i] gtsug lag khang ni bal yul e yi gtsug lag khang du grags shing sngon slob dpon chen po padma 'byung gnas kyis bal mo ku sa li [= ku sa lī] la dmyal ba bstan pa'i lo rgyus sogs thang yig gter ma 'ga' las 'byung ba'i gnas de yin par 'dug*), and Macdonald & Dvags-po Rin-po-che (1981:260). According to the ninth chapter of the *lHa 'dre bka'i thang yig*, Padmasambhava met the ruler Śīlamañju and his family in Nepal, and the encounter with the princess lHa-lcam Kun-sa zhi (*sic*) led to her descent to and later return from the hells. Together with a temple called Go-ti bi-ra'i gtsug-lag khang and the 'Phags-pa shing-kun gtsug-lag khang, the E'i gtsug-lag khang is listed as the most prominent pilgrimage place in the country; see O-rgyan gling-pa: *bKa' thang sde lnga*, pp. 16.3–24.11, and Blondeau (1971: 60–68). On the claim that the Buddha statue of Kva Bahal is a speaking Sambhogakāya image, see note 124.

122 For the earlier reference to Jo-bo U-khang as one of the Four Brothers Ārya Avalokiteśvara, see note 118. The Newar name for the statue derives from the fact that his temple is located in Bungamati, to the south of Patan. Jo-bo 'Bu-khang, the second statue (locat-

ed in Patan), is also named after his residence, namely Cakra vihāra; he is also known as Mīnanāth-Matsyendranāth. On these two Buddhist deities and their chariot festivals, see Slusser (1982:374–375). Consult Vajracharya, Michaels & Gutschow (2016, vol. 1:52–56) concerning the arrival of the second deity in Nepal—in the form a bee that entered a *kalaśa* during the reign of King Narendradeva—according to the Wright chronicle. The Tibetan name and the legend of the bee's emanation from the statue of Jo-bo U-khang is already attested in the old Tibetan guidebooks to the Ārya Wa-ti bzang-po; for Brag-dkar rta-so sPrul-sku's critical stance towards the legend, which results in the number of Brothers Ārya Avalokiteśvara being five, see Ehrhard (2004:246, and 338–339, note 44). His reservations about the name 'Bu-khang—a ray of light the size of an 'insect' (*'bu*) emanating from the heart of Jo-bo U-khang—are shared by the Fourth Khams-sprul, who refers to the Tibetan guidebooks' reporting of the Newar tradition. In a longer section in his own guidebook, he provides further details about the two Buddhist statues including the respect they received from the kings of Patan. It should be noted that he used the name Jo-bo A-kkam instead of Jo-bu U-khang; see bsTan-'dzin Chos-kyi nyi-ma: *Yul chen po'i nye ba'i tshandoha bal po'i dkar chag*, pp. 200.4–203.1, and Macdonald & Dvags-po Rin-po-che (1981:258–250). This suggests that he regarded Jo-bo A-kkam as the original Jo-bo U-khang; see note 123.

123 The text of the Sixth Zhva-dmar-pa describes a journey to Nepal undertaken in 1629/30, its starting and end point being the sacred site of La-phyi. During his stay in the Valley the hierarch of the Karma bKa'-brgyud-pa school met King Lakṣminarasiṃha (reign: 1619–1641, in Kathmandu), King Siddhinarasiṃha (reign: 1619–1661, in Patan) and King Jagat-jyotir Malla (reign: 1614–1637, in Bhaktapur); see Ehrhard (2013:283–285). Regarding his visit to Chobāra and the identification of the statue called A-kkam Jo-bo as one of the 'Five Self-Arisen [Avalokiteśvara] Brothers' (*rang byon mched lnga*), see Chos-kyi dbang-phyug: *Bal yul du bgrod pa'i lam yig nor bu spel ma'i 'phreng ba*, pp. 24a/2–3 (*de nub yam bu nas song ste dur khrod ra ma do li dang nye ba'i nags 'dab [= 'dabs] chu klung gi 'gram zhig tu gnas btab bo / sang nang par bal po'i skad du ra ma do li zhes bya rje mar pa'i mgur las kyang / byung ba'i dur khrod de dang de'i ri de'u zhig gi rtser rang byon mched lnga'i ya gyal a kkam jo bo bzhugs pa mjal nas rim par song te*), and Lamminger (2013:246–247). On the Sixth Zhva-dmar-pa's assesssment of the Five Avalokiteśvara statues and the one at Chobāra, consult also Lamminger (2013:154–155). In his guidebook to the Ārya Wa-ti bzang-po, Brag-dkar rta-so sPrul-sku compares the sizes and postures of the Chobāra statue and the Ārya U-khang-pa in Patan, and concludes that the former could not be the original Ārya U-khang-pa; see Ehrhard (2004:246).

124 The sacred objects of Patan listed in the pilgrimage guidebook of Rang-rig ras-pa's disciple are the statues of Jo-bo A-khang and Jo-bo U-khang (the former obviously referring to the Chobāra statue), the Mahābuddha temple and the Buddha in Kva Bahal, identified as a speaking Sambhogakāya image of Śākyamuni; see Ngag-dbang rdo-rje: *Bal yul mchod rten 'phags pa shing kun dang de'i gnas gzhan rnams kyi dkar chag*, p. 46.31–34 (*ye rang na maṇi bka' 'bum na gsal ba'i jo bo a khang u khang gnyis dang / sangs rgyas stong sku bzhugs / rdo rje gdan gyi zhing bkod dang sangs rgyas longs sku gsung 'byon bzhugs*). The Fourth Khams-sprul reported that the replica of the Mahābodhi temple in Bodhgaya was erected not by a trader but by the rich and powerful ancestor of a Brahmin called Rāmānanda, who also installed a stone statue of Śākyamuni in its interior; see bsTan-'dzin Chos-kyi nyi-ma: *Yul chen nye ba'i tshandoha bal po'i dkar chag*, p. 203.1–4 (*rdo rje gdan gyi gandhola'i bkod pa 'di ni da lta bram ze paṇḍita rā ma nanda zhes grags pa 'di yi pha mes bram ze zhig mnga' thang dang 'byor ba rgyas pa'i skabs yul dbus rdo rje gdan du rang gis dngos su byin nas de yi dri gtsang khang gi bkod pa 'di yang slar 'khor nas bzhengs / rdo rje gdan*

*rang nas spyan drangs pa'i sangs rgyas kyi rdo sku byin rlabs can 'di yang byang chub chen po'i tshul du bzhugs su gsol ba'o*), and Macdonald & Dvags-po Rin-po-che (1981:259). The Fourth No-min-han accords the replica the most prominent place among the many sacred objects of the city of Patan; see bsTan-'dzin 'phrin-las: *'Dzam gling rgyas bshad,* p. 2.17–18 (*grong khyer ye rang du rdo rje gdan gyi bkod pa ... sogs rten byin rlabs can mang po*), and Wylie (1970:18). According to the Wright chronicle, the Mahābuddha temple was erected by one Abhayarāja from Oṃkuli vihāra; see Vajarcharya, Michaels & Gutschow (2016:101 & 103).

125 The Lun-ti temple and the blessing-bestowing statue of Vajravārāhī are mentioned in the biography of Khro-phu Lo-tsā-ba in the context of finding a proper guide for his journey from Nepal to India; see Byams-pa'i dpal: *Paṇ grub gsum gyi rnam thar dpag bsam khri shing*, fol. 21a/5–6 (*dpon g.yog gsum pos lun ti lha khang du nye ba na rigs ngan bu mo rdo rje rnal 'byor ma'i rten la thim pa sku byin rlabs can yod pa la mchod chung byas pas ka cha kun gril te lam gyi sna khrid pa'i a tsa ra bi sham bya ba la bskur*). Another legend, of a Brahmin woman who lost her caste and whose body was cremated next to the pedestal of the Vajravārāhī statue, is related by the Sixth Zhva-dmar-pa; see *Bal yul du bgrod pa'i lam yig nor bu spel ma'i 'phreng ba*, fols. 23b/4–24a/2, and Lamminger (2013:245–246). The Fourth Khams-sprul calls this place a special sacred site that bestows siddhis, and describes the statue as a Vārāhī in flight, bearing a *vajra* and *khaṭvāṅga*. He identifies it, too, as the meditation image used by Maitrīpāda (Maitrīpa, ca. 1007–ca. 1085), and considered it possible that it also served as such for persons like the Indian [Vajra]pāṇi (a disciple of Maitrīpa) and sTong-nyid ting-'dzin [rdo-rje], i.e. the Newar master Devākaracandra; see bsTan-'dzin Chos-kyi nyi-ma: *Yul chen po nye ba'i tshandoha bal po'i dkar chag*, pp. 195.2–196.1 (*phag mo dur khrod ni dngos grub byung ba'i gnas khyad par can yin te / de yang dur khrod chen po 'jigs su rung ba nyin mo bya rgod dang dur bya 'khor zhing lding ba mtshan mo lce spyang gi ngu sgra di re ba zhig gi dbus na gtsug lag khang bkod pa legs pa'i nang du rten gyi gtso bo de ni rje btsun bcom ldan 'das rig pa 'dzin ma rnam par rtsen ma zhes phyag g.yas rdo rje zhabs g.yas dang lhan cig phyir brkyangs pa dang / g.yon pad sdong dang bcas zhabs g.yon gyi skyid khung nas bteg pa kha ṭwa phrag la bkal nas nam mkha' la 'phur ba'i tshul can gyi sku gzugs li ma byin rlabs shin tu che ba / mnga' bdag mai tri pa'i thugs dam yin nges pa / rgya gar phyag na dang stong nyid ting 'dzin la sogs pa'i rten skal du byon pa yin nam bsam*), and Macdonald & Dvags-po Rin-po-che (1981:255–256). The 'Three Khecarīs' (*mkha' spyod gsum*) refers to three forms of Vajravārāhī known as Nāro Khecarī, Indra[bhuti] Khecarī and Maitri[pāda] Khecarī; on these three khecarī lineages as the highest practices within the 'Thirteen Golden Dharmas of Sa-skya' (*sa skya gser chos bcu gsum*), see Stearns (2006:656, n. 390). The final two sentences in Brag-dkar rta-so sPrul-sku's account seem to be mutually contradictory; the actual claim made by Tibetan pilgrims may have referred to one of the two remaining Khecarīs.

126 For the location of the Ramdoli (or Ramadoli) charnel grounds according to the old pilgrimage guidebook, see note 120. The Fourth Khams-sprul mentions it as the site where the cremation of Mahāpaṇḍita Vanaratna took place, and puts its location between Kathmandu and Patan; see bsTan-'dzin Chos-kyi nyi-ma: *Yul chen po nye ba'i tshandoha bal po'i gnas kyi dkar chag*, p. 206.3–4 (*phyis mya ngan las 'das nas kyang sku gdung yam bu ye rang gnyis kyi bar dur khrod ra ma do li zhes bya na bzhugs la gzhan par bshad pa de ni da lta'ang bal po'i dur khrod du byed cing ming yang ra ma do li rang zer*), and Macdonald & Dvags-po Rin-po-che (1981:260). Concerning the Sixth Zhva-dmar-pa's stay in the vicinity of the charnel grounds and his reference to the biography of Mar-pa Lo-tsā-ba in this regard, see note 120 and Lamminger (2013:154–255); the mentioned spiritual song intoned by Mar-

pa on that occasion is contained in Sangs-rgyas rgyal-mtshan: *sGra bsgyur mar pa lotstsha ba'i rnam thar mthong ba don yod*, pp. 116.16–118.14.

[127] This account of Padmasambhava's stay at Yang-le shod and his dPal Yang-dag and Phur-ba cycle practices is based on the *Zangs gling ma*; see Nyi-ma'i 'od-zer: *Slob dpon padma 'byung gnas kyi skyes rabs chos 'byung nor bu'i phreng ba*, chapter five (*yang phur gnyis kyi sgo nas phyag rgya chen po'i rig 'dzin bsgrubs pa'i le'u*), pp. 29.16–32.13. The Fourth Khams-sprul, too, provides the Tibetan and Newari names for the site, while concerning Śeṣanārāyaṇa itself—or 'Nāga "Remainder"' (*klu lhag ma*) in Tibetan—he relates the story of Padmasambhava killing the nāga king Śeṣa with his *phur-ba* and of how at the spot where the latter was transformed into stone sacred water had been coming forth on special occasions. He also cites Kaḥ-thog Rig-'dzin Tshe-dbang nor-bu, who both confirms this and gives an explanation for this water according to oral versions of the *Rāmāyaṇa*. After a detailed description of the Śeṣanārāyaṇa temple, he again cites as an authority Kaḥ-thog Rig-'dzin, who regarded the site where Padmasambhava gained the Mahāmudrā siddhi as the most prominent of the four places of his attainment of the state of a vidyādhara; see bsTan-'dzin Chos-kyi nyi-ma: *Yul chen po nye ba'i tshandoha bal po'i gnas kyi dkar chag*, pp. 208.6–210.1 & 210.5–212.3, and Macdonald & Dvags-po Rin-po-che (1981:261–263).

[128] See *Bal yul rang byung mchod rten chen po'i lo rgyus*, chapter 8, p. 253.4–5.

[129] See *Bal yul rang byung mchod rten chen po'i lo rgyus*, chapter 8, p. 253.6.

[130] See *Bal yul rang byung mchod rten chen po'i lo rgyus*, chapter 8, pp. 255.6–256.1.

[131] See Sangs-rgyas gling-pa: *O rgyan gu ru padma 'byung gnas kyi rnam thar rgyas pa gser gyi phreng ba thar lam gsal byed*, chapter 55, p. 230.10–12. A shorter version of this account—not mentioning the name Zhi-ba'i lha—is provided by O-rgyan gling-pa: *U rgyan gu ru padma 'byung gnas kyi skyes rabs rnam par thar pa rgyas par bkod pa padma bka'i thang yig*, chapter 59, p.146.13–14 (*u rgyan chen pos bal yul zla gsum bzhugs : bal po ba su dha ra la sogs pa : bal po'i 'gro don rgya chen mdzad nas ni*).

[132] The reference to rGya-gar pham-mthing is not found in the two available versions of the *Zangs gling ma*. The source might be the autobiography of Nyi-ma'i 'od-zer, in which Pham-mthing is given as the birthplace of one Dharmarāja, a previous incarnation of the treasure discoverer; see Nyi-ma'i 'od-zer: *sPrul sku mnga' bdag chen po'i skyes rabs rnam thar dri ma med pa'i bka' rgya can ldeb*, chapter seven, pp. 35.3–39.5.

[133] Mar-pa Lo-tsā-ba's stay at Pham-mthing and his encounter with two of the Pham-mthing-pa brothers, disciples of the mahāsiddha Nāropa, is contained in his biography; see Sangs-rgyas rgyal-mtshan: *sGra bsgyur mar pa lotstsha ba'i rnam thar mthong ba don yod*, pp. 103.4–106.9. On the Pham-mthing-pa brothers, a group of four siblings, in the context of the transmission of the *Cakrasaṃvaratantra*, see gZhon-nu dpal: *Deb ther sngon po*, pp. 461.17–464.6, and Roerich (1949:380–382); consult Lo Bue (1997:646–647) concerning the eldest one, called Dharmamati, and his younger brother A-des-pa chen-po (or Vagīśvara), who was known as Pham-mthing-pa. The Fourth Khams-sprul describes the site as the birthplace of the Pham-mthing-pa brothers and provides the further fact that it was a site that hosted the nāga king Śeṣa. According to reliable historical sources, the original name of the site was Pha-na thiṅgu—or 'Nine-Hooded [Serpent]' (*gdengs ka dgu pa*) in Tibetan—which was later transformed into Pham-[m]thing, and in the centre of the village was located a temple with a terrifying statue of Bhimasena; see bsTan-'dzin Chos-kyi nyi-ma: *Yul chen po nye ba'i tshandoha bal po'i gnas kyi dkar chag*, p. 210.1–5 (*rgya gar pham thing du grags*

*pa ni klu yi rgyal po lha ma can nam śeṣa zhes grags pa sa chen po 'di yang de yi gdengs ka la brten nas yod par bshad pa'i klu yi rgyal po de yi gnas yin pas ming yang pha na thingu ste gdengs ka dgu pa zhes grags par sngon rabs mkhas pa'i lo rgyus las 'byung ba ltar yin kyang sgra zur chag pas pham thing di grags shing / dpal nā ro pa'i thugs sras pham thing pa sku mched kyi 'khrungs yul dang rje mar pa yang yun ring du bzhugs pa'i gnas de yin / grong khyer de yi dkyil na rgya phubs gser g.yab chen po bkal ba'i lha khang na bhi ma se na te 'jigs sde'i sku shin tu gnyan par grags pa de yod*), and Macdonald & Dvags-po Rin-po-che (1981:262).

[134] In the Fourth Khams-sprul's guidebook, the statue of Vajrayoginī is identified with the form known as Indra[bhuti] Khecarī. The present figure, red instead of white, is of a later date, but its predecessor may have originated during the lifetime of Pham-mthing-pa. According to the Seventh 'Brug-chen 'Phrin-las shing-rta (1718–1767) the replica was consecrated by a Newar Buddhist vajrācārya; see bsTan-'dzin Chos-kyi nyi-ma: *Yul chen po nye ba'i tshandoha bal po'i gnas kyi dkar chag*, pp. 212.4–213.1 (*yang rgya gar pham thing gi grong dang nye ba'i cha na lha khang gcig tu rdo rje rnal 'byor ma'i sku yod pa de ni phas rgol 'joms pa'i indra mkha' spyod ma yin par 'dug / 'on kyang sku mdog dkar mo yin dgos pa 'di dmar mor 'dug / pham thing pa rang gi dus kyi yin par byed kyang phyi zhig shig gsos byas shing nang pa'i rdo rje slob dpon gcig gis rab gnas mdzad pa yin ces dpal 'brug pa rin po che'i bka' las thos*), and Macdonald & Dvags-po Rin-po-che (1981:263). According to the earlier pilgrimage guidebook, it was a speaking statue of Vajrayoginī; see Ngag-dbang rdo-rje: *Bal yul mchod rten 'phags pa shing kun dang de'i gnas gzhan rnams kyi dkar chag*, pp. 46.34–47.1 (*lho nub na yang le shod kyi brag phug dang mtsho dkar nag yod / de'i nye logs na rgya gar pham mthing na phag mo gsung 'byon ma bzhugs*). Concerning the site known as mTsho dkar-nag, see note 146.

[135] For the legend of Padmasambhava's ordination under Buddha Śākyamuni's disciple Ānanda in the Asura cave in India, see Sangs-rgyas gling-pa: *O rgyan gu ru padma 'byung gnas kyi rnam thar rgyas pa gser gyi phreng ba thar lam gsal byed*, chapter 22, pp. 99.7–101.8. Compare O-rgyan gling-pa: *U rgyan gu ru padma 'byung gnas kyi skyes rabs rnam par thar pa rgyas par bkod pa padma bka'i thang yig*, chapter 26, pp. 70.4–71.6.

[136] The Fourth Khams-sprul quotes the Seventh 'Brug-chen 'Phrin-las shing-rta's report that there existed an underground way from the cave to the realm of the Asuras, its gate being only visible for persons who have reached the stage of a vidyādhara; as the place was also regarded by non-Buddhists as a site sacred to Viṣṇu, one could find sculptures of the latter's feet and his attributes before the small cave, but there were no specific Buddhist statues in its interior; see bsTan-'dzin Chos-kyi nyi-ma: *Yul chen po nye ba'i tshandoha bal po'i gnas kyi dkar chag*, pp. 214.1–5 (*dpal 'brug pa rin po che ni su ra lha dang a su ra lha min la 'jug pa'i phyir 'di nas lha min gyi yul du bgrod pa'i lam dpal gyi sgo rig pa 'dzin pa rnams kyi snang ngor yod pa yin nam snyam zhes gsungs pa thos / phyi rol pa rnams ni 'di 'ang khyab 'jug gi gnas su byed / 'on kyang brag seng lta bu'i phug chung ngu zhig las nang du sku gzugs dang lha rten ni ci yang med / sgo phyir rol gyi 'gags der rdo zhig gi steng na khyab 'jug gi zhabs gnyis dang 'khor lo ral gri sogs phyag mtshan yongs rdzogs rdo la brkos 'dug*), and Macdonald & Dvags-po Rin-po-che (1981:284). On Asura caves in the context of the Buddhist Kriyātantras and their serving vidyādharas as entrances or gateways to subterranean paradises generically called Pātāla, see Mayer (2007:3–11). There were obviously rumours of further such gateways, such as the one connecting the Asura cave and Yang-le shod; such statements were discounted by Brag-dkar rta-so sPrul-sku.

[137] In the Fourth Khams-sprul's guidebook, too, the Asura cave is noted as the place where Padmasambhava and his disciple bound the brTan-ma bcu-gnyis goddesses, the moment when the promise was made to protect the Buddhist doctrine being evoked by a phrase used during tantric rituals of the rNying-ma-pa school. It is further remarked that many great masters who travelled to either India, Tibet or Nepal had visited the site, and that it is located one or two days from the Indian border; see bsTan-'dzin Chos kyi nyi-ma: *Yul chen po nye ba'i tshandoha bal po'i gnas kyi dkar chag*, pp. 213.1–214.1 (*de nas a su ra'i brag phug ni rnying ma lugs gi sngags cho ga rnams la chad mdo bstan skyong gi skabs su / rgya gar yul gyi tshu rol na / bal po yul gyi pha rol na / a su ra yi brag phug na / slob dpon padma 'byung nas dang / rlangs chen dpal gyi seng ge yis / zhing chen bsnol ba'i gdan steng du / dmar gyi arghaṃ mchod bshams nas / lag tu rdo rje gtad nas kyang / dbang bskur gsang ba'i mtshan nas brjod / rdo rje 'chang gi gral du bzhag / zhes 'byung ba ltar / bod skyong bstan ma bcu gnyis dam la bzhag pa'i gnas dang / gzhan yang sngon gyi rgya bal bod gsum du byon pa'i grub thob ches che ba mang pos zhabs kyis bcags shing tshogs kyi 'khor la sogs pa bskor ba'i gnas de spyi khyab yongs grags la 'di rang yin par bshad 'dra rung ba'ang yod mod / 'on kyang rgya bal gyi sa mtshams la da dung nyin lam gcig gnyis tsam yod zer*), and Macdonald & Dvags-po Rin-po-che (1981:263–264). On the 'promise offerings' known as *chad-mdo* and the three sites including Yang-le shod where the 'Earth mistresses' (*sa bdag rgyal mo*) were tamed according to Mahāyoga texts, see Mayer (1996:131, note 18). Consult Cantwell & Mayer (2016:56–61) for the earliest known evidence relating to the ubiquitous rNying-ma rite of the brTan-ma bcu-gnyis goddesses and their being tamed by Padmasambhava and Rlangs dPal-gyi seng-ge.

[138] The list of sacred sites in the pilgrimage guidebook of Rang-rig ras-pa's disciple ends with Chu-mig Byang-chub bdud-rtsi, the distance of a one day's journey from the Asura cave also being given there; see Ngag-dbang rdo-rje: *Bal yul mchod rten 'phags pa shing kun dang de'i gnas gzhan rnams kyi dkar chag*, p. 47.1–3 (*de'i nye logs na a su ra'i brag phug yod / de nas lho nub tu nyin gcig gi sa na chu mig byang chub bdud rtsi yod*). The Fourth Khams-sprul referred to this distance according to the guidebook, which he characterized as a collection of Tibetan hearsay, but he himself did not undertake the journey further south; see bsTan-'dzin Chos-kyi nyi-ma: *Yul chen po nye ba'i tshandhoha bal po'i gnas kyi dkar chag*, p. 214.4–5 (*rje rang rig pa'i slob ma nas lung ngag dbang rdo rjes bod kyi gtam rnying pa rnams phyogs gcig tu bsgrigs pa'i shing kun sogs bal po'i gnas kyi dkar chag der / a su ra nas lho nub tu zhag gcig phyin pa'i sar chu mig byang chub bdud rtsi yod ces bris 'dug ste / ji bzhin rtsad ma chod pas gnas der ma phyin*), and Macdonald & Dvags-po Rin-po-che (1981:264).

[139] The modern guidebook, too, identifies Chu-mig Byang-chub bdud-rtsi with Ṛṣeśvara, locating the site on the way to India but dating the festival to the first month of the year. The naturally formed image, claimed to be that of Padmasambhava, could be worshipped at that time; see Ngag-dbang rdo-rje: *Bal yul gnas yig*, p. 41.3–5 (*chu mig byang chub la / ri ṣi shwa ra / rgya gar lam phyogs na yod / zla ba dang po'i nang dus chen bzung brag la gu ru sku rang byon mjal ba yod*), and Dowman (1981:283–284). Known as Ṛṣeśvara Mahādeva and situated at Daman in Makwanpur district, the site has a temple dedicated to Śiva where a big fair takes place on the day of Rishi Panchami.

[140] For the full quotation, see Ba-mkhal smug-po: *gSol 'debs bar chad lam gsal*, p. 73.7–15 (*rgya gar bal yul sa mtshams su : byin gyis brlabs nas byon pa'i tshe : dri bsung spos ngad ldan pa'i ri : me tog padma dgun yang skye : chu ni byang chub bdus rtsi rgyun : bde ldan de yi gnas mchog tu : skyes mchog tshul bzung chos gos gsol : phyag g.yas rdo rje rtse dgu*

*bsnams : g.yon pas rin chen za ma tog : rakta bdud rtsi nang du gtams : mkha' 'gro dam can dam la btags : yi dam zhal gzigs dngos grub brnyes*). The treasure discoverer is known especially for this prayer and for a Padmasambhava biography of the type "born from the womb" (*mngal skyes*), which has yet to surface. See Ngag-dbang Blo-bzang rgya-mtsho: *Zab pa dang rgya che ba'i dam pa'i chos kyi thob yig gangā'i chu rgyun*, vol. 3, p. 346.1–2 (*gter ston ba mkhal smug po'i gter byon bar chad lam gsal dang slob dpon chen po mngal skyes kyi rnam thar gnyis*).

141 See O-rgyan gling-pa: *U rgyan gu ru padma 'byung gnas kyi skyes rabs rnam par thar pa rgyas par bkod pa padma bka'i thang yig*, chapter 54, p. 139.2–3. For the episode of Padmasambhava taming the four goddesses and establishing them as Vajrakīlaya protectors according to the ninth chapter of the *lHa 'dre bKa'i thang yig*, see O-rgyan gling-pa: *bKa' thang sde lnga*, p. 17.7–15, and Blondeau (1971:61–62). Two of the goddesses are known as rDo-rje Ya-byin-ma and rDo-rje bSe-byin-ma; for the location of their sites see, note 144.

142 See Nyi-ma'i 'od-zer: *Slob dpon padma 'byung gnas kyi skyes rabs chos 'byung nor bu'i phreng ba*, chapter five, p. 30.1–3 (*rgya gar yul gyi tshu rol : yang le shod kyi brag phug ces bya ba na : me tog dgun yang mi skam pa bkra shis la byin rlabs che ba'i gnas der byin nas*).

143 For the full quotation, see Ba-mkhal smug-po: *gSol 'debs bar chad lam gsal*, p. 75.12–17 (*bod kyi nyi ma mdzad pa'i tshe : dad ldan 'gro ba 'dren pa'i dpal : gang la gang 'tsham skur bstan nas : gtsang kha la yi la thog tu : dgra lha'i dge bsnyen dam la btags : yul ni tsha ba shod su : lha'i dge bsnyen dregs pa can : nyi shu rtsa gcig dam la btags*). The Fourth Khams-sprul refers to Ba-mkhal smug-po's prayer in order to further identify Tsha-ba tsha-shod and the location of gTsang-kha pass. The region was known to be inhabited by powerful non-Buddhist Ma-mo deities; see bsTan-'dzin Chos-kyi nyi-ma: *Yul chen po nye ba'i tshandoha bal po'i gnas kyi dkar chag*, p. 230.2–4 (*gzhan yang sprul sku ba mkhal pa'i gter ma gsol 'debs bar chad lam sel du grags pa'i nang nas 'byung pa'i / yul ni tsha ba tsha shod ces pa dang / gtsang kha la yi la thog kyang gnas 'dir yod phyi ma 'di dang gzhan yang lung pa 'di'i gnas 'ga' zhig na phyi rol pa'i ma mo 'ga' yang gnas par thos*), and Macdonald & Dvags-po Rin-po-che (1981:270).

144 Concerning the four bSe-mo Sisters, part of a twelve-member group of Vajrakīlaya protectors tamed by Padmasambhava in Nepal, namely the four Śvāna Sisters, the four bSe-mo Sisters and the four Remati Sisters, sometimes counted as constituting the well-known brTan-ma bcu-gnyis goddesses, see Mayer (1996:130–131). On Padmasambhava's taming of the bSe-mo Sisters according to the earliest source, along with the ritual context, see Cantwell & Mayer (2016:61–65). According to the pilgrimage guidebook to Ārya Wa-ti bzang-po, one of the goddesses was known as rDo-rje bSe-byin-ma, whose seat was at bSe-thang on the border between Mang-yul and Nepal; see Ehrhard (2004:290 & 444–445, note 242). It was Kaḥ-thog Rig-'dzin Tshe-dbang nor-bu who identified this site on his first journey to Tsha-ba tsha-shod in the last Tibetan month of the year 1751. At the end of his life he was engaged in establishing a temple there; see Chos-kyi dbang-phyug: *dPal rig 'dzin chen po rdo rje tshe dbang nor bu'i zhabs kyi rnam par thar pa'i cha shas brjod pa ngo mtshar dad pa'i rol mtsho*, pp. 109.12–16 & 135.9–23. The identification of Devīghāṭ as the seat of the goddess rDo-rje Ya-byin-ma also goes back to Kaḥ-thog Rig-'dzin. This happened in the last Tibetan month of the year 1753 after he again went to Tsha-ba tsha-shod, where he finally set in motion the process to procure a *yaṣṭi* for the Svayaṃbhūcaitya; see ibid., p. 129.5–7 (*mi ring bar bal yul tsha ba tsha shod du bde bar phyag 'phebs so / de nas de vi gā ṭa zhes*

*rdo rje phur ba'i bka' bsrung ma mo bcu gnyis las se mo [= bse mo] mched bzhi'i nang mtshan [= tshan] rdo rje ya byin gnas pa der mchod rten chen po'i srog shing bsgrub par mdzad*).

145 Preparations had been made by Kaḥ-thog Rig-'dzin for the renovation of the Svayaṃbhū-caitya in the last Tibetan month of 1751. Along with the gods Gaṇapati and Kumara Kārttikeya, Viṣṇu manifested himself in a human form and gave instructions concerning the procurement of the majestic *yaṣṭi*; see Chos-kyi dbang-phyug: *dPal rig 'dzin chen po rdo rje tshe dbang nor bu'i zhabs kyi rnam par thar pa'i cha shas brjod pa ngo mtshar dad pa'i rol mtsho*, p. 108.11–13 (*de bzhin lha chen po biṣṇu bram ze'i gzugs su sprul pa zhig dngos su byung nas lha yi mchod sdong dang mtshungs pa'i srog shing chen po 'di ltar yod pa 'dren par mdzad*). Consult von Rospatt (2001:227–228) for details surrounding both Jayaprakāśa Malla and Pṛthvīnārāyaṇa Śāha being moved by the appearance of the gods, with the latter king vowing to provide a *yaṣṭi* from the Nuvākoṭ area where suitable trees could be found. Kaḥ-thog Rig-'dzin's initial journey from Kathmandu to Tsha-ba tsha-shod followed shortly afterwards; see note 144.

146 In the pilgrimage guidebook of Rang-rig ras-pa's disciple, mTsho dkar-nag is described as being located together with Yang-le shod in the south-western part of the Kathmandu Valley; see Ngag-dbang rdo-rje: *Bal yul mchod rten 'phags pa shing kun dang de'i gnas gzhan rnams kyi dkar chag*, p. 46.34–35 (*lho nub na yang le shod kyi brag phug dang mtsho dkar nag yod*). The Fourth Khams-sprul refers to this location and mentions something like spring water near Yang-le shod, but is unable to evaluate its authenticity as a sacred site; see bsTan-'dzin Chos-kyi nyi-ma: *Yul chen po nye ba'i tshandhoha bal po'i gnas kyi dkar chag gangs can rna ba'i bdud rtsi*, p. 212.4 (*gnas 'di nyid rang du mtsho dkar nag ces bya ba khron chu lta bu zhig 'dug pa gnas chen du brtsi ba'i srol ni 'dug 'ji ltar yin ma thos shing ma shes*), and Macdonald & Dvags-po Rin-po-che (1981:263). A reference to the palace of Remati, who bears the title of protectress of the region north-east of Bodhgaya, is contained in the biography of Kaḥ-thog Rig-'dzin; it is stated that the deity was first committed to an oath by him during his first journey to Nepal in the year 1728; see Chos-kyi dbang-phyug: *dPal rig 'dzin chen po rdo rje tshe dbang nor bu'i zhabs kyi rnam par thar pa'i cha shas brjod pa ngo mtshar dad pa'i rol mtsho*, p. 113.4–9 (*de nas rim par bgrod de rdo rje gdan gyi byang shar lha mo re ba ti'i [= re ma ti'i] pho brang phyi rol rig byed mkhan gyi [= gyis] lha chen po'i gnas khyad par can du rtsi ba ting wa ri'i mtsho bdag de sngar sa sprel lor bal por bgrod skabs thog mar cho 'phrul dang bcas mthar dam tshig blang ba byung bas de'i chu klung du gtor chen zhig btang*).

147 This description of the state of Buddhism in Nepal is based on a letter Kaḥ-thog Rig-'dzin addressed to the Seventh Dalai Bla-ma sKal-bzang rgya-mtsho in 1752; see Tshe-dbang norbu: *Chab shog khag*, p. 742.1–6 (*bal po'i yul der sngar sangs rgyas kyi grub mtha' mang zhing / mu stegs kyi grub mtha' nyung ba yod 'dug la / yul dbus shrī bi kra ma'i gtsug lag khang nub nas lo brgya phrag lhag tsam gyi bar du bal po'i yul du sangs rgyas kyi bstan pa lhag par dar bar 'gyur de rjes paṇḍi ta nags kyi rin chen gyi skabs dang / de yi rjes thog lo mang tsam gyi bar du yang bstan pa ma nub par yod pa snang / deng sang ni dus kyi bstan pa ming gi lhag ma tsam las thams cad phyi rol gyi grub mtha' kho nas khyab pa'o*).

148 For the renovation of the Svayaṃbhūnāth Stūpa, which lasted from 1681 to 1683 according to the Newar sources see noote 63. For a description of the events, dated to the year 1680, according to the guidebook authored by Rang-rig ras-pa's disciple, see Ngag-dbang rdo-rje: *Bal yul mchod rten 'phags pa shing dang de'i gnas gzhan rnams kyi dkar chag*, p.

47.10–23, and Ehrhard (2013:64–65). It is mentioned in particular that the initial impetus for this renovation was the gold left over from setting up a great *gañjira* on the Bodhnāth stūpa; see note 81 for the latter renovation.

149 The genealogy of the Malla rulers of Nepal down to Jayaprakāśa and the fact that the latter received tantric teachings from Kaḥ-thog Rig-'dzin are taken from the same letter; see Tshe-dbang nor-bu: *Chab shog khag*: p. 742.6–13 (*de yang sngar yul pa ṭa li su tra [= pā ṭa li pu tra] nas rgyal rigs mu stegs byed pa zhig du ru ka'i rgyal po dang 'thab pas / pham nas g.yog 'khor mang po dang bcas bros te kho khrom [= kho khom] du chags / rgyal po des bal po'i rgyal rigs rnying pa rnams gnon par byas te mu stegs kyi grub mtha' dar rgyas su gtang [= btang] / de nas mi rabs kha shas nas rgyal po de'i rigs brgyud zhig yam bu'i bdag por gyur / de nas da lta'i bar lo nyis brgya dang drug cu rtsa drug 'gro zer / de srid du rgyal rigs de rnams ram tsam sangs rgyas la ltar snang tsam du bas snying nas mos pa cher ma byung zhing / da lta'i yam bu rgyal po 'di ni sangs rgyas la mos shing / dus kyi 'khor lo gdams ngag nyan pa sogs phugs ji ltar yang da lta chos la mos 'dra ba zhig snang*). Although the royal house's origin in Pāṭaliputra, the capital city of the Mauryas and later of the imperial Guptas, is mythological, the calculation provided for the Malla rule in Kathmandu, i.e. 1486, corresponds roughly to the seizure of the city by Ratna Malla (r. 1484–1520). On the complexity of Malla political history and its last phase, from 1482 to 1769, see Slusser (1982:54–65).

150 The details concerning the rulers of Gorkha are taken from another letter of Kaḥ-thog Rig-'dzin sent to the Seventh Dalai Bla-ma from Vaṃ-le (Ladakh) in the year 1752; see Tshe-dbang nor-bu: *Chab shog khag*, p. 751.11–14 (*de yang 'dzam gling 'di na byin che ba grub pa'i gnas ne pāl la [= nepāl la] yi ljongs nas nye bar spyod de bal po rdzongs [= rdzong] gorṣa rā dza zhes phyogs de ri brag pa'i rgyal phran sngon grub pa'i slob dpon chen po gorṣa nā yi [= gorṣa nā tha'i] bsti gnas gorṣa gu ha zhes slob dpon de'i sgrub phug yod pa'i 'dabs su slas kyi mkhar bzung bas da lta garṣar [= gorṣar] grags pa kṣeṭa'i [= kṣeatriya'i] rgyal rigs su gyur pa*). The beginning of the Shah period in Nepal is generally dated to the year 1768; see Slusser (1982:76–79). Brag-dkar rta-so sPrul-sku's dating of the conquest of the three kingdoms of the Valley by Pṛthvīnārāyaṇa Śāha reflects the early phase of the warfare and is also documented in the biography of the Fourth Khams-sprul who met both Pṛthvīnārāyaṇa Śāha and Jayaprakāśa in the spring of 1756; see *Rang tshul lhug par smras pa ma bcos gnyug ma'i rang grol*, fols. 210b/5–211a/1, 213b/3–214a/4 & 215b/5–216b/2.

151 See Kun-dga' snying-po: *Dam pa'i chos rin po che 'phags yul du ji ltar dar ba'i tshul gsal bar ston pa dgos 'dod kun 'byung*, p. 344.4–6. The forty-fourth and last chapter of Tārānātha's work deals with the origin and development of Buddhist art, and was later consulted by authors like 'Jam-mgon Kong-sprul Blo-gros mtha'-yas (1813–1899); see Smith (2001: 254).

152 For the stylistic evolution of Tibetan art and the importance of Newar art in Nepal, see Jackson (2010:xix–xxiii). It is noted that the specific features of the Nepal-inspired Beri (*bal ri*) style became the universal painting style of Tibet for about a century, from the 1360s to 1450s, following the demise of the Pāla style. Consult Lo Bue (2012:49–53) concerning Tibet's heavy reliance upon Newar artists in the 15th century according to Tibetan sources.

153 For the section on Rang-rig ras-pa's reliquary shrine, see Ngag-dbang rdo-rje: *Bal yul shing kun sogs dang rje rang rig rdung rten gyi dkar chag*, fols. 4a/3–6a/4, and Ehrhard (2013:107–114). This part of the text was used for depicting the 'Brug-pa bKa'-brgyud-pa

yogin's renovation of the Bodhnāth Stūpa as well as the erection of his reliquary; see note 81. The printed guidebook by rNgog-ston Karma Blo-bzang is not extant; for his offerings to the sacred sites of the Kathmandu Valley, see Introduction, note 25.

# Bibliography

# Bibliography


*Canonical Sources*

*sKu gdung 'bar ba tsha tsha dang mchod rten gyi rgyud*, 19 fols. In "rNying ma rgyud 'bum. A collection of treasured Tantras translated during the period of the first propagation of Buddhism in Tibet", vol. 13, Thimphu: Ngodrup, 1973–1975, pp. 375.3–414.7.

*sKyes pa'i rabs kyi rgyud*, 152 fols. In "The Tibetan Tripiṭaka", vol. 88, Tokyo/Kyoto: Suzuki Research Foundation, 1955–1961, pp. 1.1.1–63.2.1

*'Phags pa glang ru lung bstan zhes bya ba theg pa chen po'i mdo*, 13 fols. In "The Tibetan Tripiṭaka", vol. 40, Tokyo/Kyoto: Suzuki Research Foundation, 1955–1961, pp. 348.1.3–353.1.1.

*'Phags pa 'jam dpal rtsa ba'i rgyud*, 254 fols. In "The Tibetan Tripiṭaka", vol. 6, Tokyo/Kyoto: Suzuki Research Foundation, 1955–1961, pp. 168.3.4–260.5.6.

*'Phags pa rdo rje sa 'og gi rgyud kyi rgyal po*, 30 fols. In "The Tibetan Tripiṭaka", vol. 8, Tokyo/Kyoto, 1955–1961, pp. 261.1.1–275.1.5.

*'Phags pa gser 'od dam pa mdo sde'i dbang po'i rgyal po zhes bya ba theg pa chen po'i mdo*, 63 fols. In "The Tibetan Tripiṭaka", vol. 7, Tokyo/Kyoto: Suzuki Research Foundation, 1955–1961, pp. 751.1–101.4.6.

*'Dsangs blun zhes bya ba'i mdo*, 171 fols. In "The Tibetan Tripiṭaka", vol. 40, Tokyo/Kyoto: Suzuki Research Foundation, 1955–1961, pp. 54.5.1–123.2.4

*Li yul lung bstan pa*, 24 fols. In "The Tibetan Tripiṭaka", vol. 129, Tokyo/Kyoto: Suzuki Research Foundation, 1955–1961, pp. 299.5.2–309.3.8.

*Bal yul rang byung mchod rten chen po'i lo rgyus*, 15 fols. In "Ta'i si tu kun mkhyen chos kyi 'byung gnas bstan pa'i nyin byed kyi bka' 'bum", vol. 7, Sansal, Dist. Kangra, H.P.: Palpung Sungrab Nyamso Khang, 1990, pp. 229–257.

*Tibetan Texts*

Karma Blo-bzang (17th cent.)
*mKhas grub chen po karma blo bzang gyi rnam thar mchod sprin rgya mtsho*, 47 pp. In "Gangs can dol po khul du byon pa'i ris med kyi bstan 'dzin skyes chen dam pa rnams kyi rnam thar phyogs gcig tu bkod pa". Taipei, 2010, pp. 474–521.

Kun-dga' snying-po, Jo-nang Tārānātha (1575–1634)
*Dam pa'i chos rin po che 'phags pa'i yul du ji ltar dar ba'i tshul gsal bar ston pa dgos 'dod kun 'byung*, 345 pp. Chengdu: Si-khron mi-rigs dpe-skrun khang, 1986.

Kun-dga' rdo-rje, Tshal-pa Si-tu (1309–1364)
*Deb ther dmar po*, 151 pp. Beijing: Mi-rigs dpe-skrun khang, 1981.

mGon-po skyabs, Gung (c. 1690–1750?)
*rGya nag gi yul du dam pa'i chos dar tshul gtso bor bshad pa blo gsal kun tu dga' ba'i rna rgyan*, 266 pp. Chengdu: Si-khron mi-rigs dpe-skrun khang, 1983.

rGyal-ba'i 'byung-gnas, 'Brom-ston (1005–1064)
*'Brom ston rgyal ba'i 'byung gnas kyis mdzad pa'i jo bo rje'i rnam thar lam yig chos kyi 'byung gnas*, 61 pp. In "Jo bo rje dpal ldan a ti sha'i rnam thar bka' gdams pha chos". Hsining: mTsho-sngon mi-rigs dpe-skrun khang, 1994, pp. 229–290.

Ngag-dbang rdo-rje, Bal-po'i dge-slong (1904–1984)
*Bal yul gnas yig*, 11 fols. In Wylie (1970:37–41 [Appendix A]).

Ngag-dbang rdo-rje, Nas-lung-pa (17th cent.)
*Bal yul 'phags pa shing kun dang de'i gnas gzhan rnams kyi dkar chag*, 10 fols. In Wylie (1970:43–48 [Appendix B]).
_______ *Bal yul shing kun sogs dang rang rig gdung rten gyi dkar chag*, 6 fols. (xylograph).

Ngag-dbang Blo-bzang rgya-mtsho, Fifth Dalai Bla-ma (1617–1682)
*Za hor gyi ban de ngag dbang blo bzang rgya mtsho'i 'dir snang 'khrul pa'I rol rtsed rtogs brjod kyi tshul du bkod pa du kū la'i gos bzang*, 3 vols., 718 pp., 532 pp., 454 pp. Lhasa: Bod-ljongs mi-dmans dpe-skrun khang, 1989–1991.
_______ *Zab pa dang rgya che ba'i dam pa'i chos kyi thob yig gangā'i chu rgyun*, 4 vols., 418 fols., 336 fols. 385 fols., 367 fols. Gangtok: Sikkim Research Institute of Tibetology, 1991–1992.

Ngag-dbang brtson-'grus, First 'Jam-dbyangs bzhad-pa (1648–1722)
*dPal rdo rje 'jigs byed kyi chos 'byung khams gsum las rnam par rgyal ba dngos grub kyi gter mdzod*, 2 vols., 735 pp. (= Gangs can rig mdzod, 66–67). Lhasa: Bod-ljongs bod-yig dpe-rnying dpe-skrun khang, 2013.

Chos-kyi dbang-phyug, Sixth Zhva-dmar-pa (1584–1630).
*Bal yul du bgrod pa'i lam yig nor bu spel ma'i 'phreng ba*, 48 fols. (manuscript). NGMPP reel-no. L 387/3.

Chos-kyi dbang-phyug, Brag-dkar rta-so sPrul-sku (1775–1837)
*Chu sbyin gtor ma brgya rtsa phan bde'i gru rdzings kyi dmigs khrid rnams bshad*, 27 fols. In „Kun-mkhyen Brag-dkar-ba Chos-kyi dbang-phyug mchog-gi gsuṅ-'bum Rin-po-che". Kathmandu: Shri Gautam Buddha Vihara, 2011, vol. 7, pp. 99–151.
_______ *Bal yul gyi gnas dang rten gyu lo rgyus nges par brjod pa 'khrul spong nor bu'i me long*, 35 fols. (incomplete manuscript), NGMPP reel-no. L376/1-L381/8 [= A]. 48 fols. In ibid, vol. 12, pp. 455–549 [= B].
_______ *dPal rig 'dzin chen po rdo rje tshe dbang nor bu'i zhabs kyis rnam par thar pa'i cha shas brjod pa ngo mtshar dad pa'i rol mtsho*, 158 fols. In „Kaḥ thog rig 'dzin tshe dbang nor bu'i bka' 'bum", vol. 1, Beijing: Krung-go'i bod-rig-pa dpe-skrun khang, 2006, pp. 1–158.
_______ *dPal ldan gzhung 'brug bka' brgyud gser phreng gyi bla ma'i brgyud pa'i rnam thar dang / phyag rgya chen po'i spyi don ngo mtshar snyan pa'i sgra dbyangs*, 104 pp. Kathmandu: Shri Gautam Buddha Vihara, 2012.

Chos-kyi 'byung-gnas, Eighth Si-tu (1700–1774)
*Ta'i si tu 'bod pa karma bstan pa'i nyin byed kyi rang tshul drangs par brjod pa dri bral shel gyi me long*, 378 fols. (= Śata Piṭaka Series, 77). New Delhi: Lokesh Chandra, 1968.

_______ & Tshe-dbang kun-khyab, Be-lo (18th cent.)
*sGrub brgyud karma kaṃ tshang brgyud pa rin po che'i rnam par thar pa rab 'byams nor bu zla ba chu shel gyi 'phreng ba*, 2 vols., 241 fols. & 350 fols. New Delhi: D. Gyaltsan & Kesang Legshay, 1972.

Nyi-ma'i 'od-zer, Myang-ral (1124–1192)
*sPru sku mnga' bdag chen po'i skyes rabs rnam thar dri ma med pa'i bka' rgya can ldeb*, 82 fols. In "bKa' brgyad bde bar gshegs 'dus pa'i chos skor". vol. 1. Gangtok: Lama Sonam Tobgay Kazi, 1978, pp. 1–163.
_______ *Slob dpon padma 'byung gnas kyi skyes rabs chos 'byung nor bu'i phreng ba*, 193 pp. In „Slob dpon padma'i rnam thar zangs gling ma". Chengdu: Si-khron mi-rigs dpe-skrun khang, 1989, pp. 1–193.
_______ *U rgyan gu ru padma 'byung gnas kyi rnam thar 'bring po zangs gling mar grags pa*, 148 fols. (manuscript). NGMPP, reel-no. AT 28/2.

bsTan-'dzin Chos-kyi nyi-ma, Fourth Khams-sprul (1730–1779)

*Yul chen po bye ba'i tshandhoha bal po' gnas kyi dkar chag gangs can rna 'i bdud rtsi*, 37 fols. In "Collected Writings of the Fourth Khamtrul Tenzin Chökyi Nyima and his disciple Khedrup Sonam Rabpel." Tashijong, Palampur, U.P.: Sungrab Nyamso Gyunphel Parkhang, 1978, pp. 307–379.

_______ *Rang tshul lhug par smras pa ma bcos gnyug ma'i rang grol*, 368 fols. (manuscript).

bsTan-'dzin nor-bu, Third Yol-mo-ba (1598–1644)

*rTogs brjod mkhas pa'i rna rgyan*, 19 fols. In "The Autobiography and Collected Writings (gSung thor bu) of the Third Rig-'dzin Yol-mo-ba sPrul-sku bsTan-'dzin nor-bu," vol. 1. Dalhousie: Damchoe Sangpo, 1977, pp. 6–44.

_______ *Rang gi rtogs pa brjod pa rdo rje sgra ma'i brgyud (= rgyud) mangs*, 102 fols. In ibid., pp. 83–267.

bsTan-'dzin phrin-las, Fourth bTsan-po No-mon-han (1789–1838)

*'Dzam gling rgyas bshad snod bcud kun gsal me long*, 297 pp. In "'Dzam gling spyi bshad dang rgyas bshad" (= Gangs can rig mdzod, 59). Lhasa: Bod-ljongs bod-yig dpe-rnying dpe-skrun khang, 2011, pp. 39–336.

sNa-tshogs rang-grol, rGod-tshang ras-pa (1482–1559)

*gTsang smyon he ru ka phyogs thams cad las rnam par rgyal ba'i rnam thar rdo rje theg pa'i gsal byed nyi ma'i snying po*, 146 fols. In "The Life of the Saint of Gtsaṅ" (= Śata Piṭaka Series, 79). New Delhi: Lokesh Chandra, 1969, pp. 1–292.

sNa-tshogs rang-grol, rTse-le[gs] (1605–1677)

*Slob dpon rin po che padma'i rnam thar chen mo las brtsam te dri ba'i lan nges don gsal byed*, 48 fols. In "The Complete Works of rGod-tshangs-pa Padma legs-grub", vol. 3. Gangtok: mGon-po tshe-brtan, 1979, pp. 397–491.

Padma dkar-po, Fourth 'Brug-chen (1527–1592)

*Chos 'byung bstan pa'i padma rgyas pa'i nyin byed*, 464 pp. (= Gangs can rig mdzod, 19). Lhasa: Bod-ljongs bod-rig dpe rnying dpe-skrun khang, 1992.

_______ *bSangs dpe bkra shis re skong*, 13 fols. In "Collected Works of Kun-mkhyen Padma-dkar-po." Darjeeling: Kargyud Sungrab Nyamso Khang, 1973–1974, vol. 19, pp. 267–292.

Ba-mkhal smug-po (12th cent.)

*gSol 'debs bar chad lam gsal*, 7 pp. In "gSang chen snga 'gyur ba'i bka' gter zhal 'don phyogs bsgrigs". Hsining: mTsho-sngon zhung-chen mtsho-lho dge-'os slob-grwa'i par-khang, 1998, pp. 71–78.

Byams-pa'i dpal, Khro-phu Lo-tsā-ba (1123–1270)

*Paṇ grub gsum gyi rnam thar dpag bsam khri shing*, 78 fols. (xylograph) [= TBRC W1KG13616]

Byams-pa phun-tshogs, gNas Rab-'byams-pa (1503–1580)

*mKhas grub chen po byams pa phun tshogs kyi rnam thar ngo tshar snang ba'i nyin byed yid bzhin nor bu dgos 'dod kun 'byung dad pa'i 'debs*, 93 fols. (xylograph) [= TBRC W25576].

gTsug-lag phreng-ba, Second dPa'-bo (1504–1566)

*Dam pa'i chos kyi 'khor lo bsgyur ba rnams kyi byung ba gsal bar byed pa mkhas pa'i dga' ston*, 2 vols., 1527 pp. Beijing: Mi-rigs dpe-skrun khang, 1986.

_______ *rJe btsun mar pa'i rnam par thar pa grub pa'i ngo mtshar brjod pa*, 69 fols. (xylograph) [= TBRC W27459]

Tshe-dbang nor-bu, Kaḥ-thog Rig-'dzin (1698–1755)

*rGya nag tu gung mgon po skyabs la dri ba mdzad pa*, 8 fols. In "Selected Writings of Kaḥ-thog Rig-'dzin Tshe-dbang nor-bu." Darjeeling: Kargyud Sungrab Nyamso Khang, 1973, vol. 1, pp. 723–732.

_______ *rGyud kyi rgyal po gdan bzhi dkyil 'khor rgyas pa yi lha'i mtshan grangs gsal ba'i me long*, 3 pp. In "Kaḥ thog rig 'dzin tshe dbang nor bu'i bka' 'bum", vol. 2, Beijing: Krung-go'i bod-rig-pa dpe-skrun khang, 2006, pp, 417–419.

_______ *Chab shog khag*, 146 pp. In ibid, vol. 1, pp. 725–871.

_______ *dPal nag po chen po phyag gnyis ba'i sku brnyan rang byung bod thang mgon por bstod cing 'phrin las gsol ba'i tshig phreng bzhed don lhun gyis grub pa'i dbyangs*. 3 pp. In ibid., vol. 2, pp. 325–327.

_______*sMon tshig sna tshogs phyogs bsdus*, 26 pp. In ibid., vol. 2, pp. 420.1–446.25.

Tshe-ring dbang-rgyal, mDo-mkhar Zhabs-drung (1697–1763)

*dPal mi'i dbang po'i rtogs par brjod pa 'jig rten kun tu dga' ba'i gtam*, 861 pp. Chengdu: Si-khron mi-rigs dpe-skrun khang, 1981.

gZhon-nu dpal, 'Gos Lo-tsā-ba (1392–1481)

*mKhas pa chen po dpal nags kyi rin chen gyi rnam par thar pa*, 37 fols. Thimphu: National Library of Bhutan, 1985.

_______ *Deb ther sngon po*, 2 vols., 1214 pp. Chengdu: Si-khron mi-rigs dpe-skrun khang, 1984.

Ye-shes dpal-'byor, Sum-pa mkhan-po (1704–1788). *'Dzam gling spyi bshad ngo mtshar gtam snyan*, 38 pp. In "'Dzam gling spyi bshad dang rgyas bshad" (= Gangs can rig mdzod, 59). Lhasa: Bod-ljongs bod-yig dpe-rnying dpe-skrun khang, 2011, pp. 1–38.

Rin-chen rnam-rgyal, lHa-btsun (1473–1557)

*Grub thob gtsang smyon pa'i rnam thar dad pa'i spu slong g.yo' ba (= g.yo ba*, 65 fols. In "Bde mchog mkha' 'gro snyan rgyud(Ras chung snyan rgyud)", vol. 1 (= Smanrtsis Shesrig Spendzod, 11). Leh: S. W. Tashigangpa, 1971, pp. 1–129.

_______*dPal ldan bla ma dam pa mkhas grub lha btsun chos kyi rgyal po'i rnam mgur blo 'das chos sku'i rang gdangs*, 54 fols. In "Biographical Material connected with the 'Brug-pa dkar-brgyud-pa Tradition." Darjeeling: Chopal Lama, 1984, pp. 165–271.

Shākya bzang-po, First Yol-mo-ba (15th/16th cent.)

*mChod rten chen po bya rung kha shor gyi lo rgyus thos pas grol ba*, 18 fols., (incomplete xylograph). NGMPP reel-no. E 2517/4.

Sangs-rgyas gling-pa, (1340–1396)

*O rgyan gu ru padma 'byung gnas kyi rnam thar rgyas pa gser gyi phreng ba thar lam gsal byed*, 488 pp. (= Slob dpon padma 'byung gnas kyi rnam thar dpe tshogs, 1). Lhasa: Bod-ljongs mi-dmangs dpe-skrun khang, 2007.

Sangs-rgyas rgyal-mtshan, gTsang-smyon Heruka (1452–1507)

*sGra bsgyur mar pa lotstsha ba'i rnam thar mthong ba don yod*, 190 pp. Chengdu: Si-khron mi-rigs dpe-skrun khang, 1990.

_______ *rJe btsun mi la ras pa'i rnam thar rgyas par phye ba mgur 'bum*, 626 pp. In „rNal 'byor gyi dbang phyug chen po mi la ras pa'i rnam mgur". Hsining: mTsho-sngon mi-rigs dpe-skrun khang, 1989, pp. 196–812.

Sangs-rgyas ye-shes, gNubs-chen (9th/10th cent.)

*sGom gyi gnad gsal bar phye ba bsam gtan gtan mig sgron*, 255 fols. (= Smanrtsis Shesrig Spendzod, 74). Ladakh: S. W. Tashigangpa, 1974.

bSod-nams dpal bzang-po (14th/15th cent),
*Dus gsum sangs rgyas thams cad kyi thugs kyi rten 'phags pa shing kun gyi dkar chag*, 5 fols. In "Rare Tibetan Texts from Nepal:" Dolanji: Tashi Dorji, 1976, pp. 81–90

bSod-nams 'od-zer, mKhan-chen (13th/14th cent.)
*dPal ldan bla ma dam pa grub chen o rgyan pa'i rnam par thar pa byin rlabs kyi chu rgyun* (= Gangs can rig mdzod, 32), 289 pp. Lhasa: Bod-ljongs bod-yig dpe-rnying dpe-skrun-khang, 1997.

O-rgyan gling-pa (b. 1323)
*U rgyan gu ru padma 'byung gnas kyi skyes rabs rnam par thar pa rgyas par bkod pa padma bka'i thang yig*, 296 pp. (= Slob dpon padma 'byung gnas kyi rnam thar dpe tshogs, 6). Lhasa: Bod-ljongs mi-dmangs dpe-skrun khang, 2011.
_______ *bKa' thang sde lnga*, 417 pp. (= Slob dpon padma 'byung gnas kyi rnam thar dpe tshogs, 7). Lhasa: Bod-ljongs mi-dmangs dpe-skrun khang, 2011.

Different authors
*Maṇi bka' 'bum*, 2 vols., 547 and 483 pp. (= Gangs can khyad nor dpe tshogs pod phreng, 135 & 136). Lhasa: Bod-ljongs mi-dmangs dpe-skrun khang, 2011.

*Western Literature*

Aris, M. (1994). *The Raven Crown: The Origins of the Buddhist Monarchy in Bhutan*. London.
_______ (1995). *'Jigs-med gling-pa's "Discourse on India" of 1789* (= Studia Philologica Buddhica, Occasioanl Paper Series, 9). Tokyo.

Bajracharya, M., Michaels, A. & Gutschow, N. (2016). *Nepālikabhūpha-Vaṃśāvalī: A History of the Kings of Nepal—A Buddhist Chronicle*, 3 vols., Kathmandu.

Blondeau, A. M. (1971). "Le Lha-dre bka'-thaṅ". In *Études Tibétains: Dédiées à la Mémoire de Marcelle Lalou*. Paris, pp. 29–126.
_______ (1987). "Une polémique sur l'authenticité des Bka' thang au 17é siècle." In *Silver on Lapis: Tibetan Literary Culture and History* (= The Tibet Society Twentieth Anniversary Celebration Volume). Bloomington, pp. 125–161.
_______ (1994). "Bya-rung kha-shor, légende fondatrice du bouddhisme tibétain." In *Tibetan Studies*, 1 (= The Institute for Comparative Research in Human Culture, Occasional Papers,1 :1). Oslo, pp. 31–48.
_______ (2002). "Les *ma mo*: mythes cosmogoniques et théogoniques dans le *Rnying ma rgyud 'bum*." In *The Many Canons of Tibetan Buddhism* (= Brill's Tibetan Studies Library, 2/10). Leiden/Boston, pp. 293–311.

Bogin, B. (2013). *The Illuminated Life of the Great Yolmowa*. Chicago.

Brough, J. (1947). "Legends of Khotan and Nepal." *Bulletin of the School of Oriental and African Studies*, 12:1, pp. 333–339.

Cantwell, C. & Mayer, R. (2016). "Representations of Padmasambhava in Early Post-imperial Tibet." *Zentralasiatische Studien*, 45, pp. 41–75.

Clemente, M. (2011). "Shedding Light upon lHa btsun Rin chen rnam rgyal (1473–1557): A Study of Two Untranslated Works from the Tucci Tibetan Collection." In *From Mediterranean to Himalaya: A Festschrift to Commemorate the 120th Birthday of the Italian Tibetologist Giuseppe Tucci*. Beijing, pp. 435–502.
_______ (2016). "The Patronage Networks of Lha btsun Rin chen rnam rgyal from Brag dkar rta so to the 'Phags pa lha khang." In *Studies in Honour of Luciano Petech: A Commemoration Volume 1914–2014* (= Rivista Degli Studi Orientali, N.S., Supplemento, 1). Pisa/Roma, pp. 103–109.

Davidson, R. M. (2002). *Indian Esoteric Buddhism: A Social History of the Tantric Buddhist Movement*, New York.

_______ (2005). *Tibetan Renaissance: Tantric Buddhism in the Rebirth of Tibetan Culture*. New York.

Dawa, P. (2016). "New Discoveries in Early Tibetan Printing History." In *Tibetan Printing: Comparison, Continuities and Change* (= Brill's Tibeta Studies Library, 39). Leiden/Boston, pp. 195–211.

Decleer, H. (1996). "Lord Atiśa in Nepal: The Thām Bahīl and Five Stūpas Foundations in the *'Brom ston Itinary* ." *Journal of the Nepal Research Centre*, 10, pp. 27–54.

_______ (2000). "Si tu Paṇ chen's Translation of the Svayaṃbhū Purāṇa and His Role in the Development of the Kathmandu Valley Pilgrimage Guide (*gnas yig*) Literature." In *Lungta*, 13 (= Special issue *Situ Paṇchen: His Contribution and Legacy*), pp. 33–64.

_______ (2011). "The Tibetan Name of Svayambhu, 'Phags pa shing kun (‚Sacred All Trees'): What Does It Really Mean?" In *Light of the Valley: Renewing the Sacred Art and Traditions of Svayambhu*. Cazadero, pp. 241–272.

Doney, L. (2014). *The Zangs gling ma: The First Padmasambhava Biography* (= Monumenta Tibetica Historica, I:3). Andiast.

_______ (2017). "Narrative Transformations: The Spiritual Friends of Khri Srong lde brtsan." In *Interaction in the Himalayas and Central Asia: Processes of Transfer, Translation and Transformation in Art, Archaeology, Religion and Polity* (= Österreichische Akademie der Wissenschaften, phil.-hist. Klasse, Denkschriften 495 / Veröffentlichungen zur Sozialanthropologie, 22). Vienna, pp. 311–320.

Dowman, K. (1973). *The Legend of the Great Stūpa*. Emeryville.

_______ (1981). "A Buddhist Guide to the Power Places of the Kathmandu Valley." *Kailash: A Journal of Himalayan Studies*, 8:3–4, pp. 113–291.

_______ (2020). *Nepāl Maṇḍal: A Pilgrims's Guide to the Kathmandu Valley*. No place.

Ehrhard, F.-K. (2002). *Life and Travels of Lo-chen bSod-nams rgya-mtsho* (= Lumbini International Research Institute Monograph Series, 3). Lumbini.

_______ (2004). *Die Statue und der Tempel des Ārya Va-ti bzang-po: ein Beitrag zur Geschichte und Geographie des tibetischen Buddhismus* (= Contributions to Tibetan Studies, 2). Wiesbaden.

_______ (2007). "The Biography of sMan-bsgom Chos-rje Kun-dga' dpal-ldan (1735–1804) as a Source for the Sino-Nepalese War." In *Pramāṇkīrtiḥ: Papers Dedicated to Ernst Steinkellner on the Occasion of His 70th Birthday*, vol. 1 (= Wiener Studien zur Tibetologie und Buddhismuskunde, 70,1). Vienna, pp. 115–133.

_______ (2008). *A Rosary of Rubies: A Chronicle of the Gur-rigs mDo-chen Tradition from South-Western Tibet* (= Collectanea Himalayica, 2). Munich.

_______ (2010). "The Holy Madman of dBus and His Relationships with Tibetan Rulers in the 15th and 16th Centuries." In *Geschichten und Geschichte: Historiographie und Hagiographie in der asiatischen Religionsgeschichte* (= Historia religionum, 30). Uppsala, pp. 210–246.

_______ (2012). "Gnas rab 'byams pa Byams pa phuntshogs (1503-1581) and His Contribution to Buddhist Block Printing in Tibet." In *This World and the Next: Contributions on Tibetan Religion, Science and Society. PIATS 2006: Tibetan Studies: Proceedings of the Eleventh Seminar of the International Association for Tibetan Studies, Königswinter 2006* (= Beiträge zur Zentralasienforschung, 27). Andiast, pp. 149–176.

_______ (2013). *Buddhism in Tibet & the Himalayas: Texts and Traditions*. Kathmandu.

_______ (2015). "A Thousand Spoke Golden Wheel of Secular Law: The Preamble to the Law Code of the Kings of gTsang." In *Secular Law and Order in the Tibetan Highland* (= Monumenta Tibetica Historica; III:13). Andiast, pp. 105–125.

_______ (2018). "Printing the Treasure Text: The 1556 Edition of the *Bya rung kha shor lo rgyus*." In *Saddharmāmṛtam: Festschrift für Jens-Uwe Hartmann zum 65. Geburtstag* (= Wiener Studien zur Tibetologie und Buddhismuskunde, 93). Vienna, pp. 75–93.

Eimer, H. (2014). *Sa skya Legs bshad: die Strophen zur Lebensklugheit von Sa skya Paṇḍita Kun dga' rgyal mtshan (1182–1251)* (= Wiener Studien zur Tibetologie und Buddhismuskunde, 83). Vienna.

Emmerick, R. E. (1967). *Tibetan Texts Concerning Khotan* (= London Oriental Series, 19). London.

Huber. T. (2008). *The Holy Land Reborn: Pilgrimage & the Tibetan Reinvention of Buddhist India*. Chicago/London.

Jackson, D. P. (1990). *Two Biographies of Śākyaśrībhadra: The Eulogy ny Khro-phu Lo-tsā-ba and Its "Commentary" by Bsod-nams-dpal-bzang-po*. (= Tibetan and Indo-Tibetan Studies, 4). Stuttgart.

_______ (2010). *The Nepalese Legacy in Tibetan Painting*. New York.

Kapstein, M. T. (2011). "*Just Where on Jambudvīpa are We?* New Geographical Knowledge and Old Cosmological Schemes in Eighteenth-Century Tibet." In *Forms of Knowledge in Early Modern Asia: Explorations in the Intellectual History of India and Tibet, 1500–1800*. Durham/London, pp. 336–364.

Karmay, S. G. (2014). *The Illusive Play: The Autobiography of the Fifth Dalai Lama*. Chicago.

Kaschewsky, R. (1982). "Zu einigen Tibetischen Pilgerplätzen in Nepal". *Zentralasiatische Studien*, 16, pp. 427–442.

Kim, H. (2013). "Sum-pa Ye-shes-dpal-'byor and the Civil War of Eighteenth Century Tibet: A Preliminary Essay on Ye-shes-dpal-'byor's Many Roles in Tibetan Civilization". In *Current Issues and Progress in Tibetan Studies: Proceedings of the Third International Seminar of Young Tibetologists* (= Journal of Research Institute, 51). Kobe, pp. 165–182.

van der Kuijp, L. W. J. (1994). "On the *Lives* of Śākyaśrībhadra (?–?1225)." *Journal of the American Oriental Society*, 114:4, pp. 599–516.

_______ (2007). "*Nāgabodhi/Nāgabuddhi: Notes on the *Guhyasamāja* Literature." In *Pramāṇnakīrtiḥ: Papers Dedicated to Ernst Steinkellner on the Occasion of His 70th Birthday, Part 2* (= Wiener Studien zur Tibetologie und Buddhismuskunde, 70.2). Vienna, pp. 1001–1022.

Kvaerne, P. (2017). "An Alternative Narrative of Tibetan History: Text and Context of the *Grags pa gling grags*." In *Musique et épopée en Haute-Asie. Mélanges offerts á Mireille Helffer á l'occasion de son 90e annviversaire*. Le Pré-Saint-Gervais, pp. 393–408.

Lamminger, N. (2013). "Der Sechste Zhva dmar pa Chos kyi dbang phyug (1584–1630) und sein Reisebericht aus den Jahren 1629/1630: Studie, Edition und Übersetzung." Ph.D. dissertation, University of Munich.

Larsson, S. (2011). "Tsangnyön Heruka's Sixteenth-Century Renovation of the Svayaṃbhū Stūpa." In *Light of the Valley: Renewing the Sacred Art and Traditions of Svayambhu*. Cazadero, pp. 208–230.

Lessing, F. D. & Wayman, A. (1968). *Mkhas grub rje's Fundamentals of the Buddhist Tantras* (= Indo-Iranian Monographs, 8). The Hague/Paris.

Lewis, T. & Jamspal, L. (1988). "Newars and Tibetans in the Kathmandu Valley: Three New Translations from Tibetan Sources". *Journal of Asian and African Studies,* 36, pp. 187–211.

Lo Bue, E. (1997). "The role of Newar scholars in transmitting the Indian Buddhist Heritage to Tibet (c. 750 – c. 1200)". In *Les Habitants du toit du Monde: Études recueillies en hommage à Alexander W. Macdonald* (= Recherches sur la Haute Asie, 12). Nanterre, pp. 629–658.

_______ (2012). "Newar Artistic Influence in Tibet and China Between the 7th and the 15th Century." In *Tibetan Art Between Past and Present: Studies Dedicated to Luciano Petech* (= Supplemento No. 1 Alla Rivista Degli Studi Orientali, N.S. 84). Pisa/Roma, pp. 25–61.

Macdonald, A.W. (1975). "A Little Read Guide to the Holy Places of Nepal, Part I." *Kailash: A Journal of Himalayan Studies*, 3:2, pp. 89–144.

_______ & Dvags-po Rin-po-che (1981). "Un guide peu-lu des lieux-saints du Népal (IIe partie)." In *Tantric and Taoist Studies in Honour of R. A. Stein*, 1 (= Mélanges Chinois et Bouddhiques, 20). Bruxelles, pp. 237–273.

Mala, G. (2006). "A Mahayanist Rewriting of the History of China by Mgon po skyabs in the Rgya gar chos 'byung." In *Power, Politics and the Reinvention of Tradition: Tibet in the Seventeenth and Eighteenth Centuries* (= Brill's Tibetan Studies Library, 10:3). Leiden/Boston, pp. 145–170.

Mathes, K.-D. (2013). "Clouds of Offerings to Lady g.Yang-ri: A Protector Practice by the First Yol mo sprul sku Shākya bzang po ($15^{th}/16^{th}$ Cent.)" In *Nepalica-Tibetica: Festgabe für Christoph Cüppers,* vol. 2 (= Beiträge zur Zentralasienforschung, 29). Andiast, pp. 37–55.

Mayer, R. (1996). *A Scripture of the Ancient Tantra Collection: The Phur-pa bcu-gnyis*. Oxford.

_______ (2007). "The Importance of the Underworlds: Asuras' Caves in Buddhism, and Some Other Themes in Early Buddhist Tantras Reminiscent of the Later Padmasambhava Legends." *Journal of the International Association of Tibetan Studies*, 3, 31 pp.

Nattier, J. (1991). *Once upon a Future Time: Studies in a Buddhist Prophecy of Decline* (= Nanzan Studies in Asian Religions, 1). Berkeley.

Pahlke, M. (2012). *Die Hagiographie des La phyi ba Nam mkha' rgyal mtshan (1372–1437): eine Studie über das Leben eines tibetischen Heiligen* (= Contributions to Tibetan Studies, 8). Wiesbaden.

Quintman, A. (2008). "Toward a Geographic Biography: Mi la ras pa in the Tibetan Landscape." *Numen*, 55, pp. 363–410.

_______ (2014). "Redacting Sacred Landscape in Nepal: The Vicissitudes of Yol mo's Tiger Cave." In *Himalayan Passages: Tibetan and Newar Studies in Honor of Hubert Decleer*. Somerville, pp. 69–96.

Roerich, G. N. (1949). *The Blue Annals*. Calcutta. Reprint: Dehli 1976.

_______ (1959). *Biography of Dharmasvāmin (Chag lo-tsa-ba Chos-rje-dpal): A Tibetan Monk Pilgrim* (= K. P. Jayaswal Research Institute, Patna, Historical Research Series, 2). Patna.

Ronis, J. M. (2009). "Celibacy, Revelations, and Reincarnated Lamas: Contestation and Synthesis in the Growth of Monasticism at Katok Monastery from the 17th through 19th Centuries." Ph.D. dissertation, University of Virginia.

von Rospatt, A. (1999). "On the Conception of the Stūpa in Vajrayāna Buddhism: The Example of the Svayaṃbhūcaitya." *Journal of the Nepal Research Centre*, 11, pp. 121–147.

_______ (2001). "A Historical Overview of the Renovations of the Svayaṃbhūcaitya." *Journal of the Nepal Research Centre*, 12, pp. 195–241.

_______ (2003). "The Sacred Origins of the Svyayaṃbhūcaitya and the Nepal Valley: Foreign Speculation and Local Myth." *Journal of the Nepal Research Centre*, 13, pp. 33–91.

_______ (2011). "The Past Renovations of Svayaṃbhūcaitya." In *Light of the Valley: Renewing the Sacred Art and Traditions of Svayambhu*. Cazadero, pp. 157–206.

_______ (2014). "The Mural Paintings of the *Svayaṃbhūpurāṇa* at the Shrine of Śāntipur and their Origins with Pratāpa Malla." In *Himalayan Passages: Tibetan and Newar Studies in Honor of Hubert Decleer*. Somerville, pp. 45–68.

van Schaik, S. (2016). "Red Faced Barbarians, Benign Despots and Drunken Masters: Khotan as a Mirror of Tibet." *Revue d'Etudes Tibétaines*, 36, pp. 45–68.

Schneider, J. (2010). *Vagīśvarakīrti's Mṛtyuvyañcanopadeśa: eine buddhistische Lehrschrift zur Abwehr des Todes* (= Österreichische Akademie der Wissenschaften, phil.-hist. Klasse Denkschriften, 394 / Beiträge zur Kultur- und Geistesgeschichte Asiens, 66). Vienna.

Schuh, D. (2012). *Contributions to the History of Tibetan Mathematics, Tibetan Astronomy, Tibetan Time Calculation (Calendar) and Sino-Tibetan Divination*, 4 vols. (= Archiv für Zentralasiatische Geschichtsforschung, 17-20). Andiast.

Schwieger, P. (1997). "Kah-thog-rig-'dzin Tshe-dbang nor-bu's Diplomatic Mission to Ladakh in the 18th Century. " In *Recent Research on Ladakh, 6*. Bristol, pp. 219–230.

_______ (1999). *Teilung und Reintegration des Königreichs von Ladakh im 18. Jahrhundert: der Staatsvertrag zwischen Ladakh und Purig aus dem Jahr 1753* (= Monumenta Tibetica Historica, III:7). Bonn.

Sernesi, M. (2019). "Writing Local Religious History: The Abbatial History of Brag dkar rta so." In *Unearthing Himalayan Treasures: Festschrift for Franz-Karl Ehrhard* (= Indica et Tibetica, 59). Marburg, pp. 387–415.

Silk, J. (2008). "The story of Dharmaruci in the *Dīvyāvadāna and* Kṣemendra's *Bodhisattvāvadanakalpalatā*." *Indo-Iranian Journal*, 51, pp. 137–185.

Slusser, M. (1982). *Nepal Maṇḍala: A Cultural Study of the Kathmandu Valley*, 2 vols.. Princeton.

Smith, E. G. (2001). *Among Tibetan Texts: History & Literature of the Himalayan Plateau*. Boston.

Sørensen, P.K. (1994). *Tibetan Buddhist Historiography. The Mirror Illuminating the Royal Genealogies: An Annotated Translation of the XIVth Century Tibetan Chronicle rGyal-rabs gsal-ba'i me-long* (= Asiatische Forschungen, 128). Wiesbaden.

Stearns, C. P. (1996). "The Life and Tibetan Legacy of the Indian *Mahāpaṇḍita* Vibhūthicandra." *Journal of the International Association of Buddhist Studies*, 19:1, pp. 127–171.

_______ (2006). *Taking the Result as the Path: Core Teachings of the Sakya Lamdre Tradition*. Boston.

Verhagen, P. (2008). "Notes Apropos to the Oeuvre of Si tu paṇ chen Chos kyi 'byung gnas (1699?–1774) (1): Belles Lettres in His Opera Minora." In *Contributions to Tibetan Literature* (= Beiträge zur Zentralasienforschung, 14). Halle, pp. 513–548.

_______ (2010). "Notes Apropos to the Oeuvre of Si tu Paṇ chen Chos kyi 'byung gnas (1699–1774) (3): The 'Editor' Si tu Paṇ chen." In *Edition, éditions, l'écrit au Tibet, évolution et devenir* (= Collectanea Himalayica, 3). Munich, pp. 465–421.

_______ (2013). "Notes Apropos to the Oeuvre of Si tu Paṇ chen Chos kyi 'byung gnas (1699?–1774) (4): A Tibetan Sanskritist in Nepal." *Journal of the International Association of Tibetan Studies*, 7, pp. 316–339.

Vitali, R. (2009/2010). "In the Presence of the 'Diamond Throne": Tibetans at rDo rje gdan (Last Quarter of the 12th Century to Year 1300)." *The Tibet Journal*, 34:3–4 & 35:1–2 (= Special issue *The Earth Ox Papers: Proceedings of the International Seminar on Tibetan and Himalayan Studies, Held at the Library of Tibetan Works and Archives, September 2009 on the Occasion of the 'Thank You India' Year*), pp. 161–208.

_______ (2012). "Grub chen U rgyan pa and the Mongols of China." In *Studies on the History and Literature of Tibet and the Himalaya*. Kathmandu, pp. 31–64.

Van Vleet, S. (2012). "An Introduction to *Music to Delight All the Sages*. The Medical History of Drakkar Taso Tulku Chökyi Wangchuk (1775–1837)." *Bulletin of Tibetology*, 49:2, pp. 55–79.

Wylie, T. V. (1962). *The Geography of Tibet According to the 'Dzam-gling rgyas-bshad* (= Serie Orientale Roma, 25). Rome.

_______ (1970). *A Tibetan Religious Geography of Nepal* (= Serie Orientale Roma, 42). Rome.

Yongdan, Lobsang (2011). "Tibet Charts the World: The Btsan po No mon han's *Detailed Description of the World*, an Early Major Scientific Work in Tibet". In *Mapping the Modern in Tibet. PIATS 2006: Tibetan Studies: Proceedings of the Eleventh Seminar of the International Association für Tibetan Studies, Königswinter 2006* (= Beiträge zur Zentralasienforschung, 24). Andiast, pp. 74–134.

Zhang, F. (2017). "Reorienting the Sacred and Accommodating the Secular: The *History of Buddhism in China (rGya nag chos 'byung)*." In *Ancient Currents, New Traditions: Papers Presented at the Fourth International Seminar of Young Tibetologists* (= edition tethys: wissenschaft, 1). Potsdam, pp. 569–591.

# Index

# Plates

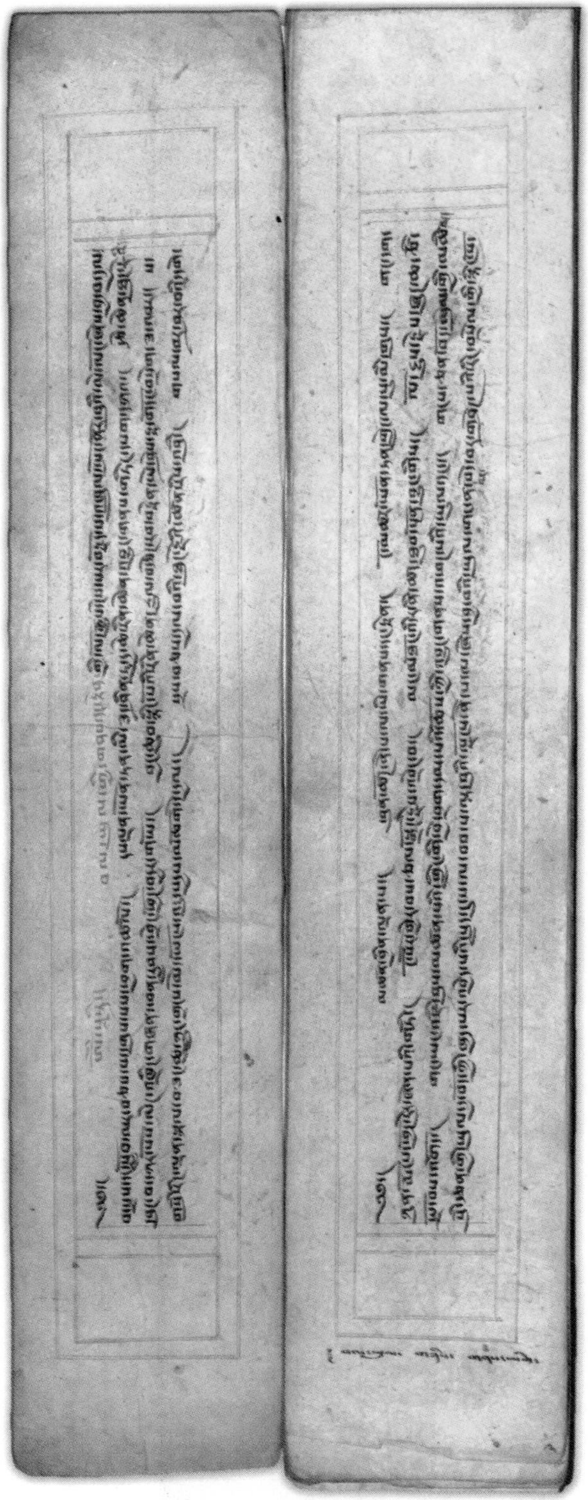

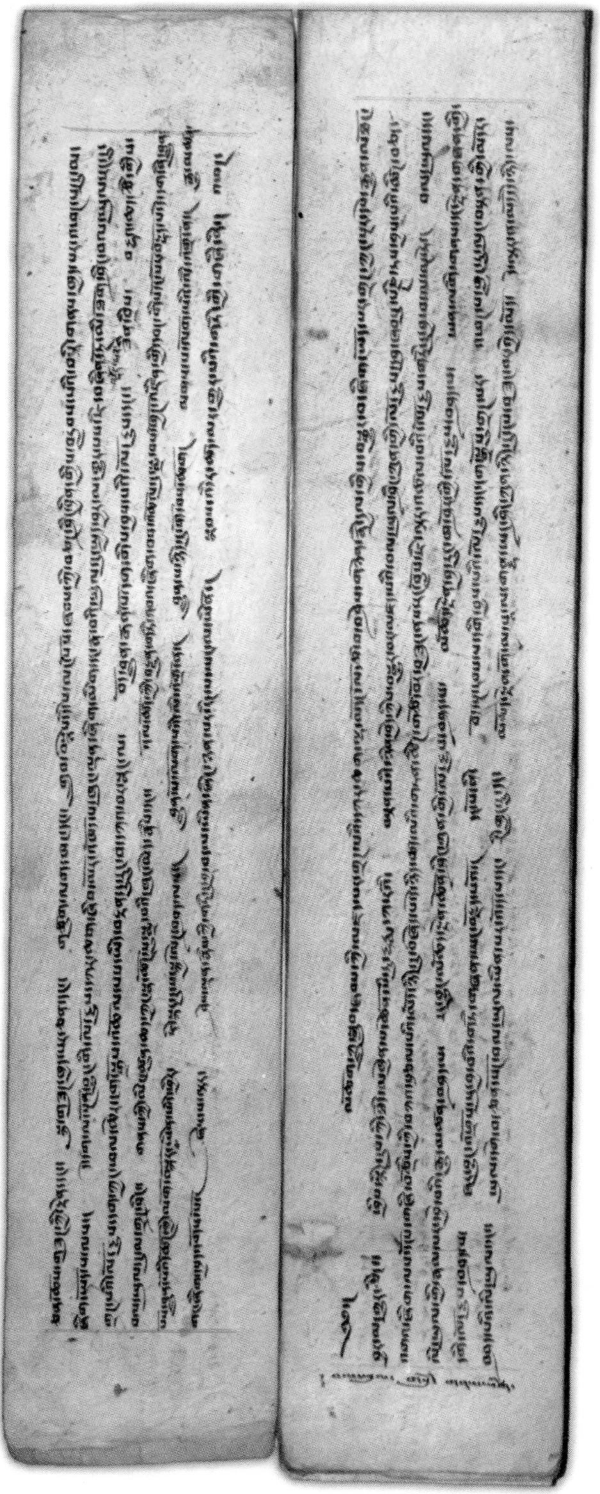

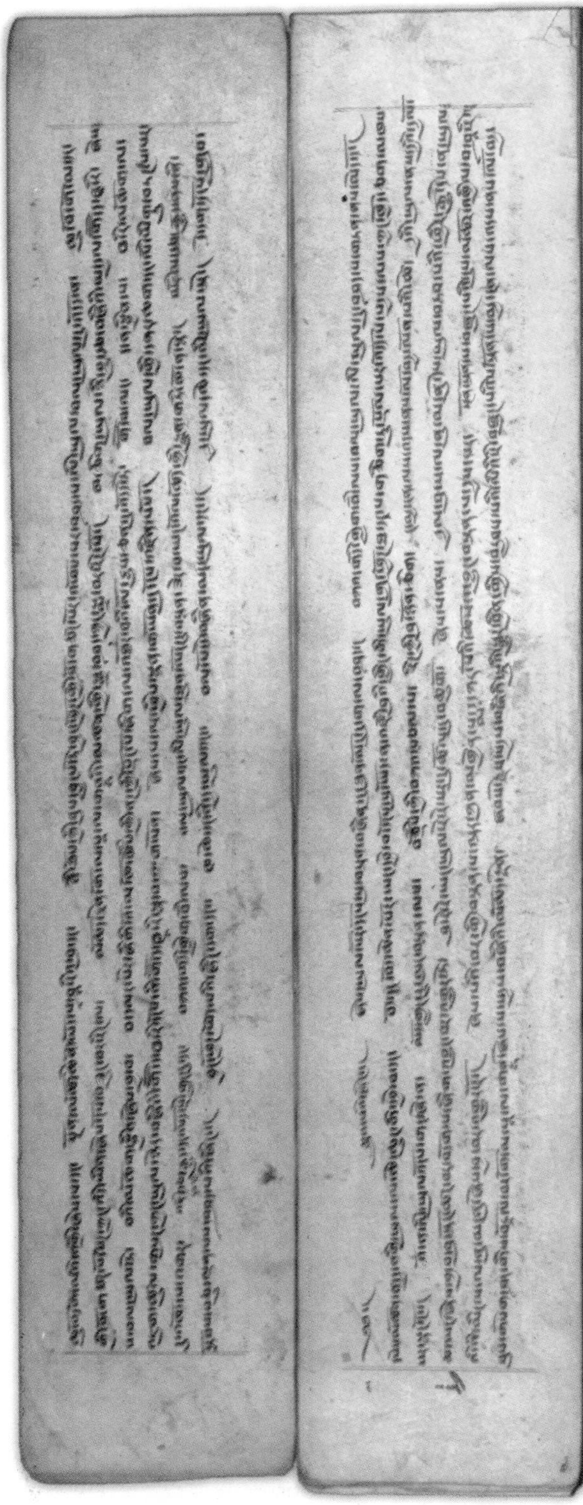

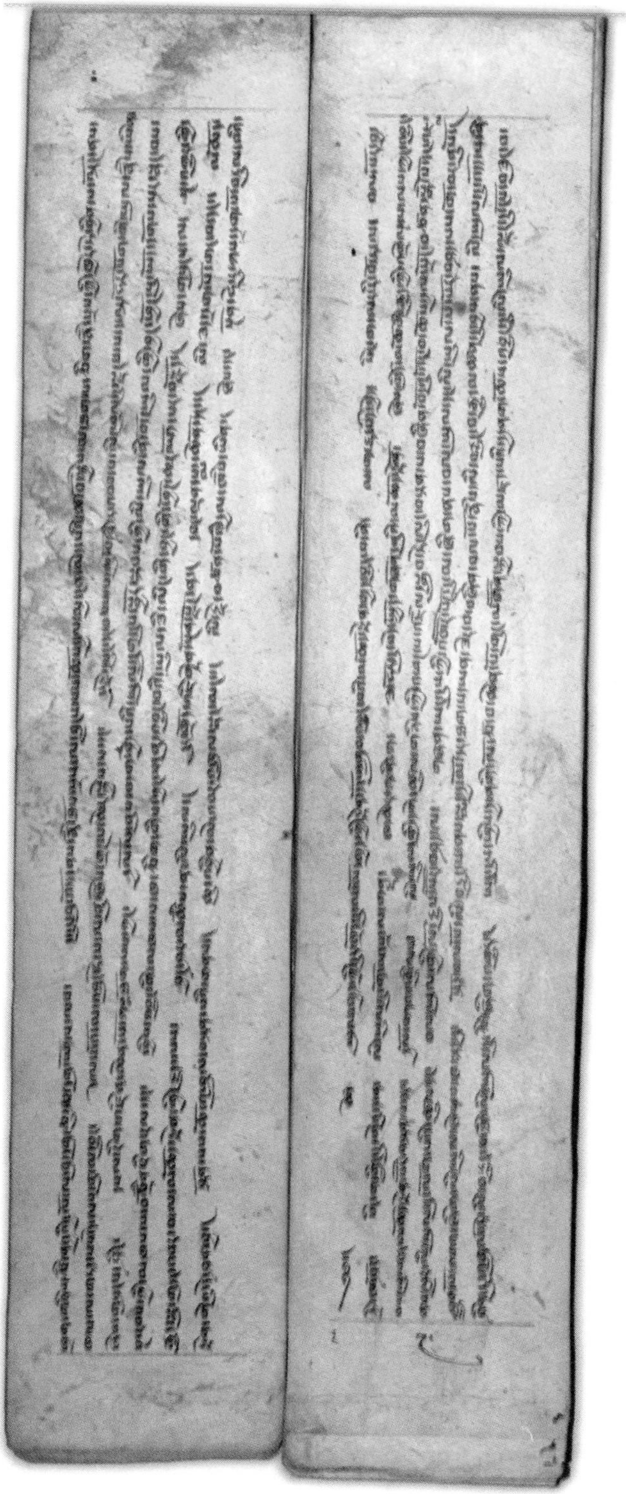

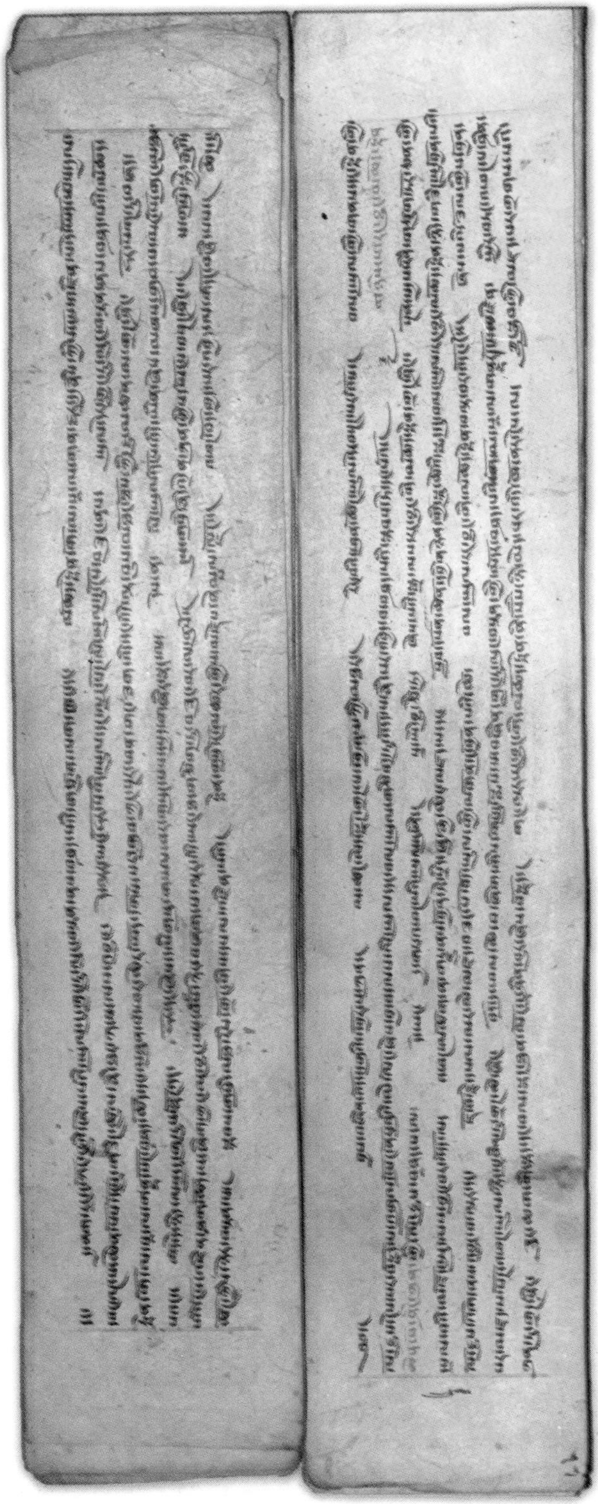

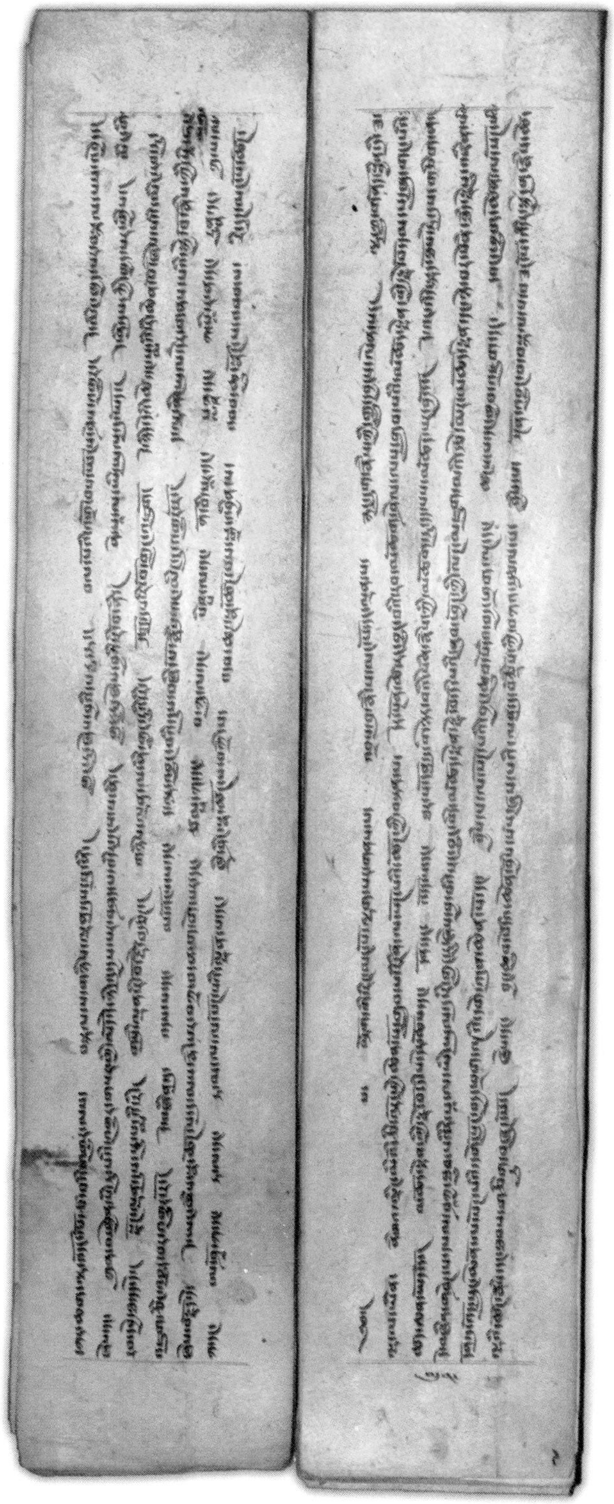

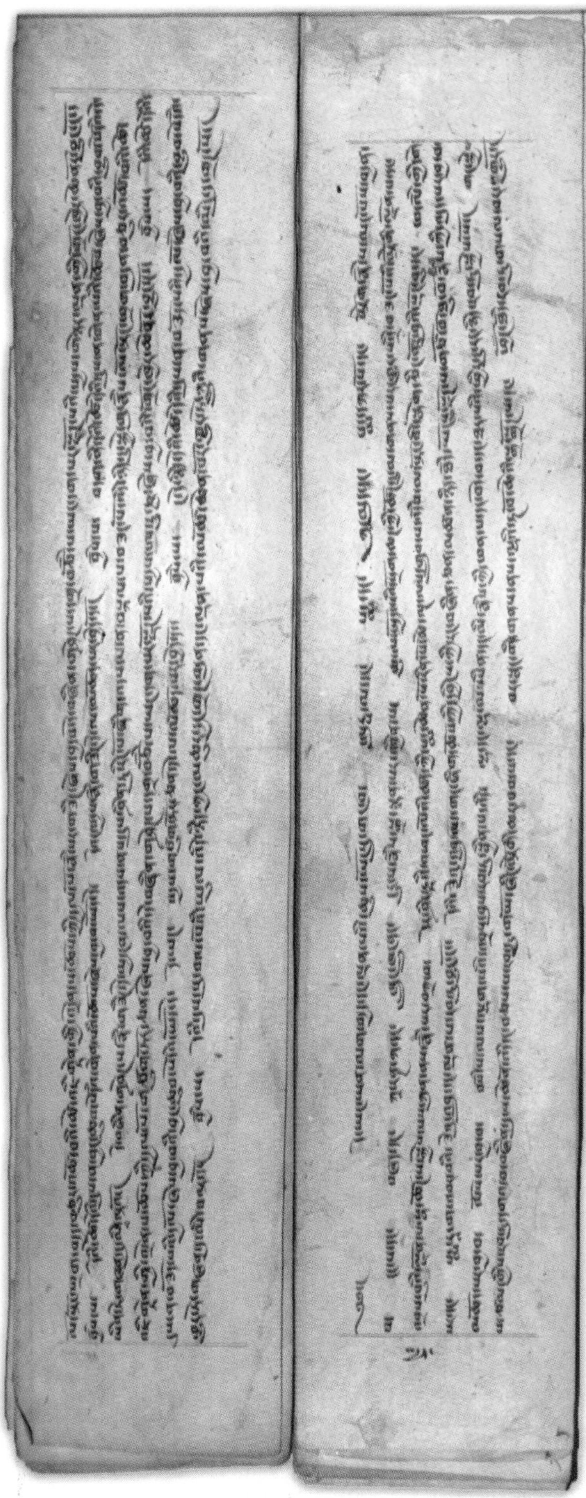

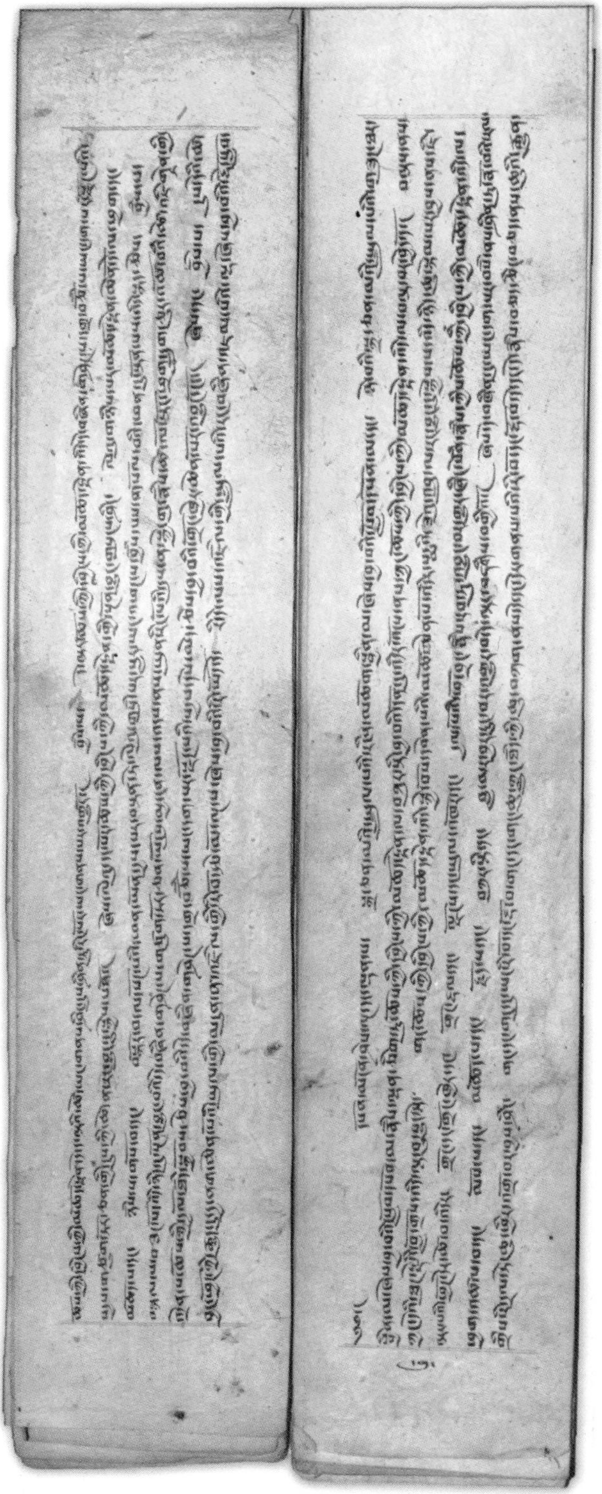

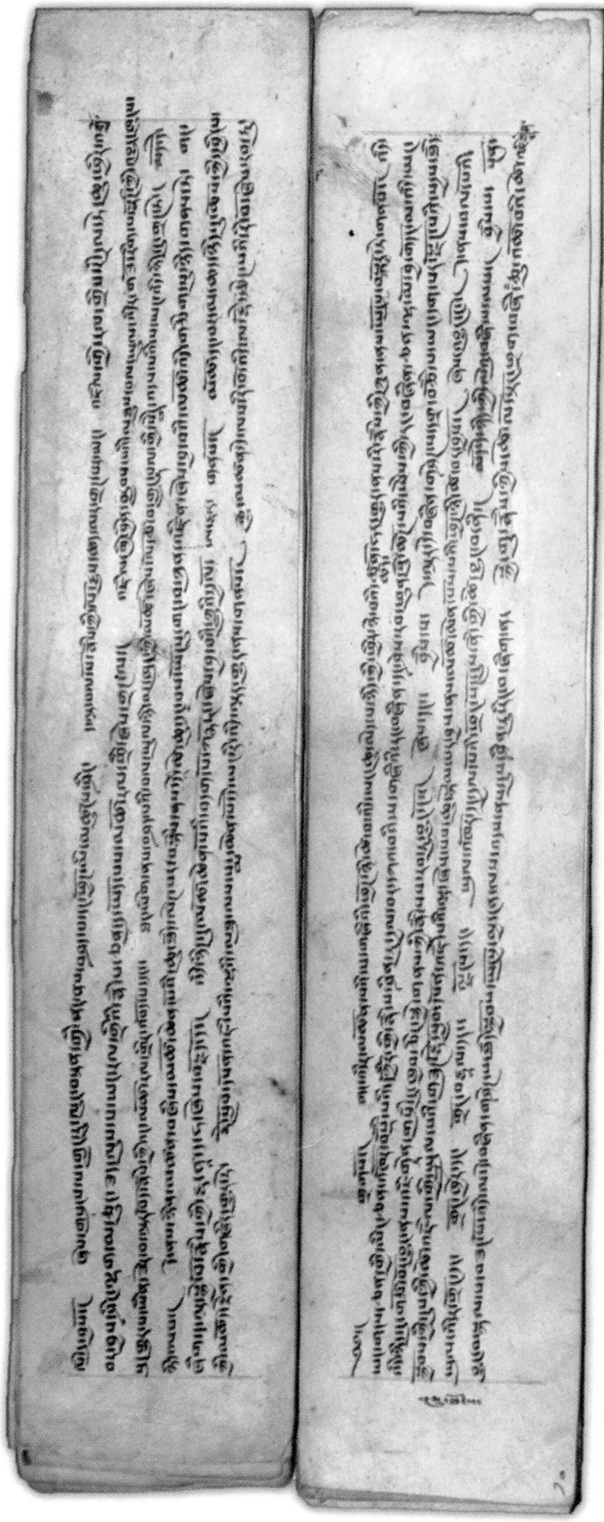

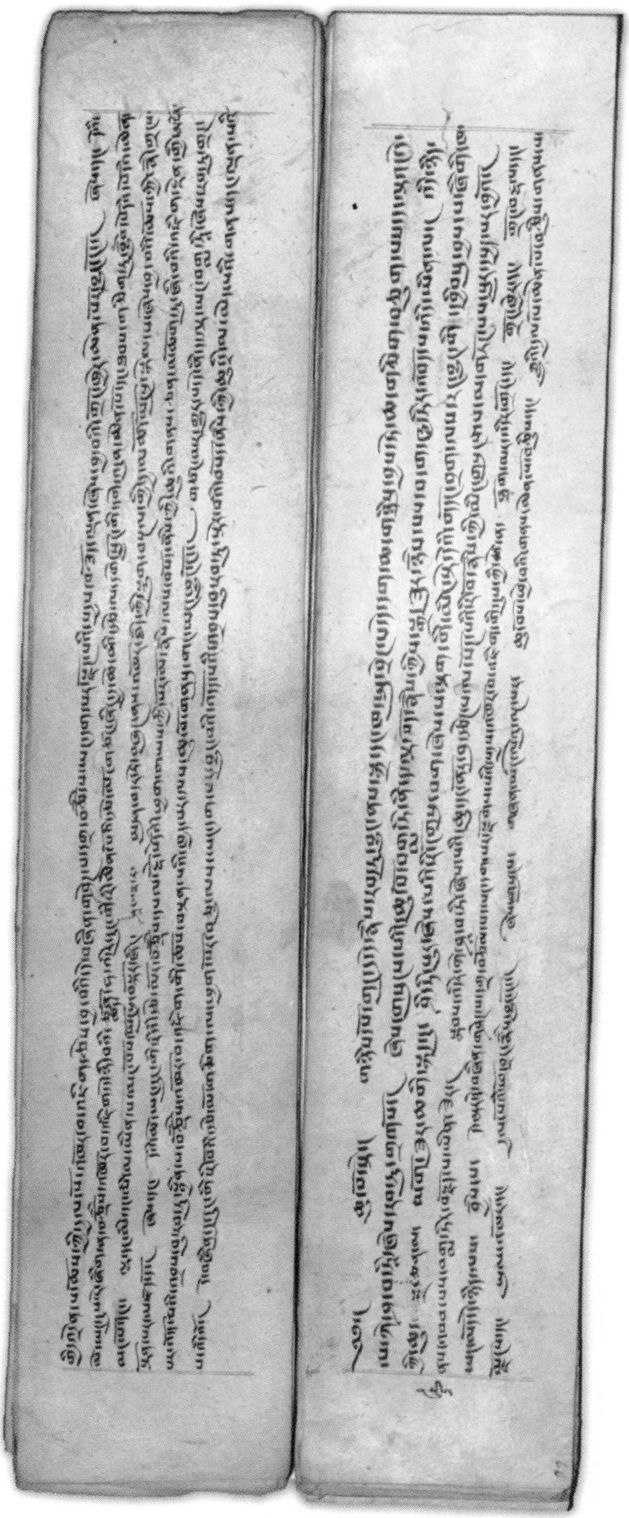

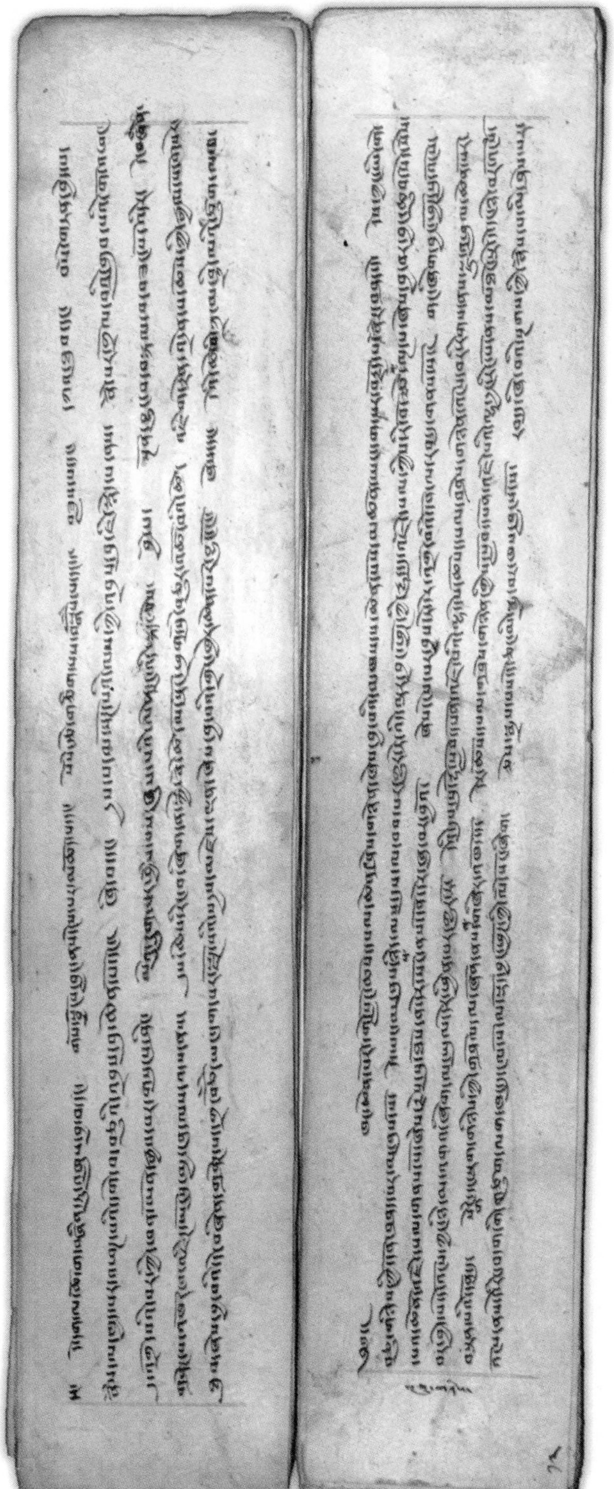

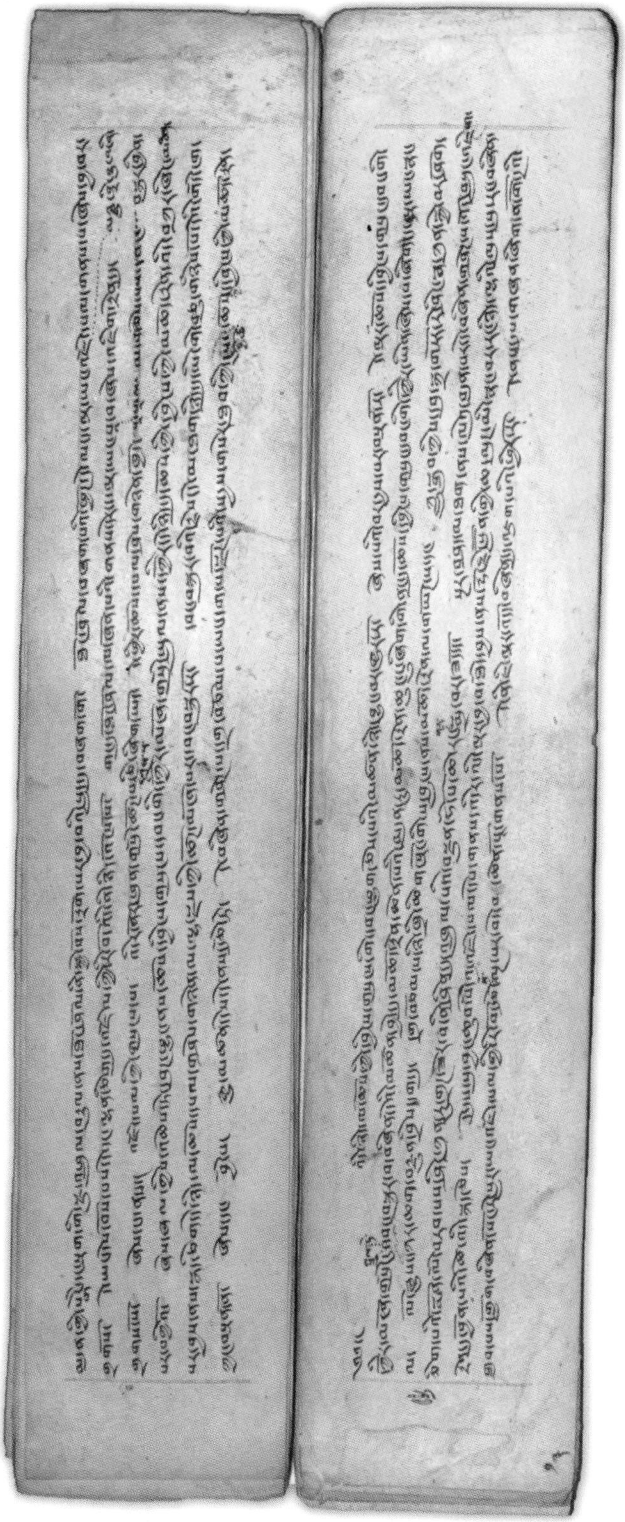

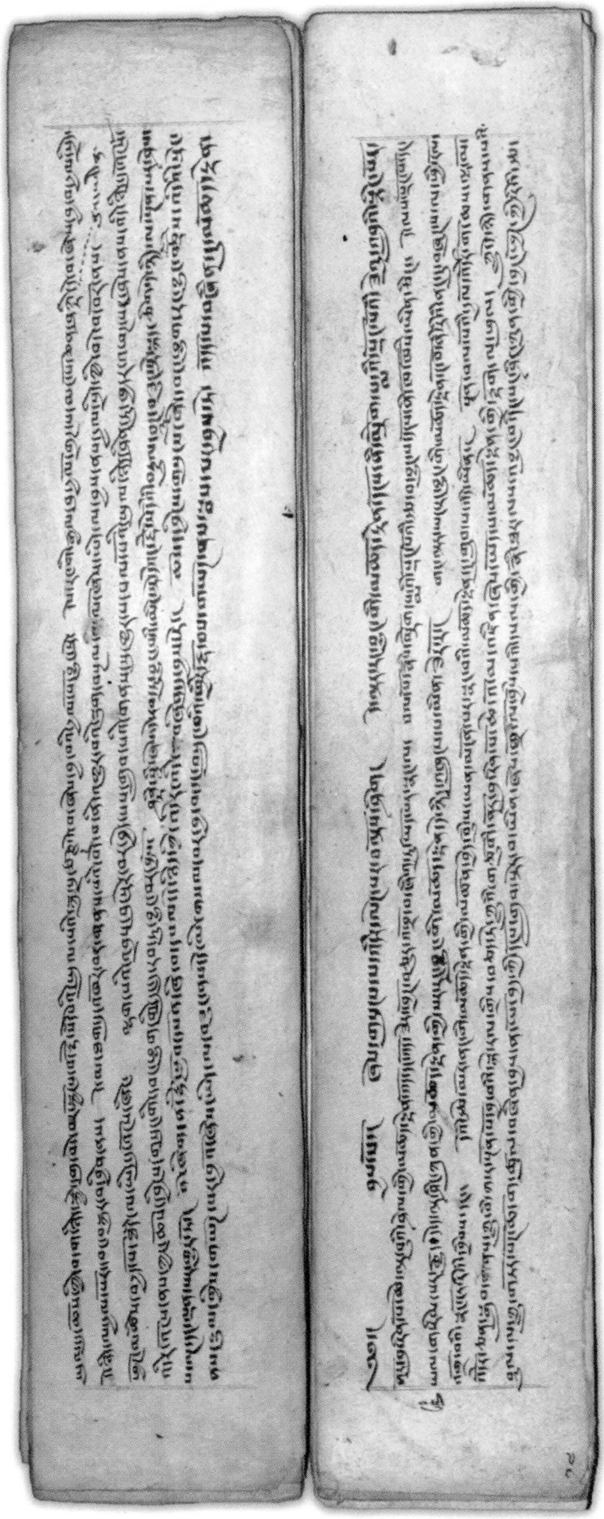

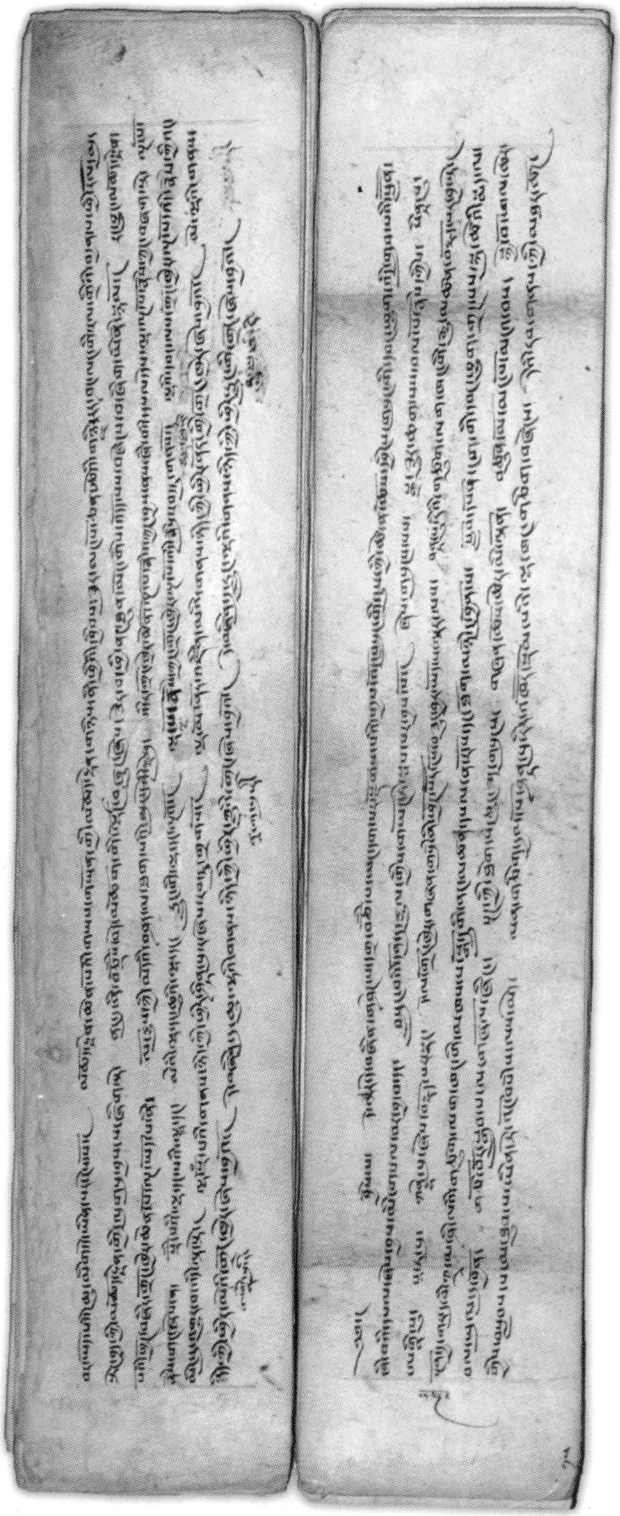

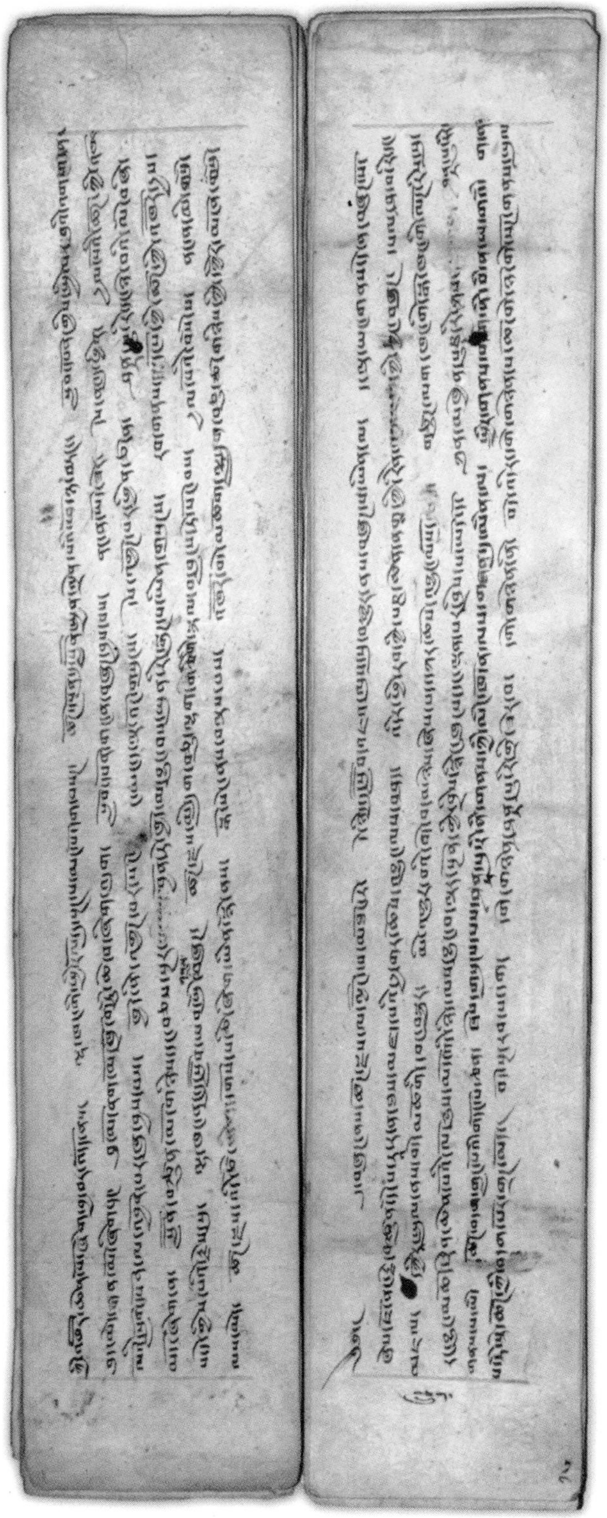

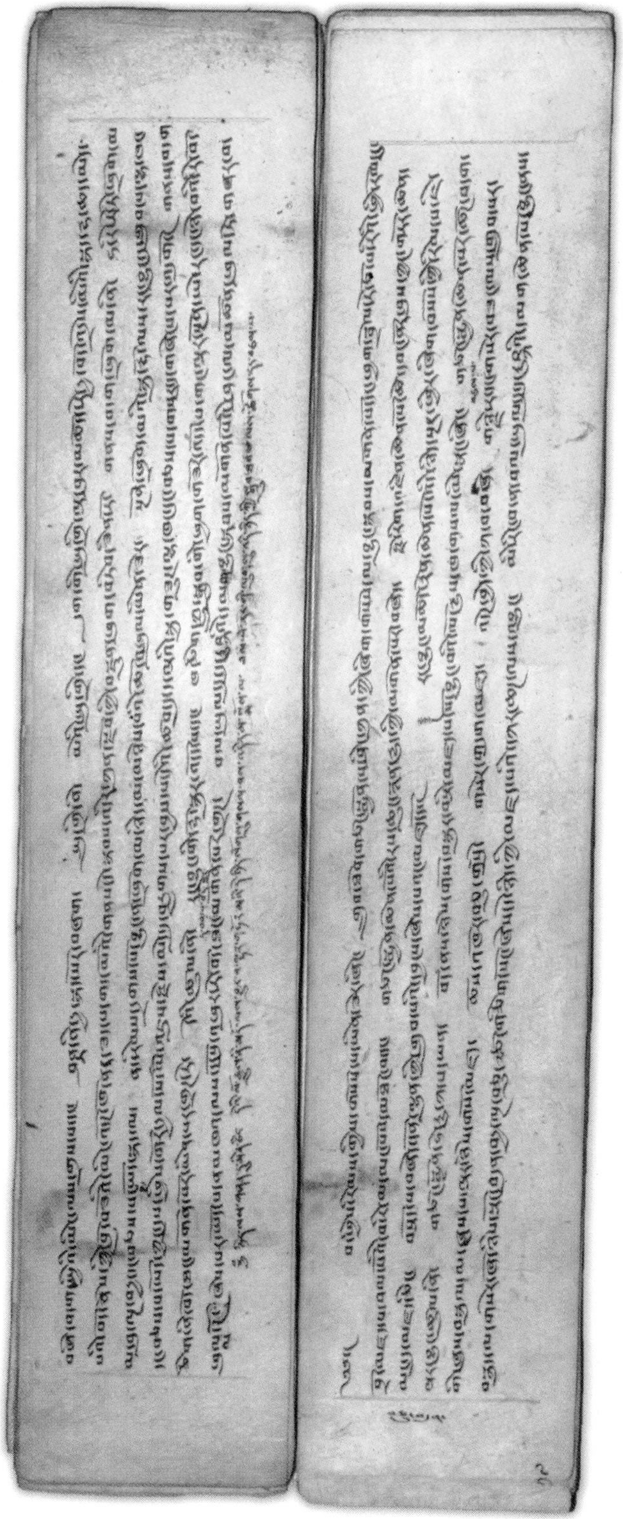

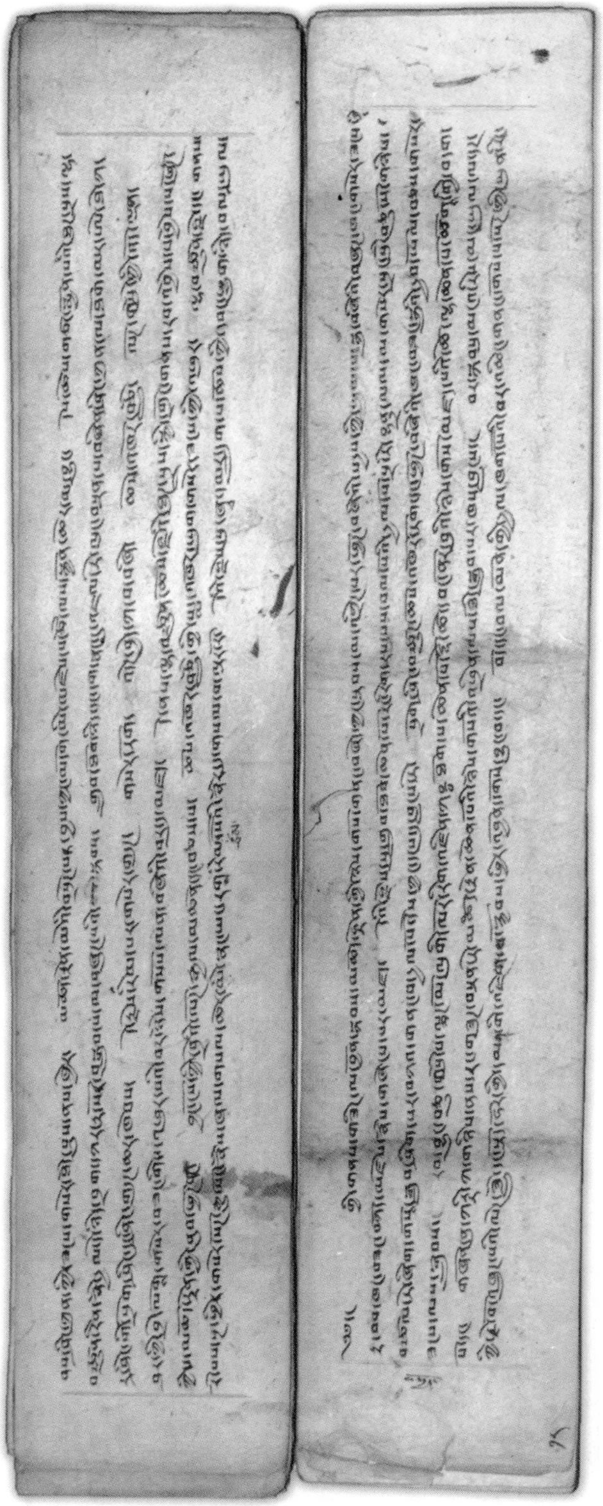

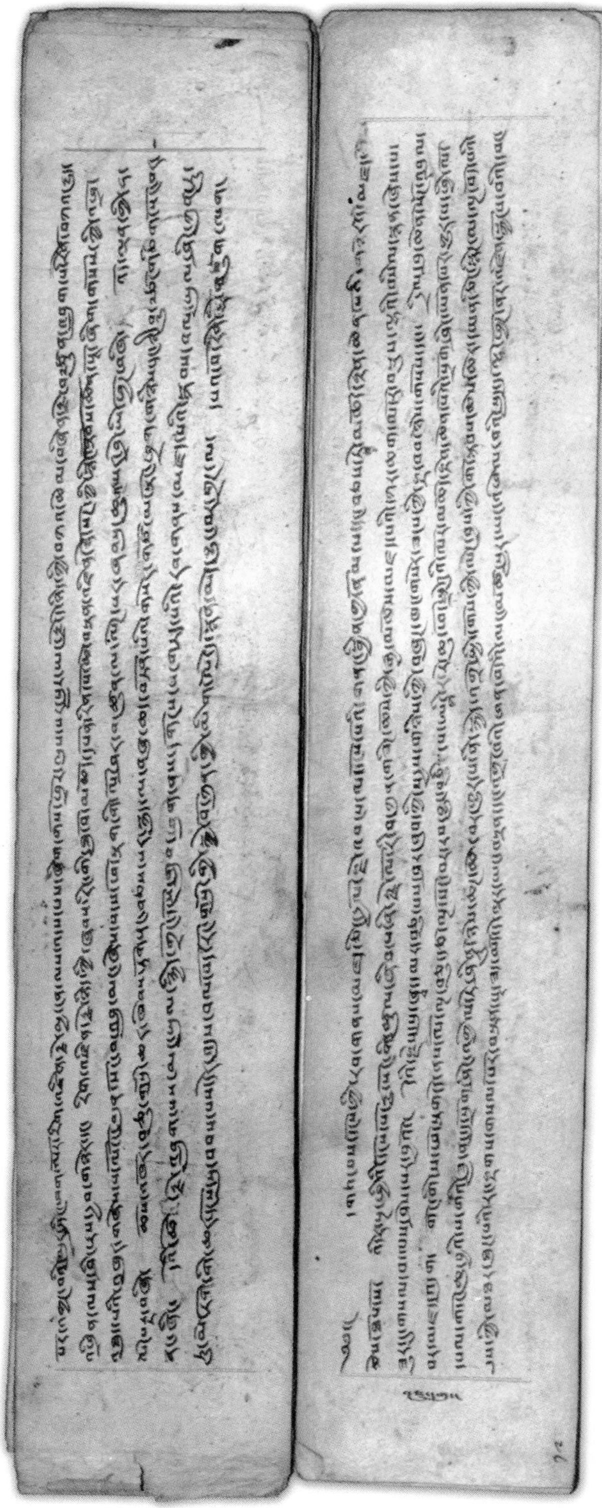

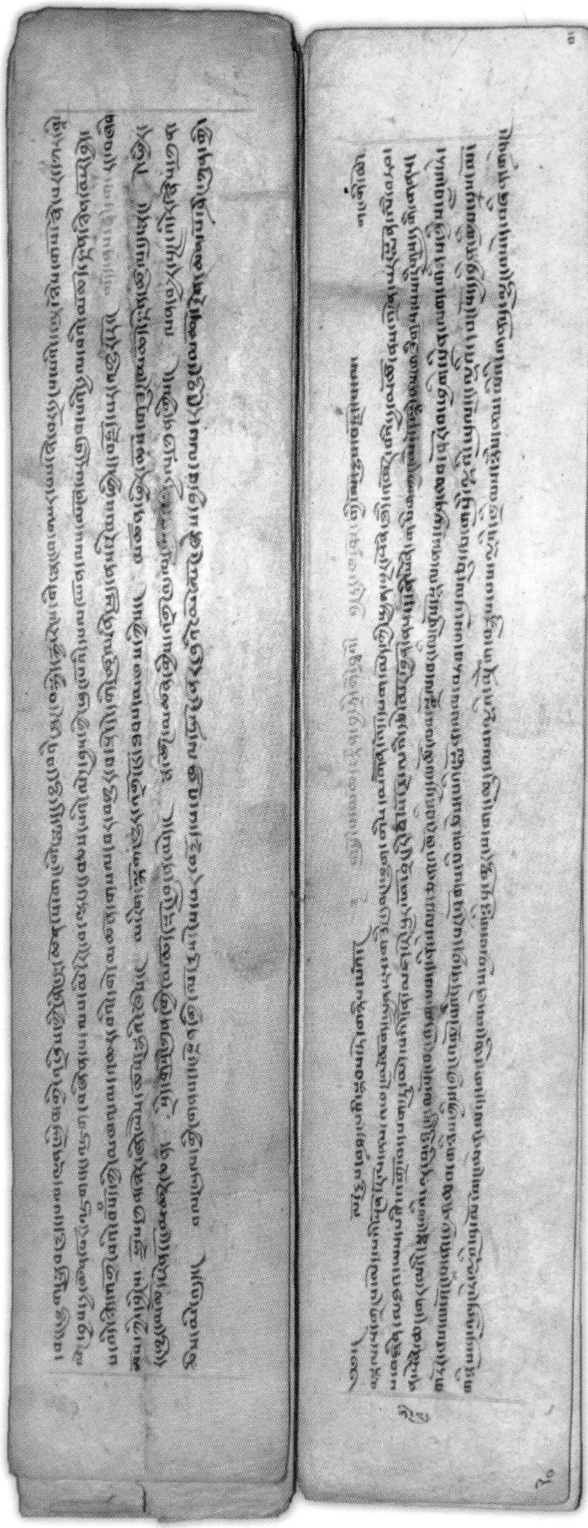

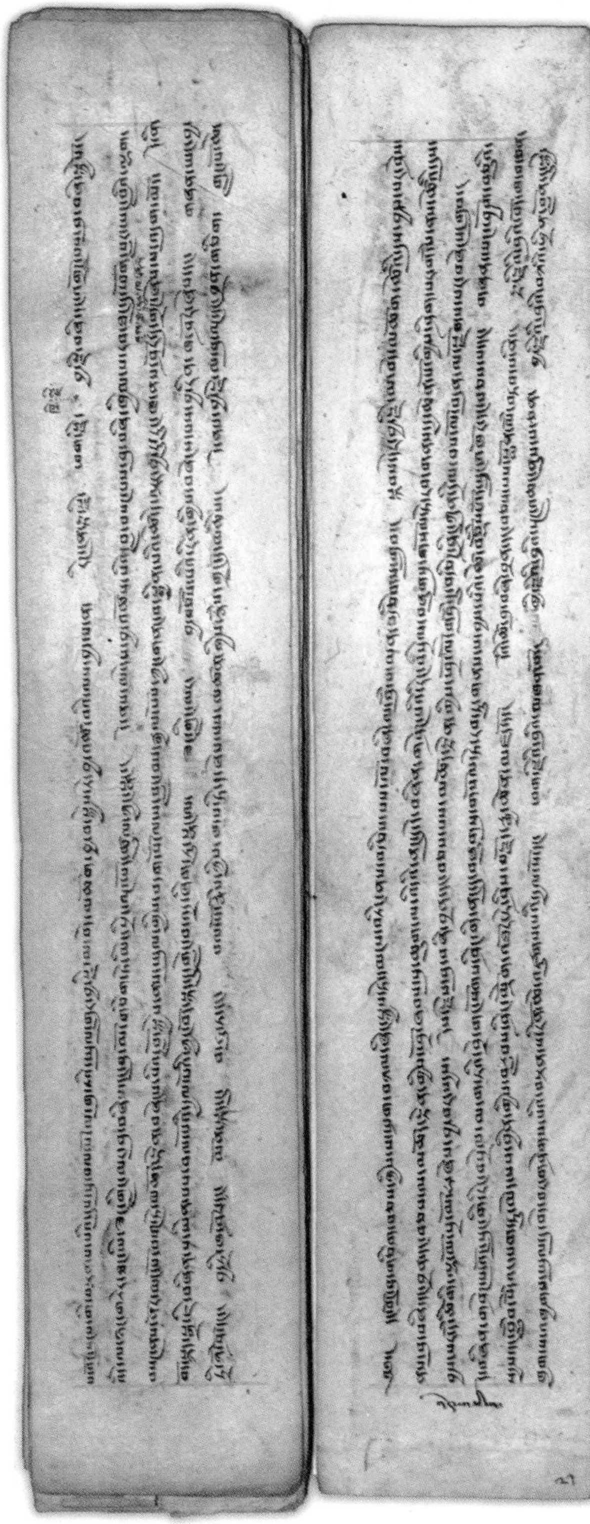

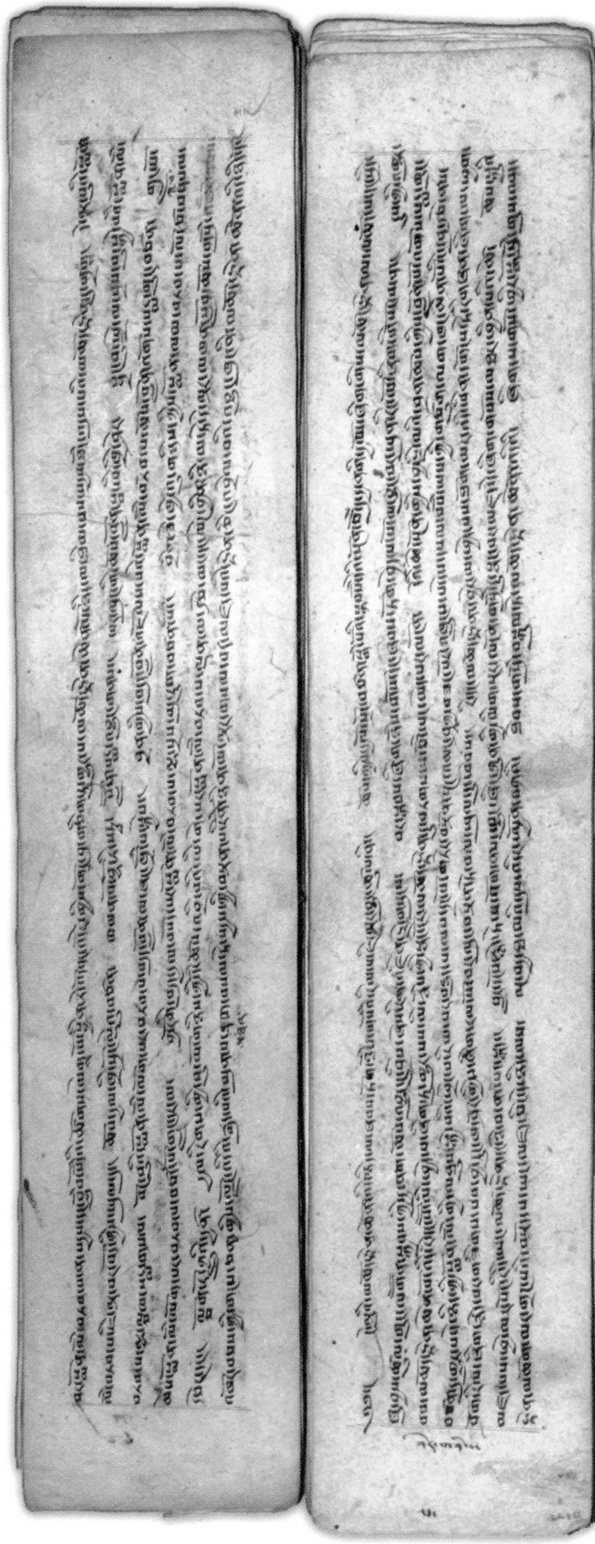

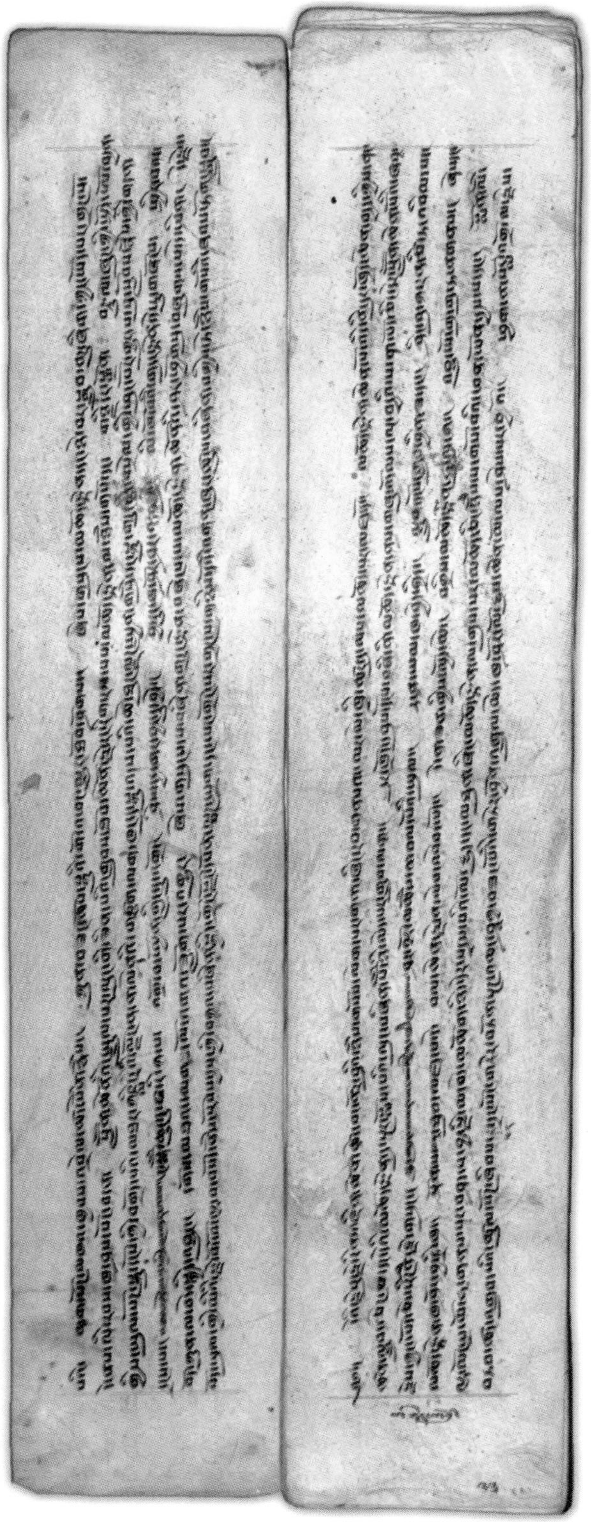

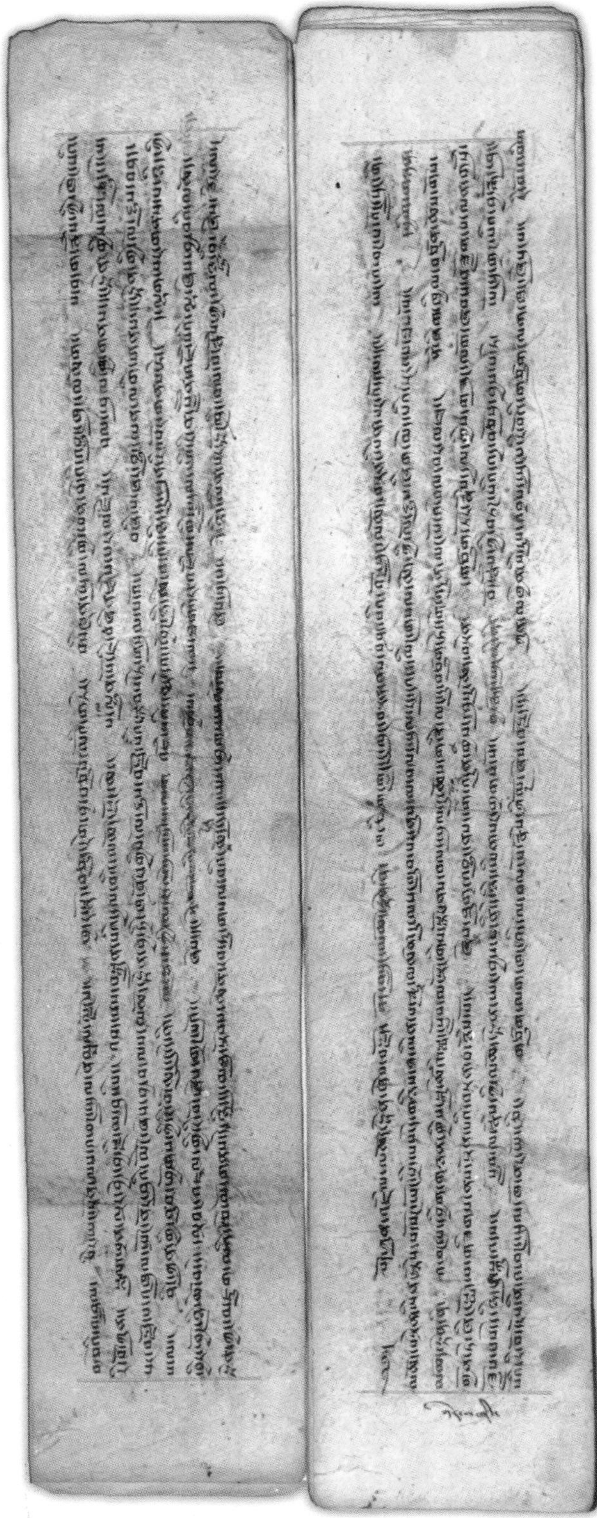

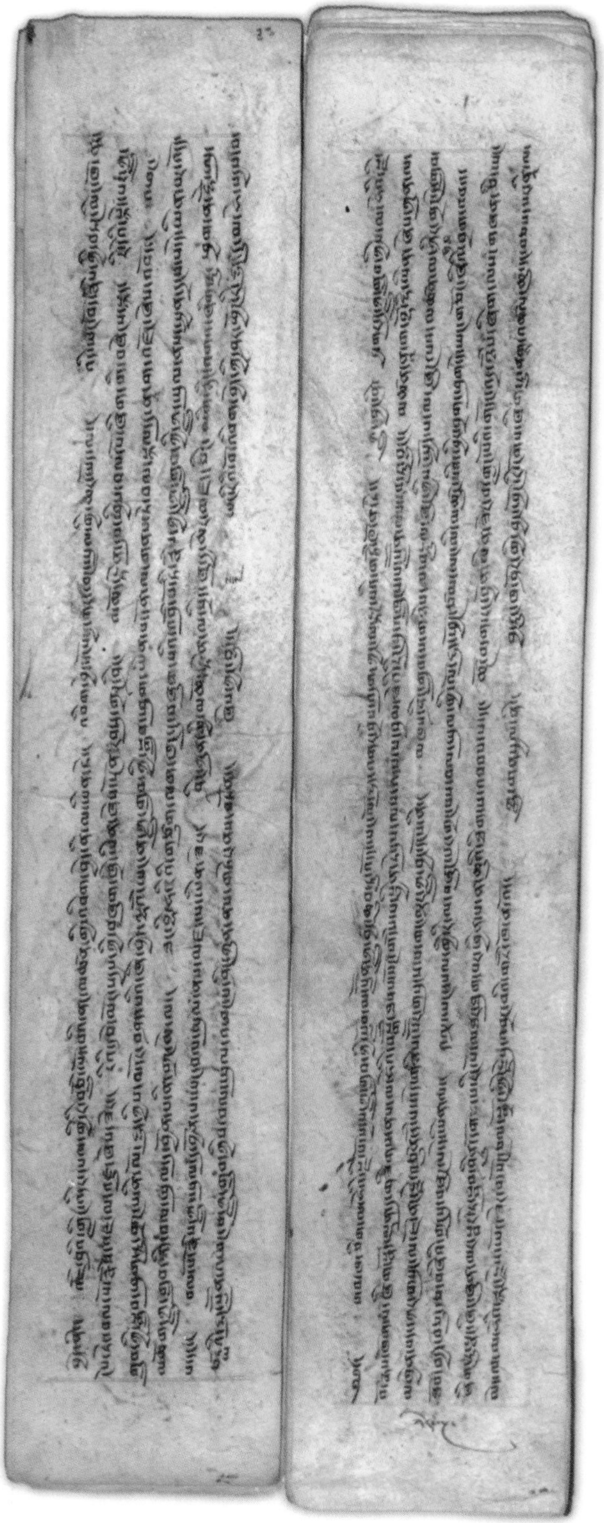

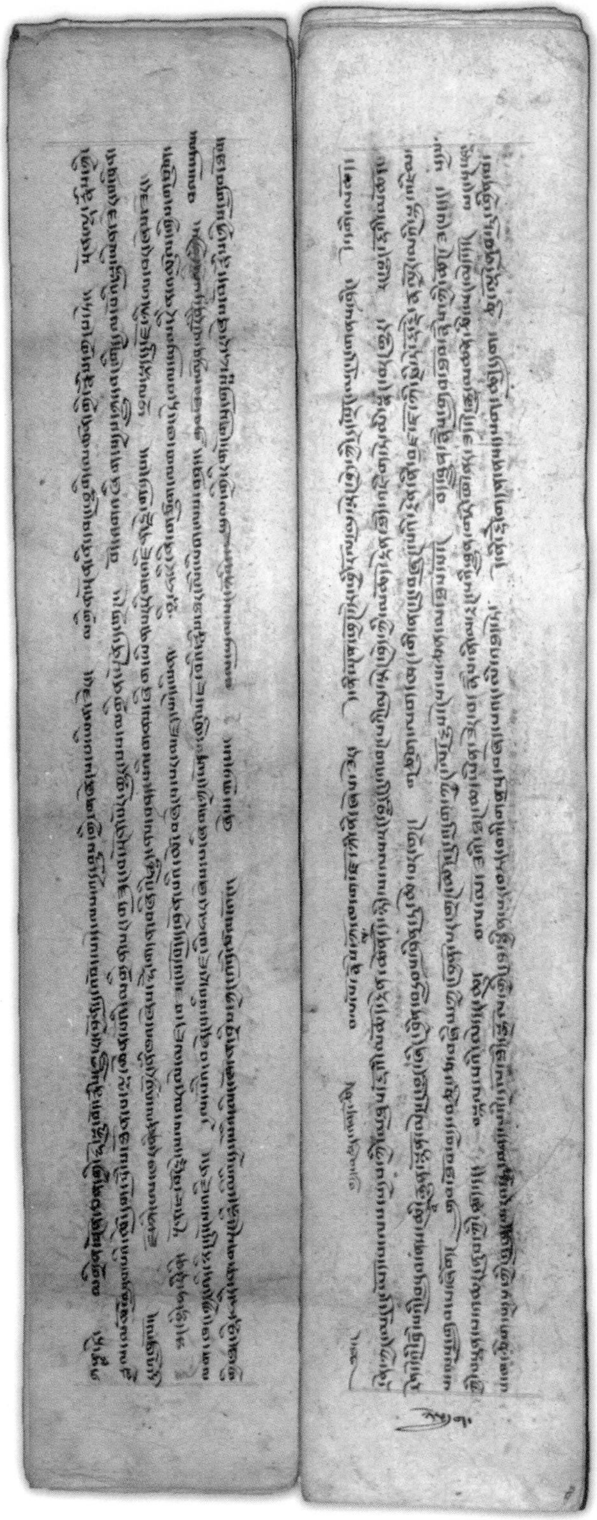

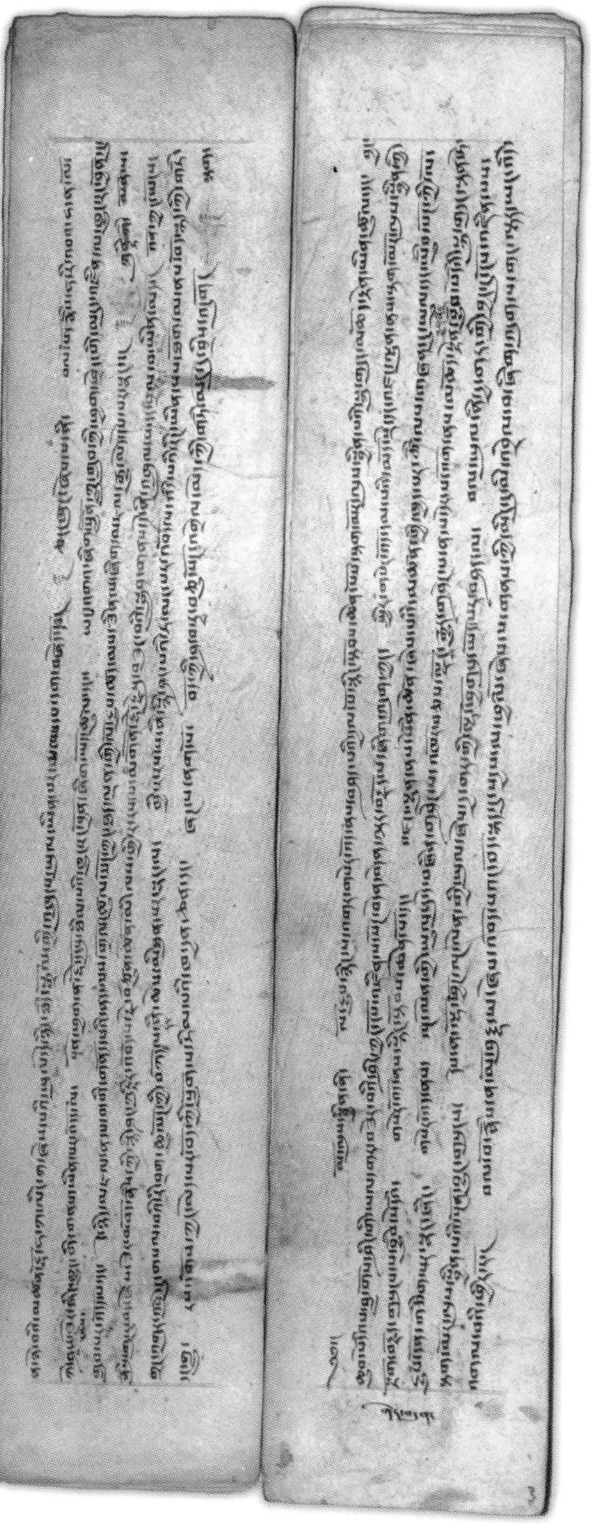

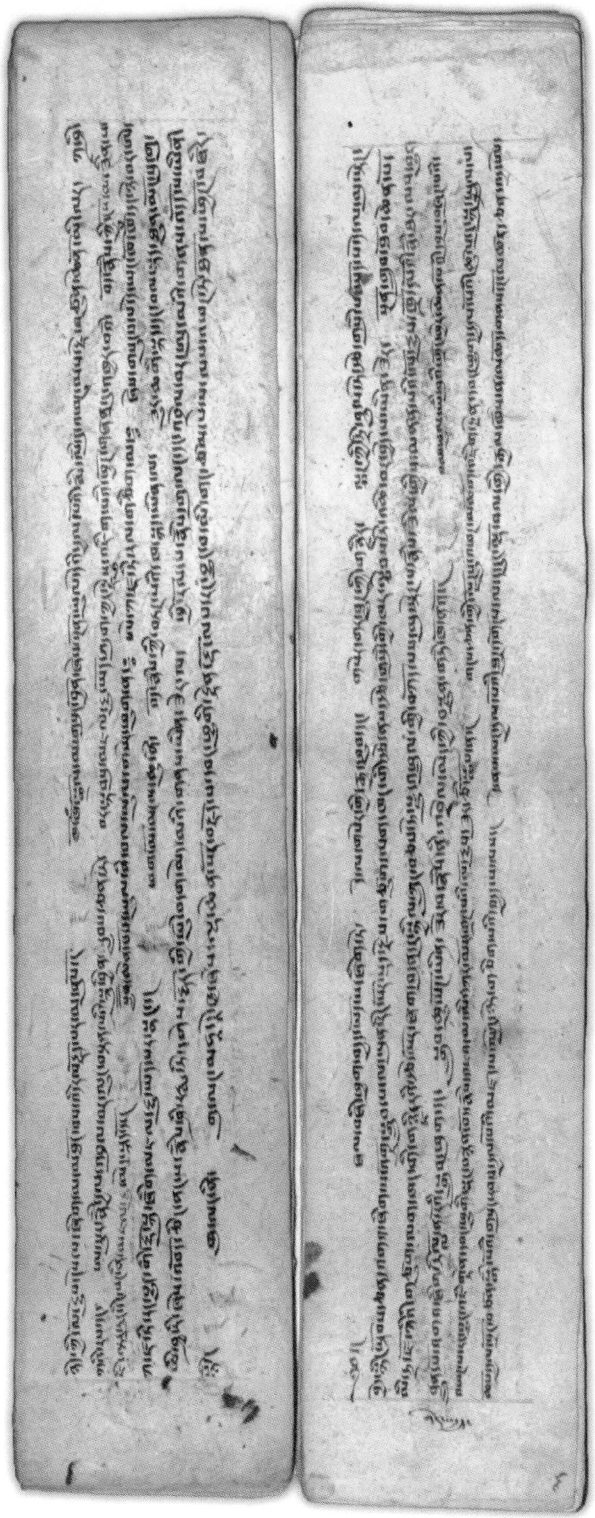

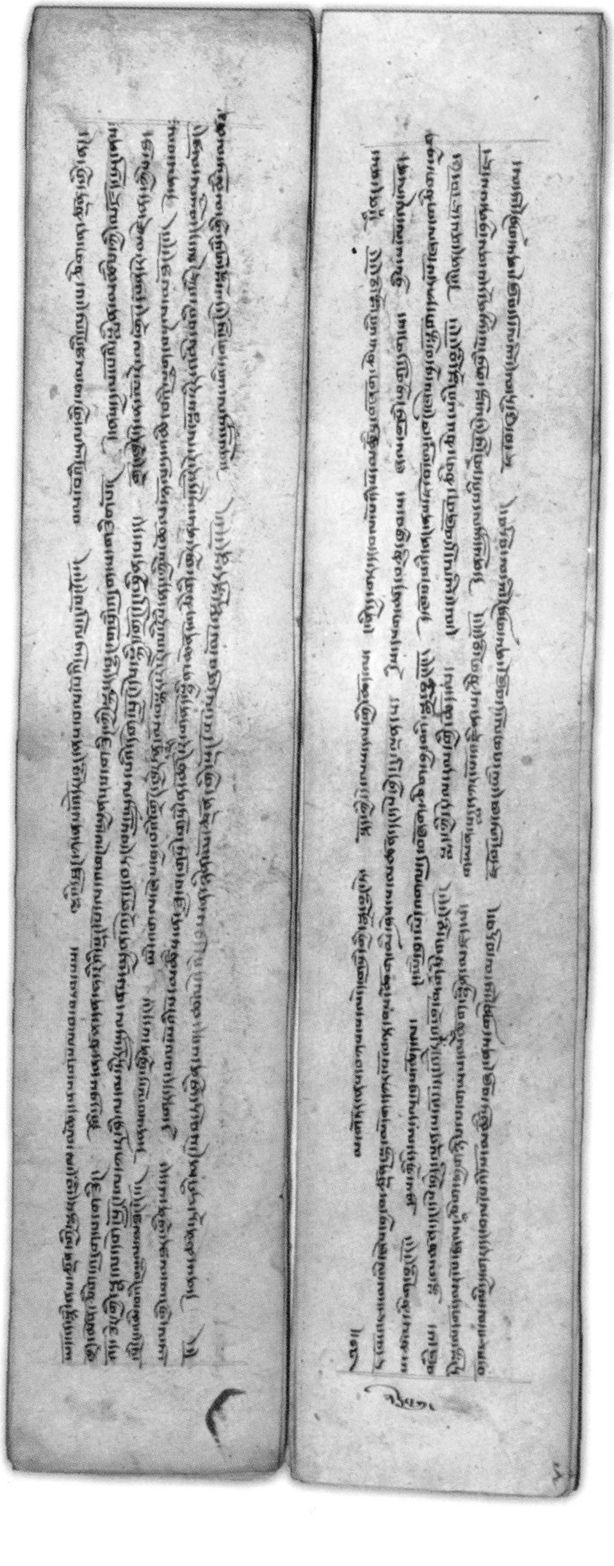

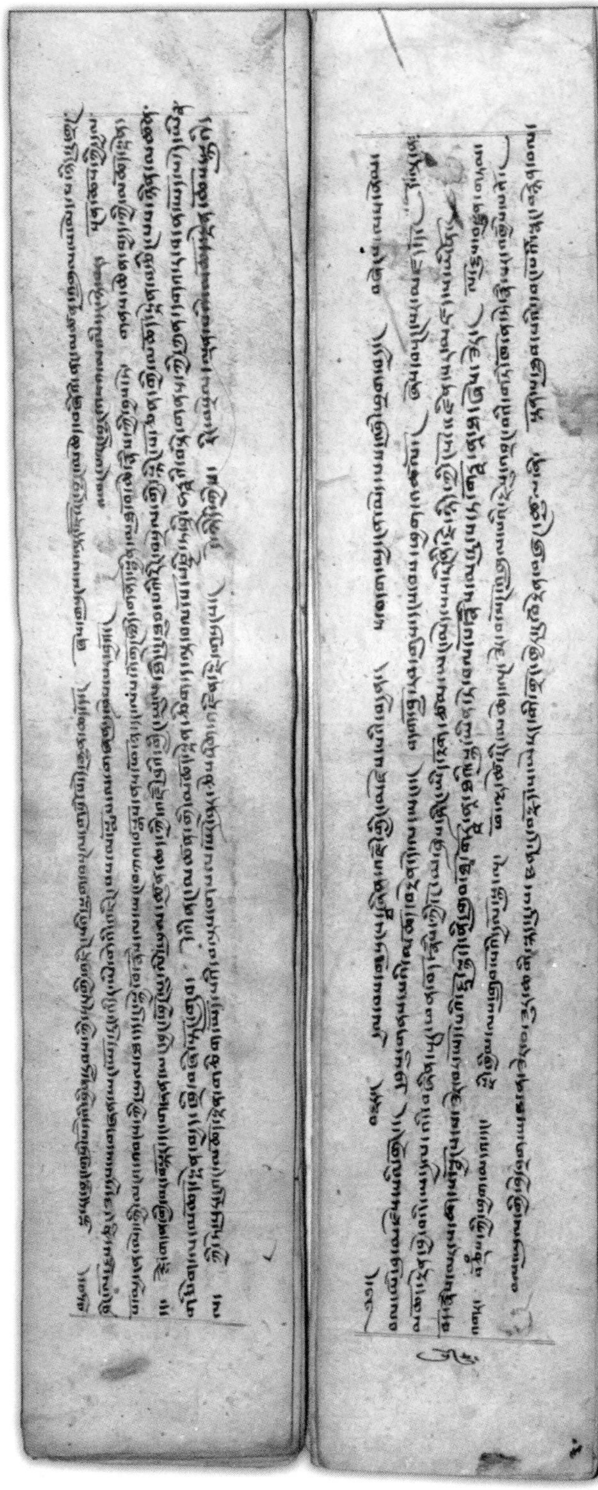

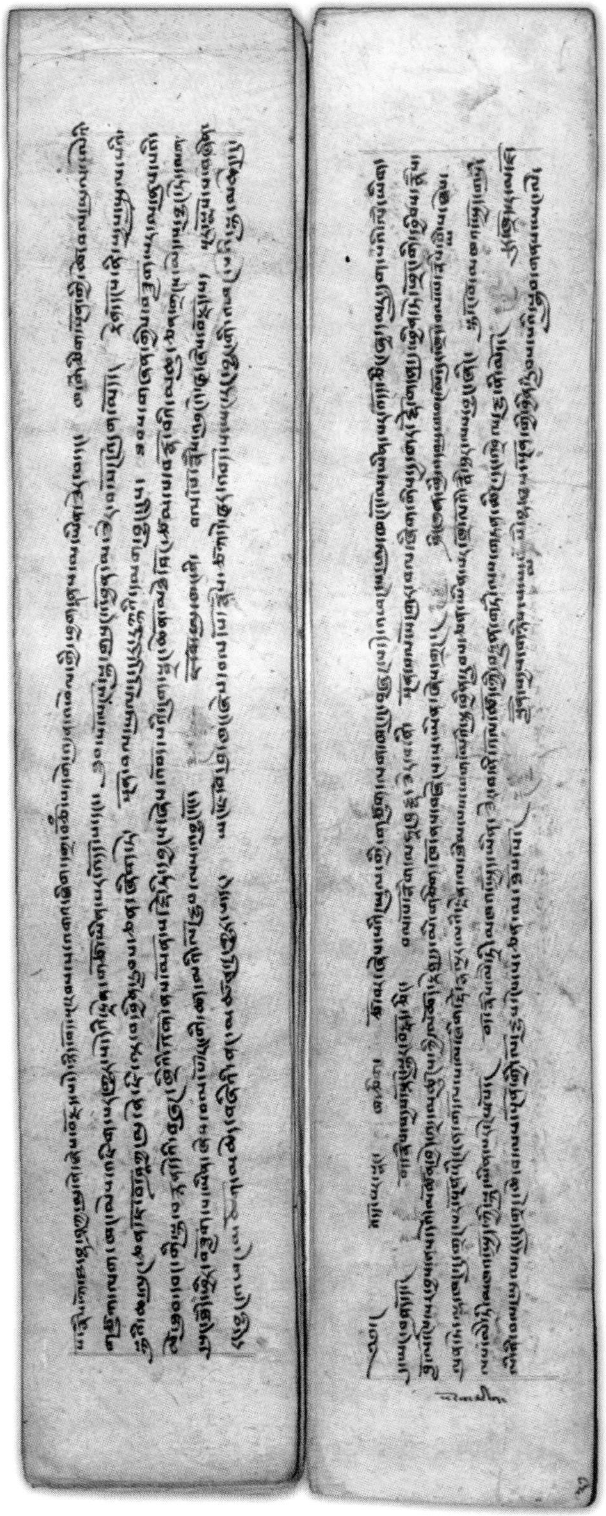

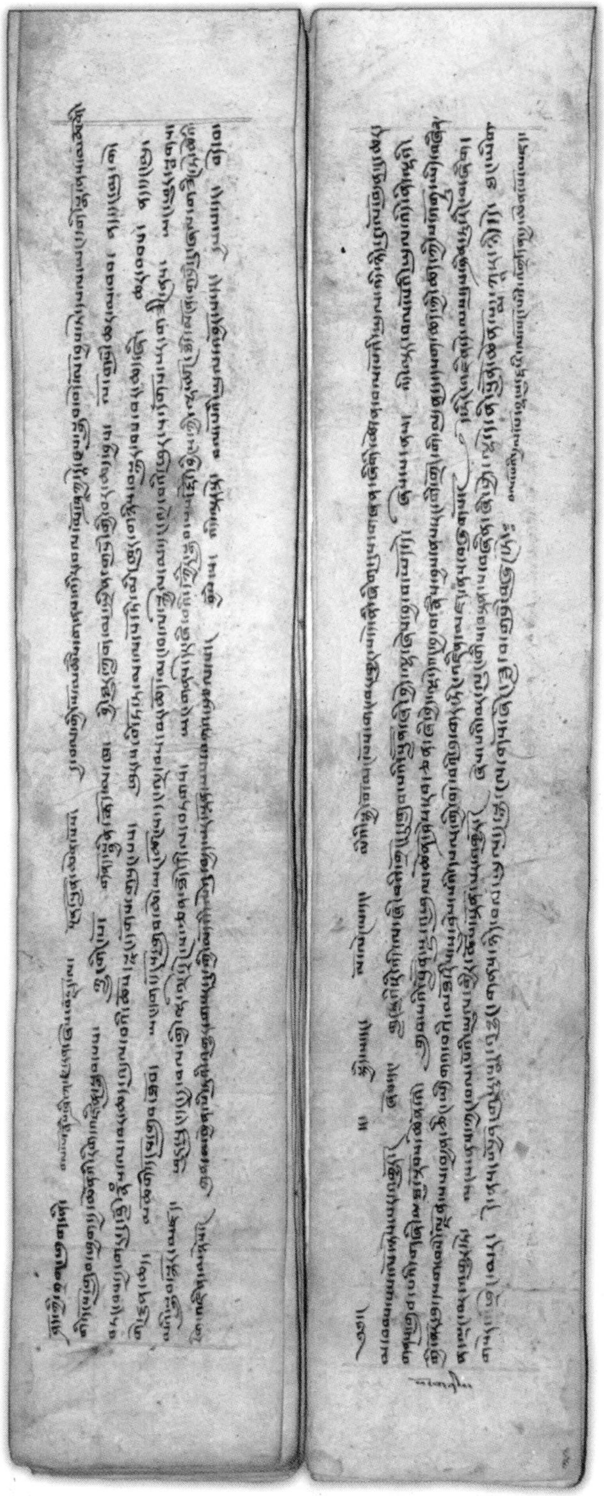

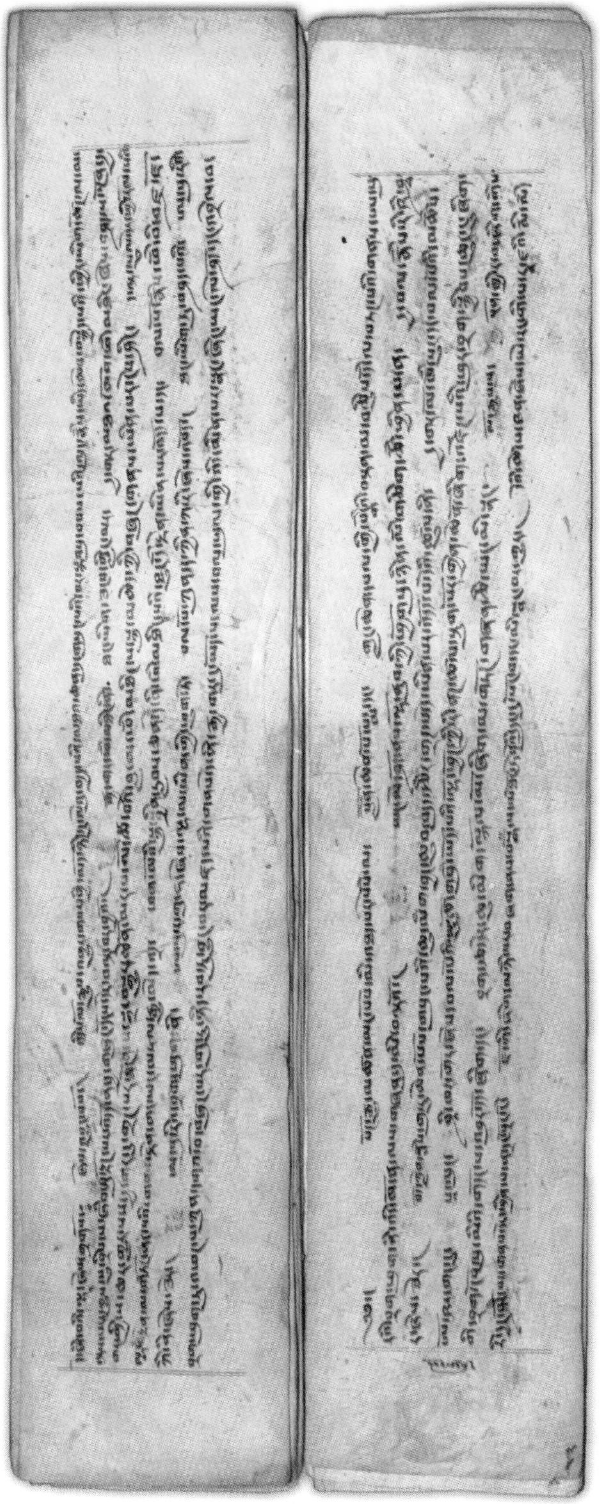

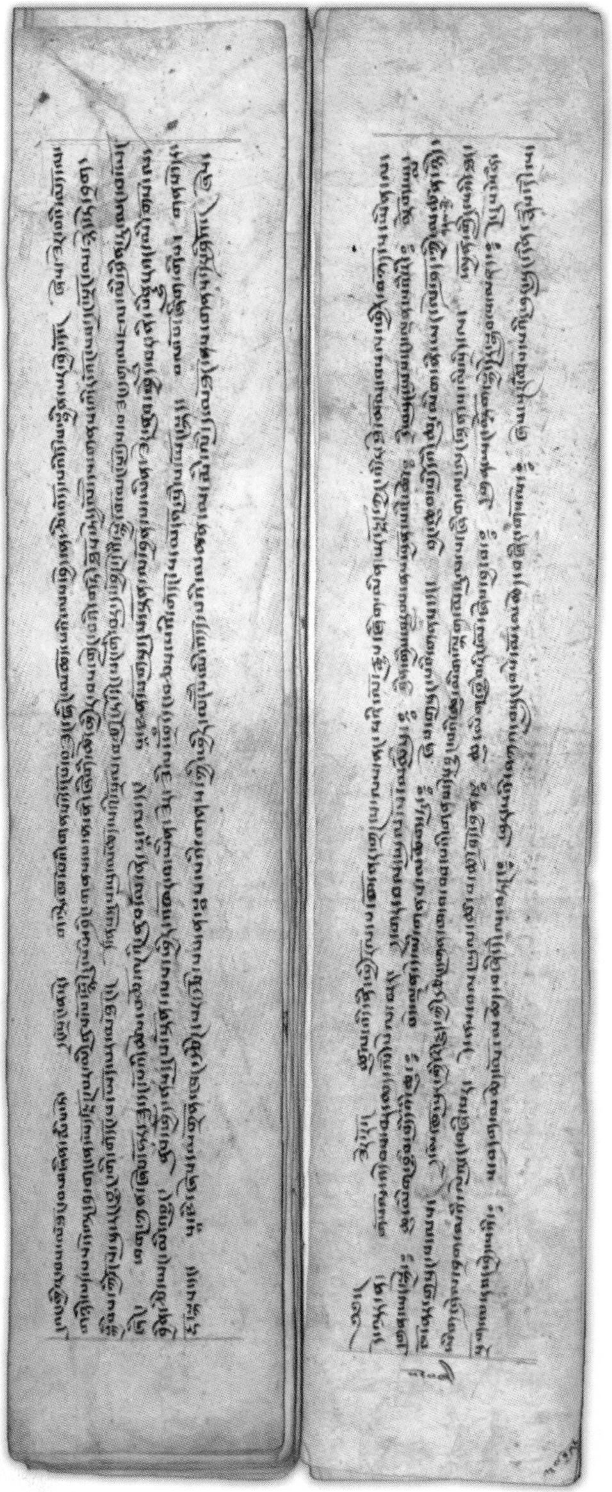

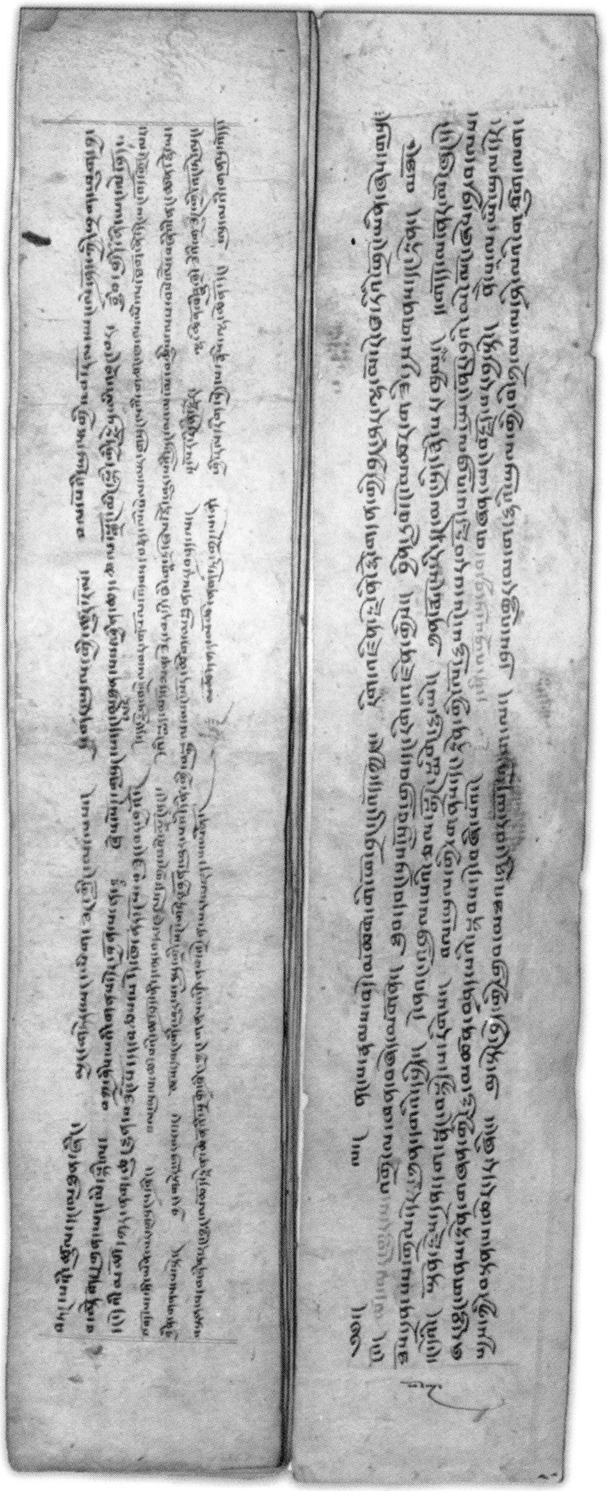